THE OTHER LOVE

THE ACT OF 25 HENRY VIII
CHAPTER 6

Le Roy le veult

'*Forasmuch as there is not yet sufficient and Condyne punishment apoynted and limited by the due course of the Lawes of this Realme for the detestable and abominable Vice of Buggery committed with mankind or beast . . . that the same offence be from henceforth adjudged felony and such order and form of process therein to be used agaynst the offenders as in cases of felony at the Common lawe. And that the offenders being hereof convict by verdict confession or outlawry shall suffer such paynes of death and losses and penalties of their goods chattels debts lands tenements and hereditaments as felons being accustomed to do accordynge to the order of the Common Lawes of this Realme. . . .*'

This measure, first enacted by Parliament in 1533, made homosexual acts an offence under English criminal law. With the exception of the penalties of death and forfeiture of property, for which life imprisonment was substituted in 1861, the Act remained in substance on the Statute Book until 1967.

Reproduced by permission from the original in the House of Lords Record Office.

THE OTHER LOVE

*An Historical and Contemporary Survey
of Homosexuality in Britain*

H. MONTGOMERY HYDE

HEINEMANN : LONDON

William Heinemann Ltd

LONDON MELBOURNE TORONTO

JOHANNESBURG AUCKLAND

First published 1970

434 35902 5

PRINTED IN GREAT BRITAIN BY
WESTERN PRINTING SERVICES LTD, BRISTOL

FOR MY WIFE

'Sweet youth,
Tell me why, sad and sighing, dost thou rove
These pleasant realms? I pray thee tell me sooth,
What is thy name?' He said, 'My name is Love,'
Then straight the first did turn himself to me,
And cried, 'He lieth, for his name is Shame.
But I am Love, and I was wont to be
Alone in this fair garden, till he came
Unasked by night; I am true Love, I fill
The hearts of boy and girl with mutual flame.'
Then sighing said the other, 'Have thy will,
I am the Love that dare not speak its name.'

Lord Alfred Douglas, 'Two Loves'
Quoted at the trial of Oscar Wilde, April 30, 1895

Contents

Acknowledgements

I wish to thank those who have generously put their knowledge of the subject of this book at my disposal and given me the benefit of their helpful advice, notably Mr Leo Abse, M.P., the Earl of Arran, Mr Antony Grey, Mr Anatole James, Dr R. S. Morton, Mr Michael Schofield, Dr D. J. West, and Sir John Wolfenden.

To Mr Antony Grey, Dr Phyllis Grosskurth, the indefatigable secretary, and the small but dedicated staffs of the Homosexual Law Reform Society and the Albany Trust, whose joint efforts have contributed so much to the important change in the English law which took place in 1967, I am under a particular debt of gratitude for making available to me a number of case histories and other relevant material from their office files, and to Mr Grey personally for reading this book in typescript and making numerous suggestions for its improvement which I have been glad to adopt.

I am also glad to thank Mrs Bridget Pym, Lecturer in Sociology at the University of Sheffield, for reading the book in proof and checking various facts and figures.

For permission to quote from the following published works which are in copyright, I am grateful to The Bodley Head Ltd, Coward-McCann Inc. and the executors of the late J. R. Ackerley, and to Martin Secker and Warburg Ltd and Mr Bryan Magee, publishers and authors respectively of *My Father and Myself* (copyright © 1968 by the executors of the late J. R. Ackerley) and *One in Twenty* (copyright © 1966 by Bryan Magee). I also wish to thank Mr Edward Colman, literary executor of the late Lord Alfred Douglas, for permission to quote part of the poem 'Two Loves'.

I am likewise grateful to the Trustees and Librarian of the London Library for allowing me to examine and make use as background material of the MS memoirs of John Addington Symonds now preserved in the Library and subject to restricted access. I also wish to thank the Keeper of the Records in the House of Lords for permission to inspect and reproduce the original of the statute of Henry VIII which appears as the frontispiece to the book.

H.M.H.

Westwell House,
Tenterden, Kent.
October, 1969.

CHAPTER ONE

The Contemporary Scene

At his trial for homosexual offences in 1895, Oscar Wilde was asked in cross-examination about 'the Love that dare not speak its name'. The phrase occurred in the poem 'Two Loves' written by his friend Lord Alfred Douglas, and prosecuting counsel put it to Wilde that the reference was to 'unnatural love' as distinct from 'natural' or heterosexual love. Wilde did not agree with counsel's interpretation, and he was invited to explain why.

' "The Love that dare not speak its name" in this century', Wilde replied, 'is such a great affection of an elder for a younger man as there was between David and Jonathan, such as Plato made the very basis of his philosophy, and such as you find in the sonnets of Michelangelo and Shakespeare. It is that deep, spiritual affection that is as pure as it is perfect. . . . It is in this century misunderstood, so much misunderstood that it may be described as "the Love that dare not speak its name", and on account of it I am placed where I am now. It is beautiful, it is fine, it is the noblest form of affection. There is nothing unnatural about it, and it repeatedly exists between an elder and a younger man, when the elder has intellect, and the younger man has all the joy, hope and glamour of life before him. That it should be so, the world does not understand. The world mocks at it and sometimes puts one in the pillory for it.'

It is on record that Wilde's words produced a spontaneous outburst of applause from his sympathizers in the public gallery, mingled with hissing on the part of the less sympathetic members of the audience. This moved the presiding judge to say that he would have the court cleared if there was any further manifestation of feeling.

In this brilliant impromptu speech at the Old Bailey, Wilde put homosexual love on the highest plane. It expressed his affectionate feelings for Lord Alfred Douglas, amongst others. Unfortunately for Wilde, there was a reverse side to the coin. Wilde's relations with his friend had not been confined to what is commonly called Platonic. There had been a physical relationship between them and, although Douglas was not a witness in the trial, there were other accomplices who gave evidence of physical intimacies, and their testimony—given in return for immunity from prosecution themselves—left no doubt of Wilde's commission of the 'acts of gross indecency' *in private* of which he was accused. In passing the maximum sentence which the law then allowed on Wilde and his confederate Alfred Taylor—two years' imprisonment with hard labour—Mr Justice Wills remarked that it was the worst case he had ever tried. 'That you, Taylor, kept a kind of male brothel,' said the judge, addressing the two prisoners in the dock, 'it is impossible to doubt. And that you, Wilde, have been the centre of the circle of extensive corruption of the most hideous kind among young men, it is equally impossible to doubt.' Incidentally, so far as Wilde was concerned, the judge's stricture was unfair, since Wilde was not proved to have corrupted any young men; on the contrary, all the youthful associates who testified against him at his trial were already practising homosexuals long before Wilde first made their acquaintance, and some of them were self-confessed blackmailers as well.

The Wilde trials and their aftermath represented the high water mark of popular prejudice against homosexuality in Victorian England, and the anti-homosexual feeling was continued into the Edwardian and neo-Georgian period. A more humanitarian climate was slow in coming. 'I have no doubt we shall win,' Wilde told the criminologist George Ives when he came out of prison in 1897, 'but the road is long, and red with monstrous martyrdoms. Nothing but the repeal of the Criminal Law Amendment Act would do any good. That is the essential. It is not so much public opinion, as public officials that need educating.'[1]

It took exactly seventy years to achieve the change in the English law that Wilde demanded. The process began in August 1954 with the appointment by the Government of a Departmental Committee under the chairmanship of Sir John Wolfenden, then Vice-Chancellor of Reading University, to consider, among other matters, the law and practice relating to homosexual offences and the treatment of persons convicted of such offences by the courts, and to suggest any changes which in the committee's opinion were desirable.[2]

Two months later, on the centenary anniversary of Wilde's

[1] *The Letters of Oscar Wilde* edited by Rupert Hart-Davis (1962), p. 726.
[2] *Report of the Committee on Homosexual Offences and Prostitution* (1957).

birth, a plaque, which had been erected by the London County Council on the front of the house in Chelsea where Wilde had lived, was unveiled by Sir Compton Mackenzie in the presence of a distinguished gathering, including several Members of Parliament. Among Wilde's surviving friends and contemporaries, who had hoped to be present, was the author and artist Laurence Housman, then in his ninetieth year, but he was too infirm to face the chilly outdoor ceremony. But he did send a message, which was read out by the chairman of the proceedings, who happened to be the present writer. Housman had been deeply moved at the time by Wilde's conviction, as indeed he remained sixty years later. 'His unhappy fate has done the world a signal service in defeating the blind obscurantists: he has made people think,' Housman said in his message. 'Far more people of intelligence think differently today because of him.'

This view found expression, three years later, in the recommendation of the Wolfenden Committee that homosexual behaviour between consenting adults in private should no longer be a criminal offence. A further decade was to elapse before this recommendation became law in England, and during the intervening period the question was frequently discussed both inside and outside Parliament. Today it remains a topic of controversy in Scotland and Northern Ireland, where the old law still prevails; but in the rest of Britain the legislative change has been generally accepted, at least among rational and liberal-minded thinkers, and homosexual conduct between grown-up males in the privacy of their homes is no longer regarded as a crime or even a disease, but simply as an alternative means of sexual gratification with a considerable minority appeal. Furthermore, it has largely put an end to the blackmailing of homosexuals by despicable scoundrels, which was for so long a standing reproach to the English criminal law.

It should be understood that the recent Sexual Offences Act does not give male homosexuals complete *carte blanche* in the matter of their behaviour. In the interests of discipline, serving members of the armed forces are excepted from the benefit of its provisions, as also are the crews of British merchant ships while they are on board their vessels. So far as other consenting adult males are concerned, no more than two persons may take part or be present, and the act must not be done in a lavatory to which the public have access. Finally, both consenting parties must be over the age of twenty-one at the relevant time. If one party is a day under that age, the other is liable on conviction on indictment to be sent to prison for five years, although the maximum sentence in such circumstances under the old law was two years. This change was made by Parliament in accordance with the Wolfenden Committee's recommendations regarding the seduction of minors by older men.

If both parties are under twenty-one—that is to say, if they are consenting adolescents instead of consenting adults—they risk going to prison for two years. In a recent case involving four teen-age youths, whose ages ranged from sixteen to nineteen, the accused pleaded through their counsel in the Court of Criminal Appeal that the Act of 1967 was intended to protect youngsters under twenty-one and not to impose upon them any liability to criminal sanctions if homosexual acts occurred between them. The appellate judge quickly disabused them of this idea when he remarked that they had 'entirely misconceived the intentions of Parliament'. In setting aside the sentences imposed by the lower court on the two younger of the youths, the judge added that 'they had developed some strength of character and had prospects of establishing normal relationships with young women'. The other two were sent for training at a Borstal institution, since the judge felt that they needed protection against 'the misery which life will have in store for them if they fail to develop natural sexual impulses and desires', although the judge did not explain how the youths could be expected to develop these impulses and desires at Borstal.[1] In this utterance the judge reflected the traditional view that homosexual acts are 'unnatural' or 'against nature', in that they cheat Nature of new offspring, rather than the more tolerant and understanding conception that homosexuals should no more be penalized for their conduct than should the left-handed or the colour-blind for being born with these eccentricities or at any rate developing them at an early age. Most men become aware of the direction of their sexual tendencies long before they reach the age of twenty-one, and there is certainly a case for reducing the age of consent for male homosexuals to eighteen or even sixteen, which is the operative age for heterosexuals.

For the time being, however, the police in Britain are zealous in the pursuit of suspected cases where there is an age difference, that is, where one or both of the parties to the homosexual act is under twenty-one. In a recent case, a youth living in the north of England was questioned for several days by the county police until he admitted having sexual relations with a local clergyman.

[1] *Stoke Evening Sentinel*, April 9, 1968.

A doctor who was called to give evidence said that in his opinion the youth had suffered far more from the interrogation than from the homosexual relationship. The clergyman was convicted and sent to prison.

Some judges and magistrates, particularly of elderly vintage, are still clearly out of sympathy with any form of sexual deviation, whatever the circumstances. A man of seventy-six, for instance, was recently sentenced to six months' imprisonment by a London court for homosexual conduct with a youngster, to which the youth consented, although a report from a probation officer suggested that the man was still emotionally and mentally disturbed by reason of his wife's death and that what he really needed was not a prison term but geriatric care.[1]

In England, from the reign of King Henry VIII to that of Queen Victoria, those convicted of 'the abominable crime' of buggery or sodomy were liable to suffer death and in practice frequently did so. In 1861 (1889 in Scotland) the maximum penalty was changed to life imprisonment. By the Criminal Law Amendment Act of 1885, homosexual acts of 'gross indecency' not amounting to buggery, which had hitherto not been regarded as a crime at all, were made subject to a maximum of two years imprisonment with hard labour. It was under this statute that Wilde was prosecuted and numerous other proceedings were brought by the police against a wide range of individual offenders over a period of more than eighty years. In 1967 all homosexual acts between consenting adults in private, subject to the two above mentioned exceptions, ceased to be criminal, whatever their character, in England.

As will be seen, popular prejudice against homosexuality throughout Britain has largely derived from the Bible and Biblical interpretation, as it has in America. But in the legal sphere, the enactments of the two principal statutes penalizing homosexual behaviour—in 1533 and 1885—were to a great extent fortuitous, and as drafted they were not primarily designed to punish homosexuals for the heinousness of their acts. The earlier statute was an example of power politics aimed at the Church by Henry VIII's minister Thomas Cromwell. The declared purpose of the Act of 1885 was to protect women and girls from the perils of prostitution and white slavery, and the clause concerning gross indecency between consenting male adults in private was only slipped into the measure as the result of an amendment moved by a Private Member in the course of a late sitting of the House of

[1] *The Observer*, August 31, 1968.

Commons, the significance of which was not generally appreciated
at the time. Neither statute was inspired by any particular wish
of the legislature to punish homosexual behaviour, but originated
in quite different considerations.

[2]

It is as well at the outset to clear up some current misconcep-
tions, which my experience shows are more widespread than
might be imagined. Many people think that 'homo' derives
from the Latin word for man, whereas in fact it stems from the
Greek word *homos* meaning 'the same'. A homosexual, therefore,
is a person who has a propensity for another of the same sex as
himself—or herself. Female homosexuals are commonly called
lesbians, from the island of Lesbos inhabited in the seventh
century B.C. by Sappho, the Greek poetess and best known female
homosexual in the ancient world, whose verses breathe the most
powerful feelings for other women, although she herself was to
marry and have a daughter of her own. Lesbian behaviour has
never been criminal in England, although an unsuccessful attempt
was made in Parliament to make it so in 1921; nor has lesbianism
ever excited the popular revulsion here and in America that male
homosexuality has.

Another common misconception is that male homosexuals
invariably practice buggery, or sodomy, as anal copulation is
known in Scotland. This is far from being the case. To some
extent this false impression may have been provided by criminal
statistics and records of proceedings brought by the police. Dr
Eustace Chesser, a most experienced psychologist and worker in
this field, doubts whether more than 15 per cent of practising
male homosexuals in this country are sodomists.[1] In fact, he is
inclined to the view that the number of husbands indulging in
this practice with their wives, as among others the poet Byron is
believed to have done, is more than 15 per cent. In an investigation which he carried out many years ago in an English provincial town, Chesser found that this practice was accepted by
many wives as an insurance against pregnancy, as still happens in
Catholic communities on the continent of Europe, where it has
been known in France as *le vice italien*, at least since the days of
the famous sculptor and goldsmith Benvenuto Cellini who experi-
mented in this fashion with one of his models, the original of the

[1] Eustace Chesser. *Live and Let Live* (1958), 31.

celebrated 'Nymph of Fontainebleau' now in the Louvre. Of course, statistics of homosexual techniques must always be regarded with caution. The percentage of practising sodomists may be a little higher than Chesser's figure, as is suggested by the survey undertaken by Gordon Westwood (Michael Schofield) for the British Social Biology Council, but probably not a great deal.[1]

Another popular fallacy is that the average homosexual is an effeminate person, who can easily be picked out for his feminine appearance and mannerisms. There are some effeminate homosexuals who ape women in their manners and even dress, just as some lesbians wear their hair short and affect mannish clothing. But it is fair to say that the great majority of homosexuals of both sexes are indistinguishable at first sight from the normal heterosexual type of man or woman. Indeed, far from being effeminate and weakling, many homosexual men have shown the greatest courage and devotion to duty and in time of war or other emergency have performed feats of outstanding personal bravery, as was abundantly proved in their service records in the two great world conflicts of arms in the present century. A story is told of a certain holder of the Victoria Cross, which he had won for leading a bayonet charge in particularly dangerous conditions in World War I, being summoned a few years ago to parade with other V.C.s before Queen Elizabeth. Before leaving for Buckingham Palace, he remarked jokingly to a friend, who was also homosexual, 'Anyway, there'll be at least two queens there!'[2]

At this point it may be asked, what do homosexuals actually do in the matter of physical relationships? There are some homosexual couples living together, who do not need, or at any rate no longer need, physical satisfaction, just as others like minded are to be found among married and other heterosexual couples. But many homosexuals of both sexes, it is true to say, do require an outlet for their physical needs.

Male homosexual techniques may be conveniently divided into four main varieties, namely, mutual masturbation, full body, oral genital, and anal; the anal method may be further subdivided into active and passive.

Physical relationships usually begin with fondling, caressing, kissing, culminating in mutual masturbation. One of the young male prostitutes who testified for the prosecution in the Wilde trials said in his evidence: 'I was asked by Wilde to imagine that I was a woman and that he was my lover. I had to keep up this

---

[1] Gordon Westwood. *A Minority* (1960).
[2] Douglas Plummer. *Queer People* (1963), 28.

illusion. I used to sit on his knees and he used to play with my privates as a man might amuse himself with a girl.' According to this witness, he later allowed Wilde to masturbate him and he did the same with Wilde.

Later the parties may proceed to more sophisticated techniques. When the police raided Alfred Taylor's rooms in London, where Wilde was introduced to various homosexual youths and male prostitutes, pairs of trousers were found with slits or vents in place of pockets, a feature plainly designed to facilitate masturbation.

'Full body' is where two men are in bed together and both experience an orgasm in close proximity to each other without employing any other stimuli. Thirdly, 'oral genital' or *fellatio*, to give this technique its Latin name, occurs where one's penis is inserted into the other's mouth and the orgasm is induced by the other sucking the organ. Mutual masturbation, 'full body' with intercrural movements, and 'oral genital' are the most frequently practised forms of homosexual intercourse in that order.

Between 1885 and 1967, the foregoing techniques were all criminal even if conducted in private. Before 1885, they were not regarded as criminal, although in certain circumstances the 'full body' technique was so regarded prior to 1828. Early in the nineteenth century the Crown lawyers argued unsuccessfully that *fellatio* amounted to buggery within the meaning of the statute of Henry VIII. In 1817, at Warwick Assizes, a man was convicted and sentenced to death for such an act committed with a boy about seven years of age. According to the report, 'it was proved very satisfactorily that the prisoner had prevailed upon the boy to go with him from the market place in Nuneaton to a rick yard in a field near the town, that he forced the boy's mouth open with his fingers, and put his private parts into the boy's mouth, and emitted in his mouth'. However, Lord Chief Baron Richards, who tried the case, postponed the execution until the opinion of his brother judges could be obtained as to whether the act constituted buggery. The judges duly met and held that it did not, with the result that the prisoner received a free pardon.[1]

The anal method—buggery (*pedicatio*)—that is the intromission of the active partner's penis into the other's anus, is the method which arouses the strongest feelings of revulsion on the part of anti-homosexuals. There are various reasons for this, as the witnesses before the Wolfenden Committee pointed out. For centuries buggery has been known as the 'abominable crime'

[1] *R. v. Samuel Jacobs* (1817), Russ. and Ry. 331.

under English statute law, on account of its condemnation in the Bible as involving coition and thus simulating more than any other homosexual act the normal act of heterosexual intercourse. Other objections to this technique are that it may sometimes approximate in the homosexual field to rape in the heterosexual, and that there is the risk of physical injury or even venereal disease resulting to the passive partner. ('Oh no, I'd never be the passive one,' was a practising homosexual's reply in a recent survey. 'I'm afraid of catching something.') The evidence received by the Wolfenden Committee suggested that cases in which physical injury results from the act of buggery are very rare. But it has been known to happen, occasionally with fatal results. For instance, Wilde's friend Marcel Schwob, the French essayist and short story writer, to whom Wilde dedicated *The Sphinx* 'in friendship and admiration', died from the effects of a syphilitic tumour in the rectum, which he acquired as the result of anal intercourse with an infected youth.

The Wolfenden Committee argued in their Report that there are other forms of homosexual behaviour which are no less likely to result in physical damage; and since the general law provided for the punishment of acts causing bodily harm, there was no apparent justification for attaching a special penalty to buggery on the ground that it might cause physical injury. It seemed probable, too, to the Committee that a homosexual act which caused bodily harm would amount in most cases to an 'indecent assault', and that the current maximum penalty of ten years' imprisonment for indecent assault allowed sufficiently for any case in which physical injury was caused. Thus the Committee considered it 'ludicrous' that two consenting parties should be liable to imprisonment for life simply because their homosexual acts took a particular form, while they were liable to only two years' imprisonment if the act took some other form which might be 'no less repulsive to ordinary people'. Anyhow this consideration of what Baroness Wootton has aptly called 'queer geography' convinced the legislators that there was no overriding reason for retaining buggery as a separate offence; and in the result as embodied in the Sexual Offences Act, 1967, no distinction was made in the various kinds of male homosexual behaviour, which apart from the armed services and the merchant navy are now no longer criminal, provided the parties are over twenty-one and the acts take place in private.

Of the male homosexuals questioned by Westwood, 39 per cent admitted that the most usual techniques which they practised

were the anal and oral; 24 per cent stated that they usually engaged in the other techniques, but were prepared to take part
occasionally in the anal and oral. 'No one thing plays an important
part in our sex,' one contact declared. 'It's mostly love with us.
I like to adapt myself. I only enjoy sex if I know the other is
enjoying it.' The remaining 34 per cent flatly objected to both
anal and oral techniques and would not take part in them at any
price. The objections of some homosexuals to the two anal
techniques, some objecting to one and some to the other, were for
such reasons mainly as physical disability, fears of venereal
disease and internal injury, impotence, difficulty in reaching
orgasm, and just lack of interest. It is worth noting that the homosexuals who preferred passive anal intercourse did not necessarily
possess either a feminine physique or feminine mannerisms.
Indeed it was found impossible to establish any apparent connection between the homosexual subject's outward appearance
and a preferred technique.

Most practising male homosexuals start with mutual masturbation and then progress to other techniques. Of a sample of
78 who began in this way, only 5 still preferred mutual masturbation when interviewed by Westwood. Of the remainder, 29
preferred full body, 17 preferred passive anal, 13 preferred active
anal, 9 preferred oral genital, while 5 did not wish to continue
their homosexual practices. Some were afraid to experiment with
the more sophisticated techniques. 'I haven't tried it yet,' said
one of those questioned on the active anal method. 'I'm too
nervous to start. I'd have to get very drunk before I'd do it for
the first time and I don't like getting drunk, so I don't know how
to start. I'm not against it or anything—just a bit afraid of starting.'

Female homosexual techniques are similar to the male except
for the use of a dildo or artificial penis by one of the partners in
imitation of normal heterosexual intercourse. The commonest
technique consists in simply kissing and manual manipulation
of the breasts and genitalia, which can lead to mutual masturbation. There are also various kinds of genital apposition approxi-
mating to the 'full body' technique of male homosexuals. The
nearest approach to the anal method practised by males, sometimes called 'lying spoons', is where one woman lies on her side
with her back turned towards the other and embraces her from
behind, fitting her thighs into the bend of her companion's legs,
so that her private parts are in close contact with the other's
buttocks, and slight movement then causes erethism of increasing
intensity which in turn induces orgasm. Contrary to popular

male opinion, an enlarged clitoris plays very little part in lesbian gratification. Mutual contact and friction of the sexual parts were common in ancient Greece, where women practitioners were known as *tribades*, from the Greek verb meaning to rub; hence the word tribadism, sometimes used like lesbianism as a synonym for female homosexuality generally.

Although the dildo was likewise known to the ancient world—the Greek women used a leather variety (*olisbos*), which is the subject of witticism in the *Lysistrata* of Aristophanes—it was also known in medieval France, where the Abbé Brantôme calls it a *godemiche* and describes its use among the ladies of the court. Its use must be regarded as comparatively rare today, in spite of Havelock Ellis's statement to the contrary when he was writing. Dr Kinsey was struck by its rarity in the case histories which he noted in America and such evidence as exists on this particular aspect points to a similar pattern in Britain.

[3]

Figures for the incidence of homosexuality, that is the proportion of homosexuals to heterosexuals in the community, are fuller and more detailed for America than for Britain. This is due to Kinsey's two monumental surveys, to which nothing comparable in extent has been undertaken in Britain, where excessive reliance has tended to be placed on criminal records and statistics. Kinsey's conclusion is that in the United States 4 per cent of adult white males are exclusively homosexual throughout their lives after the onset of adolescence. He also found evidence to suggest that 8 per cent of the white male population are more or less exclusively homosexual for at least three years between the ages of sixteen and sixty-five, and that 37 per cent of the total male population have at least some overt homosexual experience, to the point of orgasm, between adolescence and old age.

Comparable figures in the case of lesbians are considerably less, only about half to one-third exclusively homosexual and about one-third with contacts proceeding to orgasm i.e. 13 per cent as compared with 37 per cent in the case of male homosexuals. Incidentally these figures run contrary to the widespread opinion that the numbers of lesbians are proportionately higher than male homosexuals and, as Kinsey points out, may have originated in the fact that women are more openly affectionate than men in our western culture. They may hold hands in public, put their arms round each other, publicly fondle and kiss each other, and openly express their admiration for other females without being accused of homosexual proclivities, as men would be if they made such an open display of their interests in other men. The data collected by the Kinsey team showed that most of these women were not motivated by any overt homosexual attraction.

Kinsey's published findings met with much hostile criticism and abuse in England. 'It would have been a cleaner world,' wrote one doctor in a professional journal, 'if Kinsey had stuck to his rats.' In the northern provincial town of Doncaster, for example, the local bench of magistrates actually ordered the confiscation of *The Sexual Behaviour of the Human Female* on the ground that its tendency was to 'deprave and corrupt' within the meaning of the law of obscenity, but later decided against condemning it as obscene. Several national newspapers suggested that the Kinsey books were pornographic and morally subversive, but this did not prevent them from quoting the more sensational passages under provocative headlines. Unlike the press, however, the Wolfenden Committee accorded Kinsey due respect, and in their Report remarked that some of the medical witnesses had expressed the view that something very like Kinsey's figures would be established in Britain if similar inquiries were made, although the majority were of the opinion notwithstanding their lack of statistical knowledge that these figures would be 'on the high side' for this country.

The only figures relating to the systematic examination of anything like a normal sample in Britain were provided for the Wolfenden Committee by a psychologist, who gave evidence to the effect that he had examined 100 male university undergraduates and found that 30 of them had had homosexual trends and fantasies at some time in their lives and that five of these still retained them at the age of 20-plus. While certainly not prepared to say that none of the five would outgrow his condition, this witness felt that such a change was unlikely. While this sample was neither sufficiently large nor sufficiently representative of the population as a whole to enable any valid conclusions to be drawn, as the Report pointed out, it is worth while noting that subsequent samples which have been taken from cross-sections of the community tend to confirm it.

Such social surveys as have been undertaken in Britain also tend to confirm the general approximation of the Kinsey figures to the comparable figures here. In other words, there are a million or more men in Britain whose interests are predominantly homosexual—that is roughly 4 per cent of the male population or 1 in 25. For lesbians, the figures are proportionately less, although the incidence of lesbianism is even more difficult to assess—probably something between half and three-quarters of a million English women, for the most part unmarried. Of course, these figures apply to adults, and do not take into account adolescents of either sex with whom homosexuality is a passing phase at school or college and who later settle down to normal heterosexual life. Nor do all homosexuals necessarily indulge in homosexual acts. Many of them repress or sublimate their sexual feelings.

Male homosexuals tend to be more promiscuous than lesbians, and their 'affairs' are less constant and more unstable than those of their female counterparts. One reason which has been suggested for this phenomenon is that men are sexually more easily aroused than women by psychological stimuli and that, therefore, male homosexuals tend to be less faithful to their partners than lesbian women are to theirs. The sight of a good-looking youth, especially when he is undressed, can quickly produce an erection in a male homosexual just as the sight of a pretty nude woman can in a heterosexual man. Women, on the other hand, whether lesbian or heterosexual, are much less easily moved by similar sights and stimuli in the absence of physical contact and they can consequently do without sex for much longer periods than men. Fear of falling foul of the criminal law may also have contributed to the instability of the male relationships in the past and have discouraged the setting up of open and permanent establishments with the risk of denunciation to the police. It is too soon to say yet whether the 1967 Act has had any appreciable effect in this context, but by removing the apprehension of the policeman's knock on the door it cannot fail to operate beneficially and reduce promiscuity among male homosexuals. Indeed the knowledge that the consenting adult was breaking the law whenever he committed a homosexual act in private sometimes provided an additional thrill. 'It was like feasting with panthers,' Wilde wrote from his prison cell in Reading. 'The danger was half the excitement.'

Of the male homosexuals interviewed by Westwood, 16 per cent stated that they sometimes obtained extra excitement from their homosexual adventures because they were against the law, while 21 per cent replied that they believed it did add extra excitement for others but not for themselves. 'I appreciate the slight danger—the idea of being outside the law,' said one contact. 'I didn't really appreciate this in myself until I met an Argentinian who said it was much more fun in England because at home no one thinks anything of it. I think this accounts for the people one sees around who one feels perfectly sure aren't queer, but they indulge because they know it's exciting—anything for kicks.'

Compared with the males, relatively little is known about female homosexuality and there are very few published studies which are based on a representative sample of the lesbian population. As Dr F. E. Kenyon, a psychiatrist who has made such a study, has put it, many ideas on the subject are mere extrapolations from studies of male homosexuals. Dr Kenyon's study was initiated in order to obtain as representative a sample as possible of female homosexuals, and it was carried out, not from selected psychiatric patients but from 123 lesbians who belonged to an organization concerned with their interests.[1] They were then compared with an equal number of heterosexual women, belonging to various organizations for married women, such as Women's Institutes. The investigation, which was in the form of an anonymous postal survey, revealed that in spite of the lesser social stigma and greater opportunity for association between two women than is the case with men there was nevertheless considerable personal distress as reflected in the fact that approximately one in four lesbians wished to become exclusively heterosexual and one in five had experienced a 'nervous breakdown', causing them to seek psychiatric treatment with a view to change. In contrast with the heterosexual women, more lesbians had a poor relationship with their mothers, who were more likely to have had a mental disturbance or to have died. Poor relationships with the father were also more frequent in this group; fewer lesbians rated their parents' marriages as happy and there was a higher incidence of parents' separation and divorce. Also fewer lesbians remembered their childhood as happy, although later sexual adjustment does not seem to have been determined in any appreciable degree by boarding-school experience.

More lesbians than heterosexuals had gone to a university, more had a poorer work record and they showed a greater rejection of organized religion. More had been in the armed forces or police and fewer belonged to a Women's Institute. Among the lesbians 24 per cent reported a family history of homosexuality, most commonly in a brother, as compared with only 2·4 per cent of the heterosexual women. In this study, fewer lesbians had

[1] *British Journal of Psychiatry*, Vol. 114, pp. 1337–50 (November, 1968).

received any sexual instruction from their mothers and the general family attitude seems to have been one of 'outright rejection'. Only 8 per cent of the lesbians reported early seduction, while 40 per cent remembered a particularly traumatic sexual advance by a man. Over half the lesbians had experienced heterosexual intercourse, though proportionately more than in the case of the heterosexuals had found it unsatisfactory. Thirty-four per cent had been engaged to be married and nearly 20 per cent had been pregnant at the time. Half the lesbians, compared with 5 per cent of the heterosexuals, rated their sexual adjustment as poor. Nine out of the sample of 123 lesbians were still married. The mean age at which they were first aware of homosexual feelings was sixteen years and the mean age for first physical experience was twenty-one. On the other hand, only 5 per cent of the heterosexual women admitted that they had ever had any homosexual feelings.

Commenting generally on Dr Kenyon's study, which has considerably clarified the factors which deserve further research, the *British Medical Journal* remarked in a recent editorial article:

Anomalies of early relationships with parents and repressive family attitudes towards sexuality are among the most consistent findings in studies of homosexuality in either sex. Despite our inadequate knowledge of the development of sexual orientation it is possible to recognize circumstances specially apt to result in anomalous sexual development. Children reared in families which are incomplete, disturbed by distortions in personal relationships, or whose sexual attitudes are markedly clouded by repression or ignorance appear to be particularly vulnerable. Specific difficulties in relating to other people, lack of opportunity for satisfactory social contact with the opposite sex, or undue exposure to erotically stimulating contact with members of the same sex, such as may occur in single sex institutions or organizations, may result in the stirring of homosexual feelings in the adolescent. If this occurs in an individual factually or emotionally unprepared for adult sexuality it may form the basis for a life-long pattern of sexual function. It is particularly important to stress that these homosexual feelings do not inevitably imply homosexuality. However homosexual contacts are often as effective as heterosexual in the male and more effective in the female in bringing the individual to orgasm, so that once physical behaviour is established it becomes extremely difficult to displace.[1]

[1] *British Medical Journal*, February 8, 1969.

It is widely believed, as the Wolfenden Committee appreciated, that the prevalence of homosexuality has greatly increased in Britain during the present century and that homosexual practices are much more frequent than they used to be, particularly since the last war. It is true that the subject is discussed much more openly than was formerly the case, and it has been treated with increasing frankness through the media of the press, radio and television, as well as books. Recently the B.B.C. put on a play about the love of an adult homosexual for a boy, a subject which would have been unthinkable for dramatic treatment in this way a few years ago, while the recent production of John Herbert's play *Fortune and Men's Eyes* depicting the activities of homosexuals in a Canadian reformatory, including a scene in which three men are seen completely naked on the stage, would never have been licensed for public performance when the Lord Chamberlain exercised a strict censorship of the English theatre. Public interest in homosexuality has unquestionably increased, encouraged by the publicity given to the subject not only by the media already mentioned but also by the long-drawn-out discussions in Parliament before the recent Sexual Offences Act became law. Between the end of the Second World War and the passing of the Act, a sharp rise took place in the number of homosexual offences known to the police. But this may well have been due to more efficient police methods of detection and recording: it does not necessarily follow that more offences actually occurred during this period. In the years immediately preceding the change in the law, the number of indictable homosexual crimes known to the police averaged 5,000, compared with less than 1,000 in the years between the two world wars. Yet notwithstanding these figures, as the Wolfenden Committee were quick to realize, it would be dangerous to argue from the police statistics alone either that there was an overall increase or that homosexual behaviour was more prevalent in those areas where the number of cases recorded as known to the police was highest.

Those witnesses, who appeared before the Wolfenden Committe and expressed the view that there had been an increase, attributed the supposed increase mainly to three causes. In the first place, it was felt that in the post-war atmosphere of greater sexual freedom and 'general loosening of former moral standards' the increased measure of tolerance accorded to homosexual behaviour had encouraged its practice. Secondly, there was the feeling that the homosexual behaviour which was the result of war-time conditions, where men were thrown into each other's company for long periods at a time, had been carried over to some

extent into peace time. Thirdly, it was felt that the weakening
of family ties, emotional insecurity and community instability
which characterize contemporary society, must be responsible in
some measure for the supposed upward trend in homosexual
practices.

'Most of us think it improbable that the increase in the number
of offences as known to the police can be explained entirely by
greater police activity,' was the Wolfenden Committee's cautious
conclusion, 'though we all think it very unlikely that homosexual behaviour has increased proportionately to the dramatic
rise in the number of offences recorded as known to the police.'
My personal belief is that any increase attributable to the factors
advanced in the preceding paragraph is entirely minimal. I am
convinced from a study of the subject extending over the past
twenty years that there has been very little variation in the
incidence of both homosexuality and homosexual conduct in
proportion to the total population at any given period and that this
applies not only to the present century but to the previous eight
centuries, that is from the time that local chroniclers and his-
torians first began to take note of the phenomenon in English
society.

[4]

Another widely held but erroneous belief is that homosexuality
is peculiar to members of particular professions and trades such
as actors, boxers, interior decorators, sailors, waiters, Turkish
bath attendants and musicians. An old example of this prejudice
is worth recalling. In 1884, when the notorious Dublin Castle
scandals involving homosexual practices in high places were at
their height, two Irish Nationalist M.P.s, T. M. Healy and
Joseph Biggar, fell to discussing the affair on their way home from
Westminster one night. 'Have you noticed that all those buggers
were musical?' Biggar asked his colleague. Tim Healy replied with
the Shakespearian quotation that 'those who have no music in
their souls are fit for treasons, stratagems, and spoils'. But Joe
Biggar did not agree with Shakespeare: with him, according to
Healy, to be 'musical' was almost a capital offence.[1] Although an
avowed scourge of homosexuals, Biggar's own private life was
anything but reputable. He was particularly fond of bar maids,
on one occasion he had to pay a lady £400 as the result of a

[1] T. M. Healy. *Letters and Leaders of My Day* (1928), I, 195.

breach of promise action, and he had at least one illegitimate son, to whom incidentally he left the bulk of a not inconsiderable fortune made from his grocery business in Belfast.

Many aggressive anti-homosexuals are inclined to think that the majority of 'queers' come from the so-called intellectuals in the community or *intelligentsia*. In fact, as the Wolfenden Committee found, homosexuality exists among all callings and at all levels of society from the most intelligent and intellectually brilliant to the dullest and most stupid members of the community, from the high-born and socially prominent to quite obscure and ordinary folk, regardless of whether they may be Members of Parliament or factory workers. A recent police investigation in a small provincial town in Scotland revealed the callings of six homosexuals who had got to know each other— they were a miner, a labourer, a garage works manager, a book-maker, a furniture salesman and a bus conductor. Of course, some homosexuals naturally gravitate towards occupations which bring them into contact with members of their own sex or which have a reputation for tolerance, such as the theatre. Again, the arrest of an M.P. on a homosexual charge has always had greater news value than the arrest of an unknown factory worker, and the press have naturally reported the one at length and may have barely, if at all, noticed the other.

The British Medical Association, in a report which appeared in the same year as the Wolfenden Committee's proposals, stated that 'the existence of practising homosexuals in the Church, Parliament, Civil Service, Forces, Press, radio, stage and other institutions, constitutes a special problem'. The reference to Parliament angered M.P.s and several of them threatened to raise the matter as breach of privilege as bringing Parliament into disrepute. But nothing came of this gesture, those concerned no doubt thinking better of it. One wonders what revelations might have taken place if the allegation had been examined by the Committee of Privileges. During the ten years that I served as an M.P. (1950–59), which covered the publication of the Wolfenden and B.M.A. Reports, three Members of the House of Commons, one of whom was a Junior Minister, were arrested and convicted of homosexual offences, while one Member of the Upper House was sent to prison for twelve months for his part in a particularly sensational case. During the same period several other M.P.s who to my knowledge were practising homosexuals were for-tunate or prudent enough to escape detection; it was in regard to one of these that Sir Winston Churchill was supposed to have made the jocular remark that he was the kind of M.P. who 'gave pederasty a bad name'.

Two of the 'other institutions', not specifically mentioned in the B.M.A. Report, may be mentioned here. They are the police force and the prison service. It may come as a surprise to some readers to know that police are not averse from participating in homosexual acts, whether on or off duty, or in or out of uniform. The same applies to prison officers. Westwood, in his illuminating study of male homosexuality in Great Britain, gives some pertinent examples.

'The nearest I've been to trouble with the law is when I had a policemen to sleep with,' said one man whom Westwood interviewed in his home. 'He had the cheek to come here in uniform.' Another of Westwood's contacts stated that he met a man in civilian clothes during a lunch hour in London and 'we talked for a bit to see if the feeling was mutual'. As the contact had to get back to work, he asked his acquaintance for his telephone number. The man replied that he could not give him his home number as he had just moved house and the telephone had not been installed yet. He said that he would give him his 'work number' but not to be frightened by what he was going to write down. It was Whitehall 1212—the number of Metropolitan Police Headquarters in New Scotland Yard. ('I 'phoned him a few days later and we've met several times since then.')

Another contact related the story of what happened when he encountered the arm of the law on duty.

I was crossing Clapham Common one night. It was after midnight and a policeman shone his torch on me. He asked me where I was going and then he put his hand down. I wondered if anyone else was behind the tree but something told me it was all right, so we went into the bushes. The same thing happened a few months later, only this time it was an Inspector, but I didn't do anything. It's a bit unfair, isn't it? One night they want sex and the next night they'll run you in.

Westwood also gives a revealing example of a prison officer who behaved in the same way with an inmate, who related what took place.

One evening a screw came in with a form and said, 'It says here you're in for burglary.' I said, 'You bloody well know it's buggery not burglary.' He said, 'Ah, that's interesting, I'll have to come back and find out more about that.' I said,

'F— that for a lark, you'll get me into more trouble.' He said, 'Now don't you worry. I don't lock you up just yet, make your bed down and I'll come back when I've finished the floor.' He was fabulous to look at. I had sex with him six times and once on a landing with another of the boys.

A further fallacy, shared to some extent by homosexuals themselves, is that homosexuals are easily recognizable by their appearance or demeanour. Many people think they can spot 'a queer' on sight, but in reality they only recognize the relatively small minority of exhibitionists whose mannerisms and sometimes clothes stamp them as 'screaming pansies'. Masculine type lesbians, who wear men's clothes, occasionally draw attention to their proclivities. But the great majority of homosexuals, both male and female, are not immediately identifiable as such; for example, there was nothing to suggest about either Oscar Wilde or Sir Roger Casement, from their appearance, manners or conversation, that their sexual morals were otherwise than conventional, and many of their friends simply refused to believe it when their names were linked with homosexual charges; yet it is beyond the slightest doubt that they were both practising homosexuals of promiscuous tastes, Casement being specifically a pederast. It is true that homosexuals can be recognized more readily by other homosexuals than they can by heterosexuals, by intuition because they are more on the alert, as well as by such physical features or characteristics as eyes, gestures, voice and walk. But recognition is by no means invariable. 'Quite a few of the queers I've met have said they'd never have dreamt I was queer,' one homosexual told Westwood. Yet it is remarkable how the fallacy of automatic recognition persists—particularly among heterosexuals. 'I'm not recognized, I get ample proof of that,' another homosexual admitted to the same investigator. 'I remember one dinner party, where there were six of us and we got talking about homosexuality. The other two men were violently anti-queer. One of them was [an] M.P., and he addressed me like a father. "You've got no idea how many there are about. I've got a knack of recognizing them and if you'd seen as many as I have, you'd be horrified by it." '

Relatively few male homosexuals are obviously effeminate in manners and appearance, and these include the transvestite who likes to wear women's clothes and to use scent and cosmetics. The average male homosexual disapproves of the effeminate types and dislikes being seen in public with them. 'I feel sorry for them—in a rather patronizing way,' was one remark noted by Westwood. 'But I also regret it, for it gives the tribe a bad name.' Another confessed that he could not understand it. 'To me the whole situation is that a man likes another man. If he liked women he would go to them, not to an imitation of a woman.' The markedly effeminate and transvestite homosexual, it would appear, is only attractive to others in this small group. 'Their behaviour is not meant to arouse sexual desire,' remarked one homosexual in the majority grouping; 'it's more like hitting people in the face. It invites antagonism and that's what these people are seeking.' Although there have been some notable transvestite scandals in the past, as will be seen in a subsequent chapter, they have been of comparatively infrequent occurrence. While there may be an element of hermaphroditism in the make-up of the exhibitionist 'pansy' as well as of narcissism, his behaviour in public can no doubt largely be explained by the psychiatrist as an act of defiance against society.

Westwood's findings, which I accept, revealed that only 13 per cent of male homosexuals in Great Britain are recognizable by the general public. Of the remaining 87 per cent, 3 were known only to other homosexuals, 31 were not known to any one, while 25 were known as homosexual by close friends but were not recognized by casual acquaintances or at work. But some, at least, of the great unrecognizable majority may come under suspicion for other reasons of personal behaviour, such as not being seen going out with girls and being a bachelor 'with a nice flat'. On the other hand, normal heterosexual men may sometimes be suspected of homosexual activities if they are over thirty and still unmarried, and even younger men may become suspect if they decide to share a flat with another man for reasons solely of economy or companionship. Westwood also quotes one case of a wife quite unjustifiably accusing her husband of homosexuality because he was impotent, and another of a youth leader who was forced to give up his valuable social work because there had been talk of his 'unnatural' interest in boys.

Unlike Freemasons, homosexuals do not use secret signs by which they make themselves known to their like-minded fellows. But they do make use of slang terms and expressions in conversation both with heterosexuals and other homosexuals. Indeed the most popular words have sometimes been coined by heterosexuals. In Wilde's time, for example, a homosexual was said to be a *pouf* or 'so' or 'like that', an effeminate homosexual was a *Mary Ann*, and a male prostitute or a homosexual who took

money for his services was called a *renter*. Today the commonest
term in the vernacular to denote a male homosexual is *queer*, no
doubt deriving from its conventional dictionary meaning of
'strange, odd, peculiar, eccentric, in appearance or character'.
According to Westwood, the word was first used in the slang
sense in 1925 in *Variety*, the American theatrical periodical. Yet
the Americans prefer the word *gay*, used more in relation to
places than persons, for example, 'a gay bar'. *Camp*, thought to
come from the Italian *campeggiare* meaning to stand out from a
background, is commonly used to mean ostentatiously homosexual or effeminate, as also is *minny*. *Queen* or *quean* is used to
signify anyone with homosexual mannerisms, though it was
originally restricted to an elderly homosexual trying to look young.
Cottage is a public lavatory, and *cottaging* is visiting these conveniences in search of partners. An *affair* is a homosexual relationship of more than ephemeral duration, while a homosexual
partner is sometimes referred to by his friend as *my affair*. A man
who prefers active anal intercourse is a *butch*, while the passive
male homosexual is commonly called a *bitch*. Women's clothing
is *drag* and to be dressed as a woman is to be *in drag*. *To swish*
is to walk effeminately or with a mincing gait, *to take it* is to perform the passive part in anal intercourse, *to send up* is to ridicule,
and *to cruise* or *troll* is to look for a homosexual partner, and *to
have trade* is to have homosexual relations. A lesbian is a *tom* or a
dyke. A heterosexual is *normal* or *straight* as opposed to a homosexual who is *bent* and a bisexual who is *half-bent*.

Although some British homosexuals seem to accept the word
queer as a fair description of themselves, many of them strongly
object to it even if they sometimes act out its literal implication,
since (as one homosexual has pointed out in a revealing personal
confession) it is 'an unfortunately defensive word, indicating
that we are somehow beyond the pale of ordinary society'.

[5]

One final misconception, particularly prevalent among parents
whose children have developed homosexual tendencies or have
turned out to be homosexual, is that homosexuality is a 'disease'
capable of being cured by medical treatment. (In a recent Gallup
Poll, 93 per cent of those questioned regarded homosexuality as
a disease.) According to this school of thought, any male homosexual can become a heterosexual if he wishes to, but the trouble

is that many of them do not wish to. As will be seen, only the last part of this belief has any validity in practice.

The Wolfenden Committee rejected the belief that homosexuality is a disease, although they did underline the evidence of several of their medical witnesses to the effect that in some cases homosexual offences occurred as symptoms in the course of recognized physical or mental illness, for example, senile dementia or chronic schizophrenia. The Committee on the whole tended to regard homosexuality as a social rather than a medical or psychiatric problem from the point of view of treatment.

Much more important than the academic question whether homosexuality is a disease is the practical question whether a doctor should carry out any part or all of the treatment. Psychiatrists deal regularly with problems of personality which are not regarded as diseases, and conversely the treatment of cases of recognized psychiatric illness may not be strictly medical but may best be carried out by non-medical supervision or environmental change. . . . In fact, the treatment of behaviour disorders, even when medically supervised, is rarely confined to psychotherapy or to treatment of a strictly medical kind. This is not to deny that expert advice should be sought in very many homosexual cases.

The Committee came to the conclusion that a total reorientation from homosexuality to complete heterosexuality in an individual was very unlikely, and they were impressed by the fact that none of the medical witnesses was unable to provide any reference in medical literature to a complete change of this kind. It is true that occasionally such a change has been claimed, but it must be viewed with extreme caution. In their Report the Wolfenden Committee cited the case of an elderly married man, who sought advice, at his wife's instigation, for impotence. It transpired that his propensities had always been entirely homosexual. He had married 'in the hope of cure', but had achieved intercourse only with the aid of homosexual fantasies. 'To all outward appearances this would have seemed a striking example of change in sexual orientation, but it was clear that he had always been and remained a homosexual.'

Dr Desmond Curran, a leading psychiatrist who served on the Wolfenden Committee, has expressed the view that the chances of 'cure' in confirmed cases are negligible and that the psychiatrist should concentrate on making the patient a better adjusted homosexual and not aspire to convert him to heterosexuality. This view, originally derived from Freud and still regarded as heterodox and revolutionary at the time it was propounded in the Wolfenden Report a dozen years ago, is gradually gaining recognition in Britain today. Dr Curran's hand may be clearly seen in its expression in the report.

A homosexual, like any other person who suffers from mal-adjustment to society, may be regarded as successfully treated if he is brought to a more nearly complete adjustment with the society in which he lives. This can happen without any radical change in his propensity itself. It can happen by his being made more fully aware of his condition, and by processes which are directed not to changing it, but towards his fuller under-standing of it and of the problems which it raises for him in relation to society. *The object of the treatment is to relieve mental stress by producing a better adjustment.* It is perhaps worth adding that for this reason there may be good grounds, from the medical point of view, for not attempting any fundamental reorientation of the sexual propensity of a homosexual who is already well adjusted and is a useful member of society. (My italics.)

The Wolfenden Committee considered that in general practice male homosexuals formed a very small fraction of the average doctor's patients. A young man's reluctance to consult the family doctor is quite understandable, since he may well feel that the doctor may warn his parents about the homosexual tendencies of their son. Where doctors have been consulted by young homo-sexuals, there have been some astonishing instances of ignorance and lack of empathy on the part of the medical practitioner, to judge by some of the examples given by Westwood as the result of his investigation. One English doctor told his youthful patient to lie on the couch and loosen his clothing. 'Then he passed his hands over me, telling me to think beautiful thoughts and forget my evil actions.' Another English doctor told the patient 'to pull up my socks, find myself a nice girl and get married', while the advice of a third to the patient whom he described to his face as 'namby pamby', was 'to get a piece of paper and draw pictures of nude women'. No wonder the patient thought the doctor was 'off his rocker'. In another case, where the patient confided in his brother and sister and they all went off to consult their uncle, who was a specialist—we are not told in what branch of medicine—the young man was told that he 'needed more exercise' and was not surprisingly reduced to tears in consequence.

The Wolfenden Committee also argued that treatment may be directed simply towards making the subject 'more discreet or continent in his behaviour, without attempting any other change in his nature'. They felt that this was not to be despised as an objective, since, so long as homosexual acts remained criminal, such treatment, if successful, would diminish the number of homosexual offences and offenders. It is in this respect that the use of hormones (oestrogens) has its place. The hormone treatment is not designed to change the nature and object of a man's sexual desires—indeed this would be impossible—but merely to diminish their intensity. Nevertheless, as the Committee realized, there are many obstacles to success in this form of therapeutic treatment. 'Some of them do not wish to be changed, if only because they are afraid of losing, without any sure prospect of anything to take its place, the one form of sexual satisfaction which they know.' As one of them put it to Westwood, 'Not for me, thank you. I don't want to be left in a sexless limbo.' Another remarked, 'Its part of nature. You can't alter it, no matter how many pills and injections they give you.'

It is significant that out of 1,065 men in English prisons for homosexual offences, while the Committee were sitting, only 158, or 15 per cent, were regarded by the prison medical officers as possible subjects for treatment, and only 65, or 6 per cent, were ultimately accepted for treatment in the psychiatric units at Wakefield and Wormwood Scrubs. Of the remainder (907) regarded as unsuitable for treatment, 245, or 27 per cent, evinced no anxiety or real wish for treatment, while no less than 385, or 42 per cent, were found to be unsuitable 'on account of their age, inadaptability or inadequate character or intelligence'. So far, therefore, therapy in such circumstances in England can hardly be said to have produced any dramatic or far-reaching results.

'Patients', particularly those who have been referred to psychiatrists by the courts, have been known to pretend that the treatment has been successful in order to avoid being sent to prison. The only effect is that they carry on as before, only with more discretion. 'I went to the Clinic twelve times,' one 'patient' told Westwood. 'We talked about my homosexuality at great length, but I felt I was getting nowhere, so I told the psychiatrist that I was no longer attracted to men and everything was all right between my wife and myself. It wasn't true but there didn't seem any point in going on.'

Experience in Great Britain has shown that the young adult homosexual who has adjusted himself to his condition and learned

'to live with it' without outraging the susceptibilities of his
friends, neighbours and workmates, is increasingly disinclined to
change his way of life, especially after the age of thirty. If he
should run foul of the law, he may well agree to submit to
psychiatric treatment, but the purpose of this gesture is merely
to impress the court, since he has no real wish to be sexually
otherwise than he is. 'I object to the assumption that heterosexuals
are normal,' remarked one of Westwood's contacts. 'My kind of
sex is natural to me.'

The need for cultivating or inculcating discretion in the homosexual is perhaps the most valuable service which the psychiatrist
or psychotherapist can render. Now that homosexual practices
between most consenting male adults in private are no longer
illegal, this may be less important than before the recent change
in the law, but it is still not without significance, particularly with
regard to certain public conduct, if the homosexual is to avoid
being 'run in' for importuning, which is an offence still punishable on indictment by two years' imprisonment or six months on
summary conviction by a magistrate. Public lavatories, to take the
most significant example, have long been favourite meeting
places for male homosexuals, either 'for kicks' or because they
have nowhere else to go, in spite of the personal dangers involved
due to constant police surveillance of these establishments and
the deliberate use of *agents provocateurs*. It is probably true to say
that many homosexuals regard 'cottaging' as sordid and despise
homosexuals who resort to this method of finding partners. But
there are exceptions. 'Twenty-five years ago,' a contact of
Westwood's recalled, 'I met a man in a lavatory and we have
become friends for life. So, you see, out of evil came good.' But
there is a very real danger in a man known or suspected by the
police of being a homosexual of going to a public lavatory at all,
since he runs the risk of being 'framed', a possibility which does
not seem to have occurred to the Wolfenden Committee with
their implicit trust in the integrity of British police methods.

Another of Westwood's contacts had this to say on the subject:

If a policeman is there and hasn't got his quota of cases for
that day, you are his solution and there's nothing you can do
about it. It's happened to friends of mine, people who would
not be a bit ashamed to tell me if they really were cottage
crawling. They are so indignant, not because they've been
caught by the police, but because they were doing nothing at
the time. If the policeman decides to take you and you look

queer, nothing will convice the magistrate that you weren't importuning, so the only thing to do is to keep out of public lavatories.

Turkish baths, which tend to be frequented by the more promiscuous type of homosexual, who is attracted by the comparative privacy of the steam room, are scarcely less dangerous from the point of view of discovery than public lavatories. The fact that privacy is incomplete is said to heighten the excitement of those with exhibitionist tendencies. Not long ago a detective who had served for twenty years in the police force was sent to prison for indecency in a Turkish bath. He had gone to the baths with the full knowledge that others had been arrested as the result of police keeping observation through peepholes in the walls.

Clubs, pubs, and bars, including coffee bars, known to be frequented by homosexuals, are generally much safer places of rendezvous. Other towns besides London where these meeting places are known to flourish particularly are Aberdeen, Bath, Birmingham, Blackpool, Brighton, Bristol, Edinburgh, Glasgow, Leeds, Manchester, Nottingham, Plymouth and Portsmouth. In London the largest concentrations of homosexuals are to be found in the districts of Chelsea, Earl's Court and Notting Hill Gate, especially the last. As one homosexual has jocularly put it, 'Picking up queers in Notting Hill Gate is like shooting birds in a game reserve.'

When I was an undergraduate at Oxford forty years ago, and later in the nineteen-thirties, when I settled in London, the most fashionable homosexual rendezvous in the country was a public house off Piccadilly called The Running Horse, known to its patrons as 'the Horse' or 'the Mare'. Its reputation was international and it attracted visitors from all over the European continent. Although it ceased to be a pub in 1939—the premises are now a restaurant—elderly homosexuals from the Continent with nostalgic memories still occasionally inquire for its whereabouts. Similarly patronized hotel bars in my time have ranged from the *de luxe* Ritz to the more plebeian Regent Palace. Incidentally, the famous Empire music hall in Leicester Square, now a cinema, was closed down because it became a haunt of 'queers' and not, as has often been supposed, of 'ladies of the town'.

Perhaps clubs have the most advantages, particularly if they are discreetly and properly managed, as are the majority of homosexual clubs in Great Britain. Like any of the ordinary well-known men's clubs, they exist not so much with the object of enabling the members to increase their range of acquaintances as of providing a place where homosexuals can forgather and relax in an atmosphere free from feelings of apprehension and inhibition. 'I once took a normal friend of mine there who said it might be the National Liberal Club,' a member of a well-known homosexual club told Westwood. 'Everyone was so good-mannered and quiet. He said he wouldn't have suspected a single one of the people there.'

Community integration still poses the biggest problem for homosexuals in Britain today through the combination of living conditions and social pressures. In spite of the change in the law and open public discussion of the subject, there is still a large amount of ignorance and lack of understanding manifested by many members of the community. 'It's very difficult for a normal to understand,' is the opinion of a typical male homosexual. 'There are no expressions they would not use to show their disgust. It is horrifying how men and women who in every other way are decent and sensible can lose their sense of proportion on this subject. Degeneration is a mild word for them to use. I've heard people say they [homosexuals] should be castrated.'

To a great extent this prejudice is based on grounds of religion, specifically Jewish and Christian beliefs, which have exercised a profound influence upon the history of homosexuality in Britain during the past one thousand years. These beliefs, and their association with the Biblical cities of Sodom and Gomorrah, will be examined in the following chapter.

CHAPTER TWO

From Sin to Crime

[1]

Unlike the people of ancient Greece and the Arab countries in the Middle East, the Jews as depicted in the Old Testament strongly disapproved of homosexual conduct between males, and it was punishable by death, although there is no evidence that this penalty was often exacted. No doubt the basis for its condemnation was similar to that of withdrawal in coitus, or Onanism, as this primitive method of contraception came to be called from the name of its traditional originator: namely that it was the duty of the Jews to increase and multiply and any interference with the normal sexual functions to this end was to be reprobated. 'If a man also lie with mankind as he lieth with a woman, both of them have committed an abomination: they shall surely be put to death; their blood shall be upon them.' (Leviticus XX, 13.) Bestiality, whether practised by a man or a woman, was also declared to be a capital crime, but curiously enough no mention is made of female homosexuality in the Levitical law, nor for that matter anywhere else in the Bible with the exception of a single ambiguous passage in St Paul's Epistle to the Romans (I, 26.) proscribing women who 'did change the natural use into that which is against nature'. It has been suggested that this may mean no more than the reversal of the conventional coital position by which the woman lies underneath the man, and similar variations of method which were practised by Roman matrons, as we know from such pagan writers as Ovid and Apuleius. No doubt there were Hebrew women with lesbian habits in Biblical times just as there were in ancient Greece, but they would not appear to have attracted the attention of the male lawgivers.

It would certainly appear from the celebrated account of the destruction of Sodom and Gomorrah in the nineteenth chapter of the Book of Genesis that the inhabitants of these 'cities of the Plain' were given to homosexual practices, but they do not seem to have been more so than any of the other neighbouring Canaanite and Israelite towns and villages. It is clear from Lot's story that the conduct of the Sodomites which incurred divine

29

wrath was not their homosexual behaviour as such but its con-
junction with a most flagrant abuse of the Hebrew laws and
customs of hospitality to strangers. According to the testimony
of the Old Testament prophet Ezekiel (XVI, 49–50), the real
crime of the Sodomites in the eyes of the Lord was their idolatry.

Modern archaeological research has established that the fate of
Sodom and Gomorrah and the three other 'cities of the Plain' was
the result of natural causes in the shape of a great earthquake
accompanied by lightning and fire, the conflagration being spread
by the ignition of bituminous gases in the local geological forma-
tions, when the cities were eventually submerged by the waters
of the Dead Sea. It was scarcely surprising that the appalling
nature of this disaster should have been attributed at the time to
supernatural causes and should have eventually crystallized into
the familiar Old Testament story of divine punishment for
human wickedness. What, then, was the origin of the exclusively
homosexual interpretation of the delinquencies of the Sodomites
and their fellow citizens, which was later to have such a profound
influence on the thinking and legislation of Christian communities on the subject? Incidentally, it is remarkable in this
context that such scholarly sexologists as Havelock Ellis and
Kinsey among others should have accepted the homosexual
interpretation without question.

In a convincing essay entitled *Homosexuality and the Western
Christian Tradition*, published in 1955, Dr D. S. Bailey has
shown that the traditional Christian opinion that the Sodomites
were annihilated because of their homosexual practices was due
to a Jewish reinterpretation of the Genesis story which first
appeared in Palestine in the second century B.C. and was inspired
by antagonism to the Hellenistic way of life, Sodom becoming
'the symbol of the peculiar vices of Hellenism, which were
abhorrent not only in themselves, but as the depravities of an
alien and hostile culture'.[1] No doubt this antagonism contributed
to St Paul's powerful denunciation of homosexual habits as it
also did to the penal legislation of the Christian Emperors
Theodosius and Justinian. In a later age it moved Edward
Lecky, the Victorian historian of European morals, to comment
in terms of horrendous disapproval upon 'that lower abyss of
unnatural love, which was the deepest and strangest taint of
Greek civilisation'. According to the same authority, 'this vice',
which was treated by the Greeks 'with a levity we can now
hardly conceive', and 'which never appears in the writings of

[1] Bailey, 6–9, 26–27, 40.

Homer and Hesiod, doubtless arose under the influence of the public games, which, accustoming men to the contemplation of absolutely nude figures, awoke an unnatural passion, totally remote from all modern feelings. . . .'

> Artists sought to reflect the passion in the statues of the Hermaphrodite, of Bacchus, and the more effeminate Apollo; moralists were known to praise it as the bond of friendship, and it was spoken of as the inspiring enthusiasm of the heroic Theban legion of Epaminondas. . . . We can scarcely have a better illustration of the extent to which moral ideas and feelings have changed, than the fact that the first two Greeks who were considered worthy of statues by their fellow-countrymen are said to have been Harmodius and Aristogeiton, who were united by an impure love, and who were glorified for a political assassination.[1]

The conception of homosexual practices as the peculiar sin of Sodom was accepted by the early Christian Church and the word 'sodomitical' in its Latin form came into use, particularly in the pronouncements of the various Councils and Synods. In one of the Emperor Charlemagne's ordinances at the end of the eighth century there is an express condemnation of *sodomitica luxuria*. The precise treatment of homosexual offenders by the ecclesiastical authorities was set out in various manuals of penance for the use of confessors, known as the Penitentials, which originated in the Celtic Churches of Ireland and Wales and later spread to England and the European continent. Varying penances are assigned for specified forms of homosexual behaviour, ranging from kissing and embracing, with or without emission, mutual masturbation and inter-femoral (full body) to the oral genital and anal methods. The first of the known Penitentials to mention lesbianism is that of Archbishop Theodore of Canterbury, who died in 690. The majority are only concerned with male homosexuality; they make no difference between the clergy and the laity, nor between active and passive sodomy. The type of penance varies greatly in different Penitentials, ranging from a few fasts for kissing to several years of penance of different kinds. Lesbian practices were penalized in the later Penitentials, nuns being awarded seven years and lay women three, but the maximum penalties were less heavy than for sodomy, which extended to fourteen years. In one Penitential there is a reference to the use of what can only be an artificial penis, or dildo, by nuns. About

W. E. H. Lecky. *History of European Morals* (ed. 1898), II, 274–95.

the middle of the eleventh century, a monk called Peter Damiani published his so-called *Liber Gomorrhianus*, in which he called for much stiffer penalties, which generally included the degradation of clerical and monastic offenders from their orders. Among other things, he protested against the habit of culprits confessing to those with whom they had misbehaved, thereby incurring a trivial penance. However, Pope Leo IX, whose attention to the work was drawn by its author, was of the opinion that homosexual acts were not all equally sinful and therefore did not merit the same ecclesiastical censure, and he may well have thought that Damiani's charges of the increased prevalence of homosexuality in the Western Church at the time were exaggerated.

The subject was treated more dispassionately by St Thomas Aquinas, who accepted the association with Sodom and argued that, since what he called the *peccatum contra naturam* in any form was directed solely to the pursuit of venereal pleasure and excluded procreation, it clearly offended against reason and consequently fell to be considered as one of the species of lust. Even homosexual acts between consenting adults, which it might be said harmed no one, were nevertheless transgressions of the Divine Law by which Man's sexual nature was governed. This reaction of the medieval ecclesiastical mind to homosexual behaviour was endorsed in Britain towards the end of the ninth century by Alfred the Great, the legendary king of the West Saxons, on four specific grounds—'first, they proceed from a burning frenzy (*ardor*) which subverts the order of nature— secondly they are distinguished by their disgusting foulness (yet for all that are found more often among persons of high degree than among those of low estate); thirdly, those who have once become addicted to these vices seldom succeed in shaking them off, so tenaciously do they cling; and lastly, they are as contagious as any disease, and rapidly spread from one to another.' However, it may be remarked that Alfred, who was in other respects a liberal thinker, may merely have been expressing at the Church's prompting the commonly accepted views of the time.

[2]

The conquest of England by the Normans a century and a half after Alfred's death is believed by some authorities to have been accompanied by a wave of homosexuality. There is no concrete evidence of this outside the relatively narrow confines of the royal court. The Conqueror's two sons, William Rufus and Robert Duke of Normandy, have both been charged by the Norman monk and church historian Orderic, known as Ordericus Vitalis, with carrying on homosexual practices, as also have their immediate followers at court. The duke, in spite of being married and having had numerous heterosexual affairs, is said to have contracted a liking for members of his own sex as the result of his experiences in the Crusades, since Orderic records that on his return to Normandy the duke 'desperately abandoned himself to indolence and effeminacy', while 'the Venus of Sodom stalked boldly in the midst of such scenes with her wanton enticements, defiling the effeminate, who were fit only to be burnt'. The conduct of William Rufus and his court was if anything worse, according to Orderic, seeing that 'the effeminate predominated everywhere and revelled without restraint, while filthy catamites, fit only to perish in the flames, abandoned themselves to the foulest practices of Sodom'.[1]

While Duke Robert may safely be classified as bisexual, there is not the slightest doubt that his unmarried younger brother, who succeeded their father as king and reigned as William II from 1087 until his mysterious death in 1100, was an uninhibited invert. By contrast, his other brother Henry, who followed him on the throne as Henry I, was quite normally sexed. 'Into the details of the private life of Rufus it is well not to grope too narrowly,' wrote Edward Freeman, Regius Professor of Modern History at Oxford towards the end of Queen Victoria's reign. 'In him England might see on her own soil the habits of the ancient Greek and the modern Turk. His sins were of a kind from which his brother Henry, no model of moral perfection, was deemed to be wholly free, and which he was believed to look upon with loathing.' Whether the arrow which killed him while he was hunting in the New Forest was shot deliberately or by accident will probably never be known, but there is no doubt why he was buried without the religious rites of the Church. This was not because of his blatantly homosexual way of life, as some writers have supposed, but because of his blasphemy and his openly expressed contempt for holy things and persons which made him subject to this kind of popular excommunication. 'None wept for him but the mercenaries who received his pay, and the baser partners of his foul vices,' to quote Freeman again. 'A few years later the tower under which he lay crumbled and fell. Men said that it fell because so foul a corpse lay beneath it.'

[1] Bailey, 100, 119, 123.

In his study of William's reign, Freeman quotes contemporary witnesses, such as Ordericus Vitalis and William of Malmesbury, at considerable length on the vices of the court, particularly on such matters as dress and hair styles, which were cited as symptoms of the prevalent decadence.

> The gilded youth of Normandy and of Norman England began to wear long garments like women, which hindered walking or acting of any kind; they copied the walk and mien of women. Above all, their feet were shod with shoes with long curved points, like the horns of rams or the tails of scorpions. . . . The long hair and the long pointed shoes served as special subjects for declamation among the moral writers of the time. But these unseemly fashions were only the outward signs of the deeper corruption within. The courtiers, the minions, of Rufus, altogether forsook the law of God and the custom of their fathers. The day they passed in sleep; the night in revellings, dicing, and vain talk. Vices before unknown, the vices of the East, the special sin, as Englishmen then deemed of the Norman, were rife among them. And deepest of all in guilt was the Red King himself.

There is no credible evidence, as has already been suggested, that this conduct extended beyond the dissolute monarch, his courtiers, and their immediate *entourages*, who had come over from Normandy, to the mass of the English people at this time. One man was bold enough to speak out and denounce the immorality of William and his court. This was Serlo Bishop of Bayeux and Abbot of Gloucester, who had been William the Conqueror's private chaplain and was gravely shocked by the change in manners and morals from the austere and decent atmosphere which prevailed at the Conqueror's court. He is on record as having sent the king a letter on the eve of William's death telling him of a monk's dream at Gloucester in which the Holy Church had been seen calling on her Lord for vengeance on the evil deeds of the King of the English. 'I wonder at my lord Serlo's fancy for writing all this; I always thought him a good old abbot', such was William's immediate reaction when the letter was read to him. 'Tis very simple of him, when I have so much business about, to take the trouble to put the dreams of snoring monks into writing and to send them to me all this way. Does he think I am like the English, who throw up their journey or their business because of the snoring or the dreams of an old woman?' It was later that same day that the king met his death in the New Forest, a combination of circumstances not lost upon the superstitious.[1]

William's successor, Henry I, appears to have lost little time in cleaning up of the court. At a Council held in London shortly after his accession to consider the reform of ecclesiastical and moral abuses, fresh penalties were laid down for 'those who commit the shameful sin of sodomy, and especially for those who of their own free will take pleasure in doing so'. Clerics who erred were to be expelled from their orders and laymen deprived of their civic rights. At the same time Archbishop Anselm issued instructions to the clergy as to penance, directing the exercise of discretion and the taking into account of such matters as the age of the offenders, the duration of the sin and whether or not they have been married. 'It must be remembered,' wrote Anselm, 'that this sin has been publicly committed to such an extent that it scarcely makes anyone blush, and that many have fallen into it in ignorance of its gravity.' It is doubtful whether the penalties prescribed for laymen were ever put into effect, as possibly encroaching on the civil power, but it is noteworthy that the next Council held six years later did not consider it necessary to pass any further enactments against sodomy, although breaches of the rule of chastity received further attention.

Nevertheless, the legend of the sodomitical character of the Norman court lingered on, not without some foundation in fact. Just as the collapse of the tower of Winchester Cathedral upon the mortal remains of William Rufus was popularly regarded as a sign of divine displeasure at that monarch's homosexual habits, so the loss of the White Ship, which foundered on a rock outside Barfleur Harbour in 1120, when Henry I's son and heir Prince William and everyone else on board bound for England except a butcher from Rouen perished, was likewise regarded as the judgment of heaven upon sodomy. According to Ordericus Vitalis, the Prince was accompanied by 'an intemperate crowd of lascivious and showy young men', while of those who were drowned Henry of Huntingdon states that 'all or most were said to have been tainted with the sin of sodomy. Behold the terrible vengeance of God!' This view has been endorsed by two other chroniclers of the period, Gervase of Canterbury and Guillaume de Nangis. But there is no evidence that the conduct of a dissolute minority was imitated by the country at large, although there may have been a few who, as Archbishop Anselm has suggested,

[1] E. A. Freeman. *The Reign of William Rufus* (1882) I, 159, II, 330, 340–1.

followed the court example in the mistaken belief that what was
done in high places could not be so very wicked.[1]

Nothing more is heard of the subject until early in the four-
teenth century when a homosexual, or more probably a bisexual
monarch mounted the English throne in the person of Edward II,
generally known as Edward of Carnarvon. His love of low
company and his association with various favourites, of whom
Piers Gaveston was the most notorious, is fully attested. In 1327,
when being held prisoner in Berkeley Castle, he was murdered
after being tortured in a peculiarly revolting fashion at the
instigation of his French consort Isabella and her lover Roger
Mortimer. No doubt the terrible manner of his death was dictated
by common knowledge of his habits, since the contemporary
chronicler Ranulf Higden tells us that he was 'sleyne with a
hoote brooche putte thro the secret place posteriale', that is by
the insertion of a burning stake in his anus.[2] No wonder the unfortunate monarch's shrieks were heard throughout the castle
and indeed beyond the castle walls and drove many to their knees
to pray for his soul.

Half a century later, in the reign of Edward II's son Edward III,
mention is made in parliamentary proceedings, apparently for the
first time, of 'the too horrible vice which is not to be named'. The
event was noticed by the judge and law writer Sir Edward Coke,
who wrote in his *Institutes of the Laws of England* that 'it was
complained of in Parliament that the Lombards had brought into
the Realm the shameful sin of sodomy that is not to be named,
as there it is said'.[3] This was in 1376 when the so-called Good
Parliament unsuccessfully petitioned the king to banish all
'Lombard brokers' alleging that they were usurers, and other
foreign artisans and traders, particularly Jews and Saracens, on
the ground that they had introduced sodomitical practices which
would destroy the realm. It is of some significance that the vulgar
French word for usurer at this time was *bougre*, which in England
became 'bugger'. The word was also used to mean heretic.

Bougre derived from the Latin *Bulgarus* meaning native of
Bulgaria, where the Manichean and Albigensian heresies were

---

[1] Bailey, 126-7.

[2] *Cum vero ignito inter celanda confossus ignominiose peremptus est:* Rolls
Series, *Polychronicon Ranulphi Higden* (1882), VIII, 324. Bailey (*op. cit.* 170)
casts doubt upon the veracity of Higden's account, citing an article by S. A.
Moore in *Antiquity* (1887), I, 215-26, but the authorities used by Professor
Tout in his exhaustive investigation of the subject corroborate Higden. See
T. F. Tout, *The Captivity and Death of Edward of Carnarvon* (1920) reprinted
from the *Bulletin of the John Rylands Library*, Vol. 6, No. 1 (1920).

[3] Coke. *Institutes. Third Part* (ed. 1744), 58.

known to flourish. The term Bulgar or *Boulgre*, contracted to *bougre*, was gradually applied to all heretics, and from being an abusive term for heresy in general *bougrerie* (buggery) became the common appellation for the supposed sexual habits of heretics and usurers. No doubt some of the Albigensians were homosexuals, as also were the Knights Templars, who were suppressed by the Inquisition, many of the Knights confessing to their practices in the torture chambers of the Holy Office. But by and large the charge of homosexuality seems to have been part of the general 'smear' campaign employed by the Inquisition against its enemies. In England, although the word 'buggery' was no doubt previously used for some time in the vernacular, it did not become an accepted legal term until made the subject of statute in the reign of Henry VIII.[1]

The first detailed treatment of the subject 'Of Buggery, or Sodomy', by any legal authority, apart from passing mention, occurs in the Third Part of Coke's *Institutes*, which was completed in 1628. On the history of the offence, the judge had this to say:

> Our ancient Authors doe conclude, that it deserveth death, *ultimum supplicium*, though they differ in the manner of the punishment. Britton saith, that Sodomites and Miscreants shall be burnt, and so were the Sodomites by Almighty God. Fleta saith, *Pecorantes & Sodomitae in terra vivi confodiantur:* and therewith agreeth with the Mirror, *pur le grand abomination*, and in another place he saith, *Sodomie est crime de Majestie, vers le Roy celestre*. But (to say it once for all) the judgment in all cases of felony is that the person attainted be hanged by the neck, until he or she be dead. But in ancient times in that case, the man was hanged, and the woman was drowned, whereof we have seen examples in the reign of R[ichard] I, and this is the meaning of ancient Franchises granted *de Furca & Fossa*, of the Gallows, and the Pit, for the hanging upon the one, and drowning in the other, but *Fossa* is taken away, and *Furca* remains. . . .

> The Act of 25 Henry 8 hath adjudged it felony, and therefore the judgment of felony doth now belong to this offence, *viz.* to be hanged by the neck till he be dead. He that readeth the Preamble of this Act, shall find how necessary the reasoning of our ancient Authors is.

---

[1] It may be noted that in its legal sense 'buggery' was used pejoratively to mean sodomy when practised with a human being, and bestiality when practised with an animal.

As Coke suggests, the Preamble to the Act of 1533 is most important in this context, since it clearly implies that hitherto homosexual
offences had been exclusively dealt with by the ecclesiastical courts.

> Forasmuch as there is not yet sufficient and condign punish-
> ment appointed and limited by the due course of the Laws of
> this Realm, for the detestable and abominable Vice of Buggery
> committed with mankind or beast:

This Preamble also lends support to the view that the early
writers frequently stated as actual law what they thought ought
to be the law or what they had deduced from other authorities.
In this instance it is to be noted that the three writers mentioned
by Coke all flourished in the reign of Edward I, who probably en-
listed their help in his attempt to codify the domestic laws; they do
no more than state that sodomists deserved to be put to death. In
particular, Fleta's statement that sodomists and those who commit
bestiality, as well as those who have dealings with Jews or Jewesses,
should be buried alive may have resulted from a confused reading
of a well-known passage in the *Germania* of Tacitus, which describes how evil-livers (*corpore infames*) were punished by being
drowned in the marshes with a hurdle on their heads. Britton and
the Mirror, on the other hand, mention burning, possibly with
the Roman penalty under the Theodosian code of mind. However, as the jurist Stephen observes, the statute of Henry VIII
is 'wholly inconsistent' with the view that Fleta and the others
stated the law correctly, 'whereas it is not only consistent with
but suggests the notion that the offence was till then merely
ecclesiastical'.[1]

Of course, it was always open to the Church to 'relinquish'
offenders to the secular power for punishment, as was so often
done by the Inquisition in Spain, and there may well have been
some who felt that, as with sorcerers and witches, sodomists
convicted by the ecclesiastical courts ought to be handed over to
the civil authorities for burning. It is extremely improbable that
in England they were thus 'relinquished' and that their offence
was ever penalized in this way. Pollock and Maitland agree on this
point with Stephen. 'The Statute of 1533 which makes it felony
affords an almost sufficient proof that the temporal courts had
not punished it and that no one had been put to death for it for
a very long time past.'[2]

---

[1] Sir James Fitzjames Stephen. *History of the Criminal Law of England* (1883),
II, 429–30.
[2] Sir Frederick Pollock and F. W. Maitland, *History of English Law* (1895)
II, 554–5.

The statute (25 Henry 8, c. 6) was not occasioned by any
particular desire on the part of the king and his chief minister,
Thomas Cromwell, who piloted it through Parliament, to clamp
down on homosexuals. Its primary object was part of Henry's
policy in general towards the Church. Besides the seizure of its
property, this included the progressive reduction of the jurisdiction of the ecclesiastical courts, by withdrawing from them
the right to try certain offences which were now regarded as
temporal and were henceforth to become felonies triable in the
ordinary courts. No doubt buggery appeared to Cromwell as
suitable a subject as any other for the inauguration of this process
which was to continue and eventually lead to the practical abolition of all ecclesiastical courts a century later, although the
jurisdiction was later to be revived in a restricted form in relation
to the clergy.

Much of the brief parliamentary session of 1533 was occupied
with the king's matrimonial problems with Catherine of Aragon
and Anne Boleyn. Nevertheless Parliament found time to pass
twenty-two measures, ranging from the control of graziers and
butchers and selling of flesh by weight to 'the submission of the
clergy to the king', and 'the establishment of the succession on
the king's most royal majesty in the imperial crown of the
realm'. The Act 'for the punishment of the Vice of Buggery'
came immediately after an Act 'for the avoiding of deceipts in
callendering worsted' and was immediately followed by Acts
'against killing of young spawn or fry of fish' and 'for paving of
Holborn'. Nor did the Act of 25 Henry 8, chapter 6, attract any
particular attention, being as it were incidental to the principal
anti-clerical measures of the session. It was a short piece of
legislation, which originated in the House of Lords, declaring the
'detestable and abominable Vice of Buggery committed with
mankind or beast' to be a felony subject to the penalties of death
and loss of property customarily suffered by felons, without
benefit of clergy, which meant that offenders in holy orders
could not claim to be tried in the ecclesiastical courts. It was
further laid down that the offence was triable by Justices of the
Peace as were other felonies, and that the Act was to continue
in force until the last day of the following Parliament.[1]

According to Coke, the Act extended 'as well to a woman as to
a man, and therefore if she commit buggery with a beast, she is a

[1] *Parliamentary History of England* (1802), I, 572. The original engrossed on
parchment and endorsed with the Royal Assent—the traditional Norman-French
formula, 'Le Roi le veult'—is preserved in the House of Lords Record Office.
It is reproduced as the frontispiece to this book.

person that commits buggery with a beast' and so fell 'within the Purview of this Act. . . . And the rather so, for that somewhat before the making of this Act, a great Lady had committed buggery with a Baboon and conceived by it.'

During the next twenty years the Act was repealed twice and re-enacted four times, after which it was to remain undisturbed on the statute book for upwards of three centuries. Under Henry VIII, it was re-enacted in 1536, 1539 and 1541. In the first Parliament of Edward VI, it was repealed along with all other new felonies established in his father's reign, but a year later, in 1548, it was re-enacted with certain amendments, which provided that the convicted felon's property should no longer be forfeited to the Crown. Indictments should be framed within six months of the commission of the alleged act, and no person due to benefit in the event of the accused's death should be allowed to give evidence against him. On Mary's succession in 1553, there was a further comprehensive repeal of statutes passed in the previous reign, including the Act of 1548, and no attempt was made to re-enact it while Mary was on the throne, presumably because it was intended to restore the former jurisdiction of the ecclesiastical courts. It was finally revived by Queen Elizabeth in 1563 in the harsh terms of the original Act of thirty years before—not, as perhaps might have been expected, in the less severe terms of her half-brother Edward's measure—the reason given in the Preamble being that since the repeal of the previous Act ten years earlier 'divers ill disposed persons have been the more bold to commit the said most horrible and detestable Vice of Buggery aforesaid, to the high displeasure of Almighty God'.

The Elizabethan chronicler Holinshed, to whom Shakespeare was indebted for the historical background of many of his plays, estimated that no less than 72,000 executions took place in the reign of Henry VIII.[1] Many of these were for quite trivial offences such as felling a tree or robbing a rabbit warren. How many were for buggery it is impossible to say, since evidence on the point is lacking. The fact remains that, although there is a certain amount of information pointing to the prevalence of homosexual conduct among the more socially prominent in the sixteenth and seventeenth centuries, it was not until the earlier years of the eighteenth century that convictions of ordinary folk have been recorded. That is not to say that they did not occur. The only case men-

[1] Quoted by Sir Samuel Romilly in the House of Commons February 9 1810.

tioned by Coke in his *Institutes* is that of a certain Stafford whose indictment was drawn 'by great advice for committing buggery with a boy, for which he was attainted and hanged'. This was in 1608.

The first recorded instance of official action against a homosexual after the initial Act of Henry VIII was in 1541, when the Rev. Nicholas Udall, author of *Ralph Roister Doister*, a work generally regarded as the original English comedy, was involved in a homosexual scandal with two Eton schoolboys and one of his own servants. Udall, or Uvedale, as his name is sometimes spelled, was headmaster of Eton at this time, where he was notorious for the frequent floggings he inflicted on his pupils, a habit which no doubt implied a sadistic impulse. He was examined before the Privy Council and on confessing his guilt he was committed to the Marshalsea prison and immediately dismissed from his headmastership. But he only remained in prison for a few months. He had powerful friends at court and on regaining his liberty he enjoyed a number of lucrative Church livings, including that of Prebend of Windsor; and on her succession Queen Mary, for whom he had written a play, appointed him headmaster of Westminster, another great school. He died in 1556 and was buried in St Margaret's, Westminster; he is remembered today as a successful dramatist rather than as a homosexual and sadistic schoolmaster.[1]

In the field of Elizabethan literature, there were three homosexuals whose inclinations are apparent from their conduct in private life as well as from their writings—namely Christopher Marlowe, Richard Barnfield, and Francis Bacon. All three were contemporaries of Shakespeare, who has himself been mentioned by some critics as a possible invert.

In his short life Marlowe, who was the son of a Canterbury shoemaker, proved himself of outstanding brilliance as a poet and songwriter ('Come live with me and be my love') and a dramatist (*The Tragedy of Dr Faustus, The Jew of Malta, Edward II*). His most powerful drama, *The Troublesome Reigne and Lamentable Death of Edward the Second King of England*, depicts the king's relations with his favourites in graphic and at times terrifying language. The essayist and critic Charles Lamb admitted that the king's death scene moved him to pity and terror beyond any scene, ancient or modern, with which he was acquainted. Like his hero in this play, Marlowe was probably bisexual. He also delighted in shocking the 'Establishment' of his day with his

[1] *Dictionary of National Biography*, XX, 6–9.

unorthodox views. In 1593, when he was only 29, Marlowe was accused of holding atheistical opinions, and also of having openly stated that 'all thei that love not tobacco and boys are fooles'. A warrant was issued by the Privy Council for his arrest and it was only his sudden death immediately afterwards which prevented its execution. In the course of a drunken brawl, in which he had become involved in a tavern at Deptford, he was fatally stabbed, as a contemporary related, by 'a bawdy serving man, a rival of his in his lewd love'.[1]

Barnfield was a lyrical poet of high quality, some of whose compositions were for long attributed to Shakespeare. His first poetic work, *The Affectionate Shepherd*, published in 1594, when he was twenty, was addressed to a youth, to whom the poet declared:

> If it be sin to love a lovely lad,
> Oh then sin I.

It is worth noting what Edmund Gosse, the author of the article on Barnfield in the *Dictionary of National Biography*, first published in 1885, and himself a painfully repressed homosexual, had to say about his subject in this context. 'All his best early pieces,' writes Gosse, 'and especially his sonnets, are dedicated to a sentiment of friendship so exaggerated as to remove them beyond all wholesome sympathy. Even in the Elizabethan age, when great warmth and candour were permitted, the tone of these sonnets was felt to be unguarded.' Little more is known of his life beyond the fact that he wrote no more after the turn of the century, when he retired to his beautiful manor house in Staffordshire, there to live the quiet life of a country gentleman with his wife and son until his death nearly thirty years later. Like Marlowe, Barnfield was no doubt bisexual, and as not infrequently happens in such cases, to quote Havelock Ellis, 'the homosexual element developed early under the influence of a classical education and university associations, while the normal heterosexual element developed later and, as may happen in bisexual persons, was associated with the more commonplace and prosaic side of life. Barnfield was only a genuine poet on the homosexual side of his nature.'[2]

That there was also a homosexual side to Shakespeare's nature may be inferred from his sonnets to the young Earl of Southamp-

---

[1] Havelock Ellis. *Christopher Marlowe* (1883), 429.
[2] *D.N.B.* I, 1182–3. Havelock Ellis. *Studies in the Psychology of Sex*, Vol. II, Part 2, 42–3.

ton, notably the 36th with its references to 'blots', 'shame' and
'bewailed guilt' in which he despairingly declares that so much
scandal is being created by their association that it must be
broken off completely if Southampton's reputation is to be saved;
also the 72nd in which the bard utters a veritable *cri de cœur:*

> My name be buried where my body is,
> And live no more to shame nor me nor you.

There are strong homosexual undertones, too, in the relationship
of Antonio with Bassanio in *The Merchant of Venice*, the 'merchant' in this play being Antonio and not the Jew Shylock, as is
commonly supposed.[1] On the other hand, it is only right to
point out that Shakespeare is much preoccupied with women in
his other writings, particularly in the twenty-six sonnets to the
'Dark Lady', as well as in such dramas of heterosexual passion as
Troilus and Cressida, *Measure for Measure*, and *Antony and
Cleopatra*. Dare it be said that Shakespeare, too, was bisexual,
with the heterosexual element predominating?

By contrast, there is no doubt that Shakespeare's eminent
contemporary Francis Bacon was a thorough invert, as is attested
by Aubrey in his *Brief Lives* and Sir Simon D'Ewes in his
Autobiography. D'Ewes is quite precise as to Bacon's homosexual
practices with his servants, both before and after his disgrace in
1621 for taking bribes as Lord Chancellor, and even gives the
name of a 'very effeminate-faced youth' who was his 'catamite
and bedfellow'; he states further that there had been some
question of bringing Bacon to trial for sodomy. These allegations
are supported by a letter from his mother reproving him for
what she had heard about his behaviour with the young Welsh-
men in his service. Bacon is known to have had many friendships
with men, while women played little or no part in his life. He
married late in his career, and although he treated his wife with
formal consideration in public it is probable that he neglected
her in private. Nor do his writings show any interest in or
attraction towards the other sex, and it is not without significance
that his essay 'On Beauty' in the celebrated *Essays* deals exclusively
with masculine beauty.[2]

The Scottish monarch who came to the English throne in 1603
presented such a striking contrast in his personal habits that the
following Latin tag was soon going the rounds: 'Elizabeth was
King, now James is Queen.' (*Rex fuit Elizabeth, nunc est regina*

---

[1] G. P. V. Akrigg. *Shakespeare and the Earl of Southampton* (1968), *passim*.
[2] Ellis. *loc. cit.* 44–5.

Jacobus.) James I had a number of favourites, of whom the most notorious was Robert Carr, whom he advanced from being a page to Earl of Somerset. When Somerset was brought to trial before the Lords in Westminster Hall, in 1615, for complicity in the murder of Sir Thomas Overbury, the king was afraid that he might make some gravely embarrassing revelations about his relations with his sovereign. James accordingly instructed the Lieutenant of the Tower to have two men stationed beside the prisoner throughout his trial with cloaks in readiness to muffle him if he started any dangerous outburst. In the event James need not have worried, since Somerset conducted himself with dignity throughout the proceedings and said nothing about the king's homosexual love for him. Somerset was found guilty and sentenced to death, but the king immediately pardoned him, possibly fearing that after all he might speak out on the scaffold. But Somerset wisely held his tongue and was allowed to retire into obscurity.[1]

It was not until after James I's death that for the first time we hear in detail of the punishment of homosexuals by the courts.

[4]

The first reported trials for homosexual offences in England took place in the sixth year of Charles I's reign, that is almost a century after the passing of Henry VIII's penal statute. They resulted from the indictment of the thirty-eight-year-old Earl of Castlehaven on a charge of committing sodomy with one of his servants as well as a rape upon his wife. Since no modern account of this extraordinary case exists, it is perhaps worthwhile describing it and its social and legal implications in some detail. Their contemporary significance may be judged from the numerous state papers concerning the trials which have been preserved in the national archives.[2]

Mervyn Touchet, twelfth Lord Audley in the peerage of

[1] William McElwee. *The Wisest Fool in Christendom* (1958), 230.

[2] The principal source of the trial is a MS volume in the Public Record Office entitled 'The arraignment of the Earl of Castlehaven, wherein is set forth as well the manner thereof as of his death and execution, with other passages between his condemnation and time of execution'. Further information is contained in another MS work, 'Lord Stewards of England and Trials before Them' preserved in the Harleian Collection in the British Museum (Harleian MSS 2194). Contemporary published accounts, reprinted in Cobbett's *State Trials* (1909), III, 401–25, are based on these MSS. See also *Calendar of State Papers Domestic Charles I, 1629–1631, 1631–1633*, ed. John Bruce (1860–62).

England and second Lord Audley and Earl of Castlehaven in the peerage of Ireland, was the only son and heir of George Lord Audley, who as a reward for his part in the Irish wars at the turn of the century had been given an extensive grant of land in Ulster by James I during the first 'plantation' of that province with English and Scottish settlers; at the same time he was created an Irish peer with the titles of Baron Audley and Earl of Castlehaven. On his death in 1617, his son, who was about twenty-four and had inherited a considerable fortune, seems to have plunged into a life of unbridled dissipation. He spent much of his time at Fonthill Giffard, a property near Tisbury in Wiltshire, which had come from his mother, heiress of Sir James Mervyn, and Fonthill was the scene of some remarkable happenings, which might well be called orgies.

Although he had been brought up a Protestant, it appears that on coming into the Fonthill estate Lord Castlehaven 'turned to the Romish religion, at the instance of some Popish gentlemen who were neighbours'. He was married twice, each time to an heiress. His eldest son by his first wife, by whom he had several other children, was James Lord Audley, who was eventually to succeed him in his Irish titles. Castlehaven's second wife, who was about twenty years younger than her husband, was Lady Anne Stanley, daughter of the fifth Earl of Derby and widow of the fifth Lord Chandos. Shortly after she married Castlehaven a marriage was arranged between his eldest son Audley and his step-daughter, Elizabeth Brydges, who was the second Lady Castlehaven's daughter by her previous husband. Although this daughter had likewise been married before, she was little more than a child, as also was her new husband Audley.

A voyeur as well as a homosexual, Lord Castlehaven enjoyed the spectacle of others having sexual intercourse, and it was said that he encouraged the servants in his household to copulate in his presence both with his wife and step-daughter, who was also his daughter-in-law. His favourite servant for this sport was apparently a man named Henry Skipwith, who had come over from Ireland, where his parents were said to be 'very poor folks', to be the second Lady Castlehaven's page. According to Anne Lady Castlehaven, her lord 'would make Skipwith come naked into his chamber, and delighted in calling up his servants to shew their privities, and would make her look on, and commended those that had the largest'. It appears that Castlehaven encouraged the page to 'lie with' his wife, which Skipwith did, although the latter afterwards alleged that he merely pretended to do so to please his lordship. In spite of Skipwith's denial, however, there is little if any doubt that he committed adultery with Lady Castlehaven as did two other household servants. Skipwith, who had a child by his aristocratic mistress, also admitted to having seduced Castlehaven's daughter-in-law, young Lady Audley.

Lady Audley subsequently swore that 'she was first tempted to lie with Skipwith by the Earl's allurements', and that, her husband being absent from home, 'she had no means but what she had from Skipwith . . . that the Earl himself saw her and Skipwith lie together divers times; and nine servants of the house had also seen it'. She was then only twelve years old. When the earl solicited her first, 'he said that upon his knowledge her husband loved her not; and threatened that he would turn her out of doors if she did not lie with Skipwith; and that if she did not, he would tell her husband she did'—also, 'that she being very young, Skipwith had used oil to enter her body first, and it was with the Earl's privity and consent'. According to Skipwith, it was his master who produced the oil for the purpose and two applications were necessary before Skipwith 'entered her body and knew her carnally'. No wonder this performance provoked a sharp remonstrance from the young lady's husband when he learned of it; indeed as will be seen, it eventually led to the depraved earl being brought to justice.

The two servants who were proved to have had intercourse with Lady Castlehaven were a footman named Giles Broadway and a page named Ampthill, who married a daughter of Lord Castlehaven by his first marriage. Broadway, who was introduced to the household by Skipwith, had wished to go to sea and had been taken into the household at Fonthill while waiting for news of a possible voyage. Soon after the earl's second marriage, Broadway happened to be walking in the garden with his master and Skipwith. When the latter was out of earshot, Castlehaven was alleged to have said to him: 'Broadway, thou art young, lusty and well favoured, and therefore canst now prevail with any woman thou attemptest: wherefore that I am old, and cannot live long, my wife wholly delighting in lust, which I am neither able nor willing to satisfy, thou mayest do well to lie with her: and so pleasing her, after my death marry her, and thereby raise thy fortune.'

Shortly afterwards, possibly the same night, while Lady Castlehaven was in bed and asleep, her husband called out for Broadway about midnight to bring him a pipe of tobacco. When the servant did so, according to Lady Castlehaven, 'my lord pulled him into bed to him and her, made him lie next to her, and Broadway lay with her, and knew her carnally, whilst she made resistance, and the lord held both her hands and one of her legs the while: and that as soon as she was free, she would have killed herself with a knife, but that Broadway forcibly took the knife from her hand and broke it; and before that act of Broadway she had never done it.' She also deposed that her husband 'delighted to see the act done, and made Ampthill to come into bed with them, and lie with her whilst he might see it: and she cried out to save herself'. This testimony was corroborated by Ampthill and also by Broadway, who swore that while he (Broadway) was ravishing Lady Castlehaven, the earl amused himself with Broadway 'using his body as the body of a woman, but never pierced it, only emitted between the thighs'. This was held to be sodomy within the meaning of the statute, although penetration had not actually taken place.

Lawrence Fitzpatrick, another servant, who gave evidence for the Crown at the earl's trial, confessed that his master had committed sodomy twice upon his person. Like Broadway, he convicted himself out of his own mouth, and as others have done in similar circumstances declared that he had been promised immunity if he testified against Castlehaven and affected to be surprised when he himself was subsequently indicted for buggery with the earl.

Castlehaven eventually came to grief as the result of a complaint lodged by his son at court. On November 1, 1630, young Audley, who had recently come of age, wrote to his father remonstrating with him for his parental unkindness and telling him that 'in this monstrous change of a father into an enemy' he craved pardon if he appealed from his father to 'the father of their country—the King's Majesty'. He added that he 'never went about to abridge the earl's bounty to a well-deserving follower', but desired him 'not to strike out the difference betwixt a servant and a son'. He went on: 'Tis a fearful judgment to be a prisoner to bestial affections and lusts, or to think to blot out lesser sins by writing greater in their places.' Meanwhile, his father's 'own dear branches hang down their heads to see the sap and livelihood conferred upon another', namely Henry Skipwith.[1]

Six weeks later, the wicked earl was arrested and brought to London where he was confined in the Tower, pending his arraignment on charges of rape and buggery. He would have preferred to be tried by a local jury in Wiltshire, but he was

[1] *C.S.D.P. 1629-31*, 371.

informed that, since he was a peer of the realm, he must be tried by his peers in Parliament assembled. He was therefore accorded a state trial in this traditional form. The Keeper of the Great Seal, Lord Coventry, acted for the occasion as Lord High Steward, as the president of the court was known, and King Charles I took a keen interest in the proceedings throughout. The details of the charges were evidently considered so shocking that the indictment was drawn in Latin instead of the customary English, specifying 'that detestable and abominable, sodomitical sin *Anglice* buggery (not to be named among Christians),' which the accused 'devilishly, feloniously and contrary to nature did commit and perpetrate to the great displeasure of Almighty God and disgrace of all mankind . . .'

The trial took place in the House of Lords on April 25, 1631, before the Lord High Steward and twenty-seven other peers, of whom two were Catholics. Also in attendance were the principal judges, led by Sir Nicholas Hyde, Lord Chief Justice of the King's Bench, who by a coincidence came from the same part of Wiltshire as the prisoner. The prosecution was in the hands of the Attorney-General Sir Robert Heath, who was a bitter anti-Catholic. The proceedings began about nine o'clock in the morning, after the peers had taken their places on each side of a large table covered with a green cloth, the judges and counsel having seats below them. The prisoner was escorted by the Lieutenant of the Tower and a sergeant-at-arms to the bar of the court, 'where he had a place in manner of a pew lined with green, in which he stood'.

Before being called upon to plead to the indictment, Castlehaven addressed a request to the Lord High Steward. 'May it please your grace,' he said. 'I have been close prisoner these six months, without friends, without counsel or advice. I am ignorant of the advantages and disadvantages of the law, and am but weak of speech at the best, and therefore I desire to have the liberty of having counsel to speak for me.'

'For your so long imprisonment,' the Lord High Steward replied with studied courtesy, 'it hath been to you a special favour; for you have had time enough to bethink yourself, and more than ever any man had that hath been committed for such an offence, and more favour than ever had that came to this bar; and you shall demand nothing that the law can allow, but you shall have it. But for your demand, I must move it to the lords the Judges, and they shall satisfy you in it or any other thing you desire.'

The question being put to the judges, their lordships gave

what was then the correct interpretation of the law of criminal procedure, namely that 'in criminal cases, counsel is not to be admitted for matter of fact; but for matter of law they may'.

The Clerk of the Crown then proceeded to read out the three indictments, to which the prisoner pleaded Not Guilty. Asked how he would be tried, the prisoner replied with the customary formula, 'By God and my peers.'

The Attorney-General rose to make his opening speech, and he soon became so carried away in considering the nature of the charges that the prisoner interrupted him to protest. 'The person is honourable,' said the Attorney; 'the crime of which he is indicted dishonourable, which if it fall out to be true, which is left to trial, I dare be bold to say, never poet invented, nor historian writ of any deed so foul. And although Suetonius hath curiously set out the vices of some of the emperors who had absolute power, which might make them fearless of all manner of punishment, and besides were heathens and knew not God, yet none of these came near this lord's crimes.[1] The one is a crime that, I may speak it to the honour of our nation, is of such rarity that we seldom or never knew of the like, but they are all of such a pestilential nature that, if they be not punished, they will draw from Heaven a heavy judgment upon this kingdom.'

It was at this point that the prisoner made as if to protest that the Attorney-General should stick to the points in the indictment. The Lord High Steward thereupon desired the prisoner to be patient and assured him that 'he should be heard in fit time at full'.

When he came to deal with the sodomy charges, the Attorney-General raised one pertinent matter for the consideration of the judges, namely whether it was necessary to prove penetration:

> For the *crimen sodomiticum*, our law had no knowledge of it until the 25th of Henry VIII, by which statute it was made Felony: and in this there is no more question, but only, whether it be *crimen sodomiticum sine penetratione;* and the law of the 15th of Elizabeth sets it down in general words: and where the law doth not distinguish, neither must we. And I know how you will be cautious how you will give the least mitigation to so abominable a sin, which brought such plagues after it, as we may see in Genesis XVIII, Leviticus XVIII, Judges XIX, Romans I.

[1] The Attorney-General had evidently forgotten Tiberius, whose pederastic excesses in Capri are described by Suetonius in his biography of that Emperor (ch. XLIV).

Having thus appealed to Scriptural authority, the Attorney went on to inject religious prejudice into the trial when he denounced the prisoner as being 'constant to no religion, but in the morning he would be a Papist and go to mass, and in the afternoon a Protestant and go to a sermon'. The reason he advanced why a nobleman of the earl's quality should fall to such 'abominable sins' was simple. 'He believed not God, he had not the fear of God before his eyes, he left God, and God left him to his own wickedness: and what may not a man run into? What sin so foul, what thing so odious, which he dares not adventure?'

The prisoner's change of faith undoubtedly weighed against him at the trial, as also did his refusal at the outset to acknowledge the signed statement which he had made when he had been examined by the Lord Keeper and other members of the Privy Council, 'saying his eyes were bad'. In this document he had said among other things that 'Henry Skipwith had no means when he came to him, that he had given him £1,000 and that Skipwith lay with him when he was straitened in rooms'. Eventually he admitted the accuracy of the document. But his apparent prevarication drew a stern rebuke from the Lord High Steward: 'I would advise you not to deny the things that are clearly proved; for then the Lords will give less credit to the things you say.'

The first material Crown witness was the earl's wife, who confirmed the deposition she had previously made setting out her experiences with her husband and the servants, notably Ampthill and Broadway. However she denied that she had in fact committed any misconduct with Skipwith, whom she went out of her way to shield. As for her husband, 'he delighted to see the act done, and made Ampthill come into the bed to us, and lie with me in such a manner, as he might see it, and though I cried out, he never regarded the complaint I made, but encouraged the ravisher'. She went on to describe how she had been raped by Broadway, while her husband held her down.

Lawrence Fitzpatrick was the next witness to be called. Since Fitzpatrick was a Catholic, the prisoner objected that his testimony should not be heard until he had taken the oath of allegiance to the sovereign, as should any other of the Catholic witnesses. But the judges ruled against the prisoner, holding that they might be witnesses unless they were convicted recusants, i.e. if they had already suffered penalties for persistently refusing to attend the English Church services. Fitzpatrick was then sworn.

'My lord made me lie with him at Fonthill and Salisbury,' said the witness, 'and once spent his seed but did not penetrate my body, and I understand he had often done the like with others.' The witness went on to describe the orgies which took place at Fonthill, in which Skipwith was conspicuous, and how he saw Skipwith on numerous occasions fornicating with both the prisoner's wife and his daughter-in-law. Also, said Fitz-patrick, the prisoner kept a woman in his house called Blandina, who was 'a common whore to his Lordship and his servants. His house was a common brothel house, and the earl himself took delight not only in being an actor but a spectator, while other men did it.' Indeed Blandina was once 'abused' by the witness and the other servants 'for the space of seven hours together until she got the French pox'. As a result of her complaint, the earl not surprisingly 'sent her away'.

Skipwith and four of the other servants, including Broadway, then testified to the seduction of Lady Audley, 'with the earl's privity and consent', and this was confirmed by the young woman herself. Broadway also admitted to having committed sodomy with the prisoner, as well as having fornicated with the countess while her husband held her arms and one of her legs.

'My Lords, you have seen the clearness of the proofs,' said the Attorney-General in closing the case for the prosecution, 'and I know your wisdoms to be such as you well know in so dark a business, clearer proofs cannot possibly be had; for let a man be never so wicked, or never so impudent, he will not call witnesses to see his wickedness: yet you see here this point fully proved.' The Attorney went on to show how both the laws of God and man were against sodomy, and he appealed once more to the Scriptures, particularly Leviticus XVIII 25 and 27. ('And the land is defiled: therefore I do not visit the iniquity thereof upon it, and the land itself vomiteth out her inhabitants. . . . For all these abominations have the men of the land done, which were before you, and the land is defiled.') The Attorney proceeded to work himself up into a rousing peroration. 'That God may remove and take away from us his plagues,' he concluded, 'let this wicked man be taken away from amongst us.'

[5]

Before Castlehaven opened his defence, the Lord High Steward advised him to 'speak pertinently', whereupon, we are told, the prisoner 'alleged that he was a weak man, and of ill memory, and therefore desired that he might not be interrupted'. It is worth noting that, had Castlehaven been a commoner and tried before an ordinary jury, he would not have been allowed to give evidence on his own behalf. As it was, the prisoner seems to have been given considerable latitude by the court, while the Attorney-General, in the words of the report, 'pressed things very earnestly and in excellent method against the earl'.

Castlehaven began with an attack upon his wife, 'urging that she was naught and dishonest with Broadway, by her own confession'. At this the Lord High Steward intervened to point out that the prisoner 'ought not to allege for his defence that fact as an imputation to his wife, which he forced her into by compulsion and violence'.

'My wife has been a whore and has had a child, which I concealed to save her honour,' Castlehaven went on. 'She and my son, and one Mr William Wroughton, have plotted against my life, and all that's alleged against me is only their inventions and gives a dangerous example in the kingdom; for no peer or any other person can be secure of his life that has, as I have, a wife who desires a younger husband, and a son who is gaping after my estate, and has the devil and wicked servants to assist their malice in endeavouring to take away my life wrongfully. This, my Lords, is my condition, and I hope your Lordships will take care that you don't involve the peers, the gentry and the Commons under a dangerous precedent in my condemnation—for if a wife of such a character may be allowed to be a witness against her husband, no man is safe when his wife dislikes him and would have a younger husband.'

The Lord High Steward again interrupted. 'If your Lordship had proved a conspiracy to take away your life, you had urged what had been material; but for want of proof it signified nothing. However, I will propound your objections to the judges.' He then proceeded to ask the judges two questions of law. 'Can a rape be committed against a whore? And can a wife be a legal witness against her husband?'

After conferring among themselves for a few moments, the Lord Chief Justice delivered their opinion.

> If the woman on whom the crime be committed be a whore, yet it may be a ravishment, for it is the enforcing against the will that makes the rape, and a common whore may be ravished against her will and it is a felony to do it.

In civil cases the wife cannot be a witness against her husband, but in criminal case of this nature, where the wife is the party grieved, and on whom the crime is committed, she is to be admitted a witness against her husband.

The judges were also asked whether 'because Broadway doth not depose any penetration, but only that he emitted upon her belly while the earl held her, that should be judged felony as for a rape'. The answer was that it was a rape and consequently a felony.

'But, my Lord,' the Lord Chief Justice then asked the prisoner 'what do you say to what these fellows your servants have sworn against you?'

'They are persons of mean and base extraction, and suborned my wife and son to take away my life,' answered Castlehaven. 'Witnesses, according to law, should be honest men and of untainted reputation, which they are not. Fitzpatrick is a recusant, and therefore cannot be a witness. Besides, I have often beat him for his knavery and turned him away, and now he is hired by my son to swear against me.'

After further judicial consultation the Lord Chief Justice announced that it did not appear that Fitzpatrick had been convicted of recusancy, 'that all are held legal evidences for the King till they are convicted of crimes that may disable them and as to their reputation no [other] man could be witness of such monstrous inhumanities; besides which what the witnesses have sworn has put their own lives into the same danger with their Lordship's'.

Several other interesting questions of law were raised and resolved.

Prisoner: I desire to know whether the Statute intends that all kinds of pollution, man with man, is buggery or not, seeing the witnesses say there was no penetration?

Lord Chief Justice: It is buggery by the law, for the law of this land makes no distinction of buggery, if there be *emissio seminis*.

Lord High Steward: Are persons of mean extraction and of no estates sufficient evidences against a Baron?

Lord Chief Justice: Against any man.

Lord High Steward: Is a man that is *particeps criminis* (a party in the crime) a legal evidence against the accused?

Lord Chief Justice: Yes, my Lord, for otherwise facts of this nature would seldom or never be discovered; and till he is attainted he is a competent evidence.

The prisoner, who called no other witnesses in his defence, was then addressed by the Lord High Steward. 'My Lord, you have been graciously dealt with in this proceeding, for it is not a usual thing in so capital and heinous causes as this to bring the party and witnesses face to face before trial. But, my Lord, you have long before this time heard their examinations, and questioned and opposed them face to face, and are thereby the better enabled to make your defence; and His Majesty is still graciously pleased to continue his goodness towards you, and hath commanded that you should be heard at full. If, therefore, you have anything else to say for yourself, speak it.'

Apart from making 'a solemn protest of his innocency', and somewhat inconsistently at this stage imploring the mercy of God and the King, the prisoner replied that he had nothing more to say, but left himself to God and his peers, for whose consideration he presented what he called 'three woes'.

1. Woe to that man whose wife should be a witness against him;
2. Woe to that man, whose son should persecute him and conspire his death;
3. Woe to that man, whose servants should be allowed [as] witnesses to take away his life.

The peers then withdrew into an adjacent room to consider their verdict, which it took them two hours to reach. During this time they sent for the Lord Chief Justice on several occasions, and also sent two of their number to consult with the Lord High Steward. When the peers eventually resumed their places, each was asked by the Lord High Steward, beginning with the most junior in rank, to declare his finding. In the case of the indictment for rape, all twenty-seven of his peers found the Earl of Castlehaven guilty. But in the case of the two indictments for buggery, the numbers were divided—15 declared the earl was guilty and 12 not guilty. Since a majority verdict prevailed in a trial of peers, this amounted to a conviction in respect of the sodomy charges.

The Lord High Steward then sentenced the delinquent earl to death by hanging. Before the court dispersed, the prisoner, so we are told, 'very humbly besought' his fellow peers 'to mediate with His Majesty that he might not die, but be banished', or at least that His Majesty 'might not suddenly cut him off, but give him time of repentance'. Finally, the prisoner 'desired their Lordships' pardons, in that he had been so great a stain to honour and nobility'.

The King refused to reprieve Castlehaven, in spite of this plea and a petition for mercy from the prisoner's son. However, since he was 'a nobleman descended from ancestors who had done good services to the Crown', the hanging was commuted to beheading. The sentence was carried out on Tower Hill on May 14, when his head 'was taken off at one blow'. He met his end with dignity and courage, having previously been received back into the Anglican faith. In his speech from the scaffold he freely admitted that he has been 'a vicious liver, and justly deserved death', but not for 'the two heinous crimes with which I am branded, condemned, and here to suffer for', and which 'I do here deny . . . freely forgiving those who have accused me and have been the occasion of my death'. The latter included his son James Lord Audley, who was allowed to visit him in the Tower on the eve of his execution, having somewhat naïvely written to his father that he could 'with a safe conscience wash his hands of his blood'.[1]

Six weeks later, Fitzpatrick and Broadway were tried at the bar of the Court of King's Bench in Westminster Hall on similar charges before the Lord Chief Justice and three other judges. Lady Castlehaven again gave evidence that Broadway had raped her, after which, we are told, 'she departed with as much privacy as might be into her coach'. As for Fitzpatrick, the Lord Chief Justice informed him that he had accused himself sufficiently.

In the words of the judges' report on the case, 'Fitzpatrick who was arraigned for the buggery, confessed his examinations to be true, but like one very ignorant and rather senseless, would have them true against the Lord Audley [Earl of Castlehaven], and not against himself which was impossible; he pretended he was promised security from danger, if he would testify against the Lord Audley, and so sought to raise a suspicion, as if he had been wrought upon, to be a witness to bring the Lord Audley to his end.'

In reply to Fitzpatrick's protest that what evidence he had formerly given was for the King against the earl, and no further, the Lord Chief Justice observed that 'it was true, the law did not oblige any man to be his own accuser; yet where his testimony

---

[1] *C.S.P.D. 1631–1633*, 39. As a convicted felon, Castlehaven's English barony of Audley and his English property were forfeited to the Crown, and Fonthill passed into other hands. But his Irish titles, being entailed on his male heirs, went to his eldest son, James, in whose favour the English barony was also revived by Charles I in 1633. James 3rd Earl of Castlehaven, who was always a Catholic, subsequently had a distinguished military career as a Royalist in Ireland and the Continent. The Irish titles became extinct in 1777 on the death of the earl without male heirs, but the English barony of Audley, being a so-called barony by writ, descended through the female line and still subsists.

served to take away any one's life, and made himself guilty of the
same crime, therein it should serve to cut him off also'. In
answer to a query from the jury whether they could convict the
prisoner as an accessory under the statute, the judge ruled that,
'forasmuch as every accessory to a felon is a felon in law, so he
being a voluntary prostitute, when he was not only of understanding and years to know the heinousness of the sin but also
of strength to withstand his Lord, he therefore was so far guilty'.

Both prisoners were convicted, sentenced to death, and hanged
a week later at Tyburn. 'We for our parts thought it to stand with
the honour of common justice,' the judges reported to the Lord
Keeper after the trial, 'seeing their testimony had been taken to
bring a peer of the realm to his death for an offence as much theirs
as his, that they should as well suffer for it as he did, lest any
jealousy should arise about the truth of the fact and the justness
of the proceedings.'

There is something vaguely unsatisfactory about the whole
Castlehaven affair. That the earl was a voyeuristic homosexual
there can be no doubt, as also that he indulged in homosexual
acts with his servants Fitzpatrick and Broadway, in spite of his
ultimate denial. In his speech before the gallows, Fitzpatrick,
who died a Catholic, said he wished that his late master had not
uttered such a denial, 'for it was too true: his lordship had both
buggered him, and he his lordship'. Fitzpatrick also admitted
that 'he had lived an ill life, in that he had delighted in drinking,
whoring and all manner of uncleanness', adding that 'he had fallen
into these sins, and especially that which he came to die for',
because he had neglected to repair to his 'ghostly father' (the
priest), as he should have done, 'to make confession and receive
instruction from him'.

On the other hand, Lady Castlehaven's motives in coming
forward as a witness against her husband are not above suspicion.
She was undoubtedly a woman of extremely loose morals and at
one time infatuated with Skipwith, by whom she had a child.
Broadway, who was convicted as the result of her testimony,
declared that she had 'made away with the infant, which according
to him was the reason why Skipwith had come to hate her and
had transferred his attentions to the young Lady Audley. Indeed,
'the countess was the wickedest woman in the world, and had
more to answer for than any woman that lived', said Broadway.
The unfortunate earl's trial no doubt had religious overtones, as
is evident from the manner in which the aggressively Protestant
Attorney-General pressed the charges against him, and Castle-

haven's four sisters, who were Catholic, believed him to be the victim of a conspiracy. The countess and her lover certainly had good reason for seeking to get him out of the way, as also had his son.

After the trial, a pardon under the royal sign manual was issued to Anne Countess of Castlehaven 'for all offences of adultery, fornication and incontinence'.[1] Nor did her daughter Young Lady Audley's moral character improve with the years, since in 1658 she was reported as having been, with her friend Lady Petre, 'by the Constable in the Common Garden, carried to the Cage, where they lay all night'.[2]

Meanwhile the trial of Lord Castleheaven was to remain the leading case on the law of buggery for almost two centuries, that is, until the law as regards the proof of emission of seed was modified in 1828.

[1] *C.S.P.D. 1631–1633*, 182.
[2] G.E.C. *Complete Peerage*, III, 88.

CHAPTER THREE

Georgian Justice

[1]

Nine years after the Castlehaven affair the trial took place of a 'spiritual' peer, which aroused much comment at the time. In 1640, John Atherton, the Right Rev. Lord Bishop of Waterford and Lismore in Ireland, was convicted of buggery with his tithe proctor, John Childe. The bishop was convicted solely on the testimony of his alleged accomplice, who confessed on the scaffold that he had given false evidence against his employer.

Bishop Atherton, who came from Somerset, where his father was an Anglican parson, was ordained after leaving Oxford, and he owed his advancement to the patronage of the Lord Lieutenant of Ireland, Thomas Wentworth, Earl of Strafford. In 1636, at the age of thirty-eight, he was appointed to the see of Waterford and Lismore, where he is said to have 'behaved himself with prudence, though forward enough, if not too much, against the Roman Catholics in that country'. Evidently not popular with the religious majority in his diocese, it is significant that no Roman Catholics came forward to testify at his trial. It has been suggested that Atherton was the victim of a political conspiracy, as the result of a suit he brought against the powerful Earl of Cork for the return of certain tithe lands which had formerly belonged to the see of Waterford and which the Earl had appropriated when he bought Sir Walter Raleigh's Irish estates, and that he was in reality guiltless of the charge brought against him two years later. But there is a conflict of testimony. While the bishop denied the charge at his trial and repeated his denial as he was mounting the gallows, on the other hand he virtually admitted his guilt to the divine who attended him during his last days in prison. He was convicted at Cork Assizes and afterwards taken to Dublin where he was hanged on Gallows Green. His tithe proctor, who was the chief Crown witness at his trial, was himself convicted on a similar charge at the next Assizes and hanged on Bandon Bridge in Cork.[1]

[1] Anon. *Life and Death of John Atherton* (1641); Nicholas Bernard. *Penitent Death of John Atherton* (1641); D.N.B. I, 689.

No details of the evidence given at these two trials are available, but the following remarks about them from an early nineteenth century work with a strong anti-clerical bias, *The Crimes of the Clergy*, published by a certain W. Benbow in London in 1823, are relevant.

In Ireland, to this day, the collection of tithes is left in the hands of a fellow, called a Proctor, who exacts much more then his due in order to profit himself. A miscreant, named John Childe, was the Tithe Proctor to the Bishop, in every respect as complete a villain as his master. A description of the vices to which this obedient servant was pander would occupy a volume: over scenes, disgraceful to manhood, and revolting to human nature, we draw a veil, unwilling to shock and disgust our readers.

An English clergyman, who misbehaved about the same time, was treated more leniently, being merely deprived of his benefice, for attempted buggery with three of his parishioners and also a mare. He was the Rev John Wilson, Vicar of Arlington, near Eastbourne, who was disciplined 'for that he in a most beastly manner attempted to commit buggery with Nathaniel Browne, Samuel Andrewes, and Robert Williams his Parishioners, and by persuasions and violence, laboured to draw them to this abominable sinn, *that* (as he shamed not to professe) *they might make up his number eighteene;* and hath professed, *that he made choice to commit that act with man-kind rather than with women, to avoide the shame and danger that oft ensueth in begetting Bastards;* and hath also attempted to commit Buggery with a Mare . . . and hath openly affirmed, *that Buggery is no sinne.* . . .' His other offences included saying openly in church that Christ was a bastard, advocating the use of images and rosaries for prayer, and being 'a usuall frequenter of Ale-houses, and a great drinker', so that it is not surprising that he was considered unsuitable to continue in his cure of souls.[1]

A similar example of bestiality with a mare was reported some years later in Scotland. Major Thomas Weir, who commanded the town guard in Edinburgh, was presented with a mare. One day he rode her into Lanarkshire, and was detected in the act by a woman near New Mills. She reported what she had seen with the result that he was pursued by some soldiers and brought before the local bench of magistrates. But on hearing what the

[1] Pisanus Fraxi (W. S. Ashbee). II. *Centuria Librorum Absconditorum* (1879), 40.

major had to say, the case was dismissed, the magistrates at the
same time ordering the woman to be 'whipped through the town
by the hand of the Common Hangman, as a slanderer of such an
eminent Holy man'. Many years later, Major Weir, whose
conscience weighed heavily on him, confessed that he had 'dealt
carnally' with the mare, and had also 'done the same abominations' with a cow and 'three Species more'. He also admitted to
having had incestuous relations with his sister as well as having
committed adulteries and fornications with various women in
town. In 1670, he was duly brought to trial in Edinburgh, convicted and sentenced to be strangled at a stake between Edinburgh and Leith, after which his remains were to be 'burnt to
ashes'. The sentence was carried out. For her part in the incest
his sister was hanged.[1]

The Restoration of Charles II to the throne in 1660 and the
easy morals of that monarch's court were characterized by a
tolerant and even flippant attitude towards homosexual conduct.
Certainly there were no prosecutions of any prominent individuals during this period. It was the opinion of the diarist
Pepys that the court had never been as bad as it was during the
reign of Charles II for 'the most abominable vices that ever were
in the world'. The libertine courtier and poet John Wilmot,
Earl of Rochester, who died worn out by his exertions in 1680
at the age of thirty-three, is generally regarded as the author of
the play *Sodom*. Composed in heroic couplets and reputed to have
been privately performed at court, *Sodom* has been described by
Sir Sidney Lee, the author of the article on Rochester in the
Dictionary of National Biography, as being of intolerable foulness.[2]
Treating the subject as it does with marked levity, its somewhat
crude humour may be regarded as not unamusing. The somewhat slender plot, if it can be called plot, is devoted to the
happenings which result from a proclamation issued by
Bolloxinion, King of Sodom, to Borastus, his 'Buggermaster-
General', and General Buggeranthos, that in future buggery
should be the order of the day for his subjects.

---

[1] Pisanus Fraxi. II, 51–7, William Roughead, *Twelve Scots Trials* (1913),
41–62. Except for a short period under the Commonwealth, from 1650 to 1660,
incest in England was an ecclesiastical offence and unlike Scotland did not
become subject to the ordinary criminal law until 1908.

[2] Pisanus Fraxi II, 326. *Sodom* was published under an Amsterdam imprint,
probably fictitious, in 1684. No copy of this original edition is extant, but two
MS versions exist, of which one is in the Harleian Collection in the British
Museum. It has recently been reprinted by the Olympia Press in Paris. Rochester
disclaimed responsibility as author, and it has been attributed to a barrister
named John Fishbourne. However, internal evidence suggests that Rochester
had the main hand in its composition. *D.N.B.* XXI, 538.

Henceforth, Borastus, set the nation free,
Let conscience have its right and liberty:
I do proclaim that bugg'ry may be us'd
Through all the land, so cunt be not abus'd.
That's the proviso.
To Buggeranthos let this charge be given,
And let them bugger all things under heaven.

The other characters include Queen Cuntigratia; Prince Pricket
and Princess Swivia; Prince Pockenello, the King's favourite;
Pine and Twely, 'Two Pimps of Honour'; Flux, the King's
physician; and Virtuoso, 'Merkin and Dildoe Maker to the
Royal Family'; besides a crowd of 'Boys, Rogues, Pimps and
Other Attendants'.
At the outset Pockenello reveals to the King that Pine has
been familiar with the Queen, and Twely adds that 'he swiv'd
her in the time of term'. But Bolloxinion takes no offence and
declares:

With crimes of this sort I shall now dispense,
His arse shall suffer for his prick's offence;
In roopy seed my spirit shall be sent,
With joyful tidings to his fundiment.
Come Pockenello, o're my pintle burns,
In, and untruss, I'll bugger you by turns.

However, terrible misfortunes befall Bolloxinion's kingdom
and his own family as the presumed result of his edict, which his
physician Flux eventually begs him to cancel.

To Love and Nature all their rights restore,
Fuck women, and let bugg'ry be no more,
If doth the procreative end destroy,
Which Nature gave with pleasure to enjoy;
Please her, and she'll be kind, —and if you displease
She turns into corruption and disease.

But the King refuses to return to 'the old whore my wife', and
says, 'I'll reign and bugger still.' The curtain falls to the accompaniment of fire, brimstone, smoke, 'fiery demons' and other
'horrid apparitions', which now overwhelm the kingdom of
Sodom.
In the reign of William and Mary, the subject was introduced
on the stage more discreetly by the architect and playwright Sir
John Vanbrugh, whose witty comedy *The Relapse* had its first

public performance at the Theatre Royal, Drury Lane, in 1696. The play was a brilliant commentary on the manners and morals of the day and was enthusiastically received, the more sophisticated members of the audience being aware that the author was taking some risk in his homosexual allusions in view of the king's known feelings for several of his courtiers. Elizabeth, Duchess of Orleans, an acute French observer, wrote at this time: 'The King is said to have been in love with Albemarle as with a woman, and they say he used to kiss his hands before all the Court.' Perhaps the most notorious in this respect was William III's minister Lord Portland, who greatly shocked the French by his behaviour when he went to Paris as British ambassador in 1698.

'Nothing is more ordinary in England than this unnatural vice, as I was told by an Englishman himself,' remarked the Duchess of Orleans to a friend; 'and all those who followed Lord Portland to Paris led a terrible life with the debauchees of Paris. Lord Westmoreland and Lord Raby and three or four others did not hesitate to make public what their inclinations were. . . . You ask why people persist in tasting such forbidden pleasures, but since the days of Adam it has always been so, that forbidden fruits taste better than those that are allowed.'[1]

The anonymous editor of a reprint of the proceedings at the Castlehaven trial, which appeared in 1699, prefaced his account with some severe comments on the subject, which show how firmly implanted the Sodom legend had become by this date.

> Another abomination that shocks our natures and puts our modesty to the blush to see it so commonly perpetrated is the devilish and unnatural sin of buggery, a crime that sinks a man below the basest epithet, is so foul it admits of no aggravation and cannot be expressed in its horror, but by the doleful shrieks and groans of the damned. A sin that caused God Almighty to rain down hell upon Sodom and Gomorrah and turn a fruitful pleasant country into utter barrenness and desolation.
>
> The sin now being translated from the sodomitical original, or from the Turkish and Italian copies into English . . . I thought I could not more oblige the public than . . . to publish it at this juncture, that by reading the sin, so tragically delineated in its horrid shape and ugly visage by the grave and learned sages of the law, and in the death of a noble peer, other men might be terrified and scar'd from those sins that are

[1] G. S. Stevenson (ed.) *Letters of Madame* (1924) I, 217, 156–7.

attended with nothing but infamy and death in this world and eternal damnation in the next.

[2]

In Queen Anne's reign we hear for the first time of the homosexual clubs which began to flourish in London and later in the provinces. Those who supported them were known as 'mollies', from Molly, the familiar pet-form of Mary, the term being particularly applied to the effeminate type; hence 'molly-coddle'. The humourist and political pamphleteer, Edward Ward, who has recorded many pictures of low life in the metropolis at this period, has described the behaviour of this 'curious band of fellows' in his *History of the London Clubs*, which first appeared in 1709.

They adopt all the small vanities natural to the feminine sex to such an extent that they try to speak, walk, chatter, shriek and scold as women do, aping them as well in other respects. In a certain tavern in the City, the name of which I will not mention, not wishing to bring the house into disrepute, they hold parties and regular gatherings. As soon as they arrive they begin to behave exactly as women do, carrying on light gossip as is the custom of a merry company of real women.

According to Ward, they were in the habit of discoursing at length and with great impropriety of the pleasures of a 'husband' and 'children', imitating 'the petty feminine faults of women gossiping over coffee, in order to . . . encourage unnatural lusts'. This particular club was broken up through the zealous efforts of 'some agents of the Reform Society', as a result of which several of the regular frequenters of the club 'were publicly punished, and this fortunately ended their scandalous orgies'. But not for long, as other clubs soon sprang up in the town.

There are details extant of the activities of these gatherings, which were really a species of male brothels. For instance, a woman somewhat improbably named Margaret Clap was indicted at the Old Bailey summer sessions in 1726 on a charge of 'keeping a disorderly house' in Field Lane, off Holborn, 'in which she procured and encouraged persons to commit sodomy'. A police constable gave evidence that one Sunday evening in the previous November he had visited the prisoner's house, where he found between forty and fifty men 'making love to one another as they called it'. Sometimes they would sit on one another's laps, 'kissing in a lewd manner and using their hands indecently'.

Then they would get up, dance and make curtsies and mimic the voices of women, indulging in such vernacular expressions as 'O, fie, Sir', 'Pray, Sir', 'Lord, how can you serve me so?', 'I swear I'll cry out', 'You're a wicked devil', 'You've a bold face', and 'Eh! ye little dear toad!'

Then, according to this witness, they would 'hug, and play and toy, and go out by couples into another room on the same floor to be married, as they called it'. The door of that room was kept by a man called Eccleston, 'who used to stand pimp for them to prevent anybody from disturbing them in their diversions. When they came out, they used to brag, in plain terms, of what they had been doing. As for the prisoner, she was present all the time except when she went out to fetch liquor.' Among those present the witness recognized a certain Will Griffin, who had been convicted of buggery at the previous sessions and hanged. The witness added that he visited the house on several of the following Sunday nights, and the same kind of behaviour was going on as before. 'The company talked all manner of gross and vile obscenity in the prisoner's hearing, and she appeared to be wonderfully pleas'd with it.' As the result of the police raid, we learn that 'there were above forty sodomites taken from that house and committed to prison in one night'.

Since nobody came forward to speak as to the prisoner's character, Mistress Clap was asked by the judge whether she had anything to say for herself. 'I hope it will be considered that I am a woman,' she replied briefly, 'and therefore it cannot be thought that I would ever be concerned in such practices'.

However, this somewhat lame defence did not convince the jury, who found her guilty as charged. She was sentenced to stand in the pillory in Smithfield, pay a fine of twenty marks ($£13$ 6s. 8d.), and go to prison for two years.[1]

On the whole, the law seems to have been fairly, if severely, applied. In this respect the better-to-do and more socially influential accused had an advantage, since they could get bail from the committing magistrate and later abscond. Attempts to commit buggery were usually punished by the pillory in addition to fine and imprisonment. In 1721, a man named George Duffus was charged at the Old Bailey with the major offence, but 'the spermatic injection not being proved, the court directed the jury to bring in their verdict special', i.e. guilty of the attempt only.[2] Of course, where the jury found the accused guilty of the major

[1] *Select Trials at the Old Bailey 1720–1742* (1742), III, 37–8.
[2] id. I, 105–8.

offence, the court was bound to pass sentence of death, although this was not always carried out. At the sessions at which the unfortunate Will Griffin was convicted in 1726, five men including Griffin were charged, of whom four were found guilty and one was acquitted. Three of those convicted were hanged at Tyburn and one was reprieved. This appears to be the average pattern during the eighteenth century, at any rate in London. In spite of the judges' ruling in the Castlehaven case that on their construction of the Act of Henry VIII it was not necessary to prove penetration in cases of buggery and that emission of seed upon the body was sufficient, the courts usually insisted on proof of penetration as well as emission. The difficulty of proof both in buggery and rape was eventually to lead to a change, or rather a clarification, of the law, in 1828, when it was expressly enacted that 'carnal knowledge shall be deemed to be complete upon proof of penetration only'.

An early eighteenth century work of anonymous authorship entitled *Plain Reasons for the Growth of Sodomy in England* blames the custom of sending young boys to kindergartens run by women for the increase in homosexuality, besides foppish clothes, continental manners, tea-drinking and the Italian opera, observing that sodomy is considered a trivial matter in Italy, since no sooner does a stranger set foot in Rome than the procurers rush to ask if he wants a woman or a young man. English schools and universities had their share of homosexual scandals, some suppressed and others open, such as the case of the head of an Oxford college.

In 1739, the Rev. Robert Thislethwayte, Doctor of Divinity and Warden of Wadham College, Oxford, for the past fifteen years, was charged with a 'sodomitical attempt' upon the person of William French, a commoner of the college. He was then aged about fifty-two. The assault was said to have taken place in the Warden's Lodgings one February afternoon between divine service and supper time. Young Mr French, who was in his second year, told his father what had happened, and the father immediately posted to Oxford, where he appealed to the Vice-Chancellor. As a result the Warden was brought before the local bench of magistrates, who committed him for trial at the next assizes but at the same time released him on bail. In due course the Grand Jury returned a true bill against him, but he failed to appear and stand his trial.[1]

---

[1] *A Faithful Narrative of the Proceedings . . . against Robert Thistlethwayte, Late Doctor of Divinity, and Warden of Wadham College for a sodomitical Attempt upon Mr W. French, Commoner of the same College* (1739).

Apparently Mr French was not the only one whose virtue had been attacked by the Warden, since the depositions read to the Grand Jury included two compromising statements which the police had taken from the college butler and a barber who used to shave the Warden in college.

According to Robert Langford, the butler, the Warden had invited him to supper five or six years previously. They sat down, nobody else being present, and drank a bottle of wine together, 'when the Warden began to talk and act in a beastly manner, endeavouring to kiss and tongue him, and to put his hand into his breeches; that he (the butler) soon understood him and desired him to be quiet, for he did not like such usage'. On another occasion, when the butler was going home from the buttery through the college quadrangle, the Warden looked out of his study window and called him. Since there were several gentlemen in the quadrangle at the time, the butler thought it would look 'very odd' if he did not obey the Warden's summons, with the result that he went in to him and the Warden 'began his caresses, trying to know him as before'. The butler also swore that he begged the Warden to desist, adding that he would expose him if he did not; 'that upon the Warden's continuing his addresses he told him that he wondered gentlemen of his fortune did not provide themselves with women, or wives, and not act in so vile and beastly a manner; that the Warden made answer that he would not give a farthing for the finest woman in the world; and that he loved a man as he did his soul'. Having thus 'expressed his resentment', the butler left the Warden and 'never went to him after'.

The deposition of William Hodges, the barber, may be quoted in full:

That about a year and a half ago he went to shave the Warden about eleven in the forenoon: that the Warden, being dressed in his gown and cassock, he put his nightgown over him to avoid daubing him: that whilst he was shaving him he found something tickling about his breeches, but he thought at first it might be the effect of the gown's not sitting right upon the Warden, wherefore he altered the position of it and went on:

That immediately after he found the Warden trying to introduce his hand into his breeches: that thereupon he asked him what he meant:

That the Warden answered, 'There is no harm in this, my dear', and talked to the same effect so long that the barbe swore he would never shave him again, for he knew what he wanted, and that he was the wrong person for his purpose:

That when he went home he told his master of the Warden's behaviour and that he would shave him no more, that his master desired, though he did not continue to shave him, that he would go, however, for two or three days, for if he did not go, the Warden would suspect he had told him (the master), and it would be to his prejudice:

That he accordingly went again one day, and as soon as he came into the room the Warden said to him, 'How dost do, my dear barber? It's fine weather, my dear barber. Let me feel it.' And then he went to kiss him.

That upon this he said to the Warden, 'Damn you, you son of a bitch, what do you mean?' And knocked him backwards into his chair:

That Thislethwayte got up and attacked him again as lewdly as before, and that he again knocked him down, and never went near him afterwards.

It only remains to add that the unfortunate Warden, who had been a Fellow of his college since 1715 and had previously filled the post of Bursar and Sub-Warden, resigned all his offices, ecclesiastical as well as academic—he was Prebend of Westminster and Rector of Winterslow, his native parish in Wiltshire, a living presumably in the gift of his family—and he fled across the channel. He appears to have travelled no further than Boulogne, where as an absconder he was safe from the attentions of the law. He died there five years later and, having probably expressed the wish to be buried in English soil, his remains were brought to Dover where they were appropriately laid to rest in the churchyard of St Mary the Virgin.[1]

In his picaresque and partly autobiographical novel *Roderick Random*, first published in 1748, Tobias Smollett, who was a familiar figure in the London taverns and coffee houses of the period, makes his character Lord Strutwell declare that homosexuality 'gains ground apace and in all probability will become in a short time a more fashionable device than simple fornication'. This statement was amplified in a curious work, which appeared anonymously the following year under the title, *Satan's Harvest Home: or the Present State of Whorecraft, Adultery, Fornication, Procuring, Pimping, Sodomy . . . And other Satanic Works, daily propagated in this good Protestant Kingdom*. The author roundly

[1] R. B. Gardiner (ed.) *Register of Wadham College Oxford* (1889), I, 432.

condemns the habit of members of the same sex kissing each other in public, the women 'in a lascivious manner' and the men still worse squeezing each other's hands and indulging in 'other like indecent symptoms'.

> Under this pretext vile Catamites make their preposterous Addresses, even in the very Streets, nor can any thing be more shocking, than to see a Couple of Creatures, who wear the shape of Men, Kiss and Slaver each other, to that Degree, as is daily practised even in our most publick places; and (generally speaking) without Reproof; because they plead in Excuse, That it is the Fashion. Damn'd Fashion! Imported from Italy amids't a Train of other unnatural Vices. Have we not Sins enough of our own, but we must eke 'em out with those of Foreign nations, to fill up the Cup of our Abominations, and make us yet more ripe for Divine Vengeance?

The author repeats the familiar charge that Italy is 'the Mother and Nurse of Sodomy', since it is there that 'the Master is oftner intriguing with his Page than a fair Lady'. And not only in that country, but in France, which 'copies' from the Italians, 'the Contagion is diversify'd, and the Ladies (in the Nunneries) are criminally amorous of each other, in a Method too gross for Expression'. On the subject of lesbianism, which the author calls a 'new sort of sin', it has now, so we learn, 'got footing' among English women of quality, and is practised in Twickenham as well as in Turkey.

[3]

The pattern of cases in the second half of the eighteenth century showed little change from the first, except towards the end of the period, when there seems to have been a falling off in convictions for the major offence, owing partly, no doubt, to the difficulty of proof, following a judicial decision in 1781 that both penetration and emission of seed must be established.

Four years previously a man had been convicted on one species of evidence only. The trial judge, who had some reservations about the justice of the verdict, referred the matter to all the judges who used to sit informally in Serjeant's Inn. In this instance the twelve judges upheld the verdict and the man was duly sentenced and executed. A similar case arose in 1781 when a man named Hill was convicted before Mr Justice Buller. When this case came before the twelve judges, eight held that both penetration and emission of seed must be proved, while four considered that one or the other was sufficient. The Lord Chief Justice gave no opinion on the case, and the man was not executed, being held guilty of the attempt only. Consequently, from 1781 to 1828, when the law was expressly altered, the uniform practice was to require evidence of both acts before a man could be convicted of buggery.

Attempts to commit buggery were invariably punished by the pillory, where the individual was liable to be seriously injured by the mob hurling bottles and brickbats at him. In 1761, a young woollen draper of Cornhill, London, pilloried for an attempt with a boy in a court off Lombard Street, was nearly lynched; and two years later two men, similarly sentenced, were actually killed by the mob. There was a marked increase in blackmail and attempts to extort money by threatening to denounce the victim as a practising homosexual to the authorities.

In February 1779 a man named James Donally was accused at the Old Bailey of extorting money from the Hon. Charles Fielding. younger son of the Earl of Denbigh, by threats. 'You had better comply,' he said, 'or I'll take you before the magistrate and charge you with unnatural crime.' As a result he obtained a guinea and a half from young Mr Fielding. He also tried to get money from Fielding's elder brother, Lord Fielding, by using similar threats, but without success. On the jury convicting the prisoner of highway robbery, he raised a point of law, whether his action in fact amounted to street robbery, which was a capital offence. The trial judge thereupon referred the matter to all the King's Bench judges for an opinion, which was duly delivered to the effect that the prisoner's threat was 'equivalent to an actual violence and was such a method as in common experience was likely to occasion fear, and induce any man to part with his property'.

This view was warmly endorsed by Lord Mansfield, the Lord Chief Justice, who 'with great energy observed that it was a specious mode of robbery of late grown very common, invented by fraud to evade the law, but which would not suffer itself to be evaded. God knows what numberless robberies of this kind would have been perpetrated by these detestable wretches on timorous minds, if their Lordships had been of a different opinion.'[1]

Although he was the father of several illegitimate sons, the bachelor actor and dramatist Samuel Foote, who built the Haymarket Theatre, had the reputation of being homosexual. Two

[1] *Annual Register* (1779), 199–200, 208–9.

of his most successful roles were Lord Foppington in Vanbrugh's *The Relapse* and Mrs Cole, the procuress, in his own comedy *The Minor*; the character of Mrs Cole was said to be based on a well known 'Madam' called Mother Douglas, who also figures in John Cleland's *Memoirs of a Woman of Pleasure*, commonly known as *Fanny Hill*. Foote was certainly very familiar with the seamier side of London life. In 1776, an Irish clergyman named Jackson, whom Foote had satirized in his play *The Capuchin* as Dr Viper, retaliated by publicly insinuating that Foote was guilty of 'the most odious form of crime'. At the same time Jackson instigated a coachman whom Foote had dismissed from his employ to prefer a bill of indictment against him in the Court of King's Bench alleging indecent assault, and it appeared that he provided the coachman with money to conduct the case.

The only witness for the prosecution was the prosecutor himself, who swore positively that the assault had taken place on May 15, the day (so he said) on which the Haymarket Theatre opened for the season. However, it was clearly proved by several of the performers that the theatre did not open until the 22nd of the month. Foote was defended with much eloquence by John Dunning, later Lord Ashburton, and the jury acquitted him without leaving the jury box. But Foote was completely unnerved by the ordeal of the trial, from which indeed he never recovered. His acting went to pieces, and he died in the following year while on his way to the south of France in a vain attempt to recover his shattered health.[1]

Then, as in later periods, it was natural that homosexual scandals involving the aristocracy and members of society should attract more public attention than the misdoings of humbler folk, which seldom rated more than a few lines in the Old Bailey and other session records. Four members of the peerage at this time are noteworthy in this context: Earl Cowper; the Earl of Findlater, who was also Earl of Seafield; Viscount Courtenay, later Earl of Devon; and the Earl of Leicester, later Marquess of Townshend.

George Nassau Clavering-Cowper, third Earl Cowper, spent most of his life in Florence, where he died in 1789 aged forty-one. He was a Prince of the Holy Roman Empire and a noted art collector. Shortly after his death, an English journalist named Topham wrote in *The World* newspaper words to the effect that Lord Cowper 'had led a wicked and profligate course of life, and had addicted himself to the practice and use of the most criminal and unmanly vices and debaucheries'. Topham was prosecuted

[1] William Cooke. *Memoirs of Samuel Foote* (1805) I, 221-31; D.N.B. VII, 370.

at the suit of the Cowper family and duly convicted of publishing a criminal libel. Normally libel and slander are regarded by English law as personal wrongs and the right of action, therefore, dies with the person defamed. Nevertheless it is a criminal offence to publish defamatory words of any deceased person if it be done with intent to injure and bring contempt on his family, and so provoke a breach of the peace. However, the trial judge, dissatisfied with the verdict in this case, referred the matter to his judicial brethren in the Court of King's Bench, who on consideration arrested judgment on the ground that there was no allegation in the indictment that the libel was published 'with an intent to create any ill-blood, or to throw any scandal on the family and posterity of Lord Cowper, or to induce them to break the peace in vindicating the honour of the family'.

The law about libelling the dead, which still prevails, was clearly stated by Lord Chief Justice Kenyon in his judgment in the Topham case:

> To say, in general, that the conduct of a dead person can at no time be canvassed: to hold that, even after ages are passed, the conduct of bad men cannot be contrasted with good, would be to exclude the most useful part of history. And therefore it must be allowed that such publications may be made decently and honestly. But let this be done, whether soon or later after the death of the party, if it be done with a malevolent purpose, to vilify the memory of the deceased, and with a view to injure his posterity . . . then it is done with a design to break the peace, and then it becomes illegal.[1]

James Ogilvy, seventh Earl of Findlater and third Earl of Seafield, and the last of his line to hold the Findlater title, was the only surviving son of the sixth Earl, a well-known Scottish agriculturist of his time, whom Horace Walpole described as 'a mighty sensible man', though he found his 'solemn Scotchery' was 'not a little formidable'. Ogilvy's mother was born Lady May Murray, eighteenth child of the first Duke of Atholl. While an undergraduate at Oxford in 1770, he succeeded his father, who had committed suicide. Soon afterwards he left Oxford without taking a degree, and went to live abroad, whether or not as the result of some scandal is uncertain. According to Ashbee (Pisanus Fraxi), 'he was an able and learned man, but his tastes becoming known, he resided for the greater part of his life on the continent, where he could more easily indulge them'. In 1779, he married,

---

[1] *R. v. Topham* [1791], 4 T.R. 126, at p. 130.

in Brussels, a Murray kinswoman, whose father was a general in
the Austrian service. He had no children by his wife, from whom
he parted shortly after their marriage. Lord Findlater eventually
settled in Dresden, where he died without a direct heir in 1811,
aged sixty-one, being buried there, whereupon all his titles
became dormant, except the Seafield earldom, which passed by
special remainder to a cousin. After his death it appeared that he
had left the whole of his unentailed property to a Saxon family of
the name of Fischer, chiefly to a young man, who had acted first
as his page and afterwards as private secretary. The relations
refused to pay these legacies, and an action was brought by the
Fischer beneficiaries in the Court of Session in Scotland to
enforce payment. This was resisted by the relations on the
ground that the bequests had been made for an immoral consideration (*ob turpem causam*). Proceedings went on for some
time, and two commissions were appointed by the court to take
evidence in Saxony. 'But the scandal became so great, of a noble
family attempting to fix a stigma on the memory of their relative
from pecuniary motives, that friends interfered, and a compro-
mise was effected, by which the Fischers received a large sum,
£60,000 in full [settlement] of their claims.'[1]

William Courtenay was born in 1768, the only boy in a family
of fourteen. He was brought up with his thirteen sisters at
Powderham Castle, his father's seat near Exeter, which he eventually inherited. He was a singularly beautiful boy, judging by
the portrait which Romney painted of him in his early teens at
the instance of his friend William Beckford. Beckford, who is
chiefly remembered today as the author of *Vathek*, was the
wealthy and eccentric squire of Fonthill, which had once belonged
to the ill-fated Earl of Castlehaven. He was probably bisexual.[2]
He first met young Courtenay, whose senior he was by nine years,
when Courtenay was ten, and immediately fell in love with him.
The relationship which resulted, though it was largely romantic
and sentimental, at least on Beckford's side, was to prove disast-
rous for them both, when it reached a climax five years later, in
1784. By the autumn of that year everything seemed to be going
well for Beckford. He was married to an earl's daughter, he had
been elected a Member of Parliament, and it was being openly
said in the newspapers that he was about to be raised to the
peerage; indeed there is some evidence that the patent of peerage
had actually been made out and only lacked the king's signature.

[1] Pisanus Fraxi. I, *Index Librorum Prohibitorum*, 341.
[2] J. W. Oliver. *The Life of William Beckford* (1932).

Then suddenly everything collapsed while Beckford and his wife were on a visit to Powderham. Early one morning, Courtenay's tutor, who occupied a room next door, heard his pupil cry out, and he immediately went to the door of Courtenay's bedroom, which he found locked. It appeared that Beckford was within, possibly in bed with the boy. Beckford denied that he was in any such compromising position, and would not say what had been happening. It was only much later that he admitted that he had been carrying on an affair with Courtenay's aunt, Lady Lough-borough, and that Courtenay had been acting as courier in their correspondence. One of Beckford's letters or notes was said to have fallen into wrong hands, and Beckford in a fit of annoyance went to Courtenay's room to chastise him, hence his crying out.

An attempt was made to hush up the whole business. But it was soon a subject of gossip. The gossip eventually reached the ears of King George III, who is said to have wished that Beckford should be hanged; this not being feasible, the king had to content himself with cancelling the patent for the peerage. Beckford promptly went abroad, where he remained for the next ten years. In the political circumstances of those days he was able to retain his membership of the House of Commons, but even on his return to England he seldom attended Parliament, preferring to live with a physician and a French abbé in the seclusion of Fonthill, where he embarked upon a course of the most fantastic architectural extravagance, which eventually crippled him financially and forced him to sell Fonthill and much of its valuable contents.

Meanwhile Lord Courtenay, who on his father's death had inherited Powderham, where he lived a curious bachelor life with one of his unmarried sisters, became an inveterate homosexual and, as the years went on, less and less discreet in his behaviour. In 1810 it was reported by the diarist Joseph Farington that 'many of the neighbouring gentlemen refused to hold intercourse with him', although 'several respectable families' still continued to visit him. He had recently planned to build a house in Torquay for occasional residence, and indeed the walls were erected, 'but the people of the place reviled and insulted his servants in terms so opprobrious and this was done with such perseverance that the scheme of finishing the house was given up and it remains a monument of the public opinion against him'.

Meanwhile an Exeter magistrate named Morton had been diligently collecting evidence against Courtenay, although he received no support from his fellow justices on the bench, who were no doubt landed proprietors like the noble viscount. But in May, 1811, Morton obtained statements which conclusively pointed to Courtenay's guilt under the statute. At first, Courtenay, who would have normally been tried by his peers, as was Castle-haven, pooh-poohed the possibility of any proceedings, so Farington tells us, adding with characteristic flippancy that

> should he be accused before the Lords, they, most of whom were like himself, would not decide against him. . . . But, when he was informed that the Officers of Justice were ordered to pursue him, he lost all resolution, wept like a child and was willingly taken on board a vessel, the first that could be found, an American ship, and passed there under a feigned name. After he had been on board some time, he asked whether he might not be called by his own name but was told it would be dangerous on account of the sailors whose prejudice against him might have had bad effects.

Before his hurried embarkation, he made a will under which he left his sister £1,600 a year, provided she did not marry, an action which the normally sexed diarist described as 'a strong trait of his disposition and mind'.[1]

The vessel which had taken him on board eventually landed Courtenay in France, where he was to spend the remaining twenty-four years of his life in obscurity, relieved only by one incident which again brought him to public attention. In 1831 the earldom of Devon, which had been dormant for 265 years, was revived in his favour by the House of Lords. Because Courtenay was unmarried and had no brothers to inherit his viscountcy, the latter title was due to become extinct when he died. But the earldom, by the terms of its creation, would pass to a distant cousin, William Courtenay, son of the Bishop of Exeter, provided the viscount's claim to it could be established. This cousin happened to be a clerk in the House of Lords, an occupation which left him plenty of time for genealogical research, and it was the result of this activity that the erring Lord Courtenay unexpectedly found himself Earl of Devon, his industrious cousin thus becoming heir presumptive to this latter title. The newspapers of the time commented at large on the matter, remarking that the new earl 'ought to think himself happy that his tithes and estates have not been forfeited, or himself paid the debt to the law', and taunting him with the fact that he

[1] James Greig (ed.). *The Farington Diary* (1926), VI, 147–8, 273.

'never ventured to put the question of guilt to a trial', but remained 'skulking abroad, afraid to venture on taking his seat in Parliament'. But Courtenay was not to be drawn, since he had no doubt been advised that he risked immediate arrest and possible execution if he set foot in England. He prudently chose to stay on in his comfortable Paris house in the Place Vendôme until his death in 1835 and his cousin's succession to the title which Courtenay had not wanted and had never used.

Courtenay's younger contemporary George Ferrers, Earl of Leicester, who also inherited a title which he never used, was if anything more notorious than Courtenay. On going up to Trinity College, Cambridge, in 1798, where he was known by the courtesy title of Lord Chartley, he took with him an Italian servant named Neri, who had formerly been a waiter in a London coffee house. Neri, who lived in Leicester's rooms, was a most unusual servant, since we are told that he used to play the guitar and he and his master would give concerts attended by 'most of the nobility and many of the seniors of the college'. In college, not surprisingly, he passed for an eccentric. Apparently he used to shut himself up in his rooms for a week or more at a time and saw no one, except presumably the indispensable Italian. We are also told that instead of the purple gown which noblemen generally wore, Leicester wore a pink one, besides which he 'dressed his hair effeminately, and was called Miss Leicester, Lady Chartley, etc. in derision. Many gentlemen in the college, however, were like ladies.' He left the University suddenly without taking a degree, on the pretext of 'going abroad'.

Leicester was next heard of some years later in London when he began to pick up private soldiers in the Guards and used to be seen walking arm in arm with them. He was also in the habit of giving the guardsmen presents of gold watches, money and civilian clothes, which their commanding officer subsequently stated were as good clothes as he himself wore when off duty. In 1807, by which date he was styled Earl of Leicester, Farington recorded in his diary that he was 'a very effeminate young man' and 'sometimes he wore pink ribbon to his shoes', adding that 'having married a young lady only a few months ago, he is said to be on the point of separation from her'.

Early in 1809, Leicester brought an action for libel against the *Morning Herald* for two statements published in that journal. The first, which appeared on December 3, 1808, was to the effect that Lady Leicester had accused her husband of the same crimes for which Lord Castlehaven 'was convicted and deservedly executed; but in the present instance, there were circumstances of far greater atrocity'. According to the second statement, 'the wretched son of an English Marquess has absconded on a charge which Lady Leicester has exhibited against him. A special warrant has been issued for apprehending this lord, whose infamies have long rendered him a disgrace to human nature.'[1]

At the trial of this action, which was heard in the Court of Common Pleas in Westminster Hall, a good deal of dirty linen was publicly washed. The truth was that, far from Lord Leicester and his bride 'having lived happily together', as his counsel urged, 'there was nothing perhaps in the whole history of married life more wretched. Three sleepless nights were all they passed together, and after that time they were never in bed and seldom at board together.' The former waiter, Neri, whom Leicester had set up in a costly establishment of his own, frequently shared their meals, with the result that Lady Leicester 'was soon banished from his house by such conduct'. However, since the substance of the libel could not be proved, judgment was entered for the earl with £1,000 damages, the figure being reduced from the sum of £20,000, which the plaintiff had claimed, owing to Leicester's bad reputation and the fact that there were so many 'flying rumours' about his character. Indeed he did not make a personal appearance in court, since he had already removed himself abroad.

In fact, the proceedings which the countess had begun against her husband, later dropped, were for non-consummation of their marriage, she having accused him, in Farington's words, 'of impotency and of not being found as a man should be'. There does not seem to have been any question of sodomy and therefore Leicester was not in danger of arrest, as the *Morning Herald* had stated. However, he had been disinherited by his father on account of his general behaviour, and it is likely that Lord Townshend threatened to cut him off completely unless he went to reside abroad. The result was that he settled in the Villa Rostan at Pegli, near Genoa, where he lived out the remainder of his life in similar obscurity to that enjoyed by his fellow peers Findlater and Courtenay. Although he became titular Marquess of Townshend on his father's death in 1811, he never used the title, unlike his wife, nor did he continue to style himself Earl of Leicester, but took the name of Compton, which had been his grandmother's maiden name. He is said to have kept a large supply of wine at the Villa Rostan, which he gave away freely at a time when wine in the Riviera di Ligure was very scarce; and he always sat

[1] *Annual Register* (1809).

at dinner with his hat on. 'Signor Compton' died at Pegli in 1855, being described in his death certificate as '*Giorgio Feres* (sic) *Compton . . . figlio del fu Giorgio Compton*', and was buried in the local protestant cemetery of San Benigno.[1]

Meanwhile his wife, who did not go on with her divorce suit, had been living with a brewer named John Margetts of St Ives, Huntingdon, whom she evidently regarded as her 'common law' husband, since she had gone through a ceremony of marriage with him at Gretna Green and had a large brood of children by him. This offspring was all declared illegitimate by Parliament in 1833, an enactment which resulted from Lady Townshend's eldest son by Margetts having wrongfully assumed the title of Earl of Leicester and having been elected M.P. for Bodmin under that style. No doubt the news of this legislation afforded some satisfaction to 'Signor Compton' when it reached him in his Mediterranean exile.[2]

[4]

Although the decline in the number of convictions was maintained in the early years of the nineteenth century, due to the requirement that both penetration and emission of seed must be proved, the capital crime of buggery continued to be regarded with horror and execration on the part of both judges and the general public, so that reprieves were relatively rare. It was not surprising that blackmail should have continued to flourish. One such case, *Rex* v. *Passingham and Edwards*, which was tried in the Court of King's Bench in 1805, so impressed William Beckford that he had a folio copy of the proceedings made for his use and had it placed amongst his treasured MSS.[3]

George Townshend Forrester, who lived in Worcestershire, was married to a Miss Jones of the same county, where he was said to have resided with her for some years 'in the greatest harmony'. Colonel Robert Passingham and Mr John Edwards, who were both related to Mrs Forrester, were charged with conspiracy to procure her husband's consent to their separation and compel him to give her a substantial sum by way of maintenance by threatening to charge him with 'crimes of the most horrible kind'. In fact the two blackmailers did lodge information

---

[1] James Greig (ed.). *Farington Diary* (1925). V, 75.
[2] G.E.C. *Complete Peerage*, XII, Pt. 1, 813.
[3] *Annual Register* (1805), 365–6.

against Forrester before the magistrate at Bow Street, and Forrester was foolish enough to take to flight. He was arrested on the Kent coast while trying to make his way to the Continent and brought back to London. Fortunately for him, the witnesses on whom the blackmailers depended withdrew their testimony, and the blackmailers were arrested in their turn. At the trial in Westminster Hall Forrester was the principal Crown witness and spent nearly four hours under cross-examination, 'in the course of which he was frequently so agitated as to be deprived of speech, particularly when the subject of his wife and children were called in question'. Thirty witnesses in all gave evidence and the proceedings lasted for thirty hours, during which we learn from the contemporary report that 'many circumstances transpired at which human nature must shudder'. Both the defendants were convicted on all counts. Their punishment is not known, but since their offence consisted of conspiring to attempt to extort money, it would not have been capital.

It was otherwise with John Hodges and two others, who were found guilty at the Old Bailey sessions in the same month and sentenced to death for 'assaulting Mr Edmund Lodge in the highway, and under threat of accusing him of an unnatural crime taking from his person banknotes value £10 and £5 his property'. According to the *Annual Register* for 1805, Mr Lodge was 'a gentleman of unblemished character', while 'the circumstances of this case were of the most horrible nature, and it was not until the prisoners had received considerable sums of money from the prosecutor and had made a further demand for £250 that he had the courage to lay open the transaction'.

According to a Home Office return for 1811, when criminal statistics began to be scientifically compiled, four out of five convicted sodomists were executed, as against only 63 out of 471 other capital offenders. The recorded details show little change from the previous century. At Lancaster assizes in 1806 Isaac Hitchen, aged sixty-two, one of the most respectable and affluent citizens of Warrington, and four other apparently middle-aged gentlemen were indicted for 'unnatural crimes' along with other men who had turned Crown evidence to save their lives. According to the evidence, they regularly assembled at Hitchen's house on Monday and Friday evenings, and 'they called one another brother'. In passing sentence the judge advised them 'in the most impressive manner . . . to prepare to meet the fate which the laws of the country had affixed to their heinous offences'. Hitchen and one other were respited. The remaining three were hanged 'in a state of the greatest agitation . . . on the new drop erected at the back of the Castle'. No mercy was shown to members of the armed forces, particularly guardsmen, for thus offending against good order and discipline. In 1811, for instance, Ensign John Hepburn, who protested his innocence to the last, and a drummer named Thomas White 'were launched into eternity' outside Newgate before 'a vast concourse of spectators', which included the Duke of Cumberland, Lord Sefton, Lord Yarmouth, 'and several other noblemen'.

The presence on this occasion of the Duke of Cumberland, future King of Hanover and himself a professional soldier, has a curious interest, since it was strongly rumoured at this time that he had recently been involved in a horrible homosexual scandal. He had two valets named Neale and Sellis, and it was openly said that the Duke had been detected 'in an improper and unnatural situation with this Neale by the other servant Sellis, and exposure was expected'. In order to stop Sellis from talking, the duke is supposed to have murdered him. At all events, Sellis was discovered in bed in his room in St James's Palace in the early hours of June 1, 1810 with his throat cut, while Cumberland, who was at the same time suffering from severe head wounds, alleged that he had been attacked by Sellis in a fit of madness. A coroner's jury found that Sellis had committed suicide after attempting to assassinate the Duke. This 'wicked uncle' of Queen Victoria was probably the most unpopular man in England, and the legend of his infamy died hard. A journalist who published the scandalous rumour in 1813 was sentenced to fifteen months in prison and a fine of £200 for criminal libel, while another pamphleteer who repeated the story twenty years later got six months. The truth of the affair will probably never be known. All that can be said here is that this detested character was commonly regarded as having killed Sellis in order to conceal his relations with the other valet.[1]

White, the guards drummer, who was convicted at the Old Bailey in December 1810, was a conspicuous figure in the celebrated 'Vere Street coterie', a homosexual club which used to meet in the White Swan public house in Vere Street, off Oxford Street, kept by a man named James Cooke, and which was broken up by the police in July of the same year, following the arrest of White and more than twenty others. It is stated in a contemporary publication, *The Phoenix of Sodom, or the Vere Street Coterie*, that

[1] *The Trial of Joseph Phillips for a Libel on the Duke of Cumberland* (1833).

White, being a universal favourite, was very deep in the secrets of the fashionable part of the coterie; of which he made a most ample confession in writing immediately previous to his execution, the truth of which he averred to his last moments; but it is impossible to give it literally, for the person who took it, in the presence of a magistrate, said that the recital made him so sick he could not proceed.

The author of *The Phoenix of Sodom* thus described the White Swan and its patrons:

The fatal house in question was furnished in a style most appropriate for the purposes it was intended. Four beds were provided in one room: another was fitted up for the ladies' dressing room, with a toilette, and every appendage of rouge, &c. &c.: a third room was called the Chapel, where marriages took place, sometimes between a *female grenadier*, six feet high, and a petit maître not more than half the altitude of his beloved wife! These marriages were solemnized with all the mockery of *bride maids* and *bride men*, and the nuptials were frequently consummated by two, three, or four couples in the same room, and in the sight of each other. Incredible as this circumstance may appear, the reader may depend it is all provable.

The upper part of the house was appropriated to wretches who were constantly in waiting for casual customers, who practised all the allurements that are found in a brothel, by the more natural description of prostitutes; and the only difference consisting in that want of decency that exists between the most profligate men and depraved women. Men of rank, and respectable situations in life, might be seen wallowing either in or on the beds with wretches of the lowest description: but the perpetration of the abominable act, however offensive, was infinitely more tolerable than the shocking conversation that accompanied the perpetration; some of which, Cooke has solemnly declared to me, was so odious that he could not either write, or verbally relate. It seems many of these wretches are married; and frequently, when they are together, make their wives, whom they call Tommies, topics of ridicule, and boast of having compelled them to act parts too shocking to think of. . . .

It is generally received opinion, and a very natural one, that the prevalency of this passion has for its object effeminate delicate beings only: but this seems to be, by Cooke's account, a mistaken notion.

For instance, two of the most sought after of the passive homo-sexuals frequenting the White Swan were 'an athletic bargeman' who called himself Fanny Murray and 'a Herculean coal-heaver' who was known as Lucy Cooper, besides whom there were 'Black-eyed Leonora', 'Pretty Harriet', 'Lady Godiva', the Duchess of Devonshire', and 'Miss Sweet Lips', respectively a drummer, a butcher, a waiter, a blacksmith, and a country grocer.

These are merely part of the common stock belonging to the house, but the visitors were more numerous, and, if possible, more infamous, because more exalted in life and *these ladies*, like the ladies of the petticoat order, have their favourite men, one of whom was White. According to Cooke, a certain person of outward respectability frequently came to The White Swan, and stayed several days and nights together, during which time he generally amused himself with eight, ten, and sometimes a dozen different boys and men! Sunday, added the landlord, was 'the general and grand day of rendezvous', and some of the visitors came a great distance, even so much as thirty miles, to join the festivity and elegant amusements of grenadiers, footmen, waiters, drummers and all the catamite brood, kneaded into human shape, *from the sweepings of Sodom, with the spawn of Gomorrah.*

The landlord and five of his companions received prison sentences and were also condemned to stand for one hour in the pillory in the Haymarket, opposite Panton Street. Here they were mercilessly pelted with brickbats, dead cats, rotten eggs, potatoes, mud and buckets filled with blood, offal and dung, which the local butchers had considerately supplied for the use of the spectators. The unfortunate Cooke, according to a contemporary newspaper account, 'received several hits in the face, and he had a lump raised on his eyebrow as large as an egg'. The delinquents were similarly assailed on their journey by cart from Newgate, and 'as they passed the end of Catherine Street, Strand, on their return, a coachman stood upon his box, and gave Cooke five or six cuts with his whip'. In the words of the report,

it is impossible for language to convey an adequate idea of the universal expressions of execration, which accompanied these monsters on their journey. . . . Before the cart reached Temple Bar, the wretches were so thickly covered with mud that a vestige of the human figure was barely discernible. They were chained, and placed in such a manner that they could not lie down in the cart, and could only hide and shelter their heads from the storm by stooping. This, however, could afford but little protection. Some of them were cut in the head with brickbats and bled profusely. The streets, as they passed, resounded with the universal shouts and execrations of the populace.[1]

[5]

Higher up the social scale, clergymen figure prominently at this period. Because they were invariably granted bail by the local magistrates, who as a rule belonged to the gentry, it was possible for them to flee abroad rather than face trial. Of four reverend gentlemen, whose cases caused much interest in the early years of the nineteenth century, three forfeited their bail and fled abroad, while only one remained to answer the charge in court.

In 1797, the Rev. John Fenwick, Vicar of Byall, Northumberland, and member of a well-known county family, removed himself hurriedly to France after a warrant had been issued for his arrest. His homosexual behaviour had begun when he was an undergraduate at Oxford, when he was discovered by the college washerwoman in bed with a young man with whom he used to play the fiddle. The washerwoman immediately spread the story round the university, but she later refused to make a written deposition as to what she alleged she had seen, having, so it was said, 'been tampered with', otherwise bribed by Fenwick, to do so. Fortunately for Fenwick, he had got his degree, so that he was able to return home and take up the church living which was in his father's gift. Some time later a man named Harper, whom Fenwick had invited to the vicarage, jumped out of the library window so as to escape the attentions of the vicar who he alleged had assaulted him. However, the local magistrate, who was a fox-hunting friend of Fenwick's, dismissed the complaint with ridicule. On his way to the country town to seek the help of one of the assize judges, the luckless Harper was seized by the press-gang and forced into service aboard a warship, where he shortly afterwards fell in action. The eventual cause of the vicar's undoing was his action in turning his wife out of his room in the

---

[1] Pisanus Fraxi. I, 328–38. In 1816 the pillory was abolished as a punishment in England for all offences except perjury and subornation. It was finally abolished in 1837. It lasted longer in the United States, surviving in the State of Delaware until 1905.

vicarage and spending the night alone with his curate. From France, after his flight, Mr Fenwick went on to Italy, where he established himself in Naples in a fine house and was reported, somewhat surprisingly, as getting on friendly terms with Lady Hamilton, whose husband was British Ambassador in the kingdom of the Two Sicilies.

In 1812, the Rev. V. P. Littlehales, who held two livings in Lincolnshire and was a prebendary of Southwell Cathedral besides keeping a school, was staying on a visit with a certain Dr Wollaston, when he was alleged to have tried to assault his host's footman, 'who with difficulty escaped from him, and of course refused to return to his room, although the bell was repeatedly rung with great violence'. It was also reported that 'the gentleman of the house, asking his servant why he did not answer Mr Littlehales's bell, received an answer so improbable that he dismissed the servant on the spot, an imprudent step, which irritated the servant and released him from all necessity of keeping secret the infamous occurrence'. At first the local magistrates' bench refused to believe the servant's charges. However, before fleeing to America, which the anonymous author of that interesting work *The Crimes of the Clergy* described as 'that sanctuary of crime and hot-bed of guilt', the unfortunate Mr Littlehales admitted his homosexual tendencies. 'I have known that this is the rock on which I should split,' he said.

The biggest scandal in which clergymen were involved at this time concerned the Bishop of Clogher. This case had a particularly tragic aftermath in the blackmailing of the Marquess of Londonderry, the Foreign Secretary, better known by his courtesy title of Lord Castlereagh, who confessed in an audience with King George IV that he had been 'accused of the same crime as the Bishop of Clogher'; and, his mind giving way under the strain, he committed suicide shortly afterwards by cutting his throat with a razor.[1]

During the previous three weeks the affair of the bishop had made a considerable stir in London. Indeed it was a prime topic of conversation in the clubs and coffee-houses, although from the nature of the case its details were scarcely fit to be discussed in drawing-rooms. Public interest was increased by the fact that the accused person was not only a high dignitary of the Church but also a member of an aristocratic Irish family and the uncle of a

[1] *Annual Register* (1822). J. Richardson. *Recollections of the Last Half Century* (1855), I, 283–304. H. Montgomery Hyde, *The Strange Death of Lord Castlereagh* (1959), 54–8.

peer. The Right Rev. Percy Jocelyn, Bishop of Clogher, was the third son of the first Earl of Roden, a landowner whose estates by a curious coincidence were situated not far from Castlereagh's ancestral property in County Down. Although it was a suffragan bishopric, nevertheless Clogher boasted a fine episcopal palace, also in Ulster, which the bishop had occupied for the past two years. Before that he had for over a decade been Bishop of Ferns. He was about fifty-seven years of age and was unmarried.

On the night of July 19, 1822, his lordship, who was in London on a visit from Ireland, went into a public house called the White Hart in St Alban's Place, Westminster. There he was detected in the act of committing a homosexual offence with a private soldier of the 1st Regiment of Guards, named John Moverley. He was attired in his customary episcopal dress and made no attempt to conceal the nature of his calling. 'The Bishop took no precautions,' noted Charles Greville in his diary at the time, 'and it was next to impossible he should not have been caught. He made a desperate resistance when taken, and if his breeches had not been down they think he would have got away.' He was then escorted along with the soldier to the watch-house in Vine Street, being followed by a crowd, which shouted insulting remarks after them as they went along. Arrived in Vine Street, he refused to give his name to the constable of the watch. But his identity was revealed by a letter, which he took from his pocket and tore up. He threw the fragments into the fire-place, but as there was no fire burning there, they were recovered by the constable and pieced together. The letter turned out to be from his nephew, Lord Roden. This was confirmed by a note which he asked the constable to send to a friend in the house where he lodged off Portman Square, in which he wrote that he was 'totally undone' and signed himself 'P.C.'–the initial letters of his christian name and diocese.

Next day the two delinquents were brought before the local magistrate, and after they had been formally charged they pleaded not guilty and reserved their defence. The magistrate informed them that their offences were bailable, and he fixed the amount of bail each in £500 and two sureties in £250 each. Two sureties came forward on behalf of the bishop and entered into the necessary recognisances. The bishop was thereupon released, though not until he had given his name and address, which he did with considerable reluctance. No sureties appeared for the soldier, so that the unfortunate Private Moverley was remanded in custody.

Meanwhile the affair continued to be talked about and the people of the public house made a good deal of money by showing the place. According to Greville, Lord Sefton went to see the soldier in prison:

> He says he is a fine soldier-like man and has not the air which these wretches usually have . . . It seems that the soldier will be proceeded against with the greatest vigour, and the Magistrate is much blamed for having taken such small bail as that which he required. The Duke will not spare the soldier. Lord Lauderdale said the other day that the greatest dissatisfaction would pervade the public mind at the escape of the Bishop and the punishment of the soldier, and the people, who cannot discriminate, or enter into nice points of law, will only see in such apparent injustice a disposition to shield an offender in the higher classes of society from the consequences of his crime, while the law is allowed to take its course with the more humble culprit. He said he would have exacted the greatest bail of the bishop that ever had been taken. . . .

As it happened, this was not the first time that the bishop had been accused of attempting to commit such an offence. Eleven years previously in Dublin a domestic servant named James Byrne had charged his lordship with having made an immoral proposition to him. For this the servant was prosecuted for criminal libel by the bishop, and on his conviction was sentenced to two years' imprisonment and also to be publicly flogged. The latter punishment was carried out with such severity that the poor man nearly died. This incident was now recalled in connection with the bishop being granted such lenient bail, particularly when the fears expressed by Greville and others were abundantly justified and the bishop failed to appear to stand his trial at the next sessions at Clerkenwell.

While preparations were being made to deprive the bishop of his ecclesiastical dignities, he broke his bail and fled to Scotland, where he anticipated there would be difficulties in executing any warrant for his re-arrest. Here he assumed the name of Thomas Wilson and for a time, it is said, took employment as a butler, on one embarrassing occasion being recognized by one of his former acquaintances as he was handing round the dishes at dinner. He died incognito in Edinburgh in 1843. He was buried quietly in the new cemetery, at seven o'clock in the morning, followed by only five mourners in a one-horse coach. By his directions no name appeared on his coffin, but the plate bore an inscription in Latin, which he had himself devised some years previously. The translation read: 'Here lies the remains of a great sinner, saved by grace, whose hope rests in the atoning sacrifice of the Lord Jesus Christ.'

[9]

The only member of the clerical quartette mentioned above, who did not escape abroad, but remained to stand trial, was the Rev. Thomas Jephson, Tutor, Lecturer and Fellow of St John's College, Cambridge. In its way the scandal of his case was as great as that of Robert Thislethwayte at Oxford in the previous century, although in staying to face the music instead of fleeing and forfeiting his bail he displayed much greater courage than the Oxford don. The son of a London schoolmaster, Jephson, who graduated in Divinity, became domestic chaplain to the Duke of Northumberland immediately after being ordained, but soon returned to Cambridge, where he was elected a fellow in 1808. An able scientist and mathematician, he wrote an authoritative work on *The Fluxional Calculus*, and he might well have become a professor but for the unfortunate incident which occurred on Whit Sunday in 1823, when, after assisting in the celebration of Holy Communion in the college chapel, he went for a walk along the Cherry Hinton Road.

According to his own account, Jephson went into a field 'for the purpose of easing himself', and while doing so he observed a youth loitering about who 'annoyed him by being several times in his way'. Jephson thereupon 'went to a convenient place for his purpose', when the youth came so near him that Jephson thought of going into an adjoining field, and heard the youth give a peculiar whistle as if whistling for someone. The don then asked the youth what he meant by whistling, and the lad replied, 'I always whistle when I am alone'. Jephson then asked whether there was a gap in the hedge, and the youth answered in a surly manner, 'You'll find one if you look for it'. He eventually found the gap and got through it with difficulty, finding himself as a result in the corner of the field.

No sooner had he pulled down his breeches, than four or five men leaped over the hedge. 'We have found you at last!' one of them shouted as they collared him. He was then dragged along some way with his breeches still down, at which he protested violently, but they replied that 'there would be plenty of girls to look at him'. On his further remonstrating with his captors, one of them said that if he would give them some money they would let him go.

'I will give you all I have,' said Jephson, taking out three notes and some silver from his pocket and offering it to them.

'That is not enow,' said one of the men.

'It is all I have,' answered Jephson.

'Perhaps the gentleman has a watch?'

'Will you set me at liberty if I give it to you?'

'Yes.'

Jephson then gave them his gold watch and chain to which his seal and key were attached, producing them from his waistcoat pocket. He was then allowed to pull up his breeches and to go on his way without further ado. The lad went off with the men.

The college don subsequently charged the men with robbery, but after hearing what the men had to say, the magistrate dismissed the charge, whereupon Jephson was in turn arrested and accused of criminal assault and of having attempted to commit an unnatural offence. He was released on bail on his own surety of £600 and two other sureties of £300 each to come up at the summer assizes.

The trial took place in the Cambridge assize court on July 23, 1823, when the prisoner was brilliantly defended by a fellow member of St John's, Thomas Denman (afterwards Lord Chief Justice), who had been Brougham's junior in the spectacular defence of Queen Caroline. The principal witness for the prosecution was the youth, whose name was James Welch and who was nineteen years of age. He swore that he had had an earlier meeting with Jephson, in the morning, when Jephson asked him how old he was and on being told that he would be twenty on his next birthday he asked the youth whether he 'would go with him'. Welch asked him what he meant by this. His evidence continued as follows:

He took hold of me and took me where the hedge was thicker because there was a gap where we stood and folks could see us. He began to pull me about there. He says, 'You are a nice fellow', and got hold of my hand and kept putting it against him. He wanted me to put my hand in his breeches, but I would not. He asked me whether I would lay down in the ditch. I said, 'No sir, I do not like to do any such thing'. He then asked me if I would meet him at night—at nine o'clock. I said yes. He says. 'I must kiss you before I go,' and he got hold of me and he did.

Then, according to Welch, he went home, where he was asked how his trousers had come to be torn. He told several older acquaintances what had happened and asked them to come with him to the evening appointment 'for fear the gentleman should use me ill'. Three men did in fact accompany him, of whom one was a man called Joseph Hart, who subsequently laid the information against Jephson, since Welch refused to do so. When they got into the ditch, Welch went on, Jephson gave him £1 5s. 6d. and then undid his trousers down to his shoes, after which he pulled up his shirt and put it under his chin. 'Come, come, young man,' he was alleged to have said to Welch, 'you are so long—we shall not be long'. Jephson also told Welch that he was very fond of a man; he said he had not had a man for a long time. 'He wanted to reach hold of my hand, and I ran away.'

At this, one of the others who were on the far side of the hedge and had overheard what had passed, jumped into the ditch and seizing Jephson exclaimed: 'Hullo, this is a nice sport for a gentleman to be at!'

'I know I have done wrong,' Jephson replied, according to Welch. 'I will give you all I have. If it is known, it will ruin me for ever.'

In his evidence, Hart stated that Jephson had given as his explanation of being in the ditch with his breeches down that he had gone there to relieve himself.

'That excuse won't do, because we heard every word you said,' Hart deposed that he had replied. 'I will take you into Cambridge as the Bishop [of Clogher] was taken into St James's.'

This witness supplied some further details of the conversation he had overheard between Jephson and Welch at the side of the ditch. Asked by Jephson which he liked best, men or women, the youth replied, 'Men'. Jephson then asked him 'if he ever played with boys' cocks', and then, unbuttoning his breeches, asked him 'to feel his parts'. Welch answered no, he was 'not used to it'.

Jephson went on to inquire whether the women's parts he went with were hairy, following this with a request that the youth should experiment with 'his parts to feel which was the most hairy'. On Welch refusing to get into the ditch, Jephson pulled him down, tearing his trousers as he did so.

Jephson's defence counsel argued strongly that the whole

affair was a base conspiracy to extort money. After a trial which lasted for seventeen hours, the jury eventually decided to give the prisoner the benefit of the doubt, and they returned a verdict of Not Guilty.

The acquittal appears to have been received with some surprise by the university authorities. The Senate voted a petition be addressed to the Bishop of Ely praying him to deprive Jephson of his holy orders, but the bishop replied that the matter was not within his jurisdiction. At the same time the Master and Fellows of St John's ordered that Jephson should not reside in college nor hold any office or preferment in their appointment 'until his innocence was more clearly established'. No further action was taken, and, although he removed himself from Cambridge and went to live elsewhere, the Rev. Thomas Jephson continued to hold his fellowship until his death forty-one years later.[1]

[1] J. A. Venn. *Alumni Cantabiogienses* (1947). Pt. 2, III, 568.

CHAPTER FOUR

Some Victorian Homosexuals

As a reforming Home Secretary, Robert Peel was responsible in the reign of George IV for consolidating most of the English criminal law, as well as mitigating its severity. Although he succeeded in abolishing the death penalty for over one hundred offences, it was retained in respect of the more serious sexual crimes, namely buggery, rape and having carnal knowledge of girls below the age of consent (then 13). In all three cases Peel proposed to dispense with the requirement that emission of seed must be proved in addition to penetration. At first sight this may appear contrary to Peel's generally humanitarian policy, but he was concerned with the enforcement of the law, as he was at pains to make clear.

In introducing the Offences Against the Person Bill, which was largely a consolidating measure, in the House of Commons, Peel declared that from his experience during six years at the Home Office 'he was aware of the manner in which public justice was often thwarted by this unnecessary difficulty which the law had placed in its way'. Further, 'it was his strong conviction that one of those descriptions of proofs was unnecessary; and that it was not necessary to a capital conviction, to prove more than that which constituted the moral offence, as far as the offending party was concerned'. The only objection to a change diminishing the proof, in his opinion, was the possibility of increasing the number of false accusations. But he thought there was no substance in this.

If cases of rape were difficult of proof, how much more difficult was the requisite proof in the two other cases? In these cases how was it possible to prove the completion of either offence to the extent which the law required? The difficulty was so great as almost to preclude the possibility of conviction. The demand for specific evidence of the offence was a great obstruction to the end of public justice, and a great accumulation of the misery which the unhappy victim had to undergo.

Peel also pointed out that 'the alteration in the law, such as was proposed, would be only the re-establishment of the ancient law of England, as it existed'. Finally, he observed that 'he had consulted a number of authorities and found that, up to a recent period [i.e. Hill's case in 1781] one of the proofs only was deemed necessary for conviction'. This was of course quite true and long before Hill's case had been expressly laid down by the judges in the Castlehaven trial, when it was held that either penetration or emission was sufficient proof.

Since the bill had already passed the Lords, Peel indicated that he would not 'press' it through the Lower House, 'without giving ample opportunities for considering it in all its bearings'. Whether or not any observations were made about proof in cases of buggery does not appear from the record of the proceedings. Members, not to mention the parliamentary reporter, may have shared Peel's reticence in referring to the offence specifically, since whenever the minister had to mention it he did so in a circumlocutory Latin phrase as 'the crime *inter Christianos non nominandum*'. On the whole he was more concerned with revising the law of evidence in respect of sexual offences against women.[1]

The measure was duly enacted as the Offences Against the Person Act, 1828 (9 George IV c. 31). First, the original statute of Henry VIII, as continued in the reign of Elizabeth, was repealed and briefly re-enacted (section 16):

> ... That every person convicted of the abominable crime of Buggery committed either with Mankind or with any Animal, shall suffer death as a Felon.

A further clause (section 18) dealt with the question of proof:

> ... Whereas upon Trials for the crimes of Buggery and of Rape, and of carnally abusing Girls under the respective Ages hereinbefore mentioned, Offenders frequently escape by reason of the 'Difficulty of Proof which has been required of the Completion of those several Crimes': for Remedy thereof be it enacted: That it shall not be necessary, in any of those cases, to prove the actual Emission of Seed, but that the carnal knowledge shall be deemed complete upon Proof of Penetration only.

Since emission no longer constituted an essential element in the crime of sodomy, some amelioration as well as clarification of the law may be said to have resulted. A case heard four years

[1] Hansard. *Parliamentary Debates*. New Series. IX, 350–60 (May 5, 1828).

after the passing of the 1828 Act removed any doubts about the need to prove emission during penetration.

In 1832, a boy of fourteen was assaulted by a man named Reekspear on Southsea Common. The boy swore that Reekspear took him by the collar, threw him down among some furze bushes and buggered him. The circumstances pointed to penetration having taken place and also indicated emission but not during penetration, since the man had been interrupted in his act. Mr Justice Gaselee left it to the jury to say whether there had been penetration, directing them that if so the crime was complete under the new Act. The jury were of opinion that there had been penetration and found the prisoner guilty. However, in view of the fact that there had been no emission *in corpore* the trial judge referred the matter to his fellow judges for consideration. They held unanimously that the conviction was right and the man was executed.[1]

The point came up again two years later in a case involving bestiality with a ewe. Here the prisoner was interrupted by one of the prosecution witnesses who called out to him. As a result the prisoner 'withdrew himself from the animal, he then being in a state of erection'. In this case the prisoner was also convicted, but in his summing up, the trial judge, Mr Justice Parke, drew the jury's attention to the need for strict proof.[2]

> In the former state of the law, the prisoner would have been entitled to an acquittal; but as the law is now, if there was penetration, the capital offence is completed, although there has been no emission. However, as the proof is less than was formerly required, it behoves judges and juries to see that the proof now required is satisfactory.

No executions for buggery or sodomy were carried out after 1836, nor for that matter for any other capital offence remaining on the statute book with the exception of treason and murder. The abolition of the death penalty was enacted by the Offences Against the Person Act, 1861 (24 & 25 Victoria c. 100), the penalty being reduced to penal servitude for life or for any term not less than ten years at the discretion of the court. Attempts were punishable by a maximum of ten years. At the same time, the requirement of proof of penetration was re-enacted. This legislation continued in force until its repeal in 1967, together with the supplementary clause in the Criminal Law Amendment Act,

---

[1] *R.* v. *Robert Reekspear* (1832) 1 Mood. 342.
[2] *R.* v. *Cozins* (1834) 6 Car. and P. 532.

1885, which, as will be seen, made 'an act of gross indecency' with another man, whether in public or private, not amounting to buggery, an offence punishable by up to two years' imprisonment with hard labour.

[2]

The short reigns of George IV and William IV and the long reign of Queen Victoria, which together covered the greater part of the nineteenth century, had their measure of society scandals with homosexual overtones. In particular, during the earlier period, two well-known figures in the literary world were involved; they also happened to be Members of Parliament and were obliged to resign their seats in consequence of the charges brought against them.

The first was the famous book collector Richard Heber, of whom it has been said that perhaps no private individual ever collected such vast accumulations of choice volumes, in more than 150,000 of which he is supposed to have invested £100,000. 'No gentleman can be without three copies of a book,' he used to say, 'one for show, one for use, and one for borrowers'. In 1822, following his election as M.P. for Oxford University, he received the honorary degree of Doctor of Civil Law from the university. In 1824, he was one of the founders of the Athenæum Club and its magnificent library, which he helped to form. Among those he met in the course of his activities as a bibliophile was a young man named Charles Hartshorne, the son of an ironmaster in Shropshire, where Heber also had property. The publication by Hartshorne of a bibliographical essay in 1825, the same year as he graduated from Cambridge, attracted Heber's attention, and the two became intimate friends. At this time Heber was fifty-two and Hartshorne twenty-three. In the following year, a column appeared in a local newspaper in which pointed allusions were made to this intimacy. The matter might well have gone unnoticed if young Hartshorne's father had not seen fit to bring an action for libel against the newspaper. This so alarmed Heber that he fled to Brussels and immediately resigned his seat. Although no proceedings were brought against him, nevertheless Heber deemed it prudent to remain abroad for the next five years. On his return to England, in 1831, he found himself completely ostracized by society. Until his death, which occurred four years later, he lived a life of almost total seclusion either in his London

or his country house, only emerging from time to time to visit
the sale rooms and booksellers' shops. On the other hand, the
affair does not appear to have injured Hartshorne, since he subsequently had a successful career both as a clergyman and an
antiquarian, marrying the daughter of the Cambridge University
librarian, and publishing among other works *The Book Rarities
of the University of Cambridge*.[1]

The other parliamentarian was William John Bankes, the
forty-five-year-old oriental traveller and friend of the poet
Byron, who represented Cambridge University and afterwards
the County of Dorset in the House of Commons. He had the
reputation of being a witty conversationalist and according to
Samuel Rogers he could eclipse Sydney Smith by the vigour of
his table talk. In 1833, Bankes was accused of committing an
act of indecency with a soldier in a public lavatory outside Westminster Abbey. At his trial, many well-known persons, including
the Duke of Wellington, Samuel Rogers, and Dr Butler, the
Master of Harrow, came forward and testified as to his good
character, with the result that he was acquitted. Some years
later, however, in 1841, he was brought before a magistrate for
indecently exposing himself in a London park, and was set at
liberty on bail pending trial. This time he forfeited his recog-
nizances and fled to the Continent, where he died in Venice in
1855.[2]

The great homosexual scandal of the mid-Victorian period
involved another Member of Parliament, thirty-year-old Lord
Arthur Clinton, third son of the fifth Duke of Newcastle. Living
in the same lodgings as Lord Arthur were two young men,
Ernest Boulton, aged twenty-two, the son of a London stockbroker, and his inseparable companion, Frederick William Park,
aged twenty-three, whose father was a Master in the Court of
Common Pleas. Boulton and Park were both transvestite homosexuals, who liked to play female parts in amateur theatricals and
frequently appeared in public dressed as women, rouged and
painted, in low cut dresses. Boulton, familiarly known as 'Stella',
was an effeminate-looking youth, extremely musical and the
possessor of a fine soprano voice. A servant in the lodgings
deposed that she thought Boulton was Lord Arthur's wife, and
certainly his lordship did nothing to dispel this idea; on the
contrary, the evidence showed that he had visiting cards printed
in the name of 'Lady Arthur Clinton' and a seal engraved with the

[1] *D.N. B.* IX, 75, 357.
[2] *id.* I, 1004.

name 'Stella'. Park, who was known as 'Fanny' was also on terms of intimacy with Lord Arthur, as appeared from some of his letters which the police seized. 'Is the handle of my umbrella mended yet?' he asked Lord Arthur in language which caused considerable mirth when the letter was read out in court. 'If so, I wish you would kindly send it to me, as the weather has turned so showery that I can't go out without a dread of my back hair coming out of curl. . . . Ever your affectionate Fanny.'

The police, who had been watching Boulton and Park for some months, eventually arrested them as they were leaving the Strand Theatre one night in April 1870. The officer who carried out the arrests subsequently stated in evidence:

When we got to the station I saw that Boulton had on a scarlet dress and a muslin shawl over it. It was partly satin, and I believe the rest was white moiré antique. Boulton had false hair and chignon of fair colour, like the ordinary hair I have seen females wearing. He had ornaments—bracelets, rings and lockets. It was a very low dress and the arms were bare. He wore white kid gloves. I found afterwards that he wore white petticoats and stays, and a white skirt. He wore ladies' white boots. The bosom was padded to make it appear very full.

Park's costume consisted of a dark green satin dress, low necked, trimmed with black lace, of which material he also had a shawl round his shoulders. His hair was flaxen and in curls. He also had on a pair of white kid gloves and wore earrings.

Next morning the two men, dressed in this remarkable attire, were brought before the magistrate at Bow Street and charged with frequenting the Strand Theatre with intent to commit a felony. The case was adjourned, and after six further hearings both defendants were committed for trial, bail being refused.

Boulton and Park did not always appear in public in women's clothes but, not surprisingly, when they went out dressed as men they were sometimes mistaken for women. A man named Cox, who gave evidence at the preliminary police court proceedings but died before the trial (where his deposition was read), stated that he had been introduced by a friend to Boulton and Lord Arthur Clinton, M.P., in a City pub. Boulton was dressed as a man, but looked like a woman, as Cox believed him to be. He (Cox) stood them a champagne lunch. ('I kissed him, she, or it, believing at the time it was a woman.') Lord Arthur appeared to be jealous, Cox went on, and left the room, whereupon Boulton presented Cox with his photograph, 'secretly, as far as Lord

Arthur was concerned'. Later Cox learned the sex of Boulton, and meeting the pair again at Evans's Coffee House in Covent Garden (a notorious establishment which was to serve as the prototype of 'The Cave of Harmony' in Thackeray's *The Newcomes*), exclaimed: 'You damned set of infernal scoundrels, you ought to be kicked out of this place!' However, under cross-examination, Cox admitted that Boulton had never said he was a woman. ('I flirted with him, believing him to be a woman.')

As drawn by the Crown lawyers, the indictment charged the defendants with conspiring to commit a felony, which was rather stronger than the charge to which they answered at the police court. Letters found in their lodgings appeared to implicate Lord Arthur Clinton, as well as two men living in Edinburgh, Louis Charles Hurt and John Safford Fiske. The latter was an American who was his country's consular representative at Leith. All three were joined in the indictment along with Boulton and Park. But before the case came to trial Lord Arthur Clinton contracted scarlet fever, from which he died. However, the others eventually appeared in the dock at the Old Bailey.

The trial opened before Lord Chief Justice Cockburn on May 9, 1871 and lasted for six days. It aroused immense public interest. The Attorney-General and the Solicitor-General led for the prosecution and the prisoners were each defended by leading counsel of the day, Boulton by Digby Seymour, Q.C., and Serjeant Ballantine, and Park by Serjeant Parry. As the law of evidence then stood, the defendants were debarred from going into the witness-box to testify on their own behalf, so that, although they could be seen, they could not be heard by the jury. Unlike Boulton and Park, Hurt and Fiske were not female impersonators and they were in no way concerned with their transvestite activities; indeed they disapproved of them. 'I am sorry to hear of your going about in drag so much,' wrote Hurt to Boulton in one letter. In another letter Hurt refused to go to the Derby with Boulton if the latter were 'in drag'.

Although there could be no doubt that all the defendants were homosexuals, the prosecution was unable to prove that any of them had infringed the law. The letters seized by the police and read out in court, although most affectionate in tone, did not in any degree suggest that buggery had taken place or been attempted. Nor did the appearance of Boulton and Park in public places dressed as women and visiting the 'ladies' room' in various theatres and bars constitute proof that a felony had been committed by any of them. Much evidence was given about the numerous performances of amateur theatricals in which Boulton and Park had played women's parts, and it was admitted that they often went to parties after the shows in their female costume: their counsel argued strongly that there was no evidence whatever of conspiracy 'beyond the mere going about as women'. In particular, the letters addressed to Park by Fiske, which appeared the most compromising, were dismissed as light-hearted notes to 'an effeminate lad, a dainty and pleasing boy, who was generally treated as a young girl'.

Whatever he may have thought of 'Stella' and 'Fanny' and their caperings, Lord Chief Justice Cockburn strongly disapproved of the form in which the case had been brought. 'We are trying the defendants for conspiracy to commit a felonious crime,' he told the jury in his summing up, 'and the proof of it, if it amounts to anything, amounts to proof of the actual commission of crime. . . . I am clearly of opinion that where the proof is intended to be submitted to a jury, it is not the proper course to charge the parties with conspiring to commit it, for that course manifestly operates unfairly and unjustly and oppressively against the parties concerned.' The defendants, in the judge's view, should have been tried separately, and this would have excluded evidence against one being used to the prejudice of the other defendants. Yet so far as the Crown lawyers were concerned, the Lord Chief Justice's strictures were to go unheeded, and for nearly a century—that is until homosexual offences between consenting adults in private were abolished in 1967—the conspiracy device was used in many homosexual trials in Britain to draw homosexuals into the net of the criminal law.

Both Boulton's mother and Park's father gave evidence of the two defendants' theatrical interests and the various lawful occasions for the possession and use of the women's dresses, in which they had been arrested. The judge was apparently convinced since he summed up strongly in their favour. 'Was there not a solution consistent with innocence?' he asked with particular reference to the letters written by 'Stella' and 'Fanny' to Lord Arthur Clinton, and the parties they attended together. 'These parties had been mixed up together in performances in which Lord Arthur continually acted with Boulton as his lover or husband, and it may have been that, half in fun at first and then habitually, they spoke of each other in that kind of way.'

It took the jury exactly fifty-three minutes to return their verdict of Not Guilty in regard to the four defendants. The verdict was greeted with loud cheers and shouts of 'Bravo!'. It came as such a shock to Boulton, who had by this time grown a moustache in an effort to promote a more masculine appearance, that he fainted in the dock and had to be revived with water.

Next day *The Times* came out with a leading article which contained the following remarks:

> It is not without a certain sense of relief that we record this morning the failure of a Prosecution which nothing but a strong conviction would have justified the Government in instituting. THE QUEEN v. BOULTON AND OTHERS is a case in which a verdict for the Crown would have been felt at home, and received abroad, as a reflection on our national morals, yet which, for that very reason, could not be hushed up after popular rumour had once invested it with so grave a complexion. . . .
>
> Now that justice has been satisfied and the whole story thoroughly sifted, the verdict of the jury should be accepted as clearing all the defendants of the odious guilt imputed to them.

The following limerick, to which the case gave rise, was soon going the rounds:

> There was an old person of Sark
> Who buggered a pig in the dark;
> The swine in surprise
> Murmured: 'God blast your eyes,
> Do you take me for Boulton or Park?'

In all the circumstances, the four defendants, especially Boulton and Park, must be considered fortunate to have been exonerated as they were.[1]

There were many homosexuals among the Victorians, whose inclinations were known to their friends but who managed to avoid 'getting into trouble'. Two literary figures in the mid-Victorian world particularly stand out as deserving notice. Both, by a coincidence, excelled in the art of translation, one from the Persian and the other from the Italian, and both had 'unhappy' marriages. The former, Edward Fitzgerald, died in 1883, and the latter, John Addington Symonds, ten years later. Both are remembered today, and rightly so, for their literary excellence rather than their homosexual proclivities.

Fitzgerald, the translator of Omar Khayyám was a wealthy

---

[1] *The Times*, May 16, 1871. A detailed account of this extraordinary case is contained in William Roughhead, *Bad Companions* (1930), pp. 149–83, to which the present writer is indebted.

eccentric from East Anglia, who, as Havelock Ellis points out, was always out of harmony with his environment, although he was on friendly terms with some of the most distinguished men of his time. Unfortunately for him, he felt himself called upon to marry a woman, the daughter of a friend and fellow poet, with whom he had never been in love and with whom he had nothing in common. ('Her ways were not my ways, and we parted.') Indeed he was never attracted towards women, and all his affections were for men. When he was twenty-three, Fitzgerald met a teen-age youth named Kenworthy Browne, to whom he became passionately attached and whom he glorified in *Euphranor, a Dialogue on Youth*. To Fitzgerald, wrote his Edwardian biographer W. A. Wright, 'Browne was at once Jonathan, Gamaliel, Apollo—the friend, the master, the God—there was scarcely a halt to his devotion and admiration'. When Browne died as the result of a riding accident, Fitzgerald was heartbroken. As he told Browne's widow at the time, he used to wander about the shore at Lowestoft at night 'longing for some fellow to accost me who might give me some promise of filling up a very vacant place in my heart'. This happened in 1859, the same year as Fitzgerald's immortal version of the quatrains of Persia's astronomer poet was first published.[1]

Shortly afterwards Fitzgerald met a local fisherman named Joseph Fletcher, known familiarly as Posh. 'A gentleman of Nature's grandest type', was how Fitzgerald described him, six feet tall, with 'strictly auburn hair which any woman might sigh to possess', 'fit to be a leader of men, body and soul', 'a man of simplicity of soul, justice of thought, tenderness of nature and very much more ladylike than the ladies'. In fact, he was the 'greatest man' Fitzgerald had ever met, which was certainly saying something since Fitzgerald knew Tennyson, Carlyle and Thackeray, among others. Unfortunately Posh was not so absolutely perfect as this description suggests. He liked to get tipsy in the local pubs, and when he and his patron went into partnership in a herring-lugger, which Fitzgerald called *Meum and Tuum* (known locally as the 'Mum and Tum') for which Fitzgerald put up the money, Posh's unbusinesslike ways over the accounts, or rather lack of them, led to misunderstandings and eventually to the break-up of the partnership and indeed of the friendship.

Fitzgerald was himself an accomplished sailor, and he owned a smart fifteen-ton schooner, which was appropriately called the

[1] Havelock Ellis. *Studies in the Psychology of Sex*, II, Pt. 2, 50.

Scandal, and long before he met Posh he was on friendly terms with various fishermen and longshoremen on the Norfolk and Suffolk coasts, particularly with one called Lew Colby and his son 'Dickymilk', with whom he spent much of his time cruising on the river Deben and along the coast between Harwich and Lowestoft. In fact, it is remarkable that in that less democratic age, Fitzgerald's obvious interests should have been shrugged off as the whim of a well-to-do eccentric, although in a later period they would quite probably have attracted the attention of the police.

As 'a poor, old solitary and sad man', Fitzgerald would still long for the society of his 'dear Poshy' and would continue to lecture him in affectionate terms. 'I thought I had done with new likings, and I had a more easy life perhaps on that account,' he wrote in one letter. '*Now* I shall often think of you with uneasiness, for the very reason that I had so much liking and interest for you.' Many of these letters Posh either carelessly lost or destroyed until he realized after Fitzgerald's death that they had some commercial value, when he began to part with them for money, supplementing the written word with reminiscences of his old patron in return for pints of his favourite ale in the Lowestoft taverns. 'He was a master rum un, was my ole guv'nor!' Posh used to say. One visitor, who made Posh's acquaintance in this way, acquired enough material to make a book.[1]

Besides emphasizing the perennial loneliness of the ageing homosexual, Fitzgerald's letters to Posh reflect the difficulties and incongruities of such a relationship as theirs between partners with such widely differing social and intellectual backgrounds. Fitzgerald was a Cambridge-educated poet and translator of acknowledged genius, while Posh was a handsome Nordic type of fisherman, whose good looks Fitzgerald admired but whose only interest he shared with him was a love of the sea and sailing. Posh was just a plain fisherman, no better or no worse than his fellows, and as likely to get drunk on occasion as they habitually did. But in Fitzgerald's eyes he was a young god, and Fitzgerald could be intensely jealous. Once on Lowestoft pier, when Posh got into conversation with someone who may also have admired his 'Ulysses-like' appearance when Fitzgerald's back was turned, Fitzgerald was furious, and pulled Posh away by his jersey, saying as he did so, 'he is *my* guest!'. Indeed, so possessive was Fitzgerald's behaviour that people who did not know them

[1] James Blyth. *Edward Fitzgerald and Posh* (1908).

supposed that he was a tolerably harmless lunatic and Posh was his keeper. Fitzgerald was quite crazy about Posh and went so far as to commission a portrait of him in oils 'to hang with Thackeray and Tennyson, with whom he shares a certain Grandeur of Soul and Body'. Posh, it may be added, survived his benefactor by nearly thirty years and lived until the eve of the first World War, a familiar figure on the pier at Lowestoft with a frill of white beard from ear to ear.

With John Addington Symonds—'Mr Soddington Symonds', as the poet Swinburne irreverently called him—homosexuality posed a much bigger problem than in the case of Fitzgerald. In fact, it was an obsession with him throughout his life. Not only was he a practising invert with a wide range of homosexual associations, ranging from schoolboys to gondoliers, but he gave much thought to the problem, which indeed greatly tormented him and coloured everything he wrote as a professional author. Besides his works of biography, criticism, poetry and history, he produced two privately printed monographs on the homosexual problem, *A Problem in Greek Ethics* (1883) and *A Problem in Modern Ethics* (1891), each of which was described in the sub-title as 'An Inquiry into the Phenomenon of Sexual Inversion addressed especially to medical psychologists and Jurists'. The substance of the former had been embodied more briefly and discreetly in the final chapter on Greek love in his *Studies of the Greek Poets*. Nevertheless he was convinced that his implicit plea for the better understanding of the classical Greek conception of 'paiderastia' in this chapter lost him the Chair of Poetry at Oxford in 1877. The controversial chapter was in a sense a reply to the conventional Victorian view put forward ten years earlier by the historian W. E. H. Lecky in his *History of European Morals* when he described what he called 'the lowest abyss of unnatural love' as 'the deepest and strongest taint of Greek civilization', adding that 'my task in describing this aspect of Greek life has been an eminently unpleasant one'.

Among the close friends to whom Symonds sent a copy of *A Problem in Greek Ethics* was his younger literary contemporary Edmund Gosse, who was also tormented by homosexual longings at this time. In middle age Symonds began to have serious doubts about the wisdom of teaching Greek in boys' schools ('The Greek voice rings in accord with few souls now'), and he refused to regard the homosexual condition as a pathological one, rather than as a perfectly normal phenomenon, as the Greeks had done. 'To see the making of chivalry where the vulgar only perceive vice,' he wrote to Gosse, 'to recognize the physiological and psychological differences in individuals, which render this process of elevation necessary, and the process of extirpation impossible, that is the duty which Society neglects.' The significant point about the Greeks, in Symonds's view, was their attraction for both sexes: they married and went on taking boys (just as Symonds himself did).

A Problem in Modern Ethics, which appeared anonymously in 1891 in a privately printed edition limited to fifty copies, was a frank and forthright attempt to look at the subject in the context of Victorian mores. 'The one thing that seems clear is that sexual inversion is no subject for legislation, and that the example of France and Italy might be followed by other nations,' he argued. 'The problem ought to be left to the physician, the moralist, the educator, and finally to the operation of social opinion.' It should be remembered that Symonds was writing barely five years after the passing of the Criminal Law Amendment Act, 1885, which for the first time made homosexual acts not amounting to buggery a crime punishable by up to two years' imprisonment with hard labour when committed by two consenting adults in private, a statute which Symonds condemned as 'a disgrace to legislation by its vagueness of diction and the obvious incitement to false accusation'. The point was to be abundantly proved by Oscar Wilde's three trials, which were four years distant in time when Symonds wrote.

Symonds summarized his arguments in the following words:

The points suggested for consideration are whether England is still justified in restricting the freedom of adult persons, and rendering certain abnormal forms of sexuality criminal, by any real dangers to society: after it has been shown (1) that abnormal inclinations are congenital, natural, and ineradicable in a large percentage of individuals; (2) that we tolerate sterile intercourse of various types between the two sexes; (3) that our legislation has not suppressed the immorality in question; (4) that the operation of the Code Napoleon for nearly a century has not increased this immorality in France; (5) that Italy, with the experience of the Code Napoleon to guide her, adopted its principles in 1889; (6) that the English penalties are rarely inflicted to their full extent; (7) that their existence encourages blackmailing, and their non-enforcement gives occasion for base political agitation; (8) that our higher education is in open contradiction to the spirit of our laws.

Elaborating on the last of these points, Symonds suggested that higher education

> still rests on the study of the Greek and Latin classics, a literature impregnated with paiderastia. It is carried on at public schools, where young men are kept apart from females, and where homosexual vices are frequent. The best minds of our youth are therefore exposed to the influence of a paiderastic literature, at the same time that they acquire the knowledge and experience of unnatural practices. Nor is any trouble taken to correct these adverse influences by physiological instruction in the laws of sex.

The fifty copies of *A Problem in Modern Ethics*, which Symonds distributed to his particular friends and others interested in the subject, achieved a much wider clandestine circulation, since they were passed on from hand to hand and resulted in the author receiving a mass of homosexual case histories. These communications reflected Gosse's admission that 'the position of a young man so tormented is really that of a man buried alive and conscious, but deprived of speech. He is doomed by his own timidity and ignorance to a repression which amounts to death.' Although Symonds lived mostly in Switzerland for his health— he suffered from tuberculosis—and was consequently safe from the unwelcome attentions of the English law, his friends became uneasy at the prospect of his defence of homosexual behaviour becoming generally known in England. This uneasiness was increased when Symonds began to collaborate with Havelock Ellis in his *Sexual Inversion*, which became the first volume of Ellis's classic *Studies in the Psychology of Sex*. In fact, the collaboration was cut short by Symonds's sudden death in 1893, but when it eventually appeared four years later it was seen that *Sexual Inversion* owed much to Symonds, both on the historical side and in the matter of contemporary case histories.

For his part Symonds had been encouraged on the whole by the reactions which *A Problem in Modern Ethics* had produced among those who had read it. As he told his friend Graham Dakyns, 'I am quite surprised to see how ardently and sympathetically a large number of highly respectable persons feel toward a subject which in society they would only mention as unmentionable'. Among its readers—he had been lent a copy by Gosse—was Henry James, whose short novel *The Author of Beltraffio*, about a writer whose wife disapproves strongly of his writings, had been inspired by the case of Symonds. James, who

is sometimes regarded as an unconsciously repressed homosexual, found the work 'infinitely remarkable', although he had
one cogent criticism to make. 'It's on the whole, I think, a queer
place to plant the standard of duty, but he does it with extraordinary gallantry,' James told Gosse when he returned the
volume. 'If he has, or gathers, a band of the emulous, we may
look for some capital sport. But I don't wonder that some of his
friends and relations are haunted with a vague malaise. I think
one ought to wish him more *humour*, it is really *the* saving salt.
But the great reformers never have it—and he is the Gladstone
of the affair.'[1]

The official biography, which Symond's literary executor
Horatio Brown published two years after his death, contains no
hint of the subject's homosexual interests, no doubt to spare the
feelings of the family. Nor is there anything similar in the contribution on Symonds which Richard Garnett made a few years
later to the *Dictionary of National Biography*. It may be added
that Symonds supplemented his two 'studies' with an autobiographical account of his emotional experiences, which he
hoped would be published after his death, but this was also
suppressed by Brown. Of this work Dr Phyllis Grosskurth has
written in her recent biography:

> The autobiography emerges essentially as the history of
> Symonds's sexual life—it is not the lusty boasting of a Frank
> Harris but the anguished record of a man whose energy has
> been drained by the struggle to reconcile his instincts with
> the mores of society. As such, it is a profoundly moving
> document, and he earnestly hoped that its future publication
> might serve to create greater understanding for others like
> himself. It was not by his wish, but through Horatio Brown's
> decision, that it has been locked away all these years.[2]

As a schoolboy at Harrow in the eighteen-fifties, Symonds was
introduced to the pleasures of 'paiderastia', stimulated by his
study of the writings of certain ancient Greeks, notably Plato's
Symposium, which he sat reading one night until past sunrise
next morning, so fascinated was he by the subject. At Balliol he
became a practising invert, but with a sense of uneasy guilt
which remained with him throughout his life. His Oxford career

[1] H. Montgomery Hyde. *Henry James at Home* (1969), 50.
[2] Phyllis Grosskurth. *John Addington Symonds* (1964), 279. Symonds's
interesting MS autobiography is in the London Library and cannot be published before 1976. Although consequently unable to quote directly from it,
I am grateful to the Librarian and Trustees for permission to examine it.

was spectacular, since he gained a double first in classical studies, won several prizes, including the Newdigate prize for poetry, and was elected to a fellowship at Magdalen. But his career as a don was short-lived. In a fit of jealousy an undergraduate named Shorting, who shared what Symonds called his 'Arcadian tastes', sent the Magdalen Fellows several poems and letters which Symonds had written to him and which left no doubt about their feelings not only for each other but for a Bristol choir-boy named Alfred Brooke. Although he was not formally deprived of his fellowship, Symonds was severely censured by the other college dons. Shortly afterwards he had a nervous breakdown and resigned his fellowship, spending the next few years in foreign travel, which the possession of ample means enabled him to do in comfort. The *Dictionary of National Biography* attributes his breakdown to 'irritability of the brain'. Its true cause was his unrequited love for the chorister, coming on top of the college scandal.

Symonds's latest biographer, Dr Grosskirth, has carefully chronicled the tale of his numerous loves. The three principal were Norman Moor, a Clifton schoolboy ('He has not come tonight which was to have been one of our sacred nights'), Christian Buol, a sleigh-driver in Davos ('It is a splendid sight to see him asleep with the folded arms and the vast chest of a young Hercules, innocent of clothing.'), and Angelo Fusato, a gondolier, ('A very good fellow'), who accompanied him on many of his travels and stayed with him to the end. 'I do not much believe in knowing anybody, even oneself,' Symonds confessed the year before his death. 'But I am sure one can love immensely. And I love beauty with a passion that burns the more I grow old. I love beauty above virtue, and I think that nowhere is beauty more eminent than in young men.'

Symonds was initiated into homosexual practices with youths and men outside his own social class through the influence of two friends, the Hon. Roden Noel and Claude Delaval Cobham. Noel, a son of the Earl of Gainsborough, was an old Harrovian like Symonds (but before his time at the school), an indifferent poet, and an enthusiastic invert, although he was married and deeply attached to his wife. Symonds found his conversation 'poisonous' but 'pleasantly so'. Cobham, on the other hand, who was at Oxford with Symonds and played some part in the Shorting affair, had no interest in women, poetry, philosophy or religion, all of which interests Symonds shared with Noel. Cobham's sole interest appears to have been soldiers, for whom he had an inordinate passion. As a boy of thirteen a friend of his elder brother had seduced him in his mother's house, and he had never afterwards been able to experience love except in rude and masculine form. Yet he was by no means devoid of intellectual ability and, according to Symonds, had a remarkable aptitude for languages, both ancient and modern.

In 1865, the year after he had got married, Symonds was accosted by a young grenadier late one night in a passage leading off Trafalgar Square in London, after dining at his club. The soldier was a strapping young fellow and the sight of him in his scarlet uniform acted as a powerful physical magnet upon Symonds. He was strongly tempted to go to a certain house which the soldier suggested, but he resisted the temptation and hurried home while the soldier continued to plead with him. A dozen years later when the joys of being married to a middle-class M.P's daughter began to pall and his affair with Norman Moor had already run its course, Symonds yielded to renewed temptation.

In February 1877 Symonds came to London to deliver a series of lectures on 'Florence and the Medici' at the Royal Institution. One day when he was not lecturing to his frock-coated and bonneted audience, an old acquaintance, probably Claude Cobham, invited him to accompany him to a male brothel near the Regent's Park barracks. Here Symonds made an assignation to spend the afternoon with a brawny young soldier, a very nice fellow as it turned out, comradely and natural and manly, who treated the affair quite sensibly, and made no exorbitant demands upon Symonds's purse. After they had both spent themselves, they dressed and sat and smoked and talked together. They parted the best of friends, exchanged addresses and met several times later in various public places in London, but without a thought of 'vice'. Even in the sphere of a male brothel, Symonds reflected afterwards, permanent human relations were capable of finding their natural sphere, perhaps more than in conventional middle-class heterosexual marriage. After this experience it is scarcely surprising that Symonds found that his soul was not in his lectures, but on the contrary throbbed for the soldier, as it was to do in the succeeding years for a succession of equally humble folk.

Interesting as his two studies of the 'Problem' are, Symonds was probably too emotional to present a completely balanced view. 'Good Lord! in what different orbits can human souls move,' he exclaimed after a discussion of the subject with the

Cambridge philosopher Henry Sidgwick. 'He talks of sex out of legal codes, and blue books. I talk of it from human documents, myself, the people I have known, the adulterers and prostitutes of both sexes I have dealt with over bottles of wine and confidence. Nothing comes of discussions between a born doctrinaire and a born Bohemian.' But there was no doubting Symonds's sincerity. 'I am eager about the subject for its social and juristic aspects,' he told a friend on the first appearance of *A Problem in Modern Ethics*. 'You know how vitally in the past it has interested me as a man, and how I am therefore in duty bound to work for an elucidation of the legal problem.'[1] It was to remain for his collaborator Havelock Ellis with a characteristic clinical detachment to put the subject in its scientific context and perspective.

Another homosexual friend who provided Ellis with an invaluable case history was the socialist sociological writer Edward Carpenter, whose essay *Homogenic Love, and its Place in a Free Society* appeared under the imprint of the Labour Press in Manchester early in 1895. Like Symonds's *Problem*, it was a sincere plea for the tolerance and understanding of homosexuality and was printed for private circulation. The author seems to have distributed it fairly freely, and coming as it did at the time of the Wilde scandal it resulted in Carpenter's other books being rejected or boycotted by respectable publishers and booksellers, just as was Ellis's *Male Inversion*. 'The Wilde trial had done its work,' wrote Carpenter afterwards, 'and silence must henceforth reign on sex-subjects.' However, Carpenter was able to break the silence in the following decade when he found a courageous publisher named Sonnenschein who brought out his other writings on this subject, *Love's Coming of Age* (1902), *Iolaus: an Anthology of Friendship* (1902), and *The Intermediate Sex* (1908), titles which as the *Dictionary of National Biography* laconically observes 'had more vogue on the Continent that in England'.

Carpenter, who lived a markedly bohemian life in a cottage in Derbyshire was generally regarded as a socialist crank on account of his complete disregard of social and class distinctions— engine drivers, coal miners and farm lads sitting down to meals in his cottage with parsons, dons, suffragettes and sprigs of aristocracy. The faithful friend who lived with Carpenter for thirty years was a man called George Merrill who, so Carpenter tells us, was 'bred in the slums quite below civilization, but of healthy parentage of comparatively rustic origin'. According to Carpenter they first met on the outskirts of Sheffield, and

[1] Grosskurth, 281.

Carpenter had recognized at once in him 'a peculiar intimacy and mutual understanding'. They set up house together in 1898, Merrill doing the housekeeping, and they ordered their lives with sufficient discretion to escape the unwelcome attentions of the police, although some of the neighbours naturally gossiped. Carpenter described their relationship in his autobiography *My Days and Dreams*:

Thus we settled down, two bachelors: keeping the mornings intact for pretty close and rigorous work and the afternoons and evenings for more social recreation. As a rule I find the housekeeper, who is a little particular and 'house-proud' is inclined, not unnaturally, to be somewhat set against visitors— especially those who may bring some amount of dirt and dishevelment with them. But George—though occasionally disposed that way—was so genuinely sociable and affectionate by nature that the latter tendency overcame the former. The only people he could not put up with were those whom he suspected (sometimes unjustly) of being pious or puritanical. For these he had as keen a *flair* as the orthodox witch-finder used to have for heretics and I am afraid he was sometimes rude to them. On one occasion he was standing at the door of our cottage, looking down the garden brilliant in the sun, when a missionary sort of man arrived with a tract and wanted to put it in his hand. 'Keep your tract,' said George. 'I don't want it.' 'But don't you wish to know the way to heaven?' said the man. 'No, I don't,' was the reply, 'can't you see that *we're in heaven here*—we don't *want* any better than this, so go away!' And the man turned and fled. Like the archdeacon in Eden Phillpotts' *Human Boy* he flew and was never heard of again.

No doubt his objection to the pious and puritanical was returned with interest by their objection to him. Whatever faults or indiscretions he may have been guilty of, they were occasionally (in true provincial style) fastened on and magnified and circulated about as grave scandals. It was on such occasions however that the real affection of the country people showed itself, and they breathed slaughter against our assailants. George in fact was accepted and one may say beloved by both my manual worker friends and my more aristocratic friends. It was only the middling people who stumbled over him and they did not so much matter! Anyhow our lives had become necessary to each other, so that what anyone said was of little importance.

After Merrill's death in 1928, Carpenter moved into a bungalow in Guildford. He was heartbroken by the loss and survived his friend by barely a year.

Several other allegedly homosexual Victorians may be conveniently if briefly mentioned here, notably General Gordon, Cardinal Newman, Frederic Lord Leighton and Walter Pater. Gordon and Newman, who figure prominently in the homosexual Strachey's *Eminent Victorians*, were possibly of the sublimated type. Gordon, who never showed any interest in women, was fond of boys, as appears from his social work in the East End of London, but apart from a brief reference by the German sexologist Hirschfeld there is no concrete evidence that he was a pederast. Similarly with Newman, whom Hirschfeld also lists as homosexual. In his earlier years at Oxford, Newman's principal attachment was to Hurrell Froude, a fellow religious enthusiast. Thereafter he formed the closest intimacy with Ambrose St John who followed him from Oxford into the Roman Catholic Church and the Birmingham Oratory. In his celebrated *Apologia* the Cardinal hinted at his devotion to Brother Ambrose, who was fourteen years younger, and when Ambrose died at the age of sixty Newman was almost crazed with grief. He threw himself on the bed with the corpse and stayed with it all night. In later years he would burst into tears whenever Ambrose's death was mentioned, and by his express directions his own body was buried in the same grave as his most intimate friend.

Frederic Leighton, who was created a peer by Queen Victoria in 1896 for his services to painting, only lived to enjoy his honour for a single day, and, as he was a bachelor, his peerage died with him. It was said that his homosexual habits were widely known but indulged in with suitable Victorian discretion. One of his most talked-about pictures was a portrait of Sir Richard Burton, another alleged homosexual, which Leighton painted in 1876, two years before he was elected President of the Royal Academy.

In contrast with Leighton, who went out and about much in society, the bachelor Oxford don and pre-Raphaelite art critic Walter Pater kept very much to himself and his intimate circle. 'He was condemned by temperament to a certain isolation,' wrote his discreet biographer A. C. Benson after his death; 'he was outside the world and not of it. His genius was for friendship rather than for love and his circumstances and environment were favourable to celibacy and thus he passed through life in a certain mystery, though the secret of his life is told for those who can read it in his writings.'

[4]

Symonds's references to homosexuality being rife in the English public schools of the period, which he attributed to compulsory classical studies and the lack of a co-educational system, prompts a brief look at these establishments, or rather the two principal schools then as now, Eton and Harrow, with a passing glance at Marlborough.

Writing in 1866, a few years after he had left Harrow, Symonds had this to say about his old school:

> As to the boys themselves they are drawn from the lower aristocracy and the moneyed classes for the most part, idleness, plethoric wealth, hereditary stupidity and parvenu grossness combining to form a singularly corrupt amalgam. The seeds of vice, sown long ago in this fruitful soil continue to propagate themselves like mushrooms on a dunghill. A cousin of mine, Sir Thomas Abdy, not long ago settled at Harrow for the benefit of his sons' education, took a house etc. etc. Within three months he took them away and threw up his establishment, simply because he found the immorality of the school enormous. He has lived for many years in France and Germany and has had much experience of foreign schools; but he has never met with any *worse* than Harrow among the most corrupt of French academies.[1]

In Symonds's time the moral state of Harrow school indeed left much to be desired. Every boy of good looks had a female nickname, and a boy who yielded his person to an older lover was known as the elder lad's 'bitch'. According to Symonds, the talk in the dormitories and studies was of the grossest character, with repulsive scenes of onanism, mutual masturbation and obscene orgies of naked boys in bed together. There was no refinement, just animal lust, and it was little wonder that what he saw filled the young Symonds with disgust and loathing.

The headmaster was the celebrated preacher the Rev. Charles John Vaughan, Doctor of Divinity, whom a former pupil described as 'a saintly man, slow to wrath, but who, if he found himself face to face with wrongdoing, was fearless in his denunciation and punishment'. This view has been echoed in the *Dictionary of National Biography*, where it is stated that 'during the last dozen years of his rule it is probable that no school stood higher than Harrow'. Symonds came to a very different con-

[1] Grosskurth, 39.

clusion about the headmaster's character, and he considered him a thorough hypocrite, 'eager to keep up the external prosperity of the school at the cost of concealing any of its internal corruptions'. Although he was in the habit of preaching sermons on such texts as 'Cast out that evil person from among you' and once flogged a boy when he wrote a compromising note to another boy whom he addressed by a female name, Dr Vaughan was himself involved in the very type of 'internal corruption' which he publicly condemned. In 1859, Dr Vaughan resigned his headmastership. He was known to be ambitious for a seat in the House of Lords, and when shortly after his resignation he was offered and accepted a bishopric, the appointment occasioned no surprise. What did occasion surprise was the withdrawal of his acceptance a day or two later. For the first time we learn the reasons for his resignation as headmaster of Harrow and refusal to become Bishop of Rochester from the unpublished autobiography of John Addington Symonds.

A fellow pupil at the school named Alfred Pretor confessed to Symonds that he was having a love affair with the headmaster, and to prove it showed him several passionate letters which he had received from Vaughan, one of which Pretor allowed Symonds to retain. Shortly afterwards Symonds took his regular essay to the headmaster's study, and sat down beside the headmaster on a sofa which he knew to be the setting of amorous scenes between Vaughan and Pretor. Suddenly Vaughan began to stroke his thigh. The gesture greatly upset Symonds, since both he and Pretor had been prepared for Confirmation by Vaughan and both had subsequently received the sacrament of Holy Communion from his hands at the altar rails of the school chapel. He was disturbed too by the thought that such a man should be in supreme command of nearly five hundred boys, although he afterwards felt sorry for him when he realized how such a distinguished headmaster was gripped by such a powerful passion.

After he left Harrow and went up to Oxford, Symonds continued to brood over the affair until one day, while talking to Professor John Conington, he blurted out the truth of the matter. Conington advised him to tell his father, which young Symonds did. The elder Symonds, a leading Bristol physician, was horrified by the revelation. He immediately wrote to Vaughan, telling him that he had proof of his relationship with young Pretor and intimated that, if he resigned immediately, he would not expose him. The headmaster travelled down to Bristol, and when he was confronted with his letter to Pretor, he agreed that he had no alternative but to submit to Dr Symonds's terms. Vaughan was followed a day or two later by his wife, who pleaded with Dr Symonds. Catherine Vaughan was herself the daughter of a bishop, while her brother was Professor of Ecclesiastical History at Oxford. She flung herself on her knees before Dr Symonds, confessing that she knew of her husband's 'weakness' but begged the doctor to have mercy upon him because it had never interfered with his useful service to the school. Dr Symonds was said to have been profoundly moved by the suffering of this unhappy woman, but he remained inexorable.

The elder Symonds had stipulated that as part of the price of his silence Vaughan should never again accept any important ecclesiastical post. Consequently as soon as he read the announcement that Vaughan was to become Bishop of Rochester he sent him a telegram again threatening exposure unless he withdrew. Vaughan afterwards became Vicar of Doncaster, where his chief interest is said to have lain in preparing young men for ordination. Some years later he was appointed Master of the Temple, a post which the relentless Dr Symonds evidently did not consider of sufficient importance to warrant any further remonstration. After the elder Symonds's death Vaughan became Dean of Llandaff and in his last years refused the deanery of Westminster which Queen Victoria offered him. Before he died he gave instructions that all his papers were to be destroyed and that no biography of him was to be written.

The Vaughan scandal was effectively hushed up and its details never got into print. But they were something of an open secret in the higher ranks of Victorian society. The Bishop of Oxford, Samuel Wilberforce, who thought there was something suspicious about the two resignations within such a short time, was determined to get to the bottom of the matter. To his surprise a lady sitting next to him at dinner told him the whole story. Bishop Wilberforce duly passed on what he had heard to the Archbishop of Canterbury (Charles Longley) and the Prime Minister (Lord Palmerston). However, this revelation did not retard Vaughan's ultimate advancement, though he never secured the bishop's mitre which he had always coveted.

While Symonds was at Harrow, a new assistant master arrived in the person of Frederic William Farrar; then aged twenty-four, Farrar was later to become widely known as the author of a best selling school story, the biographer of Christ, a controversial preacher and theologian—he challenged the doctrine of eternal punishment in his sermons—and Dean of Canterbury. (Dean

Farrar Street in Westminster is named after him.) In 1858, the year Symonds left Harrow to go up to Oxford, Farrar, who had in the meantime taken holy orders, published *Eric, or Little by Little*, a partly autobiographical and highly moral tale of school life, which enjoyed an astonishing success, thirty-six editions being printed in the author's lifetime, and was surpassed as a best seller only by *Tom Brown's School Days*. While there are no overt references to homosexual behaviour in Farrar's novel, there are plenty of references to unclean talk and actions, and the moral is plain to see.[1] One particularly bad boy named Ball, 'who had tasted more deeply of the tree of knowledge of good and evil than any other boy' was expelled—we are not told precisely why, but it is not difficult to guess. Ball's place as the school's worst influence was taken by one Brigson, 'a fore-front fighter in the Devil's battles, who did much to ruin many an immortal soul. . . . Never did some of the Roslyn boys to their dying day, forget the deep, intolerable unfathomable flood of moral turpitude and iniquity which he bore with him.'

The novel was reviewed particularly adversely by the *Saturday Review*, a Conservative organ which disliked its mawkish sentimentality, as well as its Liberal author's evangelical puritanism.

> To say nothing of three or more violent deaths, two of which involve angelic death-beds, everything is served up with tear sauce. The boys quote hymns, and, to the infinite indignation of all English readers, occasionally kiss each other (principally, however when they are *in articulo mortis*) exchanging moreover such endearments as 'dear fellow' and the like.

Yet Farrar was able to write from Harrow that *Eric* had received 'the warm encomiums of the boys and masters here' an opinion equally warmly endorsed outside the school and agreeably reflected in the author's royalty account.

In 1871, Farrar, who had by now become chaplain to Queen Victoria, was appointed headmaster of Marlborough, where he had begun his scholastic career before going to Harrow. At Marlborough, where among the boys in Farrar's time was one named Alfred Taylor destined to stand beside Oscar Wilde in the dock at the Old Bailey, Farrar gained the reputation of being much addicted to flogging. This alleged predilection was of obsessive interest to the poet Algernon Charles Swinburne, who commented upon it to Lord Houghton, at the same time hinting that Farrar was also abnormal in another respect.

[1] Hugh Kingsmill. *After Puritanism* (1931), 30–6.

Swinburne frequently joked about homosexuality as well as flagellation. In 1878, while Gladstone was denouncing the Bulgarian atrocities perpetrated by Turkey, Swinburne published some poems on the Balkan war which attracted the unfavourable attention of Farrar in a sermon. Swinburne wrote uninhibitedly to Houghton of Farrar and the popularity in Liberal circles of the Bulgars, who it will be remembered had given the word 'bugger' to the English language.

> . . . I have consequently been preached at or verbally swished by a pedagogue parson (the Rev Flunkey Whoreson Farrar— qu[aere] Fellator?) in public before a numerous congregation of both sexes in the principal church of Glasgow, for which I trust that Mr Gladstone (unless first sent by a genuinely reformed government to the guillotine—whither God may speed him! and may I be there to see him 'sneeze in the bag' à la Marat!) will on his next return to power confer a bishopric on the Rev Mr Thwackum of Marlborough, as a fellow Christian and a fellow-Bulgar.
>
> Also there has been a sweet article on the subject in a religious Edinburgh newspaper. It is delightful to me just now to see the religious world openly avowing its Bulgarian proclivities.

Swinburne's taste for flagellation, which he attributed to his experiences of flogging at Eton, remained throughout his life. According to one of the keepers in Regent's Park, Swinburne used to pause there on his way from his lodgings in Dorset Street to a notorious brothel in St John's Wood. He would sit on a particular bench, composing the poems which afterwards appeared in *Songs before Sunrise*, after which he would continue his journey to the brothel, where, in Edmund Gosse's words, 'two golden-haired and rouge-cheeked ladies received, in luxuriously furnished rooms, gentlemen whom they consented to chastise for large sums. . . . Swinburne much impoverished himself by these games, which must have been very bad for his health'.[1]

The authoress of a recent criticial biography of Swinburne, Miss Overton Fuller, has suggested that the poet's peculiar taste was 'sodomite in character' and that it may be pertinent to ask 'whether there is not a direct connection between sodomy and punishment on the buttocks'.[2] However, the 'fearful propensity' in her son which worried Swinburne's mother was no doubt his

---

[1] *The Swinburne Letters*, ed. Cecil Y. Lang (1959–1962), IV, 45; VI, 245, 248.
[2] Jean Overton Fuller. *Swinburne* (1968), 178.

fondness for the bottle rather than other men or boys. On the contrary, in spite of his joking about the subject, Swinburne held no brief for homosexuals. When his friend Simeon Solomon was convicted on a homosexual charge, Swinburne described the unfortunate artist as 'a person who has deliberately chosen to do what makes a man and all who associate with him infamous in the eyes of the world . . . let us say, a Platonist, the term is at once accurate as a definition and unobjectionable as a euphemism'. Some years later, when he heard that Solomon had sold some letters of his, Swinburne denounced his action to Gosse as 'a thing unmentionable alike by men and women, as equally abhorrent to either—nay, to the very beasts—raising money by the sale of my letters to him in past years, which must doubtless contain much foolish burlesque and now regrettable nonsense never meant for any stranger's eye who would not understand the mere childishness of the silly chaff indulged in long ago'.[1]

Finally, there is a letter from Swinburne to his friend Theodore Watts-Dunton, when the Wilde trials were still fresh to the public memory. 'Neither Anytus and Melitus nor you and I could have felt heartier and more abhorrent loathing for Platonic Love, whether imbued with 'sweetness and light' by philosophic sentiment or besmeared by blood and dung by criminal lunacy.'[2] Whatever else he may have been, Swinburne was not a homosexual.

On the other hand, his erstwhile friend Simeon Solomon undoubtedly was. This Jewish painter of the Pre-Raphaelite school ruined a brilliant career through alcohol and what the *Dictionary of National Biography* calls 'other vicious indulgences', mostly, it may be added, with his youthful male models. In 1873 he was convicted of an indecent offence in a public lavatory and was sentenced to eighteen months, the sentence being reduced to six weeks, at the end of which he was released and placed under police supervision. Thereafter he went to pieces, eventually becoming a pavement artist in Bayswater and an habitual inmate of the workhouse, where he died of bronchitis aggravated by chronic alcoholism.

Unlike most spoilt wastrels with the artistic temperament, he seemed to have had no grievances, and had no bitter stories or complaints about former friends, no scandalous tales about contemporaries who had remained reputable, no indignant feelings towards those who assisted him . . . he enjoyed his

---

[1] *The Swinburne Letters*, II, 261, IV, 107.
[2] British Museum, Ashley MSS (July 27, 1896), cited Fuller, 268. Anytus and Melitus accused Socrates at his trial of being a corrupter of youth.

drink, his overpowering dirt, and his vicious life. He was full of delightful and racy stories about poets and painters, policemen and prisoners, of which he had wide experience. He might have written a far more diverting book of memoirs than the average Pre-Raphaelite volume to which we look forward every year, though it is usually silent about poor Simeon Solomon.[1]

[5]

That homosexuality was equally prevalent at Eton is attested by the cases of two masters who were dismissed at this period. Both were able and distinguished men, fellows of the same Cambridge college (King's), and both were unquestionable benefactors of the school in their achievements and influence on their pupils, with whom they were deservedly popular. They were William Johnson, who later changed his name to Cory, and Oscar Browning.

Johnson, who is chiefly remembered today as the author of the famous 'Eton Boating Song', began to show his poetic talent while still an undergraduate at Cambridge, when he won the Chancellor's Medal with a poem on Plato. In 1845, the year of his graduation, he became an assistant master at Eton, where he remained for the next twenty-six years. A shy, short-sighted man, he had a kind of hero-worship for many of his pupils, who numbered one future prime minister (Lord Rosebery), and he was in turn beloved by them. He wrote poems for them and about them, and also text-books to help their studies. Like Symonds, he was attracted by the ideal of 'Greek Love', and in his case it seems to have been translated into practical form. When Symonds read *Ionica*, addressed by Johnson to William Wood, later Viscount Halifax, and first published anonymously in 1858, Symonds, who had discovered the author's identity ('They are making a stir in Oxford, both on account of their true poetry and the curious personal history involved'), wrote to Johnson. According to Dr Grosskurth, he received in reply a long and passionate defence of pederasty. Symonds's biographer adds that Symonds in his suppressed autobiography remarks that the Eton master's letter was 'threaded with a wistful yearning which he had never found absent from any homosexual relationships'.[2]

In 1872 Johnson suddenly packed up his few belongings and departed from Eton, to which he was never to return, leaving his

[1] Robert Ross. *Masques and Phases* (1909), 143.
[2] Grosskurth, 48.

friends to call later for his books and furniture. At the same time he resigned his fellowship at King's and assumed the name of Cory. The precise reason for his abrupt retirement has remained something of a mystery. As usual the *Dictionary of National Biography* avoids the issue, in this instance attributing it to the fact that Johnson had inherited some property which involved changing his name. That the matter was of homosexual implication there can hardly be any doubt. It was rumoured that a parent of one of the boys had complained to Dr Hornby, the headmaster, about 'an indiscreet letter' which Johnson had written to the boy in question and which the headmaster could not ignore. Whatever its nature, the cause of Johnson's departure from the school he loved and had considerably benefited must have been pretty serious, or at any rate not of such a character that it would have been glossed over or hushed up. 'Have you heard that Johnson has left and changed his name to Cory?' Simeon Solomon wrote to Swinburne at the time. 'It is creating quite a sensation at Eton.' Incidentally, Johnson's name was at once removed from the text-books he had written and for many years afterwards these continued to be issued anonymously.

Then in his fiftieth year, Cory, as he wished to be known, retired to his native Devonshire to look after his property and marry the local vicar's daughter. She was twenty at the time and said that she always wanted to marry 'an old, clever man, tender and true'. She certainly got one in William Johnson Cory. The marriage seems to have been a reasonably happy one. They lived for some years in Madeira and later settled in Hampstead, where she presented Cory with a son. In his last years in Hampstead it is said that he devoted much time to giving oral classical instruction to ladies, for his own sake as well as theirs. 'Women are as divining rods to me,' he said; 'they relish everything that is taught.' He died in Hampstead in 1892 and was buried there.[1]

Although he never revisited Eton, neither did he ever complain about his treatment after twenty-six years of devoted service to the school. No doubt William Johnson Cory preferred to be remembered by the Boating Song and the final lines of the poem 'Academus', which he wrote at the height of his career as an Eton master:

> And when I may no longer live,
> They say, who know the truth,
> He gave whate'er he had to give
> To freedom and to youth.

[1] *The Letters of Swinburne*, II, 202. *D.N.B.* XXII, 487.

Oscar Browning had been one of Johnson's pupils at Eton, following him at King's and then returning like him as an assistant master. A drawing by Simeon Solomon done after Browning had been at Eton for a few years shows a balding, slightly effeminate profile with curling side-whiskers. His house, presided over by his mother, soon became the most popular in the school, by reason largely of the good food he provided, as well as the musical and other entertainments. He was what is sometimes known as 'good with boys'. He gained their interest and respect by his innovations in the curriculum, encouraging the study of modern history and English poetry, somewhat to the annoyance of the headmaster, who was a strong classics man. Dr Hornby also disapproved of Browning's hearing of confidences from the boys on the subject of 'esoteric anthropology' and giving them advice on sexual matters generally, for 'the O.B.' did not regard too seriously cases of 'immorality' between the boys, or what they called 'spooning'. ('Dangerous confidences' was the headmaster's acid comment on his subordinate's heretical behaviour.)

Hornby, who suspected that Browning shared Cory's habits as well as his views generally on education, determined to get rid of him. He particularly disliked Browning being on such intimate terms with some of his pupils, such as George Nathaniel Curzon, the future statesman and pro-consul, and he proceeded to extract an undertaking from Browning that this intimacy should cease. The headmaster followed this up with accusations of slackness in running his house, including some of the accounts, and finally, in 1875, he dismissed him, as he had the power to do. Although the accusations of undue familiarity with the boys under his charge were never fairly and openly advanced in such a way that Browning could have refuted them, there can be little if any doubt that he was dismissed because of his known homosexual proclivities. The matter was widely canvassed in the press at the time and in London clubs and drawing-rooms and was even raised in the House of Commons. But the governors were bound in the circumstances to support the headmaster, and so Browning retired to Cambridge where, being unmarried, he was able to subsist on his fellowship, although it involved a reduction in his annual income from £3,000 to £300. Later he was able to supplement this by lecturing and tutoring until 1908, when he left Cambridge to settle in Rome, where he died in 1923 in his eighty-seventh year.

'Do you know Oscar Browning?' Oscar Wilde wrote to his young friend and future literary executor Robert Ross, when

Wilde heard that Ross was going up to King's as an undergraduate in 1888. 'You will find him everything that is kind and
pleasant.'[1] If 'the O.B.' was as celebrated a 'character' at Cambridge as he had been at Eton, he seems to have been just as
indiscreet in his friendships with the young, although he never
fell foul of the law like such friends as Wilde and Simeon Solomon.
On the other hand, his friendships were never the intense and
soulful affairs that Symonds experienced, being mainly confined
to young working lads, sailors, blacksmiths and the like, and
nobody seemed to think it particularly odd that his rooms should
have on occasion been filled with boys bawling nautical songs
and drinking, while one lad played the violin and another dried
their host after his bath. The fact remains, however, that his
fellow dons did not consider him on the whole a healthy influence
in the college, he never achieved any high teaching or administrative post, although he was turned down for several, and in the
end he had to be eased out of the educational positions he did
hold. In Rome he continued his interest in the young, and, as
Goldsworthy Lowes Dickinson somewhat ambiguously put it in
his article on him in the *Dictionary of National Biography*, he
'assisted young Italians, as he had done young Englishmen,
towards the openings they desired'. His manifold achievements
in the fields of scholarship, teaching and teacher training were
modestly recognized three months before his death with the
award of the Order of the British Empire.

After he had completed his *Problem in Modern Ethics*, Symonds
wrote to Browning, explaining that he had written two treatises,
which he had 'diffused very sparely and cautiously', and that it
was of some importance to know into how many persons' hands
they had fallen. 'I am sure you could add a great amount of
information and critical matter,' Symonds added. 'I wish you
would write this sort of stuff.' One very important point, on
which Symonds invited Browning's opinion, was whether the
study of the classics by boys in the impressionable years of their
adolescence was harmful. 'The views of the ancient world on the
question of homosexuality were so different from those held in the
England of the Victorian era. Yet to regard the phenomenon as
pathological was beset with difficulties. Assuredly much more
light, as Symonds observed, was required on all these matters.'[2]

Browning thought it prudent to decline this invitation. He
had no objection to discussing the subject, which he would do

---

[1] *Letters of Oscar Wilde*. Ed. Hart-Davis (1962), 225.
[2] H. E. Wortham. *Oscar Browning* (1927), 261-2.

with what his biographer, Hugo Wortham, calls a strange mixture of pagan enthusiasm and moral fervour, but he refrained from writing about it. It is a pity that he did not do so, as his researches and observations would have been much more valuable than the two trivial volumes of memoirs which he composed in his last years.

[6]

There is abundant evidence to show that there was a flourishing trade in male prostitution in London from the eighteen-sixties onwards. Private soldiers, particularly guardsmen stationed in the capital, were also willing to supplement their meagre pay by obliging 'gentlemen' in this way. Symonds, for instance, during his inner struggles against becoming an invert, records how he once went into a London park with a soldier and touched him intimately, afterwards expressing his remorse for what he had done in a long confessional poem, 'The Valley of Vain Desires'. It was at this period that the word 'pouf' first came into use as a term of contempt for the male invert, particularly the kind who was in the habit of paying for his pleasures with money.[1]

A curious work entitled *Yokel's Preceptor*, published by a bookseller in Holywell Street, Strand, the centre of pornographic literature in the Victorian era, includes the following description:

> The increase of these monsters in the shape of men, commonly designated margeries, poofs, etc., of late years, in the great Metropolis, renders it necessary for the safety of the public that they should be made known. . . . Will the reader credit it, but such is nevertheless the fact, that these monsters actually walk the street the same as the whores, looking out for a chance!
>
> Yes, the Quadrant, Fleet Street, Holborn, the Strand, etc., are actually thronged with them! Nay, it is not long since, in the neighbourhood of Charing Cross, they posted bills in the windows of several public houses, cautioning the public to 'Beware of Sods!'
>
> They generally congregate around the picture shops, and are to be known by their effeminate air, their fashionable dress. When they see what they imagine to be a chance, they place

---

[1] *The Shorter Oxford English Dictionary*, which gives the year 1857 for the earliest known use of 'poof' or 'pouf', defines it as 'a sound imitating a short puff of the breath, as in blowing out a candle, hence an expression of contemptuous rejection'.

their fingers in a peculiar manner underneath the tails of their coats, and wag them about—their method of giving the office. . . .

The Quadrant is thronged by a number of the most notorious margeries, who turn out daily and nightly to look for their living, the same as the blowens. One of these was nicknamed 'Fair Eliza'. This fellow lives at Westminster, and keeps his fancy woman, who does not scruple to live upon the fruits of this monstrous avocation. Another fellow, called 'Betsy H—', who walks the Strand, Fleet Street, and St. Martin's Court, is a most notorious and shameless pouf.

In the 'seventies another word came into popular use, namely 'Mary Ann'. In 1881, the confessions of one such homosexual were published under the title, *The Sins of the Cities of the Plain; or the Recollections of a Mary Ann*. It is known that this interesting production was read by Oscar Wilde amongst others.

The writer of these notes was walking through Leicester Square one sunny afternoon, last November, when his attention was particularly taken by an effeminate, but very good-looking young fellow, who was walking in front of him, looking in shop windows from time to time, and now and then looking round as if to attract attention. Dressed in tight fitting clothes, which set off his Adonis-like figure to the best advantage . . . he had small elegant feet, set off by pretty patent leather boots, a fresh looking beardless face, with almost feminine features, auburn hair and sparkling blue eyes, which spoke as plain as possibly to my sense . . .

Thus the volume begins. The youth is accosted and willingly accompanies the writer back to his rooms in 'Cornwall Mansions, close to Baker Street Station', where they share a meal which includes 'a good rumpsteak and oyster sauce, tipped up with a couple of bottles of champagne of an extra sec brand', after which an amorous encounter takes place.

It appears that the youth, whose name is Jack Saul, is making his living as a 'Mary Ann'. In addition to satisfying the other man, he is induced to write a short account of his adventures and experiences for which he is also paid. These are almost entirely of a homosexual character and are related with considerable skill and force, although the language employed is rather crude in places. Similar details are given by other characters in the narrative. For instance, Fred Jones, who 'had been a soldier in the Foot Guards and bought out', relates his experiences while in the army.

> There are lots of houses in London, [he says] where only soldiers are received, and where gentlemen can sleep with them. The best known is now closed. It was the tobacconist's shop next to Albany Street Barracks in Regent's Park, and was kept by a Mrs Truman. The old lady would receive gentlemen and let us know. That is all over now, but there are still six houses in London that I know of.

Jack relates how he was introduced to such a house, a so-called 'club', which was in a street leading off Portland Place.

> If you had looked in the London Directory, [says Jack] you would have simply found it as the residence of Mr Inslip— a rather suggestive name, you may think, considering the practices of the members of his club. I afterwards found that no gentleman was admitted to the freedom of this establishment unless he first paid an admission fee of one hundred guineas, besides a handsome annual subscription and liberal payments for refreshments and the procuration of boys or youths like myself.

The 'special' evenings of the club lasted from shortly after 10 p.m. until 6 a.m., and there were usually about a dozen members present and a similar number of younger guests. Most of the latter were dressed as girls and assumed female names. Jack was known as 'Eveline'.

'You remember the Boulton and Park case,' Jack continued. 'Well, I was present at the ball given at Haxell's Hotel in the Strand. No doubt the proprietor was quite innocent of any idea of what our fun really was; but there were two or three dressing rooms into which the company could retire at pleasure. Boulton was superbly got up as a beautiful lady, and I observed Lord Arthur was very spooney about her . . . Park was there as a lady, dancing with a gentleman from the City, a very handsome Greek merchant.'

Jack goes on to describe how Lord Arthur, to whom he had just been introduced by Mr Inslip, sat down with Boulton, who on this occasion was known as 'Laura' and, turning to Jack, said: 'Allow me to introduce you two dears to one another. Miss Laura—Miss Eveline.' After excusing himself for a few minutes, Lord Arthur went off, leaving the other two together. 'Boulton seemed to take to me at once,' Jack subsequently admitted.

The upshot of this meeting was that, when the ball was over, Jack returned with Boulton and Park to their rooms in Eaton Square, where he stayed the remainder of the night. 'As soon as we got to Boulton's place, he gave me a drop of his invigorating cordial, which seemed to warm my blood to the tips of my fingers; then we went to bed and slept till about twelve o'clock, had breakfast all dressed as ladies. (I believe the people of the house thought we were gay ladies.) Boulton assured me they hadn't a rag of male clothing in the place, all their manly attire being in some other place.' Afterwards Boulton and Jack became close friends.

Although some of the details of the incidents described in *The Sins of the Cities of the Plain* may be exaggerated for effect, the work is based upon fact and no doubt gives a faithful enough picture of a seamy side of contemporary London life. As the author remarks, 'the extent to which pederasty is carried on in London between gentlemen and young fellows is little dreamed of by the outside public'.

[7]

Towards the middle of the 'eighties a male brothel was opened by a certain Charles Hammond in a house at 19 Cleveland Street, off the Tottenham Court Road. It was soon doing highly successful business, its patrons including various aristocratic and well-to-do homosexuals, including, so it was rumoured, a member of the British royal family. (The suspected royalty was the twenty-five year old Prince Eddy, later Duke of Clarence, eldest son of the Prince of Wales.) A particular speciality of the house in Cleveland Street was telegraph boys, who were willing to go to bed with the customers, besides delivering telegrams, for which in those days they only earned a few shillings a week. There was also more than a hint of blackmail about the place.

The police got on to Hammond's trail after being called in by the postal authorities to investigate the disappearance of some money from the General Post Office in the summer of 1889. Suspicion fell on one of the telegraph boys, who was observed to have more money to spend than his modest weekly earnings permitted. The boy was questioned by the police and under interrogation confessed that he had got money from Hammond, and that he was not the only one to receive payment for obliging Hammond's customers. Other lads were questioned in turn, among them one called Algernon Alleys, who had received a number of compromising letters from a certain 'Mr Brown'.

A police constable was set to watch the house and, on July 9, a few days after the first telegraph boy had been questioned, he reported that he had seen 'a great many gentlemen' entering and leaving it. Next day he noted that furniture was being moved out. This belonged to Hammond who was preparing to flee to the Continent. Shortly afterwards the police raided the place. Hammond, it appeared, had already made good his escape, but the police arrested two men named Veck and Newlove. Veck was a forty-year-old clergyman, and Newlove was a clerk, aged eighteen. Both men subsequently pleaded guilty at the Old Bailey to the commission of 'acts of impropriety' and received relatively mild prison sentences, Veck getting four months and Newlove nine. The case being barely reported at first caused no public interest.

The fact that it was noticed at all was due to the initiative of a reporter on the *North London Press*, a recently founded weekly, which was edited by a young Radical journalist named Ernest Parke. The journal was mainly devoted to local government affairs and had been ventilating the grievances of such poorly paid members of the community as dockers, postmen and insurance agents. When the editor read his reporter's story about Veck and Newlove, he made up his mind that the case was worth further investigation. Why had they been let off so lightly? And why had Hammond been allowed to get away? The inference was that there was a conspiracy behind the scenes to hush up the goings on at No. 19 Cleveland Street, and that Hammond, who knew too much about the highly placed visitors to his establishment, had received a hint from the authorities to clear out.

Parke, who had his own contacts with the police, now learned that in the course of their raid the police had discovered a much more socially prominent person than either Veck or Newlove. This was Lord Arthur Somerset, son of the Duke of Beaufort and an ex-Guards officer, who managed the Prince of Wales's racing stables. It also appeared that he was the 'Mr Brown', who had written such compromising letters to young Alleys, some of which the lad had by this time destroyed. Realizing that he would be charged with a homosexual offence if he remained in the country, Lord Arthur prudently removed himself from the jurisdiction of the English courts by crossing the channel to Boulogne, an action which the authorities tacitly permitted. (He subsequently moved on to Constantinople, where he is said to have offered his services to the Sultan, though in what capacity has not been disclosed.) The Prince of Wales, who used to call Lord Arthur 'Podge' and had always treated him as an intimate friend, was horrified when he heard this news. 'I won't believe it,' he said, 'any more than I should if they accused the Archbishop of Canterbury', adding that any man addicted to such a filthy vice must be regarded as an 'unfortunate lunatic'. When he was convinced of the truth of the matter, the Prince wrote to the Prime Minister, Lord Salisbury, expressing satisfaction that 'Podge' had been allowed to flee the country, and asking that, if he should 'ever dare to show his face in England again', he should be allowed to visit his parents quietly in the country 'without fear of being apprehended on this awful charge'.[1]

A few weeks later, on November 16, there appeared an article in the *North London Press* in which it was stated that among the number of aristocrats who were mixed up in 'an indescribably loathsome scandal in Cleveland Street' was another ducal off-spring, the Earl of Euston, the eldest son and heir of the Duke of Grafton, and that it was believed he had departed to Peru. The article proceeded to comment on men of position being allowed to leave the country and defeat the ends of justice, because their prosecution would inculpate more highly-placed and distin-guished personages. A fortnight later the editor referred to the subject again, and published photographs of both Lord Euston and Lord Arthur Somerset.

The forty-one-year-old earl was a 'stage door johnny' type, who had married the variety theatre actress Kate Cooke, from whom he had recently been divorced. According to Frank Harris, he was a big, well-made fellow, some six feet in height and decidedly manly looking, 'the last person in the world to be sus-pected of any abnormal propensities'.[2] He immediately began proceedings against the editor of the *North London Press* for criminal libel. Although he had not in fact been out of the country for several years, Euston admitted that he had been to Cleveland Street on one occasion. Walking home late one night along Picca-dilly, he said he had been accosted by a man who had thrust a card into his hand. Printed on the card was 'C. Hammond, 19 Cleveland Street' and written on the top were the words '*Poses plastiques*'. A few nights later, having nothing better to do, on leaving the Garrick Club, where he had dined, he took a hansom

[1] Sir Philip Magnus. *King Edward the Seventh* (1964), 214.
[2] Frank Harris. *My Life and Loves* (1963), 369. Magnus Hirschfeld states that Euston was homosexual: *Homosexualität* (1920), 662. But I can find no evidence to support this allegation.

cab to Cleveland Street, where he imagined he might see some female nudes. He was admitted by a man, apparently Hammond, who asked him for a pound, which the earl gave him. Euston then inquired where the *poses plastiques* were going to take place. 'There is nothing of that sort here,' said the man, who then proceeded to make what Euston called 'improper proposals' to him. Euston threatenend to knock him down if the man would not let him out of the house at once, on which the man opened the door and Euston left. The earl afterwards swore in court that he had never visited the house either before or since that one occasion.

In the written plea of justification which Parke put in before the case came on, the editor attempted to justify the libel by citing at least five witnesses who were prepared to identify Lord Euston as a regular customer of the Cleveland Street establishment. At the same time, the allegation about visiting Peru was withdrawn, and in its place it was suggested that his lordship had visited other foreign parts, notably Boulogne, for the purpose of seeing Lord Arthur Somerset, who, as we have seen, had fled the country—the subject of a homosexual charge resulting from his visit to the brothel.

The case was tried before Mr Justice Hawkins, one of the best known of Victorian judges from the nickname 'Hanging Hawkins', somewhat unfairly bestowed upon him from the numerous murder trials at which he presided.[1] It is noteworthy that the defence witnesses included one John Saul, an Irishman, who was no doubt the same Saul, whose spicy reminiscences contributed to *The Sins of the Cities of the Plain*. It also appears that Saul, who lived for a time with Hammond in Cleveland Street and also touted for him, was the same man who accosted Lord Euston in Piccadilly and handed him the card, which was the cause of all the ensuing trouble. Giving evidence, Saul stated that he had introduced many people to the house in Cleveland Street, among them Lord Euston, whom he pointed out in court. However, under cross-examination, Saul's credibility was badly shaken. He admitted that for the past fifteen years he had led 'a grossly immoral life' and since coming over from Dublin he had not done much to earn an honest living in London. He had been employed in a couple of theatres and had kept apartments for women of bad character, besides working for Hammond, who was strongly suspected of being a blackmailer. As to this witness, Mr Justice Hawkins remarked in his summing up, 'a more melancholy or a more loathsome object' he could not imagine. Mr

[1] *The Times*, January 16–17, 1890.

Justice Hawkins hoped, 'for the honour of the police of the metropolis, that what this witness had sworn was not true, namely that the police had behaved kindly to him whilst he was taking his walks at night. He swore that they behaved kindly, and as a proof of that he said that they advised him to give up the disreputable course of life he was leading'.

The other defence witnesses, who lived in the Cleveland Street district and seem to have been indifferently coached like Saul by a private detective agency employed by the newspaper editor, all swore that they had seen Lord Euston going into the house on numerous occasions. But when it came to cross-examination, they contradicted each other, getting Euston's height wrong, with other inaccurate details. For his part, Euston in his evidence swore that he had only been to Cleveland Street once, in the circumstances already described, and further that he had not travelled abroad for the past eight years. Euston was apparently not a homosexual and there is little doubt that what he said was true. At all events the jury believed him and brought in a verdict of guilty against the editor of the *North London Press*. Mr Justice Hawkins sentenced Parke to twelve months' imprisonment, a sentence which Frank Harris subsequently described as 'infamous and vindictive', only possible in England, and a 'preposterous penalty' which 'discovers a weak and bad side of the aristocratic constitution of English society'. If Lord Euston had been Mr Euston of Clerkenwell, argued Harris, his libeller would have been given a small fine, but not imprisonment, 'though the imputation of even ordinary immorality would have injured him in purse and public opinion grievously, whereas it could not damage Lord Euston in any way'.

Less partially, and more in accordance with legal precedent, Mr Justice Hawkins, in passing sentence, expressed the hope that, besides being a punishment to the offending editor, it would be 'a warning to others not to publish atrocious libels upon others without justification'. In those days certainly no more horrible libel could be imagined than charging a man publicly with frequenting a male brothel for the purpose of indulging in 'unnatural vice'.

[8]

The other great homosexual scandal, or rather series of scandals, in the eighties, had as their venue Dublin Castle. Although they took place in Ireland, their effects reverberated across the Irish Sea and were the subject of embarrassing questions in Parliament. Like the activities in Cleveland Street, the Dublin Castle scandals involved people in high places, against whom the law was never invoked, thus placing, in the words of John Addington Symonds, 'a vile weapon in the hands of unscrupulous politicians to attack the Government in office'.[1] The iniquities in 'the Castle' were brought to light largely as the result of the exertions of two Irish Nationalist Members, William O'Brien, the editor of the militant Home Rule journal *United Ireland*, and T. M. ('Tim') Healy, the leading literary propagandist of Irish Home Rule at this time and later the first Governor-General of the Irish Free State. Dublin Castle, it is hardly necessary to add, was the seat of the local administration, that is the English Government in Ireland, headed by the Lord Lieutenant and the Chief Secretary, who were invariably Englishmen. During the period in question these offices were filled by Earl Spencer and George Otto Trevelyan, the historian nephew of Lord Macaulay. Both were able and cultured men, but they were ignorant of what was taking place under their noses, their ignorance of Irish affairs, as O'Brien was to put it, having been 'imposed upon by the mad ex-Indian officers, roguish lawyers, and scurvy *agents provocateurs* who had control of the machinery of Law and Justice in Dublin Castle'.[2]

O'Brien and Healy first got wind of what was going on from a District Inspector of the Royal Irish Constabulary in County Cork, who confided in Healy that it was common gossip at the R.I.C. depot. This informant mentioned in particular the head of the Criminal Investigation Department in Dublin Castle, Detective Director and County Inspector James Ellis French, as a homosexual deeply involved. Consequently Healy wrote an unsigned leading article in *United Ireland*, hinting that it was high time that 'the life and adventures, and what is known as the "private character" of various Crown Employees in Ireland' were 'fully laid bare to the universe', notably County Inspector French. The latter immediately issued a writ for libel against O'Brien as the editor, claiming £5,000 damages. He did this, so it was said, at the instigation of his superiors in the Castle.

However, Irish police officers, when approached by O'Brien with a view to giving evidence in the libel suit, refused to talk, no doubt fearful of losing their jobs. O'Brien then went to see

[1] J. A. Symonds. *A Problem in Modern Ethics*, 103.
[2] William O'Brien. *Evening Memories* (1920), 19.

Sir George Lewis, the leading London solicitor with a great experience in handling awkward 'society' cases. Lewis advised him to employ a private detective agent, and he recommended a man named Meiklejohn, who had formerly worked at Scotland Yard. This private detective had not been in Dublin a fortnight, to quote O'Brien, 'before he got into his hands the clues of a criminal confederacy, which for its extent and atrocity, almost staggered belief. It included men of all ranks, classes, professions, and outlawries, from aristocrats of the highest fashion to outcasts in the most loathsome dens.' The two 'principal aristocrats' were Mr Gustavus Charles Cornwall, Secretary of the General Post Office and a brother-in-law of the Scottish baronet Sir Robert Dalyell, and Captain Martin Kirwan of the Royal Dublin Fusiliers, who was a cousin of Lord Oranmore. Cornwall, who had spent forty-three years in the public service, was sixty-two and due to retire in 1884; he was described by Tim Healy as 'a dapper old beau with a waxed moustache, who strolled into his office about 11 a.m., dawdled till lunch, and left at 4 p.m.'.[1] As the result of Meiklejohn's investigations, four young men agreed to come forward and give evidence of their relations with Cornwall and Kirwan, although they must have realized that they would run the risk of incriminating themselves if they did so. One was a man of independent means named Johnston, two others in their thirties named M'Kernan and Taylor worked in a bank and a shipping office respectively, and the fourth was an army officer.

O'Brien now felt strong enough to raise the matter in Parliament, which he did by notice of motion, referring specifically to charges of 'certain felonious practices' by. Cornwall and French and also mentioning the Crown Solicitor, George Bolton, who was French's superior officer and in O'Brien's opinion was endeavouring to shield the C.I.D. chief. Publication of this notice would normally have been protected by parliamentary privilege, but in reproducing it in *United Ireland* a sub-editor had added the caption 'A Precious Trio'. Accordingly Cornwall and Bolton both began proceedings for libel against O'Brien and launched separate actions, claiming enormous damages, which with French's pending claim amounted to over £70,000. Shortly afterwards, however, French got into serious financial difficulties through speculation in real estate and resorted to a variety of devices to delay his action, with the result that O'Brien succeeded in getting it dismissed through want of prosecution. But the other two actions remained on the file, and the fact that they were *sub*

[1] T. M. Healy. *Letters and Leaders of My Day* (1928), I, 196.

judice did not prevent O'Brien from commenting on them in his journal. For this he was fined £500 on each count for contempt of court, the 'contempt' in Cornwall's case consisting of the publication of his photograph above the words 'Yours affection-ately, G. Cornwall.'

The case of *Cornwall* v. *O'Brien* was tried before Mr Justice O'Brien and a special jury in the old Nisi Prius Court in Dublin. It lasted for five days and caused an immense sensation at the time.[1]

In his opening speech, Cornwall's leading counsel, Serjeant O'Brien (nicknamed 'Peter the Packer' for his skill in picking juries for the Crown in political cases), described the private detective Meiklejohn as a convicted swindler who was employed to 'hound down' his client, thus echoing the Chief Secretary's denunciation of O'Brien in the House of Commons for having used 'a scoundrel to go over to Dublin and trump up infamous charges against innocent men'. The plaintiff's first witness was his brother-in-law the baronet, who testified to Cornwall's ir-reproachable character. He was followed into the witness box by the plaintiff himself. 'A man of imposing stature,' was how William O'Brien described Cornwall, 'of a dignity that did not deign to argue and of an iron nerve, he delivered his answers with a majesty that seemed to fascinate the Court . . . and he left the witness-chair without a break in the superb chain of his perjuries.'

In his opening speech for the defence, Serjeant Boyd, a tough Ulsterman whose Orange sympathies did not prevent him from exerting himself to the utmost on behalf of a Nationalist client, 'completely turned the tables', in William O'Brien's words, and had the jury 'panting with impatience to hear the proofs he promised to shower upon them'. But no sooner had he sat down, than his instructing solicitor was seen squeezing his way into the crowded court room and whispering something in the leading counsel's ear, which made Serjeant Boyd momentarily turn pale. His message was relayed to O'Brien on a piece of paper, on which the following words were written in a trembling hand: 'Our witnesses refuse to appear.' This was what O'Brien had been dreading all along, and indeed one of the crucial witnesses from whom statements had been taken, the army officer, had already developed cold feet and had fled to France.

A hurried consultation took place between defence counsel and the solicitor, and it was agreed that the case must be kept going

[1] *The Times.* July 3, 4, 5, 7, 8, 1884.

at all costs, while the solicitor returned to the witness room and tried to persuade the three key witnesses to change their minds. Serjeant Boyd called a handwriting expert to prove that an anonymous letter which had fallen into the detective Meiklejohn's hands was written in a disguised hand by Cornwall with the object, as counsel put it, 'of one of the witnesses being got rid of'. Counsel took the expert through the technicalities of calligraphy at what seemed interminable length, and when he could elicit no more information he called another handwriting expert to corroborate in repetitive detail what his colleague had said. These tactics irritated the judge, who guessed that something was wrong. 'Come, Serjeant Boyd,' he said, 'this is not the sort of evidence we have a right to expect from your client!' This reproof led to a heated exchange between counsel and the Bench, after which Serjeant Boyd undauntedly resumed the examination of his witness.

Just when leading defence counsel felt that he could go on no longer, the solicitor reappeared in court with what O'Brien called 'a face of triumph there could be no misreading'. In a voice he intended not to be confidential, he cried out to Serjeant Boyd: 'It's all right. Call Malcolm Johnston!' The sudden change of mind in the witnesses seemed unaccountable. O'Brien attributed their initial refusal to testify as due to 'one of those sudden gusts of fretfulness which are apt to sweep over persons of their peculiar mentality'. He could hardly blame them, seeing that 'they had only to call a cab to be in a few minutes safe from the brand of shame which must scorch their brows the moment they stepped into the witness-box'. Then, with equal suddenness, 'they fell into a fit of hysterical merriment, quizzed each other over their passionate explosion of a few minutes before as though it had been some grisly practical joke at the expense of the dismayed lawyers, and now only quarrelled in a competition who should be the first to reach the witness-chair'.

Before Johnston was half way through his evidence, the crisis was over. This witness described with some particularity how he had driven from the Botanic Gardens on one occasion with Cornwall and Captain Kirwan and how Cornwall 'showed great familiarity with him', and on other occasions was guilty of 'very reprehensible conduct'. Johnston was followed by the young bank clerk, Alfred M'Kernan, who gave intimate details of how Cornwall had invited him to his house in Harcourt Street, given him a drink, and misconducted himself with him after he had sent the servants away. He mentioned other occasions when similar things had happened until he was warned by the judge that he need not say anything which might incriminate him, after which he refused to answer any more questions. Similar advice was given by the Bench to the shipping office employee, George Taylor, whose evidence strongly corroborated the other two.

The judge put a number of questions to the jury for their consideration. After an hour's deliberation they returned to deliver their answers. 'These findings mean a verdict for the defendant,' snapped Mr Justice O'Brien, who had summed up strongly in Cornwall's favour. 'Judgment for the defendant with costs.'

This verdict naturally caused great jubilation in the Irish Nationalist camp, and this was increased when O'Brien also won the action brought against him by the Crown Solicitor Bolton. Meanwhile, Cornwall, French, Kirwan, and a number of others were arrested, Cornwall being apprehended in his brother-in-law's house in Linlithgow, where he had taken refuge. All were remanded in custody on the basis of statements taken from O'Brien's witnesses in the libel actions and also witnesses in humbler walks of life, who included two unemployed labourers and a cooper.

After they had been committed for trial, the Grand Jury returned True Bills against Cornwall, French, Kirwan, and seven other defendants. In doing so the foreman of the Grand Jury forwarded the following resolution for the consideration of the senior trial judge, Baron Dowse:

> In the interest of public morality, we most respectfully suggest that Your Lordship should prevent and forbid the publication of any part of the evidence in the felony cases which have just come before us, and if possible make a ruling that any such publication be a contempt of court.

The judge was careful to refrain from expressing any opinion as to whether he had the power or not to adopt the Grand Jury's unprecedented suggestion—as the law then stood he probably had not. What he did was to commend the resolution to 'the discretion and Christian forbearance of the Press', adding that he would 'do all consistent with the law' to carry out their wishes. Consequently in the ensuing trials none of the evidence was published either in the Irish or the English newspapers, and as all the court records were destroyed in the Irish civil war, it is impossible to state the allegations in any detail. As a student forty years ago in Dublin, the present writer heard a few snatches of the evidence from those who remembered the trials: in particular, there was a house in Golden Lane near the Liffey, apparently a male brothel, to which the accused were in the habit of resorting.

The trials took place in the Court House in Green Street, the Irish equivalent of the Old Bailey. Cornwall and Kirwan were tried jointly on a number of counts charging them with conspiracy to commit buggery. Although the evidence of O'Brien's witnesses in the libel action was repeated, the jury was not satisfied beyond all reasonable doubt of the defendants' guilt and the trial ended in a disagreement. Immediately afterwards another of the prisoners named James Pilar pleaded guilty and was sentenced by Baron Dowse to twenty years penal servitude. French was then put up, and the jury again disagreed. The three principal defendants were tried again at the next sessions, when among other matters revealed in evidence was the fact that Meiklejohn had told Taylor, who was a witness for the Crown, that he (Taylor) 'was liable to penal servitude for life, but that it would be his salvation if he could give evidence that would implicate Cornwall'. On this occasion Cornwall and Kirwan were acquitted, the jury adding an explanatory rider to the effect that the evidence produced by the Crown was 'not considered sufficient'. The verdict is said to have been received with mingled hisses and applause by the spectators in court. There was some doubt whether French could be able to stand trial a second time, since he had suffered a complete mental breakdown in the meantime. However, he did eventually take his place in the dock, and once more the jury disagreed. Finally, such was the vindictiveness of the authorities, he was put up a third time, and on this occasion he was convicted and sentenced to two years' imprisonment.[1]

The widespread belief that homosexual 'vice' was rampant in official circles in Ireland did much to discredit Gladstone's Liberal administration at this time. The Prime Minister showed his confidence in Chief Secretary Trevelyan during the Dublin trials by taking him into the Cabinet and giving him a new job. Meanwhile the 'Red Earl', as the Lord Lieutenant was nicknamed from the colour of his bushy beard, carried on until the Government was defeated in the following year. On his resignation a Dublin wit suggested that Spencer should be given a couple of steps in the peerage by Queen Victoria with a new title—'Duke of Sodom and Gomorrah'.

[1] *The Times.* August 7, 24, October 29, 30, December 2, 1884.

CHAPTER FIVE

'Monstrous Martyrdoms'

[1]

It is possible that Parliament may have been influenced by the example of the Dublin Castle scandals when in the following year it passed the measure which for the first time made 'indecencies' between adult males in private a crime punishable by up to two years' imprisonment with hard labour. As originally drafted this measure was designed in the words of its title 'to make further provision for the protection of women and girls, the suppression of brothels and other purposes', and it was brought in by the Government as the direct result of a powerful press campaign carried on by the Liberal journalist W. T. Stead against juvenile prostitution and white slavery.[1] Its principal provision was the raising of the 'age of consent' for young girls from thirteen to sixteen. In its original form, as introduced in the House of Lords, the Criminal Law Amendment Bill made no mention of homosexual acts, since it was not concerned with this subject at all. After going through all its stages in the Lords, the bill went to the Commons, where it was referred to a committee of the whole house after passing its second reading. The committee stage was taken late at night on August 6, 1885, which was to prove a fateful date in the history of English criminal jurisprudence.

Henry Labouchere, the Liberal-Radical M.P. and editor of the popular journal *Truth*, had put down an amendment on the order paper to insert the following new clause:

> Any male person who, in public or private, commits, or is a party to the commission of, or procures or attempts to procure the commission by any male person of, any act of gross indecency with another male person, shall be guilty of a misdemeanour, and being convicted thereof, shall be liable, at the discretion of the court, to be imprisoned for any term not exceeding one year with or without hard labour.

[1] Details of Stead's campaign, which led to his abduction of a thirteen-year-old girl, who had been supplied by a former brothel-keeper, and which in turn resulted in his own arrest and imprisonment, will be found in the present writer's *Cases that Changed the Law* (1951), 27–37.

When Labouchere rose to move his amendment, another backbench member intervened on a point of order to ask the Speaker whether 'the clause about to be moved by the Hon. Member for Northampton, and which dealt with a totally different class of offence to that against which the Bill was directed, was within the scope of the Bill'. The Speaker replied that, at this stage of the bill, anything could be introduced into it by leave of the House.

Labouchere, in moving the amendment, explained briefly that at present any person on whom 'an assault of the kind here dealt with' was committed must be under the age of thirteen to involve punishment, and the object with which he had brought forward the new clause was 'to make the law applicable to any person, whether under the age of 13, or over that age'. He went on to say that he did not think it necessary to discuss it at any length, as he understood the government was willing to accept it. He therefore left it for the House and the government 'to deal with as might be thought best'. The Attorney-General, Sir Henry James, did accept it on behalf of the government, subject to an amendment which he moved increasing the maximum penalty from one year to two years, imprisonment with or without hard labour. Labouchere had no objection to this minor change, and the clause, which was somewhat illogically entitled 'Outrages on public decency', was agreed to without any further discussion and incorporated in the bill, which became law on January 1, 1886, as the Criminal Law Amendment Act, 1885 (48 & 49 Vict. c. 69)[1]

The implications of Labouchere's 'gross indecency' amendment were not realized, except by the Attorney-General, when it was passed by a thinly attended House in the small hours of an August morning on the eve of the parliamentary recess. 'Labby' afterwards admitted that he had taken the new clause '*mutatis mutandis*' from the French penal code, an admission which suggests that he must have had in mind primarily the corruption of youth (*détournement des mineurs*), since the French code did not penalize homosexual acts between consenting adults in private, and in fact had not done so since the Revolution: but it did protect children and juveniles against sexual interference, whether heterosexual or homosexual. However, Labouchere's clause had no age limit. If 'Labby' had stuck to the term 'indecent assault' in preference to the vague and undefined 'act of gross indecency', a vast amount of unnecessary trouble and suffering which followed

---

[1] Hansard. *Parliamentary Debates* (August 6, 1885), 1397–98.

from the wide interpretation given to Section 11 of the 1885 Act might have been avoided. Also the expression 'in private' in this context was particularly unfortunate, since it was to open the door wide to the practice of blackmail on a considerable scale.

Sir Travers Humphreys, the well-known English criminal judge—his father was Wilde's solicitor and he himself had a junior brief in the three Wilde trials—, looking back in old age, had some pertinent remarks to make about the 1885 Act.

It is doubtful whether the House fully appreciated that the words 'in public or private' in the new clause had completely altered the law, but as soon as the Royal Assent had been given and the Act was published, there began a spate of correspondence in the newspapers, both legal and lay, and references to the subject on various public platforms, which were duly reported. A learned Recorder dubbed it 'The Blackmailer's Charter', and an eminent Q.C. prophesied that juries would refuse to convict where the alleged acts were in private and not visible to any member of the public. On the other hand, those interested in the welfare of girls welcomed the Act as a whole so warmly (and indeed it was an excellent Act apart from section 11), and it was so clearly impossible to do anything except to let the law take its course, that after a few weeks the clamour died down and the public interest became centred upon some more savoury topic. The criticisms proved to be not without foundation. The reluctance of juries to convict in such cases is notorious, while no one having experience in such matters would deny that the words 'in private' have materially assisted the blackmailer in his loathsome trade.[1]

As might be expected from their identity of views on the subject of homosexuality, the two most outspoken contemporary critics of the controversial Section 11 were John Addington Symonds and Havelock Ellis. 'The whole subject', wrote Symonds to Ellis in 1891, after the appearance of *A Problem in Modern Ethics*, 'ought to be scientifically, historically, impartially investigated, instead of being left to Labby's inexpansible legislation', which he denounced as a disgrace.[2] A few years later Ellis expressed himself forcefully in his *Sexual Inversion*, first published in 1897, when the Wilde case was still fresh in the public memory:

[1] Foreword by Sir Travers Humphreys to *The Trials of Oscar Wilde* (1948) edited by the present writer, at pp. 5–7. The reluctance of juries to convict was not borne out by later trials in the present century.
[2] Grosskurth, 286.

With the omission of the words 'or private', it [Section 11] would be sound and in harmony with the most enlightened European legislation, but it must be pointed out that an act only becomes indecent when those who perform it or witness it regard it as indecent; it would become so if carried on in public. If two male persons, who have reached years of discretion, consent together to perform some act of sexual intimacy in private, no indecency has been committed. If one of the consenting parties subsequently proclaims the act, indecency may doubtless be created, as may happen also in the case of normal sexual intercourse, but it seems contrary to good policy that such proclamation should convert the act itself into a penal offence.[1]

Incidentally, Ellis's work was held at the Old Bailey in the trial of a bookseller for selling three copies of *Sexual Inversion* to be a 'lewd, wicked, bawdy, scandalous and obscene libel'.[2]

Symonds and Ellis were pioneers, whose reasoning at the time made no impression upon Parliament or other organs of public opinion. Yet their views were practically identical with those of the Wolfenden Committee sixty years later. The intervening road was indeed to prove, in Wilde's words, 'long, and red with monstrous martyrdoms'.

[2]

The first 'monstrous martyrdom' of a public figure under the new law was remarkably enough that of an Irish M.P. named de Cobain, one of the Belfast members. Edward Samuel Wesley de Cobain was the son of a Methodist Minister in Belfast and as a young man had entered the service of the City Corporation, where he became cashier. Here he acquired a detailed knowledge of local affairs, at the same time like other Conservatives in politics he joined the Orange Order, eventually becoming Grand Master of the Grand Lodge of Belfast and a Deputy Grand Master for Ireland. At the General Election of 1885, when he was in his middle forties, he challenged the local party caucus in East Belfast, standing as an Independent or 'Democratic Conservative' and defeating the official nominee by over a thousand votes. He was again returned, at the Election in the following year, after the rejection of Gladstone's first Home Rule

[1] Ellis. *Sexual Psychology*. II, Pt. 2, 349.
[2] *Homosexual Laws in History. The Times* January 14, 1958.

Bill for Ireland. The Bill's rejection led to rioting in Belfast and a commission of inquiry sat at which de Cobain gave evidence, boldly denouncing police brutality in connection with the riots. He thus incurred the enmity of the police force as well as that of the Conservative party caucus, whose power he had successfully challenged. His undoing seems to have been the work of a blackmailer, convicted forger and embezzler named Heggie, with whom he admitted that he had 'swapped a handkerchief once or twice because he admired the perfume on it'. There seems little doubt that de Cobain was a homosexual, but it is equally clear that he was the target of a blackmailing conspiracy engineered by Heggie. The atmosphere was poisoned against him, the East Belfast Member declared, 'by the babbling of the police and his enemies in the city'. In May 1891, while he was in London attending to his parliamentary duties, he received a telegram from a friend in Belfast advising him to take a trip abroad for the benefit of his health. De Cobain thereupon crossed the Channel to Boulogne.

Afterwards the unfortunate M.P. said somewhat implausibly that he thought the telegram was really sent in the interests of his health, though he must have quickly been disabused of this idea when he read in the local papers that a warrant had been issued for his arrest. While at Boulogne he also received a summons from the Speaker of the House of Commons to return to Westminster and explain his conduct. It appears that he was suffering from some kind of nervous breakdown, since he was confined to bed when the Speaker's summons was served upon him. However, when he recovered he did not immediately return to England, but went instead to America, where he remained for the next eighteen months. Meanwhile, since he had ignored a resolution of the House of Commons to appear in his place and answer the charges which had been brought against him, he was expelled. Eventually he returned to Belfast early in 1893 and after a delay of five weeks, during which the authorities were making up their minds what to do, he was arrested and charged on ten counts with the commission of acts of gross indecency with five persons in Belfast during 1887 and the three succeeding years. He was tried at the next Belfast assizes in March before Mr Justice Johnson, convicted and sentenced to twelve months' imprisonment with hard labour.[1]

The next prosecution under the new law to make prominent newspaper headlines and to provide a public sensation for many

[1] *The Times*, March 22, 1893.

weeks was that of Oscar Wilde and Alfred Taylor in 1895. The defendants were originally placed in the dock together on charges which included conspiracy. At this trial the jury disagreed and Wilde and Taylor were put up again at the next sessions. On the second occasion, they had separate trials, and both were found guilty and received the maximum sentences. Sir Travers Humphreys, who had a brief for Wilde in all three trials, has recalled that there was a belief in some minds at the time that the unpopularity of the new law with juries would assist Wilde. However, as a legal friend of Humphreys put it: 'We shall see which the jury dislike most—Section 11 or Oscar Wilde.' Humphreys always doubted whether the jury, before coming into court, knew anything about Wilde apart from his reputation as a successful dramatist. 'I think we are bound to assume,' he said afterwards, 'that the jury convicted Wilde as another jury had convicted Taylor—upon the evidence in the case.'

Wilde's association with Taylor was particularly unfortunate for the playwright, since Taylor was a transvestite homosexual, who had previously come up against the law, indeed only a few months before he stood beside Wilde in the dock at the Old Bailey. Alfred Waterhouse Somerset Taylor, who was aged thirty-three at this time and thus seven years younger than Wilde, was the son of a successful cocoa manufacturer. Educated at Marlborough public school, he was intended for the army, but on inheriting a fortune of £45,000 when he came of age, he followed what he later admitted to be 'a life of pleasure', in the course of which he ran through his inheritance within a few years. He lived in rooms in Little College Street, Westminster, where he shared his bed with a succession of homosexual friends and acquaintances, some of whom he introduced to Wilde. With one, a young man named Charles Spurrier Mason, he was alleged to have gone through a ceremony of 'marriage'. Although Taylor denied this, he admitted that Mason had slept in the same bed with him the first time he stayed in Little College Street. There is no doubt, too, that Taylor liked dressing in women's clothes, of which the police found a considerable collection in his rooms, described by Edward Carson, Q.C., as 'nothing more than a shameful den'. At his first trial, it was suggested to Wilde that Little College Street was not the sort of street he would usually visit in. 'Rather a rough neighbourhood, isn't it?' asked prosecuting counsel. 'That I don't know,' was Wilde's characteristic reply. 'I know it is near the Houses of Parliament.'

As the result of a midnight raid by the police on a house in

Fitzroy Street in the Bloomsbury district of London in August
1894, eighteen men were taken into custody, among them Taylor
and an unemployed valet named Charles Parker, who had been
introduced to Wilde by Taylor and who was to be the first of the
string of Crown witnesses to testify against Wilde at his trials.
Another of those arrested was a female impersonator named
Arthur Marling, who appeared in court next morning dressed in
'a fantastic female garb of black and gold'.[1] After a week's
remand, five of those charged were bound over to be of good
behaviour, and the remainder, including Taylor and Parker,
were discharged unconditionally. In announcing his decision,
the magistrate stated that he had had a number of letters in-
forming him that many of the men were of 'the vilest possible
character', but no one had come forward to give evidence to that
effect, although most of those charged were said to be already
known to the police. 'Poor Alfred Taylor,' wrote Wilde at the
time. 'It is a dreadful piece of bad luck.'[2]

When the police afterwards searched Taylor's rooms, they
found a letter from Mason to Taylor in an old hat box which
Taylor had left behind when he moved. Taylor described Mason
at his trial as a man of independent means who was 'connected
with a newspaper' in which he held a number of shares, but
although the letter was written from an address in Fleet Street,
it hardly fitted Taylor's description of his friend. 'As soon as you
can afford it do let me have some money and I shall be pleased
and obliged,' Mason had written. 'I would not ask you if I could
get any myself, but you know the business is not so easy. There
is a lot of trouble attached to it. I have not met anyone yet. Come
home soon, dear, and let us go out sometimes together.'[3]

'You are an old public school boy?' the Solicitor-General (Sir
Frank Lockwood) asked Taylor in cross-examination.

'Yes.'

'Was it not repugnant to your public school ideas, this habit
of sleeping with men?'

'Not to me,' replied Taylor. 'Where there is no harm done I
see nothing repugnant in it.'

There is no doubt that Taylor acted as a procurer for Wilde.
('I'm glad you've made yourself pretty,' Taylor told one youth in
arranging an introduction. 'Mr Wilde likes nice clean boys.')
Ironically Taylor originally met Wilde through a young homo-

---

[1] In 1897 Marling was sentenced to five years penal servitude for receiving
stolen goods.
[2] Letters of Oscar Wilde, 363.
[3] Trials of Oscar Wilde, 287.

sexual named Maurice Schwabe, who happened to be a nephew of the Solicitor-General's wife. Efforts were made to keep Schwabe's name out of the trials, but without success. However, it must be added in Taylor's favour that he was offered immunity from prosecution if he would agree to turn Queen's evidence and testify against Wilde, like the other Crown witnesses, but he refused to do so.

It is likely that Wilde first became a practising homosexual in 1886 as the result of his meeting Robert Ross; the latter subsequently admitted to Frank Harris that he was 'the first boy Oscar ever had', and there seems no reason to doubt this statement, confirmed by a similar admission to Arthur Ransome, for whose well-known 'critical study' of Wilde Ross supplied considerable information. No doubt, too, that in his Oxford days, Wilde was a latent homosexual, showing an inquisitive interest in male inversion, which, as Havelock Ellis has observed, is sometimes the sign of an emerging homosexual impulse. At Oxford he saw a good deal of two artistic homosexuals, Lord Ronald Gower and Frank Miles. Gower, a younger son of the second Duke of Sutherland, was a highly cultivated 'queer', who had a host of friends but always managed to steer clear of the criminal law, and was eventually to publish a volume of respectable memoirs. With Miles, a successful portrait painter, who was later to commit suicide in a lunatic asylum, Wilde shared rooms in London for a time after leaving Oxford, and once succeeded in holding the police at bay when they were in hot pursuit of Miles for an alleged offence with boys.

Later in the 'eighties, after he had met Ross, some curious evidence of Wilde's tastes came to light. A French bookseller named Charles Hirsch came over from Paris to London and opened a bookshop, the *Librairie Française* in Coventry Street for the sale of French publications. Among his first customers was Oscar Wilde, who used to buy the works of the leading French authors of the day, such as Zola and Maupassant. After a while, when he got to know the bookseller better and had taken him into his confidence, Wilde would order 'certain licentious works of a special *genre*' which he euphemistically described as 'socratic' and which the bookseller was able to obtain not without difficulty. Most of these works were in French, like *Monsieur Venus* by 'Rachilde', but at least one, as the bookseller recalled afterwards, was in English. This was *The Sins of the Cities of the Plain*, the autobiographical account of a male homosexual's experiences in London, which has previously been mentioned.

One day, in 1890, Wilde came into the bookshop, carrying a small package, which was carefully wrapped up and sealed. 'A friend of mine will call for this manuscript and will show you my card,' he told the Frenchman, to whom he also gave the name of the prospective caller. Some few days later, a young man, whom the bookseller had previously seen in Wilde's company, appeared and took the package away. After a while, he came back with it, saying in turn: 'Please give this to one of our friends who will call for it on behalf of the same person.'

This procedure was repeated three times. The last borrower, who was not so careful as the others, returned the manuscript unwrapped and simply tied round with a piece of ribbon. The temptation to open it and read it was too great for M. Hirsch to resist. On the greyish paper cover which held together the pages of the MS, there was a single word, 'Teleny'. The same evening the bookseller read through the whole of the MS, which proved to be the story in the form of an erotic novel of a well-to-do Parisian called Des Grieux—the author had given his hero the same surname as Manon Lescaut's lover—and his love for a young male pianist named Teleny. What particularly struck the bookseller about the MS was the extraordinary mixture of different handwriting, erasures, interlineations, corrections and additions obviously made by different hands. 'It was evident to me,' M. Hirsch noted at the time, 'that several writers of unequal literary merit had collaborated in this anonymous but profoundly interesting work'. The bookseller subsequently told C. R. Dawes, the English authority on erotic literature, that in his opinion *Teleny* was mainly the work of various friends of Wilde, who had himself looked over and corrected the MS, adding touches of his own here and there. Dawes subsequently admitted that *Teleny* was 'better written than most English erotic books', but that if Wilde really had a hand in it, as apparently he must have done, 'perhaps it may be regarded as an outlet for the worst and most sensational side of Wilde's artistic nature'.[1]

For several years after his first meeting with Robert Ross, Wilde's interest in male inversion was theoretical rather than practical. 'I do not think that people who do these things derive as much pleasure as I do from talking about them,' he used to say,

[1] *Teleny* was published under an anonymous imprint in 1893 by Wilde's latter-day publisher Leonard Smithers, who ran a profitable sideline in erotica. 'It is a book which will rank as the chief of its class,' wrote Smithers in advertising it, 'and it may truthfully be said to make a new departure in English amatory literature'. Hirsch brought out a French translation in 1934. The original English text with some omissions and an Introduction by the present writer was published by Icon Books in London in 1966.

in discussing the subject. According to André Raffalovich, who heard him hold forth, he was fascinated by the story of James I and his favourite Robert Carr, Earl of Somerset, who, on the eve of his trial for the murder of Sir Thomas Overbury, threatened to reveal publicly that 'the King had slept with him', and the precautions taken at the trial to prevent any embarrassing revelations of this kind.[1] In this context he studied the lives of Plato and Michelangelo, and he conducted an ingenious piece of research into the origins of Shakespeare's sonnets to 'Mr W. H.', whom he claimed to be a boy actor named Willie Hughes whom the dramatist admired.[2] In Wilde's only novel, *The Picture of Dorian Gray*, in which the character of the cynically decadent Lord Henry Wooton was based on the real life Lord Ronald Gower, there is a pervading atmosphere of homosexuality. John Addington Symonds, who resented 'the unhealthy, scented mystic, congested touch which a man of this sort has on moral problems', described the work as 'an odd and very audacious production, unwholesome in tone, but artistically and psychologically interesting', on its first appearance in *Lippincott's Magazine* in 1890. ('If the British public will stand this, they can stand anything.')[3] At his first trial, when Wilde prosecuted the Marquess of Queensberry for having criminally libelled him by leaving a card at his club on which Queensberry had written the words 'Oscar Wilde posing as a sodomite', Carson, who defended Queensberry, was to put several passages to Wilde with devastating effect, particularly since the passages in question were omitted when *Dorian Gray* appeared in book form.

It was in the early summer of 1891, a few weeks after the book publication of *Dorian Gray*, that Wilde, then in his thirty-seventh year, was introduced by the poet Lionel Johnson to Queensberrys' twenty-two-year-old younger son Lord Alfred Douglas, then an undergraduate at Oxford. It was the intimate friendship that immediately sprang up between them that Queensberry was determined to break at all costs. In his old age I had some acquaintance with Douglas, and I questioned him about the exact nature of his relations with Wilde. In his various writings, which appeared after Wilde's death, Douglas had always denied that there was anything improper between them. This he now retracted on the ground that he owed it to his family and

---

[1] See above, p. 43–4.
[2] *The Portrait of Mr W. H.* originally appeared in *Blackwood's Edinburgh Magazine* for July, 1889.
[3] *Letters and Papers of John Addington Symonds*, ed. Horatio Brown (1923), 240.

friends to deny it and that, as he put it to me, 'convention demands that what is perfectly well known to all men and even at a public school and a university should be kept quiet as far as the public acknowledgement of it goes'. He admitted to me that when he first met Wilde he was not any more innocent than other young men of his age.[1]

From the second time he saw me, when he gave me a copy of *Dorian Gray* which I took with me to Oxford [Douglas went on] he made overtures to me. It was not till I had known him for at least six months and after I had seen him over and over again and he had twice stayed with me in Oxford, that I gave in to him. I did with him and allowed him to do just what was done among boys at Winchester and Oxford. . . . Sodomy never took place between us, nor was it attempted or dreamed of. Wilde treated me as an older one does a younger one at school. . . .

Much as I was fascinated by Wilde and much as I really in the long run adored him and was crazy about him, I never liked this part of the business. It was dead against my sexual instincts which were all for youth and beauty and softness. After a time he stumbled to the fact that I did not like it at all and only consented to it to oblige him, and he very soon cut it out altogether. For at least six months before he went to prison no such thing happened between us, nor was it as much as hinted at after he came out two years later.

In fact, both Wilde and Douglas were pederasts, and they were in the habit of pursuing youths and boys, sometimes acting together as in one instance mentioned in the trials when they were both staying in the Savoy Hotel. It was Douglas's careless-ness in leaving a compromising letter addressed to 'my own boy' by Wilde in a suit of clothes which he had given to one such youth, an unemployed clerk named Alfred Wood, that was the beginning of Wilde's undoing, when a copy of it came into Queensberry's hands after Wilde had succeeded in recovering the original from two blackmailers. ('. . . it is a marvel that those red rose-leaf lips of yours should have been made no less for the music of song than for madness of kisses. . . . I know Hyacinthus, whom Apollo loved so madly, was you in Greek days.')

Meanwhile Wilde's relations with a series of characters in London's homosexual underworld, out-of-work stable boys,

[1] See my Introduction to *Oscar Wilde and the Black Douglas* by the Marquess of Queensberry and Percy Colson (1949).

clerks, domestic servants and the like, proceeded with an increasing and almost unbelievable recklessness. It seems to have been only the fact that he was regarded as a great poseur, which indeed in many respects he was, that postponed the day of reckoning for so long. He habitually wore as a buttonhole a carnation artificially coloured green, an emblem which he knew to be the distinguishing mark of homosexuals in Paris, and this was speedily imitated by his youthful admirers on this side of the channel. Indeed the cult of the green carnation led the novelist Robert Hichens to write an amusing skit, in which the two chief characters were admittedly based on Wilde and Douglas. And as late as the autumn of 1894, when *The Green Carnation* made its original anonymous appearance, people were still saying: 'It's only Oscar. He likes to talk about it, but he doesn't do anything.' Yet he had already done a great deal, for which he was soon to be called upon to answer at the Old Bailey.

With his literary friends in Paris, Wilde was particularly candid. 'He makes no secret of it,' Henry de Régnier told Edmond de Goncourt in 1893. 'He admits that he is a homosexual.' Goncourt records in his journal that a friend of his who went to see him in a London hotel (presumably the Savoy), where he was staying with Lord Alfred Douglas, afterwards told de Goncourt that 'there was only one bed in the room, with two pillows, and that while he was there Wilde's wife, who brings him his post every morning, arrived in tears'.

'I've been married three times in my life,' Wilde confessed at this period, 'once to a woman and twice to men.'[1]

[3]

Such full accounts of the Wilde trials have been published—among others by the present writer—and the details are now so familiar that it is not intended to repeat them here beyond indicating some features which are not generally known or appreciated. For instance, after the jury had disagreed at the second trial and before the last trial, at which the Crown had briefed the Solicitor-General, Sir Frank Lockwood, to lead the prosecution, the great Irish advocate Edward Carson, who had defended Queensberry in the first trial but had refused to take any part in the subsequent prosecution of Wilde, went to see

---

[1] *Pages from the Goncourt Journal.* ed. Robert Baldick (1962), 384. The men were, of course, Robert Ross and Lord Alfred Douglas.

Lockwood in his chambers. 'Cannot you let up on the fellow now?' he pleaded. 'He has suffered a great deal.'

'I would, but we cannot,' replied Lockwood. In fact, the Solicitor-General went on, the government dared not drop the prosecution for the simple reason that, if they were to do so, 'it would at once be said, both in England and abroad that owing to the names mentioned in Queensberry's letters we were forced to abandon it'.

In the first trial—that is the private prosecution for criminal libel instituted by Wilde against Queensberry—Queensberry had given the jury the impression from the witness box that it was solely his love for his son Alfred that had led him to the vulgar course of action he had followed in trying to save his son from Wilde's baleful influence. To rebut this evidence, Wilde's counsel put in letters written by Queensberry to his son Alfred and the latter's maternal grandfather Alfred Montgomery, whose daughter had married Queensberry but had subsequently divorced him for adultery and cruelty, to show that in reality Queensberry heartily detested his son. 'Your daughter is the person who is supporting my son to defy me,' wrote Queensberry to Montgomery in one of these letters. Wilde he described in the same letter as a 'damned cur and coward of the Rosebery type', adding that he was now 'fully convinced' that his former wife had 'worked' what he called 'the Rosebery–Gladstone–Royal insult that came to me through my other son'. He concluded his outburst, which was written from Skindle's Hotel, Maidenhead, with a characteristic disregard for the rules of grammar 'I saw Drumlanrig here on the river, which much upset me. It shall be known some day by all that Rosebery not only insulted me by lying to the Queen, which makes her as bad as him and Gladstone, but also has made a lifelong quarrel between my son [Drumlanrig] and I.'[1]

Queensberry had previously sat in the House of Lords as an elected representative peer of Scotland, but after some years had failed to secure re-election, due to his refusal to take the customary oath of allegiance to the Queen which he denounced as mere 'Christian tomfoolery'. In 1892 his eldest son Francis, Viscount Drumlanrig, a twenty-five-year-old bachelor, described by Walburga Lady Paget at the time as 'an excellent amiable little man', was appointed assistant private secretary to Lord Rosebery, then Foreign Minister in Gladstone's government. Rosebery, who (so gossip said) had a particular liking for

[1] *Trials*, 155.

amiable young men with good looks, took a considerable fancy
to young Drumlanrig, and in the following year persuaded the
Prime Minister to make him a lord-in-waiting, a junior minis-
terial post which involved answering for the government on
occasion from the front bench in the House of Lords. To make
this possible in Drumlanrig's case, it was necessary he should
have a seat in the Upper House, and consequently the Queen, on
Gladstone's recommendation, created him a peer of the United
Kingdom under the title Baron Kelhead, much to the indignation of his father, who was no longer entitled to sit in the Lords.
Whether Queensberry suspected that there was anything out
of the ordinary in the relations between his eldest son and the
Foreign Minister is not definitely known since the letters which,
according to his grandson the late Lord Queensberry, he wrote to
Rosebery, Gladstone and the Queen to the effect that Rosebery
was 'having a bad influence on Francis', are not available.

One October afternoon in 1894 shortly after his father's ill-
mannered letter to Alfred Montgomery, Drumlanrig was the
victim of a shocking tragedy. He was a guest at a shooting party
in Somerset and was found dead from a gunshot wound. It
looked on the face of it like an accident, and this was confirmed
by the verdict of 'accidental death' subsequently brought in by a
coroner's jury at the inquest. Nevertheless there were rumours
at the time that Drumlanrig was implicated in a homosexual
affair with Rosebery and had committed suicide rather than face
a public scandal which in the event was hushed up.[1]

Some corroboration of Lockwood's statement to Carson was
provided by Lord Alfred Douglas, who retired to France before
the trials on the advice of Wilde's counsel, as it was felt that his
continued presence in London might embarrass his client. In an
article on *l'affaire Wilde*, which he wrote for a French journal
about a year after the trials, Douglas declared that Rosebery,
who by this time had succeeded Gladstone as Prime Minister,
had told the Home Secretary, then Mr H. H. Asquith, that if the
Wilde prosecution were dropped following the jury's disagreement this would create a most damaging impression among the
voters at the next General Election and that this would undoubtedly result in the defeat of the Liberals at the polls. Hence
the decision to instruct the Solicitor-General to prosecute at the
last trial and so make sure that Wilde would be convicted.

[1] Queensberry. *The Black Douglas*, 52. Francis, 11th Marquess of Queensberry died in 1954. He told the present writer that he was positive his uncle
Drumlanrig had taken his own life in the shadow of suppressed scandal.

According to Douglas in an article he wrote in the *Revue Blanche* (June 1, 1896), the Liberal Party at this period contained a number of homosexuals, and the 'maniacs of virtue' threatened to launch further actions unless the case against Wilde went on. 'It was a degrading *coup d'état*—the sacrifice of a great poet to save a degraded band of politicians.'

How many members of the Liberal Party were homosexual at this time it is impossible to say. But two prominent young Liberals who reached cabinet rank were subsequently involved in homosexual affairs. One was Lewis ('Lulu') Harcourt, later Viscount Harcourt, son of Sir William Harcourt, the Leader of the House of Commons, whose private secretary he was. At the same time Harcourt was active in the party organization and afterwards served in the 1906 Liberal Government as First Commissioner of Works, in which capacity he did much to improve the amenities of the Houses of Parliament, where there is a room named after him. One February morning in 1922 he was found dead in bed by his valet in his London home in Brook Street (now the Savile Club), from the effects of an overdose of bromidia, a sleeping draught which he had taken, so it was said, to avoid arrest on a homosexual charge. On the other hand, when asked by the coroner at the inquest whether he was in any trouble, his widow said no, adding that 'he was most cheerful'. The coroner's jury returned a verdict of 'death by misadventure'.

The other young Liberal at the time of the Wilde trials, who besides attaining cabinet office eventually became party leader in the House of Lords, was William (Lygon) Earl Beauchamp. In 1931 he suddenly resigned his offices and went to live abroad, at the insistence, so it was said, of King George V, who otherwise wished him to be prosecuted. One of his offices was that of Lord Warden of the Cinque Ports, and it was alleged that he had mis-conducted himself with various youths, fishermen and the like at Walmer Castle, the Lord Warden's official residence. He was also in the habit of inviting his homosexual friends to visit him at Walmer. Lady Aberconway recalls in her memoirs calling on Lord Beauchamp there with her husband and Sir William Jowitt, then Attorney-General, one Sunday afternoon. On their arrival they were shown into a garden surrounding a grass tennis court. To her surprise Lady Aberconway saw the actor Ernest Thesiger 'nude to the waist and covered with pearls: he explained that he had the right type of skin to heal pearls'. Her ladyship also met two or three other young men, including 'a nice young man whom Lord Beauchamp introduced as his tennis coach', although it turned out that he could not even pat a ball over the net. Some time later Lady Aberconway read in a newspaper that the Lord Warden had gone abroad 'to have mud baths'. Somewhat naïvely she wrote him off as 'an eccentric' in need of therapeutic treatment. ('Perhaps, poor man, when I saw him he was physically ill.') Lord Beauchamp died a lonely exile in New York in 1938.

The verdict and sentence upon Wilde were almost without exception welcomed by the English press at the time, not only as well deserved but as a salutary warning to others like-minded. 'No sterner rebuke could well have been inflicted on some of the artistic tendencies of the time than the condemnation of Oscar Wilde at the Central Criminal Court,' the *Daily Telegraph* pontificated on the morning after Wilde's conviction. 'Young men at the universities, silly women who lend an ear to idle chatter which is petulant and vivacious, novelists who have sought to imitate the style of paradox and unreality, poets who have lisped the language of nerveless and effeminate libertinage—these are the persons who should ponder with themselves the doctrine and career of the man who has now to undergo the righteous sentence of the law.'

Ironically the only public figure who had anything to say on Wilde's behalf was W. T. Stead, the man more than anyone else responsible for getting the Act of 1885 on to the statute book, although he had nothing to do with the section under which Wilde was convicted. He wrote in *The Review of Reviews*, which he had recently founded:

> The heinousness of the crime of Oscar Wilde and his associates does not lie, as is usually supposed, in its being unnatural. It would be unnatural for seventy-nine out of eighty persons. It is natural for the abnormal person who is in a minority of one. . . .
>
> At the same time it is impossible to deny that the trial and the sentence bring into very clear relief the ridiculous disparity there is between the punishment meted out to those who corrupt girls and those who corrupt boys. If Oscar Wilde, instead of indulging in dirty tricks of indecent familiarity with boys and men, had ruined the lives of half a dozen innocent simpletons of girls, or had broken up the home of his friend by corrupting his friend's wife, no one could have laid a finger upon him. The male is sacrosant: the female is fair game. To have burdened society with a dozen bastards, to

have destroyed a happy home by his lawless lust—of these things the criminal law takes no account. But let him act indecently to a young rascal who is very well able to take care of himself, and who can by no possibility bring a child into the world, as the result of his corruption, then judges can hardly contain themselves from indignation when inflicting the maximum sentence the law allows. Another contrast, almost as remarkable as that which sends Oscar Wilde to hard labour and places Sir Charles Dilke in the House of Commons, is that between the universal execration heaped upon Oscar Wilde and the tacit universal acquiescence of the very same public in the same kind of vice in our public schools. If all persons guilty of Oscar Wilde's offences were to be clapped into gaol, there would be a very surprising exodus from Eton and Harrow, Rugby and Winchester, to Pentonville and Holloway.[1] It is to be hoped that our headmasters will pluck up a little courage from the result of the Wilde trial, and endeavour to rid our Protestant schools of a foul and unnatural vice which is not found in Catholic establishments, at all events in this country. But meanwhile public schoolboys are allowed to indulge with impunity in practices which, when they leave school, would consign them to hard labour.

Among those who read and pondered these remarks was Lord Alfred Douglas, and he wrote to the editor from his place of exile in France what was in effect a spirited defence of male homosexuality and which Stead not unnaturally declined to publish. In this letter, which was preserved and ultimately came into the hands of the present writer, Douglas underlined what he considered the injustice of the law which allowed lesbians and male seducers of women and girls to go free, while the male invert was liable to suffer heavy penalties.

Perhaps you are not aware that 'Lesbianism' exists to any extent in London, but I can assure you that it does, and though of course I cannot mention names, I could point out to you half a dozen women in society or among actresses who would be considered as 'dangerous' to young girls as Oscar Wilde will I suppose henceforth be considered to boys.
Why on earth in the name of liberty and common sense a man cannot be allowed to love a boy, rather than a woman when his nature and his instinct tell him to do so, and when he has before him the example of such a number of noble and

[1] Holloway was not then a women's prison, as it is today.

gifted men who have had similar tastes (such as Shakespeare, Marlowe, Michael Angelo, Frederick the Great, and a host of others), is another question and one to which I should like to hear a satisfactory answer. Certain it is that persecution will no more kill this instinct in a man who has it, than it killed the faith of the Christian martyrs. I am not pleading for prostitution, but I think if a man who affects female prostitutes is unmolested it is disgraceful that a man who prefers male prostitutes should be thus barbarously punished. The only difference is that the man who brings bastards into the world, who seduces girls or commits adultery does an immense amount of harm, as you have yourself pointed out, whereas the paederast does absolutely no harm to anyone.[1]

After he had been in prison for rather more than a year, Wilde addressed a powerfully worded petition to the Home Secretary, praying for his release partly for reasons of health and partly because he felt that he had already suffered sufficient punishment, although he made it clear at the outset that he did not desire

to attempt to palliate in any way the terrible offences of which he was rightly found guilty, but to point out that such offences are forms of sexual madness and are recognised as such not merely by modern pathological science but by much modern legislation, notably in France, Austria, and Italy, where the laws affecting these misdemeanours have been repealed, on the ground that they are diseases to be cured by a physician, rather than crimes to be punished by a judge.[2]

Wilde's plea was rejected, and he was made to serve out the whole of his sentence without a day's remission.

The futility of punishing homosexuals with imprisonment was never so abundantly demonstrated as in Wilde's case. On his release from Reading jail, Wilde lost no time in resuming his former sexual habits. Lord Alfred Douglas assured me that it was Robert Ross who 'dragged Wilde back to homosexual practices' during the summer of 1897 which they spent together in Berneval near Dieppe. ('Oscar told me this himself one night after dinner in Paris when he had had a great many drinks. I did not mention it in my *Autobiography* because I thought everyone would think I was inventing it to get even with Ross.') But Wilde probably did not require much persuading. 'As for Wilde's last years in Paris,' Douglas went on, 'the manner of his life there was notorious

[1] *Trials*, 359–61.   [2] *Letters*, 401.

and he was quite open about it. He was hand in glove with all the little boys on the Boulevard. He never attempted to conceal it. Oscar believed, as many other eminent people do, that he had a perfect right to indulge his own tastes. He would not thank you for trying to make people believe it was otherwise. In fact nothing irritated him more than to meet—as he occasionally did—admirers who refused to believe that he was addicted to the vices for which he was condemned. This used to infuriate him.'[1] In this respect Douglas's statement is amply borne out by Wilde's recently published letters, particularly those to Ross.

'Today I bade good-bye, with tears and one kiss, to the beautiful Greek boy. . . . He is the nicest boy you ever introduced to me,' Wilde wrote to Ross a few months before his death. 'How evil it is to buy Love, and how evil to sell it! And yet what purple hours one can snatch from that grey slowly-moving thing called Time! My mouth is twisted with kissing, and I feed on fevers. The Cloister or the Café—there is my future. I tried the Hearth, but it was a failure.'[2]

[4]

Many English homosexuals were alarmed by the Wilde scandal and deemed it prudent to leave the country for a time. Wilde's friend and biographer Frank Harris later described the immediate result of his arrest:

Every train to Dover was crowded, every steamer to Calais thronged with members of the aristocratic and leisured classes, who seemed to prefer Paris, or even Nice out of season, to a city like London, where the police might act with such unexpected vigour. The truth was that the cultured aesthetes . . . had been thunderstruck by the facts which the Queensberry trial had laid bare. For the first time they learned that such houses as Taylor's were under police supervision, and that creatures like Wood and Parker were classified and watched. They had imagined that in 'the home of liberty' such practices passed unnoticed. It came as a shock to their preconceived ideas that the police in London knew a great many things which they were not supposed to concern themselves with, and this unwelcome glare of light drove the vicious forth in wild haste.

[1] *Trials*, 372–3.   [2] *Letters*, 828.

Never was Paris so crowded with members of the English governing classes; here was to be seen a famous ex-Minister; there the fine face of the president of a Royal society; at one table on the Café de la Paix, a millionaire recently ennobled, and celebrated for his exquisite taste in art; opposite to him a famous general. It was even said that a celebrated English actor took a return ticket to Paris for three or four days just to be in the fashion. The mummer returned quickly; but the majority of the migrants stayed abroad for some time. The wind of terror which had swept them across the Channel opposed their return, and they scattered over the Continent from Naples to Monte Carlo and from Palermo to Seville under all sorts of pretexts.[1]

Lord Alfred Douglas, who was already abroad at the time of Wilde's conviction, also did not return to England for several years.

The man who was to a great extent responsible for this exodus, was the actor-playwright Charles Brookfield. It is said that he was jealous of Wilde's theatrical success. At all events he was friendly with Queensberry, and he probably did more than anyone else to collect evidence against Wilde which he handed over to Douglas's father. Indeed, his zeal in hunting out homosexuals did not stop with Wilde and Taylor and was continued after they went to prison. Eventually his conduct became an embarrassment to the authorities, and it is said that the London Metropolitan Police Commissioner got hold of him and advised him in the interests of his personal safety to 'lay off', pointing out that there were influential homosexuals in high places who resented Brookfield's laudable but misguided endeavours and that if Brookfield were to persist in them his dead body might be found floating in the Thames one morning.[2] Brookfield took the hint; he was subsequently appointed to the post of censor of plays in the Lord Chamberlain's office—a singular piece of irony, since he himself had written one of the 'riskiest' plays of the period.

The most notorious aristocratic homosexual at this period was the young Henry Paget, Earl of Uxbridge, who succeeded his father in 1898 as fifth Marquess of Anglesey. He married his cousin, the beautiful red-headed Lilian Chetwynd, who left him on their honeymoon on discovering what his particular propensities were. A year or so later, she obtained a decree of nullity from the courts. Anglesey was an extreme example of the

[1] Frank Harris. *Oscar Wilde* (1938), 171-2.
[2] Communicated by Sir Seymour Hicks.

effeminate transvestite type, and was a gifted female impersonator. He was in the habit of rouging and powdering his face in order, so it was said, 'to look paler and more interesting'. When he walked along Piccadilly or the Champs-Elysées, he invariably carried a snow-white, pink-ribboned poodle in his arms, who was just as abundantly scented with patchouli and *eau d'Espagne* as his master. Within six years of his coming into his inheritance, he had incurred debts of over half a million pounds, notwithstanding that his income amounted to £110,000 a year. Consequently, his creditors made him bankrupt, and his personal effects were sold up for their benefit. They included what was described at the time as a 'preposterous accumulation' of clothes and jewellery, mostly women's, which realized no less than £88,000. By this time Anglesey had withdrawn to the Continent. He settled in Monte Carlo, where he died in 1905, shortly after his thirtieth birthday.

Very different from Anglesey was the rich philanthropist and founder of the Polytechnic, Quintin Hogg, who, as sometimes happens with social workers whose interests bring them into frequent contact with youth, was said to have become involved with a boy; he was also said to have been about to be exposed when he suddenly died. The cause of his death, which occurred in January 1903, a few weeks before his fifty-eighth birthday, was officially given as heart failure, but it was whispered at the time that, fearing his arrest was imminent on a homosexual charge, he had taken his own life. His life was insured for a large sum, and it was said that the insurance company's immediate reaction was to declare the policy void and refuse to pay on it as the company was entitled to do in the case of deliberate suicide. A board meeting was called to discuss the matter. One of the directors, who had a high regard for Hogg's work, pointed out the immeasurable value of the Polytechnic in providing young men and women with instruction, recreation and cheap holiday tours, and he urged his fellow directors in the light of Hogg's outstanding philanthropic record to regard the assured's death as the result of natural causes and thus to avoid the public scandal, not to mention the pain to Hogg's family, which their refusal to honour the policy would undoubtedly produce. Fortunately these humanitarian arguments prevailed, and to their credit the company paid the family the full amount due on the policy.

It is only fair to add that the case against Hogg has never been proved. Opinion is similarly divided about Sir Richard Burton, the explorer and translator of *The Arabian Nights*, who like another Arabist in a later generation (T. E. Lawrence) is thought to have been homosexual, as also is Cecil Rhodes, the imperialist and millionaire philanthropist. Burton was probably bisexual. His wife, who disapproved strongly of her husband's writings, as did Mrs J. A. Symonds of her husband's, destroyed all his diaries and other papers after his death, so that we are unlikely to discover the truth about this eccentric scholar. His passion for Oriental erotica—Lady Burton also destroyed the manuscript translation of *The Perfumed Garden* upon which he had been working in the last year of his life—would seem to indicate that his interests were predominantly heterosexual. That he was interested in homosexuality appears from the terminal essay on 'Pederasty' which he wrote for the final volume of *The Arabian Nights*. This was later published separately as *The Sotadic Zone* in 1887 and gravely shocked some of his contemporaries, particularly by his reference to a number of well-known homosexuals in history, which latter incidentally he would appear to have copied from the privately printed bibliography of pornographic books by Henry S. Ashbee (Pisanus Fraxi).

About this time Dublin Castle was the scene of another scandal with homosexual undertones. This centred round the theft of the Irish crown jewels from the safe in the library of the College of Heralds in the Castle during the summer of 1907. The jewels, which had once belonged to Queen Charlotte, wife of George III, and later to their son George IV, who lent them to his mistress Lady Conyngham, were used as insignia for the Order of St Patrick. The officer responsible for their safe-keeping was the Ulster King of Arms, Sir Arthur Vicars, a homosexual aged forty-three. Sir Arthur shared a house with his assistant, the Athlone Pursuivant, Francis Shackleton, also homosexual, whose brother Ernest was the well-known Antarctic explorer. Vicars was known to be in the habit of entertaining his homosexual friends at drinking parties in the Office of Arms, and furthermore he made no secret that he kept the keys of the strong room in his pocket. One of his friends, whom apparently he had met through Shackleton, was a certain Captain Richard Gorges, a blackguard who had literally been kicked out of his regiment in the South African War for having been caught red-handed with a drummer-boy. Gorges had subsequently become an army musketry instructor and had come to Ireland for the annual militia training, which gave him an easy entrée to the Castle. Shackleton and Gorges first plied Vicars with whisky until he was insensible, then took the keys from his pocket, and made wax impressions of them, subsequently replacing the keys. Then one evening in June the two conspirators got into the safe with the counterfeit keys they had made and removed the jewels. Shackleton immediately took them to Amsterdam, where he pawned them for £20,000, about a quarter of their real value, afterwards returning to Ireland.

The theft was discovered on July 6, when Vicars wished to replace a collar belonging to one of the Knights of St Patrick who had died, and found the safe empty. It was not long before the Dublin police were on the track of the thieves, who made no attempt to flee from justice. In fact they dared the authorities to arrest them, and said that if they were arrested, they would reveal so many scandals that 'they would shake the Government'. This was confirmed by Vicars, who wrote to a friend that 'Shackleton, when he was suspected, worked the alleged scandal for all he was worth and even blackened his own character, threatening to produce a social scandal and involve high persons'. Meanwhile a Royal Commission was appointed to inquire into the disappearance of the jewels, but after sitting for a week and examining a number of witnesses it was indefinitely adjourned and never met again. It was said that this was due to the direct intervention of King Edward VII, who was alarmed at possible disclosures affecting highly placed individuals, including his own brother-in-law, the Duke of Argyll.

There may well be some truth in this. The police inquiries revealed that Shackleton acted as a link between Vicars and a homosexual clique of which Lord Ronald Gower was the moving spirit. Lord Ronald, whose association with Oscar Wilde has already been noted, was sixty-two at this time and was living quietly in the country with his devoted companion Frank Hird, whom he had first met when Hird was Rome correspondent of the *Morning Post* and had adopted as his son. Shackleton was a frequent visitor to his house at Penshurst in Kent, as also was the Duke of Argyll, who was his first cousin as well as being the king's brother-in-law. In fact, both Shackleton and the duke spent the week-end at Penshurst immediately before the theft of the jewels was discovered. The king was naturally anxious to prevent the press and public from learning that his brother-in-law had been associating with 'an abandoned ruffian' like Shackleton in the house of two other homosexuals. For all the king knew, there might be a link with the homosexual scandals which had broken at the court of his nephew, the German Kaiser William II, where the Kaiser's favourite, Prince von Eulenberg-Hertzfeld, had recently been dismissed, along with the Master of Ceremonies, three Imperial *aides* and the Commandant of Berlin, for their homosexual activities. Not even the Hohenzollerns had behaved as stupidly as this before, declared Edward VII, when he heard of the ensuing trials. Thus the king had every reason for wishing the affair to be hushed up.

The immediate upshot was that Shackleton resigned his post as Herald, and Vicars was summarily dismissed. No arrests were made. Nor were the jewels ever recovered. But the two conspirators eventually met with their deserts. Shackleton and Gorges were both given long sentences of penal servitude, Shackleton for fradulent conversion and Gorges for attempting to murder a policeman who had come to arrest him on another charge. As for the unfortunate Sir Arthur Vicars, he retired to his country estate in Kerry, where he lived out the remainder of his life in obscurity, until he was murdered by a roving band of Sinn Feiners during the Civil War in 1921.[1]

One of the most remarkable homosexuals at the turn of the century was the first and last Lord Farquhar, whose rapid advancement in business and court circles is said to have been due to his skill in exploiting his physical charms. The fifth son of a Scottish baronet by an illegitimate daughter of Lord Reay, Horace Brand Farquhar began his career as a clerk in the East India commercial house of Forbes, Forbes & Co., and through the Forbes family was introduced to the Marlborough House set of the Prince of Wales and so to Queen Victoria, who took a fancy to him and created him successively a baronet and a peer. Previously he had been a Liberal Unionist M.P. and had married the wealthy widow of the banker Sir Edward Scott. He then took up banking in Scott's Bank (later absorbed in the Westminster) and with the help of the Duke of Fife, who was a partner in the bank and son-in-law of the Prince of Wales, became the prince's financial adviser and made considerable sums of money for His Royal Highness. Like the Duke of Fife too, Farquhar was one of the founders with Cecil Rhodes of the Chartered Company of South Africa, until the complications caused by the Jameson raid necessitated their retirement.

[1] The late Desmond Fitzgerald, Minister of External Affairs in the Irish Free State Government from 1922 to 1927, told me that while he was minister the jewels turned up in Paris and were offered for sale to the Irish Government, which not surprisingly showed no interest in these former relics of British rule. Further details will be found in the present writer's *Cases that Changed the Law* (1951), *Vicious Circle* by Francis Bamford and Viola Bankes (1965), and Bulmer Hobson's *Ireland Yesterday and Tomorrow* (1968), 85–90.

On the prince's accession to the throne, Farquhar was put in charge of the royal household, whose affairs he managed for some years, and he also served as a court official under George V. At the same time he became treasurer of the Conservative Party and as such was responsible for the management of the party's finances. He supported the Lloyd George coalition government during the First World War and was advanced a step in the peerage. On the break-up of the coalition in 1922 he was made an earl, at the age of seventy-eight. On his refusal to hand over £20,000 in connection with the recent election to the Conservative Party on the ground that the money had been subscribed expressly for the coalition, he was summarily dismissed by Bonar Law, the new Conservative leader, who had been told that Farquhar was 'so "gaga" that one does not know what to make of him'.

There can be little doubt that Farquhar gave this sum to Lloyd George and other sums for his account, as well as £40,000 from the Party Fund to a charity nominated by the king (which Farquhar had in turn received from Lord Astor), and his transactions can only be regarded as embezzlement. But he continued to be seen at court and the king received him in audience a fortnight before his death in 1923. In the past he had been a lavish entertainer at Castle Rising, his estate near Sandringham, and he had no doubt let it be known that he had not forgotten various members of the royal family in his will. Indeed, when this fantastic document was opened, it was seen that he had made the most generous bequests, among them £100,000 to Princess Arthur of Connaught and a similar sum to her son, besides substantial legacies to the king's private secretaries and others connected with the court. But when the executors came to distribute the estate, they had a disagreeable surprise. Farquhar was bankrupt. His personal fortune, if it ever existed, had disappeared like the Party Fund. Perhaps it was as well that he left no heir and his titles died with him.[1]

The condition of the armed forces seems to have changed little in the Edwardian period as compared with the experiences of J. A. Symonds half a century before. Xavier Mayne, a pseudonym which cloaked the identity of the American Edward I. Stevenson, quotes a letter from a British naval officer in the early 1900s.

[1] Robert Blake. *The Unknown Prime Minister* (1955), 497; *The Times* August 31, 1923; private information. Farquhar's extraordinary career would seem to entitle him to a place in the *Dictionary of National Biography* but his name does not appear there.

I have been stationed, as you know, in two or three ships, and I think they have been thoroughly representative of the best sort of British seamen. On the D . . . homosexuality was rife, and one could see with his own eyes how it was going on between officers. I have been told that in some services (the Austrian and French for instance) nobody ever remarks about it, taking such a thing as a natural proceeding. That may be so or not; but in any case nobody was 'shocked' on board either the A— or the B—. There were half a dozen ties that we knew about.

To my knowledge sodomy is a regular thing on ships that go on long cruises. In the war-ships I should say that the sailor often preferred it. In the circumstances I have described the intimacy was spoken of slyly. The friendship between men, in all grades of service at sea, tend to be much closer, more sentimental than when ashore. Everything makes for confidentiality, one is shut away from the world, and so much in pairs with his friends, in watches, and so on. Of course, when the forecastle men come ashore they are keen after the girls, but sometimes the interest quite disappears, I am told. That it does in the case of many sea-friendships between homosexual officers, I know.

On the subject of military prostitution, particularly by guardsmen, at this period, Mayne is equally frank.

The hypocrisy, or the ignorance—or the pride—of Englishmen whichever it may be, frequently asserts, if so recondite a topic is touched, that 'British soldiers, thank God, never do that sort of thing! That's a vice they leave to the Continent, sir!' Such an illusion is admirably English.

The skeptic has only to walk around London, around any English garrison centre, to stroll about Portsmouth, Aldershot, Southampton, Woolwich, large cities of North Britain, and of Ireland, to find the soldier prostitute in almost open self-marketing. Certain private resorts of British homosexuals 'deal' in such an element. It holds its ground against the cheap and dangerous pederasty of England, which is so common. On any evening, the street corners or the promenades of the big music halls and the cheap theatres of London and other cities show one the fine flower of British soldier prostitute, dressed in his best uniform, clean shaven, well groomed and handsome with his Anglo-Saxon pulchritude and vigour, smilingly expectant. He is sure to be approached by some admiring stranger or regular 'friend', and asked to take a drink or offered a cigar; and so is brought delicately to a bargain, at a tariff from the modest five shillings or three-and-six to a sovereign.

Sometimes a criminal trial will point at cynically London soldier prostitution.[1]

Such a trial, or rather inquest, since the killer was never brought to justice, followed the so-called 'Studio Murder', which caused a big sensation in the spring of 1906. A young homosexual painter named Archibald Wakley was discovered dead early one morning in his studio at 76A Westbourne Grove, Bayswater. His body showed that he had suffered multiple injuries, 'terrible in character', including a fractured skull, which had been smashed in with a hammer. There were also some peculiar marks on his right thigh. Wakley's father, a wine and spirit merchant, stated in the coroner's court that his son was a 'quiet, amiable young man, by profession an artist'. In fact, young Wakley had exhibited his paintings at the Royal Academy, but however quiet and amiable he may have been, there is no doubt that he was in the habit of inviting soldiers to his studio. Sometimes they served as models, as appeared from a number of sketches found there, but they also had homosexual relations with Wakley for which they were paid. Between thirty and forty names and addresses were also found written on various pieces of paper in the studio. The doctor who carried out the autopsy stated at the inquest that he 'did not think it would be to the public advantage to give the whole result' of his findings on the dead man's injuries, among them the marks on the thigh. These turned out to have been made with spurs, and suspicions immediately turned towards the mounted regiments stationed in London. These suspicions were confirmed by another witness, an employee of Whiteley's stores nearby, who said he had seen Wakley entering the studio about 11.15 in company with a trooper of the Royal Horse Guards on the night of the murder, adding that the trooper was in uniform and wearing spurs. One of the names found among Wakley's papers was that of a certain trooper named Walker in the Royal Horse Guards; he was easily identified and called to give evidence before the coroner.

Trooper Walker described how about four months previously he had struck up an acquaintance in Hyde Park with the unfortunate artist who had invited him round to his studio for a

[1] Xavier Mayne. *The Intersexes* (1910), 186. The term used in the Navy for buggery was 'a feed of arse' or, just 'a feed'. In the Guards homosexuals were known as 'fitters' or 'twisters'.

drink. The trooper went and the invitation was repeated for the following Sunday, but for some reason not clear he did not keep the appointment. He swore that he never saw Wakley again and for the night of the murder he was able to produce a satisfactory alibi. The jury brought in a verdict of murder by person or persons unknown. The murderer, unquestionably a soldier, was never traced. It was said at the time that 'a royal command cut short the search'.[1]

A more distinguished soldier than Trooper Walker, whose abnormal condition, like General Gordon's, was not known to the general public at this period, was Field Marshal Lord Kitchener. 'They say he dislikes women,' remarked Queen Victoria, 'but I can only say he was very nice to me.' In his later years, Kitchener found a deep and lasting friend in Captain Oswald Fitzgerald, of the 18th Bengal Lancers, whom he appointed his aide-de-camp. Fitzgerald, in the discreet words of Kitchener's latest biographer,

> established himself so securely in the affection of his chief that Kitchener never looked elsewhere, and their intimate association was happy and fortunate. Fitzgerald, like Kitchener, was a bachelor and a natural celibate; he devoted the whole of the rest of his life exclusively to Kitchener, and except for a brief period early in 1910, he never quitted Kitchener's side until they met death together on the fatal voyage to Russia in June, 1916.[2]

Although Kitchener's body was never recovered, the king and queen, both Houses of Parliament and other national leaders went in solemn procession to St Paul's Cathedral to honour his memory.

Less fortunate than Kitchener was Major-General Sir Hector Macdonald, K.C.B., who had commanded the Egyptian Brigade under Kitchener in the Nile campaign against the Dervishes, where his bravery and resourcefulness earned him the thanks of Parliament and the appointment of A.D.C. to Queen Victoria, an honorary post continued by Edward VII. Macdonald had previously served for nine years in the ranks as a private soldier, being promoted to commissioned rank during Lord Roberts's famous march from Kabul to Kandahar, and his bravery gained him his popular nickname of 'Fighting Mac'. He later commanded the Highland Brigade during the Boer War, in which he was wounded in action. In 1902 Macdonald was appointed to the command of the troops in Ceylon. Nine months later, what

[1] Mayne, 499–500. *The Times* May 28, 29, June 3, 1906.
[2] Philip Magnus. *Kitchener* (1958), 235.

the *Dictionary of National Biography* calls 'an opprobrious accusation against him' was reported to the governor of the colony.
The governor sent for Macdonald and immediately granted his
request for leave to go home and discuss the matter with the
War Office authorities. The latter directed a court of inquiry to
be held in Ceylon and ordered Macdonald to return there to face
it. Macdonald set out by the overland route to Marseilles, where
he was expected to catch the next steamer to Colombo. But he
got no further than Paris. There, in a hotel bedroom, 'Fighting
Mac' fought his last battle—this time with himself—when he put
and end to his life with a bullet, a month before his fiftieth birthday. At the request of his widow his body was brought back to
his native Scotland, where it was interred with full military
honours.

At this date there was a young member of the British consular
service, named Roger Casement, on special duty in the Congo.
When he heard the news of Macdonald's suicide, Casement
noted in his diary:

> The reasons given are pitiably sad. The most distressing case
> this surely of its kind and one that may awake the national
> mind to saner methods of curing a terrible disease than by
> criminal legislation.[1]

It is significant that the writer of the foregoing lines was himself an obsessive pederast. Abundant evidence of this is provided
by Casement's diaries, in which he recorded his homosexual
experiences in minute detail. These compromising diaries were
seized by the police at the time of Sir Roger Casement's arrest
for high treason in 1916, and some typical pages were photographed and the copies circulated by the British intelligence
authorities among local and American journalists with the object
of counteracting popular sympathy for him and his cause. After
his execution Casement's Irish sympathizers alleged that the
diaries had been fabricated by the British and that the homosexual references were forged interpolations. This is completely
contradicted by internal evidence, as well as by Casement's
admission to Serjeant Sullivan, the leading defence counsel at his
trial, that he was a homosexual and, according to Sullivan,
'gloried in it'. But, however that may be, Sir Roger Casement
was by his public conduct a great humanitarian and a courageous
patriot, who gave his life for a political cause in the justice of

[1] April 17, 1903: Peter Singleton Gates and Maurice Girodias. *The Black
Diaries* (1959), 121.

which he passionately believed. In 1965, forty-nine years after he was hanged as a traitor, his remains were exhumed from his un-marked grave in Pentonville Prison and handed over to the Irish Government for a hero's funeral and reinterment in Glasnevin, Cemetery, Dublin, with the blessing of the Catholic Church, into which he had been received on the eve of his execution.[1]

[5]

Besides Lord Alfred Douglas, several literary homosexuals who survived well into the twentieth century had links with Wilde, notably John Gray, André Raffalovich, Reginald Turner, Robert Ross and Christopher Millard.

John Gray, one of nine children of a journeyman carpenter in Woolwich Dockyard, was a junior clerk in the Foreign Office when his first and best-known volume of poems, *Silverpoints*, appeared under the imprint Elkin Mathews and John Lane, 'at the Sign of the Bodley Head', in 1893. The volume, with characteristic typography and binding designed by Charles Ricketts, was a typical *avant-garde* production of the 'nineties, whilst its contents, which included translations from French poets like Verlaine and Baudelaire, had a definitely 'camp' ring about them. Four years earlier, when Gray was twenty-three, he had been picked up by Wilde in a bar off Shaftesbury Avenue and through Wilde had been introduced to Aubrey Beardsley, Pierre Louÿs, and others of Wilde's circle. It was said that Wilde based the name character in *The Picture of Dorian Gray* on John Gray, but when this was repeated by a London evening newspaper (*The Star*) Gray successfully sued the paper for libel. On the other hand, it is known that Gray signed letters to Wilde as Dorian and was known to other young men at the time by this pseudonym. However, although Wilde was attracted to Gray, as he indicated in *De Profundis*, he never fell in love with him as he did with that other poet, Lord Alfred Douglas. The man who fell in love with Gray was André Raffalovich, already mentioned in connection with Wilde.

André Raffalovich, a wealthy Jew of Russian origin whose sister Sophie married the Irish nationalist leader William O'Brien, was a minor poet as was Gray, though his poems, like his friend's

[1] The question of the diaries has been exhaustively reviewed against the background of the subject's life in my editions of *The Trial of Sir Roger Casement* (1960 and 1964), which contain extracts from the previously unpublished diary for 1911.

are forgotten today; he is remembered chiefly as the subject of Wilde's quip: 'Poor André! He came to London with the intention of founding a *salon*, and he has succeeded only in opening an eating house!' A native of Paris, where his father was a rich and influential banker, Raffalovich had been brought up in the French capital. Besides poetry and letters he became profoundly interested in homosexuality as a social phenomenon and he contributed several studies of the subject to the scientific series edited by the French criminal anthropologist Dr A. Lacassagne. The most substantial of these was *Uranisme et Unisexualité*, which was published in Paris in 1896; it contained an interesting account of the Wilde case as well as much other material on the history and prevalence of male inversion in England. The term uranism, or *uranismus* in German, had been coined in the 1860s by a Hanoverian lawyer named Carl Heinrich Ulrichs, who under the pseudonym 'Numa Numantius' had publicly pleaded for the amelioration of the homosexuality laws in Germany, taking the term from the Uranos of Plato in the *Symposium*. Uranism, Ulrichs claimed, was a congenital abnormality in which a female soul was encased in a male body, and the resultant homosexual he called an *urning*. The pioneer work of Ulrichs to a great extent inspired John Addington Symonds and Havelock Ellis to their investigations as well as Raffalovich. Raffalovich also collaborated with his friend Gray in writing a play which they called *The Blackmailers* on the theme of the blackmailing of a young homosexual of good family by two scoundrels. Like Rousseau's *Confessions*, the joint work, according to *The Times* dramatic critic, was 'without precedent and may very well hope to remain without imitators'. It only achieved a single matinée performance at the Prince of Wales's Theatre.[1]

After the Wilde scandal, both Gray and Raffalovich were converted to the Roman Catholic faith, as indeed Wilde himself was to be at the last. But unlike Wilde, the two friends renounced the life of cultured ease which they had both previously led. The story of their conversion was a favourite one of W. B. Yeats, who no doubt embellished it in the telling. According to the Irish poet, Gray and Raffalovich were cruising in the Mediterranean in a yacht which they had painted black and called *Iniquity*. They put in at a small Italian port, where some religious festival was being held, and the two friends were so impressed that they experienced a sudden change of heart. Gray indeed went a step further, when he resigned his Foreign Office job and entered the

[1] *Two Friends*. Ed. Brocard Sewell (1963), 7–49.

Scots College at Rome as a candidate for holy orders. During Gray's long novitiate, Raffalovich spent part of each year in the Eternal City so as to be near his friend.

Gray's path to ordination was not so easy. There was the unfortunate example of another homosexual at the college some years previously, the notorious Frederick William Rolfe, self-styled Baron Corvo, an errant and erring 'spoiled priest'. It was said that, because so many of the so-called 'decadent' writers of the 'nineties who led scandalous lives subsequently became Catholic converts, the Pope decreed that John Gray must not follow his vocation in England after he had been admitted to holy orders. However, the ban did not extend to Scotland, and it was in Edinburgh as a humble priest that Fr Gray spent the remainder of his life engaged in good works. Needless to add, Raffalovich followed him to Edinburgh, where he bought a house and settled. He also provided the funds for St Peter's Church on a plot of land, which he had likewise donated, and it was here that Fr Gray officiated after serving a hard apprenticeship as a curate in Cowgate, one of the city's poorest and roughest districts. So 'this one-time young man of fashion became noted as the priest who would go anywhere, do anything for anyone and would be welcomed anywhere. . . . And the later the hour and the dirtier the night, the more gladly he went on his errands of mercy and devotion.'[1] The Church authorities recognized his saintly work by making him a canon.

Fr Gray also found time for literature. In 1904 there appeared *Last Letters of Aubrey Beardsley*, edited with an introduction by him. Most of the letters were addressed to Raffalovich, who had helped Beardsley with money and in other ways towards the end of his brief life. A few were to Gray, but the canon considered it advisable to withold the names of both recipients, since Beardsley was still popularly identified with some of the worst aspects of the 'nineties decadence, in spite of his having also embraced the Catholic faith.

John Gray and André Raffalovich—theirs was a truly touching mutual devotion and dependence, marked at least as outsiders were concerned with a certain old-world courtliness, a homosexual relationship sublimated to the highest level. 'Dear Canon, how kind of you to call!' Raffalovich would greet his friend on a Sunday evening, while in the presbytery the canon would apologize to his guests for not having any cigarettes ('André has forgotten to replenish the box'). Every morning a taxi called at

[1] Moray McLaren in *The Universe*, May 26, 1961.

Raffalovich's house in Whitehouse Terrace to take him to Mass at St Peter's, which the canon celebrated. On Ash Wednesday, 1934, Raffalovich was found dead in bed, having died suddenly in his sleep. Gray, heartbroken by the loss of his friend, survived him by only a few weeks.

'I see more beauty in the world as I grow older,' wrote Fr Gray on completing a quarter of a century in the priesthood. 'I hope to write less and better with time.'

> Enough of the world is mine,
> more than the envious know.
> I have dug in a deeper mine
> than depths where rubies glow:
> I have sailed in a fairer ship
> the rim of a vaster sea
> than sleep or companionship
> ever were sweet to me.

Reginald ('Reggie') Turner, journalist, novelist and dilettante, whom Somerset Maugham and Sir Compton Mackenzie have both described as the wittiest man they ever knew, was thought by some to be the illegitimate son of the first Lord Burnham, principal proprietor of the *Daily Telegraph*; but his putative father is more likely to have been Burnham's uncle Lionel Levy-Lawson, who also owned a substantial interest in this newspaper as well as two London theatres and a prosperous printing-ink factory in France, of which country Turner's mother was apparently a native. After leaving Oxford, Turner took chambers in Clement's Inn and joined the staff of the family paper, where he inaugurated 'London Day by Day', a pioneer gossip column of its kind which is still a feature of the *Daily Telegraph*. At the same time he became friendly with Wilde and his circle, particularly Douglas and Ross, an association which worried Max Beerbohm, who had taken a liking to him when they were Oxford undergraduates in the same college. Before leaving on a trip to America early in 1895, Max wrote to Ross imploring him not to lead Reggie astray during his absence. 'He is very weak and you, if I remember, are very wicked. . . . Also keep Bosie away from him. . . . Bosie is more fatal to Reg than you—if anything. All this is quite serious. I really think Reg is at a crucial point of his career, and should hate to see him fall an entire victim to the love that dares not tell its name.'[1] Unfortunately for Turner this good advice went unheeded.

---

[1] Stanley Weintraub. *Reggie* (1966), 57, 99. 'Bosie' was Lord Alfred Douglas.

Turner seems to have developed quickly into a pederast—
indeed Wilde jokingly nicknamed him 'The Boy Snatcher of
Clement's Inn'—and he himself used to joke about homosexuality. Once, when discussing a controversial play which had
homosexual implications, he was surprised to learn that its author
denied it. 'Silly fellow,' quipped Turner, 'knocking the bottom
out of his play!'

In 1900, Turner was mixed up in some affair which obliged
him to leave England for a time. Whatever it was, it aroused the
curiosity of Wilde in his Paris exile, where Turner shortly joined
him. 'Do tell me about Reggie,' Wilde wrote to Ross at this time.
'Was he the victim of a painful and unfounded charge? I know
such charges are constantly made, and always against innocent
people.' A few days later, Wilde wrote again: 'From your silence
about Reggie my worst suspicions are confirmed: is it a sprightly
lady-journalist who led him astray? Or was it one of those typical
Englishwomen with their "fatal gift of duty"?' But Turner was
anything but a 'mulierast', to use Ross's expression. Sir Compton
Mackenzie has recalled meeting him and Ross shortly before the
outbreak of the First World War at the Earl's Court Exhibition,
when Mackenzie was waiting for a pretty girl whom he was
expecting. Hurriedly breaking off his conversation with the two
men as the lady appeared, Mackenzie went off to join her to the
accompaniment of Ross's comment to his companion: 'Alas, dear
Reggie, you and I cannot compete with nymphs!'[1]

Turner became attached to Italy, where he eventually settled.
Once, when he was ill in Rome with a fever, he wrote to Max
Beerbohm: 'I suppose I shall not yet be laid beside Keats and
Shelley and within call of John A. Symonds (not that I ever should
call)'.[2] Most of the last twenty-five years of his life he lived in
Florence, happy hunting ground of many other English expatriate homosexuals in the years between the two world wars.
Turner died there in 1938, leaving the bulk of his fortune, over
£40,000, besides his books, drawings and papers to his homosexual friend the Florentine bookseller and publisher Pino Orioli,
who promptly sold them at Sotheby's.

Robert ('Robbie') Baldwin Ross, journalist, art-critic, and
administrator of Oscar Wilde's estate, was a Canadian who had
been born in France and brought to England as a child. Although
more discreet in his associations than Wilde, Robbie Ross
could not indefinitely withstand the implacable hatred of Lord

[1] Weintraub, 99. *Letters of Oscar Wilde*, 830–1. Mackenzie, II, 268.
[2] Weintraub, 153.

Alfred Douglas, who was unable to forgive him for having (as he thought) poisoned Wilde's mind and turned his old friend against him in prison, as evidenced by the portions of De Profundis which Ross 'suppressed' and which consisted of a devastating attack by Wilde upon Douglas.

In 1911 Douglas followed Gray and Raffalovich into the arms of the Catholic Church, having seen the light and given up his homosexual habits. During the next three years he wrote to a number of distinguished people including the Prime Minister, Mr Asquith, two High Court judges, the Public Prosecutor and others, denouncing Ross as 'a filthy bugger', 'a notorious sodomite', 'an habitual debaucher and corrupter of young boys down to the present day', and 'a blackmailer'. Ross was consequently forced to prosecute him for criminal libel at the Old Bailey in 1914, just as Wilde had prosecuted Douglas's father almost twenty years before in the same court. In the written plea of justification which he put in, as he was legally bound to do, Douglas gave a string of names and dates, which he followed up by calling a dozen witnesses to establish the nature of Ross's habits. Unlike Wilde, however, Ross proved a hesitant and unconvincing witness, from whom the trial judge, Mr Justice Coleridge, as he pointed out to the jury in his summing up, 'waited in vain for any moral expression of indignation or horror at the practice of sodomitical vices'. However, the jury disagreed—it was said that one juror stood out and flatly refused to bring in a verdict which would have the effect of publicly branding Ross as a homosexual—and Douglas was bound over to come up again at the next sessions. But Douglas was not retried, as Ross dropped the case and agreed to pay Douglas's costs, a course to which Douglas unwillingly consented as he was on the verge of bankruptcy. Nevertheless his plea of justification remained on the court file, a standing invitation to the authorities to prosecute Ross as they had done Wilde when he withdrew his case against Queensberry.

That the authorities did not respond to this invitation and took no action against Ross was due, in some measure at least, to a change in the climate of public opinion, which, while still reprobating homosexual conduct, no longer, with some conspicuous exceptions like Mr Justice Darling, held it in the extreme abhorrence that it had done at the time of Wilde's conviction. Furthermore Douglas was generally regarded as a cantankerous nuisance and busybody, while his anti-homosexual zeal coming as it did from a former uninhibited invert was not unnaturally frowned upon. Ross, on the other hand, was generally liked; his conscientious administration of Wilde's estate for the benefit of Wilde's children, besides his encouragement of Wilde's literary rehabilitation through his edition of Wilde's collected works, was admired in literary circles, and he was a respected figure in the art world, holding the post of picture valuer to the Board of Trade. What is more, he kept his private life to himself, and although most of his friends—and he had many—knew he was homosexual, he was left in peace. Indeed, his friends, who included the Prime Minister and Mrs Asquith, several Members of Parliament, a bishop, H. G. Wells and Bernard Shaw, presented him with a testimonial drawn up by Edmund Gosse and a substantial sum of money in recognition of his 'services to Art and Literature', which included help and encouragement for young writers. In handing over the money to the University of London, Ross showed a certain wry sense of humour, since the declared purpose of the gift which the University gratefully accepted was the foundation of a *scholarship for boys* to be called 'The Robert Ross Scholarship'.

As Rupert Croft-Cooke remarks in his biography of Douglas, 'it is good to find that things had changed a little since the failure of Wilde's action against Queensberry and that in 1914 a man proved homosexual by no means became an outcast'. Nevertheless Ross never recovered from the adverse publicity. He worried himself into a state of chronic ill-health and died suddenly of heart failure in his rooms in Bury Street, St James's, four years later, at the age of forty-nine. A month or two previously his friend and former secretary, 'poor Chris Millard', had been sent to prison for the second time for a homosexual offence.[1]

Christopher Sclater Millard was the only member of this literary quintette who never knew Wilde personally, although Wilde's example and works were to colour much of his own life, during which he became well known as Wilde's industrious bibliographer under the pseudonym 'Stuart Mason'. He came of a respectable Hampshire family with titled connections; his father was an Anglican canon and his mother, whose maiden name was Sclater, was a sister of Lord Basing. But he did not get on well with his family and, shortly after coming down from Oxford, he left home; he too became a Catholic, and he was by turns private tutor, schoolmaster, assistant editor of the art magazine edited by Robert Ross, a clerk in the War Office, and finally a bibliographer and rare book dealer. His monumental bibliography of Wilde's writings, which it took him ten years to produce and

[1] Rupert Croft-Cooke. *Bosie* (1963), 275.

which came out in 1914, contains much curious and interesting information. More than once he ran foul of the law and he served several prison terms, which had the effect of making him a convinced socialist. His friends included Frederick Rolfe and A. J. A. Symons, whom he introduced to *Hadrian the Seventh* and inspired to write his famous *Quest for Corvo*, which incidentally contains a faithful character sketch of himself. He lived by himself in a bungalow tucked away behind a faded Victorian mansion in Marylebone, where he cooked his own meals, made his own bed, patched his own clothes, and conducted an extensive correspondence with American book collectors on the nicer points of bibliographical research. He died in 1927, aged fifty-five, and with a final characteristic gesture left the money from the sale of his existing stock of rare books to the local hospital which had nursed him in his last illness.[1]

Millard's views on homosexuality and its treatment by the law were expressed in a letter which he wrote as a young man at the time of Wilde's conviction in 1895 over his initials C.S.M. to *Reynold's Newspaper*, the only paper besides the *Daily Chronicle* which, in Millard's words, had 'ever given the poor wretch in prison a fair hearing'.

> Mr Oscar Wilde has been sentenced to two years' imprisonment with hard labour. What for? For being immoral? No. A man may commit adultery with another man's wife or fornication with a painted harlot who plys her filthy trade in the public streets unmolested with impunity. It is because this man has dared to choose another form of satisfying his natural passion the law steps in. Yet he has not injured the State or anybody else against their will.
>
> Why does not the Crown prosecute every boy at a public or private school or half the men in the Universities?
>
> In the latter places 'poederism' is as common as fornication, and everybody knows it. . . .
>
> Prosecuting a man on such a charge as this does not tend to diminish this form of immorality; it rather increases it tenfold.

[1] The latest information on Millard will be found in Timothy d'Arch Smith's Introduction to the new edition of Millard's *Bibliography of Oscar Wilde* (1967), and the sources there mentioned. See also the present writer's edition of *The Trials of Oscar Wilde* (1948) 383-4, and his *Cases that Changed the Law* (1951), 190-203.

CHAPTER SIX

Onward to Wolfenden

[1]

During the last year of the First World War, an extraordinary story gained considerable belief in Britain to the effect that the Germans possessed a list of English men and women, many of them occupying prominent positions in public life, who were sexual perverts, mostly sodomites and lesbians, and that the Germans through their secret service were in a position to blackmail them. It was rumoured that the intermediary used by the Germans to relay the names to Berlin was none other than the late King Edward VII's mistress, Mrs George Keppel. The story was given widespread publicity by the eccentric M.P. named Noel Pemberton Billing, who had been elected as an Independent, pledged to support a more vigorous prosecution of the war, particularly in the air. Then in his late thirties, Pemberton Billing wore a monocle and a long pointed collar without the usual accompaniment of a necktie, and he used to drive about in a light yellow Rolls-Royce car. To further his political aims he had founded a weekly newspaper which he called *Imperialist*, and it was in this journal, on January 26, 1918, that the story appeared of the list that was supposed to be a 'Black Book' in the possession of Prince William of Wied, who had become King of Albania in the spring of 1914.

There exists in the *Cabinet noir* of a certain German Prince a book compiled by the Secret Service from the reports of German agents who have infested this country for the past twenty years, agents so vile and spreading debauchery of such a lasciviousness as only German minds could conceive and only German bodies execute.

The officer who discovered this book while on special service briefly outlined for me its stupefying contents. In the beginning of the book is a précis of general instructions regarding the propagation of evils which all decent men thought had perished in Sodom and Lesbia. The blasphemous compilers even speak of the Groves and High Places mentioned

in the Bible. The most insidious arguments are outlined for
the use of the German agent in his revolting work. Then more
than a thousand pages are filled with the names mentioned
by German agents in their reports. There are the names of
forty-seven-thousand English men and women.

It is a most Catholic miscellany. The names of Privy
Councillors, youths of the chorus, wives of Cabinet Ministers,
dancing girls, even Cabinet Ministers themselves, while
diplomats, poets, bankers, editors, newspaper proprietors, and
members of His Majesty's household follow each other with
no order of precedent.

The Royal Navy, according to Mr Pemberton Billing, was a
particular target for these nefarious agents, who 'under the guise
of indecent liaison, could obtain information as to the disposition
of the Fleet'. At the same time, 'wives of men in supreme positions
were entangled. In Lesbian ecstasy the most sacred secrets of
State were betrayed. The sexual peculiarities of members of the
peerage were used as a leverage to open up fruitful fields of
espionage.' It was all part of the Hun's demoniacal plan to
exterminate the British race. 'The story of the contents of this
book has opened my eyes,' Pemberton Billing declared, 'and
the matter must not rest.' Nor did it.

It may seem incredible that people should have swallowed
such a far-fetched tale, but in the popular mood of war hysteria
which prevailed at the time anything was possible. Some months
previously a society had been formed in London called the
Vigilantes with the object of promoting 'purity in public life',
and to some extent the *Imperialist* had become the organ of this
society. Pemberton Billing thereupon changed the title of his
paper to *The Vigilante* to mark its association with that movement,
whose supporters believed wholeheartedly in the existence of the
'Black Book'.

About the same time an interesting event was announced in
London's theatrical world. Two private performances of Oscar
Wilde's tragedy *Salome* were to be given under the auspices of
Mr J. T. Grein's Independent Theatre Society. Although it had
often been played on the Continent, where it had inspired the
German composer Richard Strauss to set its words to music as
an opera, in England *Salome* had come under the ban of the Lord
Chamberlain, who, in his role of censor of plays, had refused to
license it for public performance. Consequently Mr Grein's
production had necessarily to be confined to members of the

society, but membership was open to anyone who cared to join by applying and paying a small subscription. For the name part the producer had secured Maud Allan, a Canadian and well-known as a classical dancer, whose previous rendering of 'The Vision of Salome' had created quite a sensation by reason of her dispensing with more clothing than was generally considered proper at that time. In this production she was to dance 'The Dance of the Seven Veils', which is mentioned though not described in detail by Wilde in the stage directions. She had the reputation of being lesbian.

The first number of *The Vigilante*, which appeared on February 16, 1918, contained the following paragraph in the editorial:

The Cult of the Clitoris

To be a member of Maud Allan's private performance in Oscar Wilde's *Salome* one has to apply to a Miss Valetta, of 9, Duke Street, Adelphi, W.C. If Scotland Yard were to seize the list of these members I have no doubt they would secure the names of several thousand of the first 47,000.

The innuendo that Miss Allan was a lesbian was sufficient to justify her in prosecuting Pemberton Billing for criminal libel. The case which lasted for six days, was tried by Mr Justice Darling at the Old Bailey and provoked some astonishing scenes in the court room.[1]

It was unfortunate for Miss Allan that her case was never properly put to the jury, since the trial was almost entirely taken up with the 'Black Book' and the merits and demerits of *Salome* and its author. The defendant was, of course, unable to produce the alleged book or a copy of it in court. The best he could do was to call two witnesses who were supposed to have seen it and to be able to testify as to its contents. The first of these witnesses was an unprepossessing woman named Mrs Eileen Villiers Stuart, who was to reappear a few months later at the Old Bailey on a charge of bigamy for which she was sent to prison for nine months. She had been shown the 'Black Book' or a copy of it, she said, by the late Neil Primrose, M.P., Lord Rosebery's son, in the company of another officer, Major Evelyn Rothschild,

---

[1] May 29, 30, 31, June 1, 3, 4, 1918: *Rex* v. *Pemberton Billing. Verbatim Report of the Trial* (1918). In a later civil action for slander it was held that the imputation of lesbianism in a woman is an imputation of unchastity within the meaning of the Slander of Women Act, 1891, and therefore it was not necessary for the plaintiff to prove actual pecuniary damage: *Kerr* v. *Kennedy* [1942] 1 K.B. 109.

both of whom had subsequently been killed in the war. Asked by
Pemberton Billing, who conducted his own defence, about the
names of prominent people in the book, she electrified the court
by admitting that it contained the name of Mr Justice Darling
himself. Other names she mentioned were those of the ex-Prime
Minister, Mr Asquith and the ex-War Minister, Lord Haldane.
Mrs Villiers Stuart was followed into the witness box by a certain
Captain H. S. Spencer, the officer anonymously referred to in
the original article as having discovered the 'Black Book'. He
swore he had done this while serving as A.D.C. to Prince William
of Wied, who occupied the throne of Albania for a short time in
1914. The book was in the king's private rooms in the royal
palace at Durazzo, he said, and His Majesty had displayed a
'morbid curiosity' in its contents. Captain Spencer confirmed
that the controversial volume contained the names of Mr
Asquith and Lord Haldane. He added that he subsequently
passed on his findings to the British Naval Intelligence branch
of the Admiralty. This witness was alleged to have put Neil
Primrose on to obtaining a copy of the 'Black Book'.

The other defence witnesses included Lord Alfred Douglas,
who had translated the play into English from the French in
which it was first published. Wilde he described as 'the greatest
force for evil that has appeared in Europe during the last three
hundred and fifty years'. Douglas added that he intensely regretted
having met Wilde and having helped him with the translation,
which he now regarded as 'a most pernicious and abominable
piece of work'.

Since Wilde's trial Douglas had turned against his erstwhile
friend, whose homosexual practices he now condemned. That
Douglas had sought to defend these practices at the time of the
trial, Miss Allan's counsel reminded him by quoting the text of a
letter which Douglas had written at the time to Henry Labouchere,
the editor of *Truth* and author of the notorious Section 11 of the
Criminal Law Amendment Act of 1885. In his summing up of
the evidence to the jury, Mr Justice Darling commented
caustically on Douglas and this (in the judge's view) unedifying
communication.

There was a letter, stupefying in its effrontery and abusing
Mr Labouchere, the editor of *Truth*, because he ventured to
disapprove of sodomy, telling him that he was a prejudiced,
narrow-minded man, who objected to practices which were a
perfect credit to those who were guilty of them; and advocating

the repeal of the laws, and telling Mr Labouchere that by the next generation (and that is our generation—because that time has gone by, or very soon it will) he would be quite out of date and that these practices which he condemned would be looked upon as creditable to those who practised them, honourable and beautiful.

Well, gentlemen, you may know it, I daresay you do, that this crime of sodomy, which Oscar Wilde and Lord Alfred Douglas gloried in, is known in our law books as a crime not to be mentioned among Christians—'inter Christianos non nominandum'—and the reason was that it was a common offence—it was a common practice of which no one was ashamed among the Pagans of ancient Greece and Rome, very cultivated people in many ways; people capable of writing beautiful verses, beautiful plays and building buildings which are even more glorious than this Court—the Parthenon and so on, and making statues such as we cannot approach and all the time society was permeated by this vice.

And Lord Alfred Douglas points out to Mr Labouchere that its glories will return, that this will be no longer condemned by public opinion, that all the lies against them will be refuted, and calling attention to Von Krafft-Ebing, I think, who was trying to abolish the law against it in Austria so that vice should flourish and the world be what it was in those distant and forgotten days when Greece was living Greece. Mr Labouchere did not live to see the dawn of this delightful epoch; that is what the man Douglas meant. That was his idea when he translated Oscar Wilde's play from the French into the English. . . . The letter which he wrote to Mr Labouchere is very very strong confirmation of his statement to you, that that is what was meant because it expressed his deliberate opinion in unmistakable language.

Mr Justice Darling was so blinded by prejudice that he could not bring himself to realize that neither Wilde nor Douglas ever 'gloried' in 'the crime of sodomy', nor was Wilde ever accused of it—otherwise he would have risked a life sentence on conviction. One wonders what the judge would have said had he lived to see the dawn of the 'delightful epoch', at the prospect of which he expressed such disgust. But this was half a century distant, and like Henry Labouchere, Mr Justice Darling died long before the publication of the Wolfenden Report and its legislative results. Otherwise he might have had an apoplectic fit.

Although it is true that Mr Justice Darling endeavoured to dis-
abuse the minds of the jury in the Pemberton Billing trial that
they were trying Oscar Wilde and his play rather than the
defendant's libel upon Maud Allan, the result would most probably have been the same however the jury regarded the case,
since the judge made it clear that he disapproved both of Miss
Allan's style of dancing and her opinion of Wilde, whom she
had described in the witness box as a great artist. ('Well, gentlemen, it is possible to regard him as a great artist, but he certainly
was a great beast; there is no doubt about that.') The defendant
stated that he had nothing against Miss Allan in her private
character and indeed it was never suggested that she was a
lesbian, although she may well have had lesbian tastes. But the
dancer never had a chance with the jury, who viewed Pemberton
Billing in the light of a national hero and were determined to
acquit him if they possibly could. It took them just over an hour
to find him not guilty—in other words, that what he had published about Maud Allan was true and that it was in the public
interest that he should have done so.

The announcement of this palpable miscarriage of justice was
wildly cheered by the spectators in court, and Pemberton Billing
was given a similarly tumultuous ovation by the crowd waiting
outside when he emerged a free man. But for the unprecedented
temper of the times, it seems safe to say that this ardent anti-
homosexual campaigner would have been convicted of criminally
libelling a distinguished artiste, against whom no evidence of
lesbian proclivities had been adduced, although there seems no
doubt that she was homosexual.

[2]

Shortly after Pemberton Billing's acquittal, an attempt was
made in Parliament to penalize lesbians in the same way as male
homosexuals had been penalized by the Labouchere Amendment.
In 1921 a new Criminal Law Amendment Bill was introduced
into the House of Commons and passed through all its stages. It
differed from the 1885 Act in that it was a Private Member's
measure, but since the Government approved of its primary
purpose, which was to give a further measure of protection to
children and young people, it provided the Bill's backbench
sponsors with the necessary parliamentary time to facilitate its
passage through the Lower House. Pemberton Billing had just

retired from Parliament through ill-health, or otherwise, no doubt, he would have been in the forefront of the move made to amend the law. It was during the report stage, after the Bill had been considered by a standing committee, that a Scottish Conservative lawyer and son of the manse, Frederick Macquisten, who represented one of the Glasgow divisions, moved the following new clause under the heading of 'Acts of indecency by females':

> Any act of gross indecency between female persons shall be a misdemeanour and punishable in the same manner as any such act committed by male persons under section eleven of the Criminal Law Amendment Act, 1885.

'It is long overdue in the criminal code of this country,' said Mr Macquisten of the proposed new clause, adding that he had had professional experience of 'very calamitous and sad cases due to gross practices indulged in of the kind specified' in it. 'These moral weaknesses date back to the very origin of history,' he went on, 'and when they grow and become prevalent in any nation or in any country, it is the beginning of the nation's downfall. The falling away of feminine morality was to a large extent the cause of the destruction of the early Grecian civilization, and still more the cause of the downfall of the Roman Empire.'

Having delivered himself of this fallacious misreading of history, Mr Macquisten observed that 'there is in modern social life an undercurrent of dreadful degradation, unchecked and uninterfered with. I believe that if the sanction—that is the punishment—of the law were imposed upon it, it would go a long way to check it, and I believe that it would be possible to do a great deal in that way to eradicate it.' In the course of his experience, he continued, he had seen happy homes wrecked in this way. Only that night he had been speaking to a recent acquaintance who told him how his home had been ruined by 'the wiles of one abandoned female, who had pursued his wife'. Later some other misconduct happened with a male person which enabled him to get a divorce. 'But for that he would have been shackled for life to that abandoned person, who had forgotten all the dictates of Nature and morality.' He enlarged upon what he called 'this horrid grossness of homosexual immorality', which he felt it was the duty of the law-givers to grapple with. 'It is only right that this House, which has the care of the law and to a large extent the morals of the people,' he concluded, 'should consider it to be its duty to do its best to stamp out an evil which is capable of sapping the highest and best in civilization.'

In the short debate which followed, Mr Macquisten was strongly supported by a fellow lawyer and future judge, Sir Ernest Wild, who described the clause as 'simply an attempt to grapple with a very real evil'. He went on:

I can quite understand that many Members of this House, whose good fortune it is not to have to know about these things, may hesitate to believe that such things do take place. If they were to consult any neurologist, any great doctor who deals with nerve diseases, they would soon be told that this is a very prevalent practice. I have the authority of one of the greatest of our nerve specialists—I do not wish to mention names—who has told me with his own lips that no week passes but some unfortunate girl does not confess to him that she owes the breakdown of her nerves to the fact that she has been tampered with by a member of her own sex.

We do not want to pollute the House with details of these abominations. I have consulted many asylum doctors and they assure me that the asylums are largely peopled by nymphomaniacs and people who indulge in this vice. I have also consulted the criminologists, and they say that these practices take place. . . . If you consult chief officers of the police you will find the same thing. In one case I was told of a case similar to the one told to the House by Mr Macquisten, where a man said the whole of his married life was ruined because his wife had been taken from him by a young woman. It is idle to deny, although I will not say the vice is rampant in society, that there are people in society who are guilty of it.

. . . This vice does exist, and it saps the fundamental institutions of society. In the first place it stops child-birth because it is a well-known fact that any woman who indulges in this vice will have nothing whatever to do with the other sex. It debauches young girls, and it produces neurasthenia and insanity. Anyone who is really interested in the punishment of vice would desire that the law should be clothed with power which can only be exercised if there be proper proof to put down a vice that must cause our race to decline.

On the other hand, Colonel Josiah Wedgwood, later Lord Wedgwood, then a Labour Member, whose recent divorce case had created a considerable public stir, opposed the clause vigorously. 'You cannot make people moral by Act of Parliament,' he pointed out. Anyhow, he asked, how on earth could convictions be obtained if the law was to be altered in this sense?

'For one conviction that could be got in ten years, you may have, on the other hand, endless blackmail. . . . This clause must inevitably involve far more blackmail than any other suggestion that has ever been made for an addition to the criminal law.' Wedgwood was supported by the Conservative Lieutenant-Colonel J. T. C. Moore-Brabazon, later Lord Brabazon of Tara, best known as a pioneer motorist and aviator, who begged the House to remember that on this subject they were not dealing with crime at all. 'We are dealing with abnormalities of the brain, and we have got to look on all these cases from that point of view. We want to decide whether it is wise to deal with mental cases in the Law Courts. If we do so, and are to go on logical lines, we should soon be introducing measures into this House to give penal servitude for life to the hermaphrodite.' Colonel Moore-Brabazon did not think that lesbian practices did 'very much harm to society at large', and accordingly he urged the House to leave the question alone and drop the clause.

However, the House did not heed this advice and shortly before midnight on August 4, 1921 proceeded on a free vote to pass the clause by 148 votes to 53. It is worth noting that the only woman member of the house at that time, the American-born Viscountess Astor, voted with the minority, although she did not speak in the debate. Two future Conservative Prime Ministers, Stanley Baldwin and Winston Churchill, as well as a future Conservative Minister of Education, Lord Eustace Percy, and the leading authority on materia medica, Sir William Whitla, also voted with the minority. The less enlightened majority included the leading lay churchman Lord Robert Cecil, later Lord Cecil of Chelwood, and the two Chamberlain brothers, Austen and Neville, the latter likewise a future Conservative premier.[1]

The Bill was thereupon sent to the House of Lords, and there the new clause received short shrift. Its rejection was moved by the Earl of Malmesbury, member of a well-known political family connected for generations with public affairs. He argued that the clause went beyond the scope of the original Bill, and in the select committee which had recommended its initial provisions no evidence had been given on it. He would only support it, if he were convinced it were needed after careful inquiry, which had not so far taken place. 'There is ample time and ample scope for legislation to be introduced on this subject into the House at an early date,' he said, 'and I am not going to believe that the whole

[1] Hansard. *House of Commons Debates.* Vol. 145, cols. 1799–1807 (August 4, 1921).

morality of this country is going to be abandoned because a few
months delay takes place before further legislation of this sort
can be introduced.' He went on:

> Let me point out to your Lordships that in passing a clause
> of this sort you are going to do a great deal more harm than
> good. You are going enormously to increase the chance of
> blackmail, without in the slightest degree decreasing the
> amount of this vice. I think your Lordships will bear me out
> when I say—and it requires some moral courage to discuss a
> subject of this sort—that the domestic habits of men and of
> women are entirely different. Women are by nature much more
> gregarious. For instance, if twenty women were going to live
> in a house with twenty bedrooms, I do not believe that all the
> twenty bedrooms would be occupied, either for reasons of fear
> or nervousness, and the desire for mutual protection. On the
> other hand, I know that when men take shooting boxes the
> first inquiry is that each shall have a room to himself if
> possible; and a comfortable room too.

Lord Malmesbury was earnestly supported by the Earl of
Desart, a former Director of Public Prosecutions—as the Hon.
Hamilton Cuffe, he had started the proceedings against Oscar
Wilde. He pointed out that the clause had been introduced at a
late hour in the House of Commons. It was not discussed at
length, and it was supported by a small number of members
relative to the normal size of the House. This was not unusual,
but in a matter of this kind he suggested that it was not immaterial.
A clause altering the criminal law, creating a new offence of this
gravity, he said, should be introduced with the full responsibility,
if introduced at all, of the government, after full consultation
with their law officers and the police authorities. They were in
possession of information which could not be at the disposal of
private members of either House of Parliament.

Lord Desart went on to emphasize the possibilities of blackmail and its consequences.

> It is very disagreeable talking about these things, but we all
> know of the sort of romantic, almost hysterical friendships
> that are made between young women at certain periods of their
> lives and of its occasional manifestations. Suppose that some
> circumstance gave to some young person who knew of it the
> idea: 'How easy it now is for me to make a charge. Perhaps they
> do not know what the law is.' Do you suppose any woman

with anything in the world to lose would ever face such a charge as that? It would not be a question of defending themselves against it, it would be a question of facing it, of being brought into a public Court to meet a charge of that kind. They would pay anything sooner than that. I believe that blackmail would not only be certain, but that it would inevitably be successful. . . .

Suppose there was a prosecution, as there might be. In my judgment the results would be even more appalling. It would be made public to thousands of people that there was this offence; and there was such a horror. It would be widely read. We know the sort of publicity that sort of thing gets, and it cannot be stopped.

At this point the speaker interjected a reference to a celebrated prosecution for a homosexual offence. Although he did not mention the accused by name, there can be no doubt that it was Wilde he had in mind.

If I may draw on my own experience, I should like to tell your Lordships of the case of another offence of a horrible character that is already on the Statute Book. I remember one which attracted very great public attention. At that time I had access to the Chief Constable's reports of all the counties and towns in England. After that prosecution there was, for about eighteen months, according to my recollection, a perfect outburst of that offence all through the country.

I am sure that a prosecution would really be a very great public danger. Is there any necessity for it? How many people does one suppose really are so vile, so unbalanced, so neurotic, so decadent as to do this? You may say there are a number of them but it would be, at most, an extremely small minority, and you are going to tell the whole world that there is such an offence, to bring it to the notice of women who have never heard of it, never thought of it, never dreamed of it. I think that is a very great mischief, and I came here determined to do all I could to help my noble friend, Lord Malmesbury, to get this clause removed from the Bill.

It only remained for the Lord Chancellor, Lord Birkenhead, to deliver the *coup-de-grâce*.

If you except a sophisticated society in a sophisticated city [he declared from the Woolsack] I would be bold enough to say that of every thousand women, taken as a whole, 999 have never even heard a whisper of these practices. Amongst all these, in the homes of this country, where, in all innocence, and very often as a necessary consequence of the shortage of small houses, they have to have the same bedroom, and even sleep together in the same beds, the taint of this noxious and horrible suspicion is to be imparted, and to be imparted by the Legislature itself, without one scintilla of evidence that there is any widespread practice of this kind of vice.

The Bishop of Norfolk, who had formally moved the acceptance of the clause at the beginning of the debate, now admitted that he had been convinced by the arguments of its opponents. Consequently there was no vote, and Lord Malmesbury's motion was in effect carried without a division.[1] The House of Commons made no attempt to reintroduce the clause either then or on any subsequent occasion.

[3]

In the past there had been cases of strongly emotional friendships between women in England, and where the individuals belonged to well-known families the attachment naturally provoked comment, the more charitable critics attributing it to a mutual desire for companionship and the sharing of common interests. Pioneers in this type of lesbian relationship were two Irishwomen, Lady Eleanor Butler, whose brother was Earl of Ormonde, and Miss Sarah Ponsonby, a cousin of the Earl of Bessborough. They became friends at school in Ireland in the second half of the eighteenth century and after an unsuccessful 'elopement' they were brought home in disgrace and forbidden to correspond with or see each other. But their relatives eventually relented and agreed that they could live together, providing them with a minute allowance. They settled in a cottage in the Vale of Llangollen in north Wales, where they spent their time in what Lady Eleanor, the elder and masculine member of the partnership, called 'sweetly enjoyed retirement'. 'The Ladies of Llangollen', as they were universally known,—sometimes they were called 'The Platonists'—became the two most celebrated virgins in Europe and were visited by many public and literary figures of the time, including Sir Walter Scott, Wordsworth, De Quincey, Madame de Genlis, the Duke of Wellington and Lord Castle-

[1] Hansard. *House of Lords Debates*. Vol. 46, cols. 567–77 (August 15, 1921).

reagh. It was Castlereagh who provided Madame de Genlis and her pupil Mlle d'Orléans with an introduction to the 'Ladies', as the result of a conversation in 1788 in which the French woman writer and educationalist had said that she would willingly undertake a long journey for the sake of seeing two persons who had long been united in a sincere bond of this quality. 'Then, madame,' Castlereagh told her, 'you should go to Llangollen, where you will see a model of perfect friendship between two young women who are in every respect charming.' Lady Eleanor, who was ten years older than her friend, invariably wore men's clothes, and from the reference in the journal she kept to 'our bed' it is clear that they slept together. Until the elder of the 'Ladies' died in 1829, neither left their cottage for a single night throughout the fifty years that they lived together.[1]

Eleanor Butler and Sarah Ponsonby were regarded by their contemporaries as eccentrics who preferred each other's company to getting married and having children. But it was never suggested by any of their visitors who left accounts of the Llangollen establishment that there was anything improper in the relationship. It was otherwise with two Englishwomen who set up house together a century later and were to become as notorious in their way as the Ladies of Llangollen had been 'celebrated'— namely, Radclyffe Hall and Lady (Una) Troubridge. Radclyffe Hall—known to her family and friends as John—was a writer of distinction and she had already been the recipient of several literary prizes before the appearance, in 1928, of her controversial novel *The Well of Loneliness*. Una Troubridge, with whom the novelist had been living for the past dozen years, was the daughter of Captain Harry Taylor, a King's Messenger in the Foreign Service, and her grandfather on her mother's side was the Irish peer Lord Monteagle. Her husband, Admiral Sir Ernest Troubridge, whose second wife she was, was nearly twice her age, and after a short unhappy marriage, in the course of which she bore him a daughter, they separated in 1915. At this date Lady Troubridge was twenty-eight and Radclyffe Hall, whom she met shortly after she left her husband and came to live in London, was thirty-four and for some years had been in love with a much older married woman named Mabel Batten, well known socially as a patroness of young musicians like Mischa Elman and Percy Grainger. For Una Troubridge it was a case of

---

[1] Lady Eleanor Butler died in 1829 and Sarah Ponsonby two years later. See G. H. Bell (ed.). *The Hamwood Papers of the Ladies of Llangollen and Lady Caroline Hamilton* (1931).

love at first sight. 'I was swept along on a spate of feeling, of learning the endless aspects of this strange personality,' she was to confess long afterwards, 'and all I knew or cared about was that I could not, once having come to know her, imagine life without her.' Fortunately for both of them, the existence of a lesbian *ménage à trois* was rendered unnecessary by Mrs Batten's sudden death a few months later from a heart attack.

Written as fiction, *The Well of Loneliness* was to a considerable extent autobiographical, the heroine Stephen Gordon being like her authoress the only child of solid county parents who dearly wanted a son, given a boy's name and brought up as if she had been a boy. Stephen's emotional experiences were described coolly and sympathetically, and the whole formed a sincere and dignified plea for the toleration of lesbian relationships in English society. 'I wrote the book from a deep sense of duty,' Radclyffe Hall explained at the time. 'I am proud indeed to have taken up my pen in defence of those who are utterly defenceless, who being from birth a people set apart in accordance with some hidden scheme of Nature, need all the help that society can give them.' Havelock Ellis, who wrote a brief foreword to the novel, described it as possessing a notable psychological and sociological significance:

So far as I know [he observed] it is the first English novel which presents, in a completely faithful and uncompromising form, one particular aspect of sexual life as it exists among us today. The relation of certain people—who while different from their fellow human beings, are sometimes of the highest character and the highest aptitudes—to the often hostile society in which they move, presents difficult and still unsolved problems. The poignant situations which thus arise are here set forth so vividly, and yet with such complete absence of offence, that we must place Radclyffe Hall's book on a high level of distinction.

Another writer to whom the book made an immediate appeal was Radclyffe Hall's friend and fellow novelist Naomi Jacob, who bought it on the day of publication and 'found its sincerity very touching and fine'. Miss Jacob, who lived at Sirmione on Lake Garda and kept Pekingese dogs, made no secret of her own lesbianism. According to Vera Brittain, 'her style of dressing was far more aggressively masculine than that of Radclyffe Hall; she wore dress suits in the evening, and few men had a greater addiction to the whisky bottle'. One of the original suffragettes,

Naomi Jacob had been in charge of a munitions factory during the First World War before she emigrated to Italy, where she spent her time writing two novels a year, 'telling people how to cook', lecturing on the theatre and literature, 'working for the animals' cause', and never taking exercise. Reading *The Well of Loneliness* when she did, Miss Jacob wrote afterwards, 'it would never have occurred to me that there was a single sentence or phrase which could be criticized on the ground of being immoral or offensive'.

The novel attracted a number of favourable reviews, notably by Arnold Bennett, who praised it in the London *Evening Standard*. Unfortunately a puritanical journalist named James Douglas took a contrary view and attacked it with characteristic invective in a sensational article in the *Sunday Express*.[1] 'It is a seductive and insidious piece of special pleading designed to display perverted decadence as a martyrdom inflicted upon those outcasts by a cruel society,' Mr Douglas fulminated. 'It flings a veil of sentiment over their depravity. It even suggests that their self-made debasement is unavoidable because they cannot save themselves . . . I would rather put a phial of prussic acid in the hands of a healthy girl or boy than the book in question . . . What then is to be done? The book must be at once withdrawn.'

On the advice of the Home Secretary, Mr William Joynson-Hicks, who held equally puritanical views, the publishers withdrew the book, hoping to forestall prosecution. However, publication was continued in Paris and copies imported into Britain. The next step was for the Director of Public Prosecutions to apply to the Chief Magistrate for an order for the destruction of any copies of the book 'held for sale or distribution by the publishers' on the grounds that it was an obscene publication. Since the case was brought against the publishers, on whom the onus lay to show cause why the copies in their possession should not be forfeited and destroyed, Radclyffe Hall was not a party to the proceedings. But, needless to say, she took an intense interest in them and was present in court throughout with her friend Lady Troubridge.

The Chief Inspector from Scotland Yard, who had bought a copy of the book in the normal way, gave evidence to the effect that he considered the whole theme offensive because it dealt with physical passion. 'The book is indecent because it deals with an indecent subject.'

[1] *Sunday Express.* August 19, 1928.

The defence was led by Norman Birkett, later the well-known judge, and then at the height of his powers as an advocate. *The Well of Loneliness*, he said, was concerned not with perversion but with what the medical profession called inversion, that is emotions and desires which with most people are directed towards the opposite sex but in this instance are directed towards their own.

'Do you mean to say,' the magistrate asked, 'it does not deal with unnatural offences at all?'

'I say not,' replied counsel. 'Nowhere is there an obscene word or a lascivious passage. It is a sombre, sad, tragic, artistic revelation of that which is an undoubted fact in this world. It is the result of years of labour by one of the most distinguished novelists alive, and it is a sincere and high-minded effort to make the world more tolerable for those who have to bear the tragic consequences of what they are not to blame for at all.' Birkett went on to refer to the views of the literary critics, 'which constitute a chorus of praise from those qualified to speak upon matters affecting literature in general', adding that there were in court 'people of every walk of life who desire to go into the witness box and to testify that this book is not obscene and that it is a misuse of words for the prosecution to describe it as such'.

As the law of obscenity then was in England, such evidence was inadmissible, and the magistrate was bound to refuse to hear it. At the same time he left no doubt in the minds of the publishers and the author what he thought of the book. 'There is not one word which suggests that anyone with the horrible tendencies described is in the least degree blameworthy. All the characters are presented as attractive people and put forward with admiration. What is more serious is that certain acts are described in alluring terms.' When the magistrate went on to refer to a passage describing how 'some women of standing and position, engaged as ambulance drivers at the front', in the First World War, were, as he put it, 'addicted to these practices', Miss Hall could contain herself no longer and protested loudly, for which the magistrate threatened to have her removed if she could not behave herself.

In giving judgment, the magistrate had no hesitation in finding that *The Well of Loneliness* was obscene, and he accordingly made the necessary destruction order. His decision was upheld on appeal, when the judge of the superior court described the book as 'most dangerous and corrupting'.

A number of leading writers publicly protested against the banning of Radclyffe Hall's book in a letter which they jointly addressed to the principal Liberal daily newspaper in the country. They included Bernard Shaw, Rose Macaulay, John Buchan, Arnold Bennett, Lytton Strachey and Laurence Binyon.[1] Nevertheless more than twenty years were to elapse before any publisher dared to defy the ban. But when the book was re-published in England after the Second World War, no attempt was made by the authorities to enforce the ban. 'It is an indication of the world of rapid change in which we live and of the vagaries of taste,' wrote Norman Birkett, by then Lord Justice Birkett, 'that *The Well of Loneliness* is now on sale in every bookshop without the slightest interference from the police or the Director of Public Prosecutions or anybody else. The phials of prussic acid can be taken freely without apparent injury to the citizen or the State.'

Meanwhile the book had come out without any trouble in America, where it had quite a triumph. Following its initial re-publication in Paris, it was translated into eleven languages and sold a million copies in the author's lifetime. Unfortunately Radclyffe Hall did not live to see it again on sale in her native country, since she died of cancer during the war. Throughout her long and painful last illness, she was nursed with touching devotion by the faithful Una Troubridge, who afterwards wrote a moving account of their deep and rare friendship. 'God keep you until we meet again . . . and believe in my love which is much, much stronger than mere death . . .'[2]

The official view at the time of the prosecution of *The Well of Loneliness* seems to have been that it was all right to introduce lesbian associations into a novel provided that they were either condemned, as in Naomi Royde-Smith's *The Tortoiseshell Cat*, or else satirized, as Compton Mackenzie had done in *Extraordinary Women*. Mackenzie's hilarious tale of the lesbian love affairs of the expatriate inhabitants of the island of Capri appeared at the height of the public outcry over *The Well of Loneliness*, and the author was rather hoping that his book would likewise be prosecuted, as he planned to appear for his own defence, which would have enabled him to cross-examine the Crown witnesses and raise some 'good laughs' at the expense of the puritanical Home Secretary and his minions. But the authorities decided, no doubt wisely, not to prosecute. This in turn prompted

---

[1] *Manchester Guardian*, November 22, 1928. See also for details of the trial the present writer's *Norman Birkett* (1964), 254–60, and *Radclyffe Hall a Case of Obscenity* by Vera Brittain (1968), 84–138.

[2] Una Lady Troubridge. *The Life and Death of Radclyffe Hall* (1961). Lady Troubridge survived her friend by twenty years and died in 1963.

the Labour *Daily Herald* to call upon the Home Secretary 'to explain why he had suppressed an earnest and serious book like *The Well of Loneliness* and not taken proceedings against *Extraordinary Women* which treated the theme with "cynical flippancy" '.[1]

In the prevailing literary climate of the time, no publisher dared to bring out a further book devoted to a compassionate treatment of lesbianism as its main theme. It had to be done more subtly and incidentally. Two women who treated it in this way were Virginia Woolf in *Mrs Dalloway* (1925) and *To the Lighthouse* (1927), and Victoria Sackville-West in *The Dark Island* (1934). Clarissa Dalloway with her feeling for Sally Seton and Shirin le Breton with her feeling for Christina Rich bear a striking mutual resemblance. *Mrs Dalloway* is admittedly autobiographical, and it is conceivable that the character of Sally may have been based, at least partly, on Miss Sackville-West (Lady Nicolson) with whom Mrs Woolf was on terms of intimate friendship.

> The strange thing, on looking back, was the purity, the integrity, of her feeling for Sally. It was not like one's feeling for a man. It was protective on her side; sprang from a sense of being in league together, a presentiment of something that was bound to part them (they always spoke of marriage as a catastrophe), which led to this chivalry. . . .
>
> [Sally] stood by the fireplace talking, in that beautiful voice which made everything she said sound like a caress . . . when suddenly she said, 'What a shame to sit indoors!' and they all went out on to the terrace and walked up and down. She and Sally fell a little behind. Then came the most exquisite moment of her whole life passing a stone urn with flowers in it. Sally stopped; picked a flower; kissed her on the lips. The whole world might have turned upside down!

Similarly, in *To the Lighthouse*, there is a poignancy about Lily Briscoe's longing for the older Mrs Ramsey ('to want and want and not to have'), which the latter misunderstands when she urges Lily to marry. Lytton Strachey, a conspicuous member of the so-called 'Bloomsbury set', of which Virginia Woolf and her husband Leonard were the central figures, preferred *To the Lighthouse* to *Mrs Dalloway*, although he failed to understand it fully. 'It is the lack of copulation—either actual or implied—that worries me,' he told a friend after he had read it. 'I suppose there is some symbolism about the lighthouse etc.—but I can't guess

[1] Sir Compton Mackenzie. *My Life and Times Octave Six* (1967), 148.

what it is. With anyone else, the suggestion would be fairly obvious, but it won't fit into the sexless pattern by any manner of means.'[1]

Most remarkable of all in the context of her relationship with Victoria Sackville-West was Virginia Woolf's fantasy novel *Orlando*, which appeared in the same year as *The Well of Loneliness* and *Extraordinary Women*. The name character is a timeless individual, alternately male and female ('She enjoyed the love of both sexes . . . for her sex changed far more frequently than those who have worn only one set of clothing can conceive'), who is introduced as a page at the court of the first Queen Elizabeth and after a number of metamorphoses in different ages is finally left as a woman of thirty-six in 1928, married to a literary traveller who is often absent from home on his adventurous voyages, while leaving Orlando free to 'write and write' and win literary prizes. The latter description exactly fits Victoria Sackville-West, who was busy writing novels at this time, while her husband Harold Nicolson held various diplomatic posts abroad. The descriptions of Orlando's ancestral home with their accompanying illustrations are plainly based on Knole, the great Elizabethan property in Kent where Victoria Sackville-West was brought up and which she would have inherited with the title of Lord Sackville, had she been a boy, as indeed she often regretted. Victoria Sackville-West helped to choose the pictures from Knole for Orlando ('That book sounds more fantastic the more I hear of it!') and she later accepted the original manuscript of the work for permanent display at Knole, where it is now on public view.[2]

[4]

Towards the end of his life, Somerset Maugham confessed to his nephew Robin that the greatest mistake he had ever made was trying to persuade himself that he 'was three-quarters normal and that only one quarter of me was queer—whereas really it was the other way round'. No doubt only a small fraction of the immense following which enjoyed his novels and plays were aware of his homosexual tastes, but of course the fact was known to those in authority who recommend the award by the sovereign of

[1] Michael Holroyd. *Lytton Strachey* (1967-8), II, 531.
[2] Harold Nicolson. *Diaries and Letters 1930-39.* ed. Nigel Nicolson (1966) 32, 350; *Diaries and Letters 1939-45* (1967), 157; *Diaries and Letters 1945-62* (1968), 247.

honours for services to literature. There can be no other reason why William Somerset Maugham had to wait until the occasion of his eightieth birthday to receive his first and only such award, Companion of Honour, an Order of comparatively recent foundation which carries with it no title, ranks below that of knighthood, and is usually given to retired politicians and generals. He was already established as a novelist and dramatist half a century previously when he had four plays running in London at the same time, and the least he might have expected was to be dubbed a knight by the time he was fifty.

Not only did Maugham's homosexuality delay official recognition of his literary merits, but it ruined his marriage and resulted in his living outside England for long periods. His *éminence grise* was a young American about half his age named Gerald Haxton, whom he met while serving in a Red Cross ambulance unit in France early in the First World War, and who was to become his secretary and constant companion until his death thirty years later. In 1915, Haxton came to London, where he was arrested on an indecency charge. He was duly tried and acquitted. Shortly afterwards he was deported as 'an undesirable alien' and was never allowed to return to England. Travers Humphreys, later the well-known judge, who prosecuted at Haxton's trial, was convinced that he was guilty; indeed it is possible that Humphreys was responsible for his deportation. 'He's a bad lot,' Humphreys told Robin Maugham some years later. 'I can't see what your uncle sees in him.'[1]

Somerset Maugham was devoted to Gerald Haxton and would hear no ill of him in spite of his fecklessness (he was a forger and a cheat), his reckless gambling and drunken exploits such as diving into the empty swimming pool at Maugham's Riviera villa, a feat which did not noticeably improve his stability. On the other hand, as Robin Maugham points out, one of the less endearing features in his uncle's character was that he was socially ambitious and this led him to keep up a heterosexual pretence in public to the end of his life. In his final work of autobiography, *Looking Back*, Somerset Maugham put all the blame for the failure of his marriage on his divorced wife, while at the same time dismissing Gerald Haxton as merely 'a very useful companion' who accompanied him on his travels.

Beverley Nichols, who knew both men well and had many

[1] Robin Maugham *Somerset and all the Maughams* (1966), 36–7, 201. Somerset Maugham's *A Writer's Notebook* (1949) was dedicated: 'In Loving Memory of My Friend FREDERICK GERALD HAXTON, 1891–1944.'

opportunities of observing their relationship in action, has described it in a short book he wrote in defence of Mrs Syrie Maugham, whose memory her husband had so bitterly and brutally traduced.

There was something akin to black magic in Gerald's domination, something uncanny in the way in which he caused the Master to dance to his tune—sometimes, quite literally, with a flick of his fingers, summoning him across a crowded room to replenish his cocktail glass, when he knew, and I knew, and everybody else knew, that by obeying him the Master was performing an act of public humiliation, even as he tipped the cocktail-shaker. There were the two of them. The handsome young man, lolling in his arm-chair, with one bare leg thrown over the arm, holding up his glass, demanding his poison. The ageing genius, standing before him, pouring out the libation, as if he were making a sacrifice to a young god whom, in his heart of hearts, he despised even while he loved him, whom he feared, even while the whip was in his hands.[1]

By way of contrast there were other homosexual expatriate writers, like Norman Douglas and C. R. Scott-Moncrieff who nurtured no such ambition and were content to live their lives with their boy friends in the sunshine of Florence or Capri unconcerned by any censorious critics. In 1916 Norman Douglas, who had spent the previous five years in England mainly as assistant editor of *The English Review*, volunteered for war work. Humbert Wolfe was deputed by the authorities to tell him 'that he had the alternative of getting out of England at once or of facing arrest on a certain charge'. Douglas withdrew to the Continent, where he wrote his best-known novel, *South Wind*, first published in 1917, and he did not return to England for a quarter of a century.[2]

Notable literary-cum-political observers at this time are conspicuously silent on the subject of the homosexual tastes of their fellow writers and others in the public eye. Two such observers whose names readily come to mind are Harold Nicolson, who was married to Victoria Sackville-West, and Henry ('Chips') Channon, both writers and Members of Parliament and movers in high society. They both kept diaries, but in these documents, or at any rate in the carefully edited versions as published, which 'take us as it were on an immense tour of London society between the two

[1] Beverley Nichols. *A Case of Human Bondage* (1966), 144–5.
[2] Richard Aldington. *Pinorman* (1954), 148.

World Wars', to quote Mr Goronwy Rees, a member of the
Wolfenden Committee, 'none of the sights are omitted except one
of the most prominent features of the landscape'. Incidentally in
the matter of honours they did rather better than Somerset
Maugham; both were knighted, though they both wanted peerages
and were disappointed at not getting them. Not only are Nicolson
and Channon noticeably reticent about the sex lives of expatriates
like Maugham, but they likewise ignore domestic resident writers
such as E. F. Benson and Sir Edward Marsh, 'the little squeaky'
who was a close friend of Ivor Novello. Indeed the Channon
diaries are so discreetly edited that the few sexual references leave
the less knowledgeable reader in doubt as to what is meant. For
instance, when Channon met Maugham in 1950, the latter 'twitted'
him about his sex life, 'or apparent lack of it', and later in the same
year, when Channon was staying at Maugham's villa in the south
of France, the diarist simply recorded that his host 'has had a long
amorous career, and now at 75 is still lusty', and left it at that.[1] One
also searches in vain for any revealing references among the official
biographies of the period, like Sir Rupert Hart-Davis's life of the
novelist Hugh Walpole and Sir Roy Harrod's life of the economist
Lord Keynes, to the homosexual activities of their subjects. Nor
does Laurence Housman, in his memoir of his brother A. E. Housman, the homosexual poet and Cambridge don, say anything more
about the latter's feelings for his friend Adalbert Jackson other
than quoting his brother as saying that Jackson was 'the man who
had more influence on my life then anybody else'. (Like J. A.
Symonds, Housman also befriended a gondolier in Venice.) The
disappearance of this reticence broadly coincided with the repeal
of the Labouchere amendment in 1967 and the legalization of
homosexual acts between consenting male adults. The pioneer in
the new style of official biography who was to reveal the subject's
feelings and actions in considerable detail was Michael Holroyd in
his massive study of Lytton Strachey and his times.

Giles Lytton Strachey, who established a brilliant reputation
as the biographer of Queen Victoria and four of her 'eminent'
contemporaries with a peculiarly subtle, ironic and disillusioning
method of writing, was the son of a peppery general in the Indian
Army, Sir Richard Strachey, who was also a scientist, explorer,
botanist, engineer and mathematician. Strachey's forbears, both

[1] Goronwy Rees. 'A Case for Treatment: The World of Lytton Strachey' in
Encounter (March 1968), at p. 81. *Chips: The Diaries of Sir Henry Channon*, ed.
R. Rhodes James (1967), pp. 416, 436. Mr Nigel Nicolson, who has edited his
father's diaries, informs me that there are no references to homosexuality in the
unpublished portions.

on his father's and mother's side, were very much men and women of the stamp of heroic 'deeds that won the Empire'. His homosexual inclinations, which may have been part of an instinctive and unconscious reaction against this family tradition, were already pronounced by the time he went up to Cambridge, in 1899. He found that there were many undergraduates who shared his interests, particularly in the Cambridge Conversazione Society, better known as the Apostles, of which he eventually became secretary. 'The members—past and present—are sufficiently distinguished,' he wrote to his mother on becoming an Apostle. So also, he might have added, was Tennyson's dearest friend Arthur Hallam, whose premature death evoked *In Memoriam*, which had originally appeared anonymously and incurred the censure of *The Times* for its tone and content. Prominent among the Apostles was the future economist John Maynard Keynes, who competed strongly with Strachey for the favours of their good-looking contemporaries. Theirs was indeed a curious comedy of sexual or rather homosexual errors, as Strachey's latest biographer discloses in the extraordinary correspondence which passed between Strachey and Keynes, 'surely one of the oddest that has ever been published between two men of such distinction', as Goronwy Rees rightly observed. 'Reading it even today one cannot but be taken slightly aback by the unabashed frankness with which the two friends and rivals reveal the physical and erotic basis of their interest in the young men who successively captured their attention,' a process in which Keynes usually came off best. Strachey's greatest passion was for his cousin Duncan Grant, whose lips he described as 'incomparably lascivious'. 'I've managed since I saw you last to catch a glimpse of Heaven,' Strachey wrote to Keynes on August 3, 1905. 'Incredible, quite—yet so it's happened—I want to go into the wilderness of the world, and preach an infinitude of sermons on one text—"Embrace one another". It seems to me the grand solution. Oh, dear, dear, dear, how wild, how violent, and how supreme are the things of this earth! I am cloudy, I fear almost sentimental. . . . Oh yes, it's Duncan.'

It came as a terrible shock when he learned that not only was Keynes in love with Grant but Grant was in love with Keynes. 'Though I like Maynard, I cannot think of him as you do,' Strachey told Grant at this time, 'or else, I suppose, I should be in love with him too! . . . Oh lord, lord, why do we live in such a distorted coagulated world? I feel all topsy-turvy and out of place, as if I were a pocket handkerchief that somebody had dropped on the top of Mont Blanc. It's all too preposterous, and what's worse, I'm well aware that I do very little but add to the preposterousness.' Yet Strachey himself was by no means enamoured of the physical side of homosexual affiliations, certainly if it were not accompanied by genuine affection and companionship. 'I know there's a sort of passion—an animal feeling,' he wrote, 'a passion without affection, which is merely bodily pleasure, and doesn't count.'[1]

Duncan Grant's place in Strachey's affections were eventually filled by the artist Henry Lamb, whom he met through Lady Ottoline Morrell. The latter had been born a Cavendish-Bentinck and was descended from the first Earl of Portland, the homosexual Dutchman who had accompanied his homosexual master William III when the latter took over the English throne, becoming notorious as the king's catamite. Once when Lady Ottoline had carried Lamb off to the country under Strachey's 'very nose', he was left 'wishing that Dutch William and his friends had never come to England'. Unlike Victoria Sackville-West, who hated 'the drooping Lytton' for having, as she thought, done the 'cause of the Bloomsbury group a great deal of harm', Ottoline Morrell found him 'a charming companion—his feminine quality making him sympathetic and interested in the small things of life'.[2]

At this time his devotion to Henry Lamb was very great, and tossing him about on a sea of emotion. Lamb enjoyed leading him forth into new fields of experience. They would sit in pubs and mix with 'the lower orders', as Lytton called them, picking up strange friends. And so great is the imitative instinct in the human breast that he even altered his appearance to please Lamb, wearing his hair very long, like Augustus John, and having his ears pierced and wearing ear-rings. He discarded collars and wore only a rich purple silk scarf round his neck, fastened with an intaglio pin. They were a surprising pair as they walked the streets of London, as Lamb wore clothes of the 1860 period with a square brown hat, Lytton a large black Carlyle felt hat and a black Italian cape.

Homosexuality in others particularly interested him. Some years later he chanced to read the first detailed account of the

[1] Michael Holroyd. *Lytton Strachey. The Unknown Years* (1967), 226, 262, 342. Strachey's erotic *Ermyntrude and Esmeralda* was written to amuse Lamb in 1913.
[2] Harold Nicolson. *Diaries and Letters 1930–1939*. ed. Nigel Nicolson 351. Lady Ottoline Morrell. *Early Memoirs*, ed. Robert Gathorne-Hardy (1963), 214–15.

Wilde trials, which had been anonymously edited by Christopher Millard. 'It is very interesting and depressing,' he noted. 'One of the surprising features is that he [Wilde] very nearly got off. If he had, what would have happened I wonder? I fancy the history of English culture might have been quite different if a juryman's stupidity had chanced to take another turn.'[1]

He had no faith in psycho-analysis as a cure for homosexuality, at least as practised by a doctor from Freiburg, whom he met with some of his patients at Lady Ottoline Morrell's house outside Oxford, where the guests who were not having 'treatment' were playing Bach. ('My brain totters. Soon I shall be playing Bach myself.') One of the musical patients who had submitted to the Freiburg treatment was Edward Sackville-West, a cousin of Victoria's and later the fifth Lord Sackville, then an undergraduate at Christ Church. 'After four months and an expenditure of £200, he found he could just bear the thought of going to bed with a woman,' noted Strachey. 'No more. Several other wretched undergraduates have been through the same "treatment". They walk about haggard on the lawn, wondering whether they could bear the thought of a woman's private parts, and gazing at their little lovers, who run round and round with cameras snapshotting Lytton Strachey. . . . Probably after playing Bach this evening, I shall hurry to Freiburg myself. I shall certainly be badly in need of some "treatment". But I admit that I would rather receive it at the hands of P. Ritchie than of the German doctor.'

'P. Ritchie' was the Hon Philip Ritchie, eldest son of Lord Ritchie of Dundee, and soon Strachey was writing him passionate love poems. Unfortunately, this affair was suddenly terminated when Ritchie died as the result of an operation for tonsillitis. Meanwhile Strachey had transferred his affections to Ritchie's friend Roger Senhouse, whose romantic good looks, 'with a melting smile and dark grey eyes', completely captivated Strachey. It was to be his last major affair, and like all his others its course did not run uniformly smooth. At this time he was also at work on his final literary work, *Elizabeth and Essex*. 'I lead a dog's life, between Queen Elizabeth's love affairs and my own,' he wrote. Senhouse was the recipient of equally passionate poems and in a light-hearted vein Strachey would even inscribe the envelope of his letters in verse for the instruction of the postman:

> Deliver this to SENHOUSE (Roger)
> I prithee, postman debonair!

[1] Michael Holroyd. *Lytton Strachey: The Years of Achievement* (1968), 444.

> He is the handsome upstairs lodger
> At number 14 BRUNSWICK SQUARE.

Throughout his life Strachey continued to be tortured by homosexual yearnings, many of which were only satisfied in fantasy when he would see the

> forms of golden boys
> Embraced seraphically in far lands
> By languid lovers. . . .

'But you know, my dearest,' he wrote to Senhouse after Ritchie's death, 'it is impossible not to feel an undercurrent of sadness—more than before—about Philip, and about more general things—the dangers and difficulties of all human life—the miserable pain of separations and misunderstandings—the wicked power of mere accident over happiness and goodness. I know you feel all this and as for me, when I reflect upon these things, I can't help crying, and then Roger, I sink into our love which comes like the divine resolution of a discord, and all is well.'

Of course, Strachey was not always in such sombre mood. In 1931, when already gripped by the cancer which was to kill him in the following year, when barely fifty, he jokingly told Senhouse that he was thinking of writing a book moulded on the anthropologist Malinowski's *Sexual Life of Savages in North-Western Melanesia*, to be called *The Sexual Life of the English*. 'It would be a remarkable book,' he added, 'but no doubt would have to be published in New Guinea'. He had previously communicated a more detailed erotic homosexual theme to his young friend, this time in satirical verse.

> How odd the fate of pretty boys!
> Who, if they dare to taste the joys
> That so enchanted classic minds,
> Get whipped upon their neat behinds
> Yet should they fail to construe well
> The lines that of those raptures tell
> —It's very odd, you must confess—
> Their neat behinds get whipped no less.

Lytton Strachey never quite came to terms with his homosexual nature, though he did best to live with it, his attitude being fundamentally that of a cynical philosopher. 'What is love?' he asked the young Cambridge English literature don George

Rylands, and like another celebrated jester in history did not wait for an answer. ' 'Tis not hereafter—no; but it also isn't heretobefore. Is it even here? Ah, well! But the odd thing is (among all the other oddities) that one occasionally manages to enjoy oneself.'[1]

[5]

In the decades between the two World Wars, homosexuality in England came to the surface of society for the first time, although what was visible was only a portion of what was still a largely submerged iceberg. With the older generation the subject was still taboo as a topic of conversation. 'I thought that men like that shot themselves,' said King George V, when told that someone he knew quite well (possibly Lord Beauchamp) was homosexual. I remember an incident in the early 1930s when I was private tutor to a young man who belonged to an upper-class family, and working with him in the house of his aunt, a distinguished old lady and the sister of a peer. I happened to mention casually in their presence the suicide of Lord Harcourt, which had taken place a dozen years previously. I was thereupon taken aside by her ladyship and given a stern lecture on the impropriety of my reference, particularly when uttered in the hearing of my pupil. She did not realize that, as her nephew had been to Eton, he knew all about 'queers' and their habits. Amongst the younger post-war generation, particularly the so-called Bright Young People, the old taboos and reticences about sex had broken down. Debutantes and other upper and upper-middle-class girls were discovering to their consternation that numbers of eligible young men whom they fancied as potential husbands were primarily interested in their own sex. In vain they flattened their chests and cut their hair short in a 'bob' or 'Eton crop' in an attempt to compete with the 'pansies'. Their disappointment led them to become an easy prey to the heterosexual philanderer. Douglas Goldring, in his interesting survey, *The Nineteen Twenties*, recalls how a young lovely confided in him, tearfully, at a party that a certain youth at whom she had been setting her cap was 'nothing but a heartless he-vamp'.[2]

The fact that prior to 1914 the subject of homosexuality was

[1] Holroyd. *Lytton Strachey: Years of Achievement*, 468, 477, 495, 543, 545–6, 658.
[2] Douglas Goldring. *The Nineteen Twenties* (1945), 226.

never mentioned in mixed society meant that most women knew little or nothing about it. This had made it much easier than it subsequently became for the better-to-do type of male homosexual to indulge his tastes unhindered by feminine curiosity. No one thought it 'funny' if a 'toff' took an 'interest' in some working-class man or lad. He was only regarded as being 'good natured' and 'helpful' by the other's family, as for example Edward Fitzgerald had been with the fisherman Posh. From time to time some accident would produce a scandal as the Dublin Castle or Cleveland Street or the Oscar Wilde affair, but by and large homosexual behaviour between 'toffs' and their lower-class friends in private or in such places as unattended public lavatories was permitted to flourish without inconvenient interference on the part of the police, although blackmailing cases increased considerably after the passing of the Labouchere Amendment. Apart from blackmail, however, of which there was relatively little before 1885, it was very rare for one of the 'lower orders' to refuse a request for homosexual relations with one of his 'betters', whom he naturally looked up to with expectations of reward in money or kind, such as employment. The unskilled labourer of those days earned £1 a week, sometimes less, and when times were hard a working man would do anything rather than face the disgrace of applying for public assistance in the 'workhouse'. It was thus relatively easy for any 'queer' with an income of a few hundreds of pounds to have any attractive young working man or farm lad that he fancied.

World War I put an end to this state of affairs, when for the first time women found themselves working alongside men in the services. The women would tease a man they saw being unduly 'chummy' with a private soldier or naval rating. This development, and the ease with which a man could get almost any girl to allow him to copulate or sleep with her gradually made it more difficult for the homosexual to find a suitable partner in a different social class, while the cheap beer and cigarettes provided for the armed forces was an inducement for the ratings and other ranks to seek the company of women of their own class rather than the homosexual 'toff', as they had previously been in the habit of doing.

This did not prevent homosexuality from continuing to flourish in the public schools and universities still largely populated by the 'toff' class. That English public schools had not changed much in this respect since the days of Harrow's Dr Vaughan and John Addington Symonds is well brought out in

Flannelled Fool by T. C. Worsley, a remarkable account of the
author's experience as an assistant master at a well-known public
school in which the homosexual proclivities of both boys and
staff are fully described. The school is not mentioned by name,
but it is not difficult to recognize it as Wellington College, a mid-
nineteenth-century academy founded in memory of 'the Duke'
with the object of encouraging his soldier-like qualities in English
youth. One point which Worsley underlines is that in homosexual relationships between masters and boys it was the boys
as much if not more than the masters who made the running.

> There was one attractive, yellow-haired boy who over a space
> of time regularly used to barge into my bedroom in shorts and
> singlet, when he knew I was changing back from games and
> when I met him later at a party in London, he wanted to know
> why on earth I hadn't taken advantage of his arrival. That
> was what he had come for! And this was far from an isolated
> incident.

On another occasion, when Worsley was coaching a boy in the
holidays at his mother's house in London, his pupil got his
mother out of the house for the night on the faked pretext that
his brother was ill in the country. 'Well,' said the boy quite
brazenly, when Worsley expostulated with him, 'you didn't
think my brother was really ill, did you? I fixed it up on the
telephone this morning to get mother away, so you could sleep
with me. Please, you must.'[1]

Lytton Strachey's account of the Oxford undergraduate scene
is supplemented in detail by Marie-Jacqueline Lancaster's biography of Brian Howard, the writer and promiscuous homosexual playboy, whom Evelyn Waugh characterized as 'mad, bad
and dangerous to know'. Among his friends was the wealthy

---

[1] T. C. Worsley. *Flannelled Fool* (1960), 124, 179. How the homosexual pattern in boys' schools appeared in the post-Second World War period has been
graphically described as the result of an investigation carried out by Dr Royston
Lambert and a team of research workers from Cambridge University, quoting
the language of the boys themselves. 'You get sex starved and look twice at
younger boys and have to keep yourself in hand,' admitted one 17-year-old,
while another wrote: 'You have to exert strong will power not to be a practising
queer here.' The main cause of their homosexual awareness or tendencies was
summarized by a boy of 15, who told Dr Lambert: 'We go to bed at night and sit
on Peoples Bed [*sic*] and then your hands start to wander. Now (Just use your
imagination). This is because the school is all male.' Nevertheless Lambert concluded that, while there may be more homosexual activity in boys' schools than
the school authorities know, there is at the same time 'much less of it than is
commonly imagined outside': Royston Lambert. *The Hothouse Society* (1968),
318–19, 340. Possibly this finding may be explained, in part at least, by the
greater freedom with which teen-age boys and girls mix in the school holidays
today with a consequent increase in heterosexual associations.

homosexual Evan Morgan, later Lord Tredegar, who on one
occasion in London gave 'the most horrible party' which Howard
attended and 'which began at the Eiffel Tower [Restaurant] and
ended in somebody's bedroom at Prince's Hotel in Jermyn
Street'. Howard, who succeeded in extricating himself from this
orgy, 'clutching my remaining bits of virtue', as he put it, subsequently admitted that he had never seen anything 'so stupen-
dously naughty, even in Oxford'. And there was certainly plenty
of it going on at Oxford. In those days, as I well remember, the
restaurant frequented by undergraduates who wished to be in
the fashion was The George in Cornmarket Street, now no more.
Normally a restaurant of such standing would employ waiters
and at an earlier date did so. However there were so many complaints from the waiters about the invitations they received from
the restaurant's undergraduate patrons that waitresses had to be
substituted: their virtue was regarded as quite safe, as indeed it
was. Howard, who mixed both with the 'aesthetes' and the
'hearties', has described how, after a Bullingdon Club dinner, at
which he drank a lot of champagne and was toasted as 'Brian
Howard—that rare combination, the intellectual and the horse-
man', he broke most of the windows in Christ Church (at a cost to
himself of £60), after which he 'had a tumultuous sleep with someone who remained extremely chilly until we actually got "between
the sheets". ' Howard's uninhibited feelings on the subject were
expressed in a letter which he wrote to his mother at this time.

> People should be left alone, dear. As long as children are
> protected, it really doesn't matter going to bed with a lamp-
> post. Napoleon and Lenin thought so, Rome and Greece
> thought so, the modern psychologists think so—and so do I.
> Certainly it isn't a virtue to be homosexual. As society is now
> constituted it is excessively inconvenient. But it certainly
> isn't a vice.[1]

I arrived in Oxford a year after Brian Howard had gone down,
but John Betjeman was a contemporary of us both and is a
pertinent witness on the prevalence of homosexuality in the
Oxford of the 1920s. 'But *everybody* was queer at Oxford in those
days!' Betjeman declared in a recent radio programme. Betjeman,
of course, exaggerated, but as Goronwy Rees has aptly pointed
out, there was truth as well as exaggeration in his remark, and
this I can endorse from my own personal experience.

[1] Marie-Jacqueline Lancaster. *Brian Howard. Portrait of a Failure.* (1968),
144, 167, 348.

It would be fair to say that, as in Strachey's Cambridge, so in Oxford in the '20s and early '30s homosexuality was, among undergraduates and dons with pretensions to culture and a taste for the arts, at once a fashion, a doctrine and a way of life, and, as with the Apostles, exercised an influence which extended far beyond the boundaries of the university. It could, of course, be said that no more people were affected by it than are today addicted to marihuana, LSD or Flower Power, and the comparison would be just, because homosexuality was very largely the particular form which the revolt of the young took at the universities at that time. But the effect of a cult on an institution or a society is not limited to the number of its actual adherents, any more than the influence of Catholicism is limited to those who go to Mass.[1]

So far as the law went, there were the general run-of-the-mill cases of buggery and indecency, as there always had been, but provided a reasonable modicum of discretion was exercised homosexuals were still not unduly troubled by the police. There was no open scandal involving any society figure during this period, if one excepts the relatively minor case of Sir Almeric Fitzroy, a former Secretary of the Privy Council, who was convicted of importuning in South Kensington Underground Station. It is true that the police got on the trail of the two ex-Cabinet Ministers, Lords Harcourt and Beauchamp, but as the former committed suicide and the latter fled the country before any proceedings could be initiated against them the general public knew nothing about their cases. In the higher social echelons there was Sir Edward ('Eddie') Marsh, patron of the arts and Winston Churchill's secretary for twenty-three years, whom Max Beerbohm has described as 'undeniably one of the ornaments of his time'. There was also the Right Honourable Sir James Tynte Agg Gardner, Lord of the Manor of Cheltenham, who represented Cheltenham as a Conservative in the House of Commons intermittently from 1874 until his death fifty-four years later. A discreet bachelor, he lived in the luxury Queen's Hotel in his constituency and carefully avoided getting into any trouble. In a rather different category was the writer and radio producer J. R. Ackerley, whose autobiography gives a touching account of a homosexual's constant longings and search for the Ideal Friend, presented with a sense of humour and without the least self-pity. Indeed this work is probably the fullest and frankest account of a

[1] Goronwy Rees, *loc. cit.*, 80.

homosexual's confessions to have been published in the English language.

Ackerley's friends in the 'twenties and 'thirties were mostly guardsmen, but sometimes sailors and occasionally waiters and other youths of that class. He does not seem to have had many affairs with men of his own social standing, except in the theatrical profession—for instance, he admits that the well-known actor and composer of light musicals, Ivor Novello, took him to bed twice. His longest attachment, with a sailor, lasted for about four years, although it was necessarily intermittent through the sailor's periodic absences at sea. Most of his affairs were of a casual kind, some extremely casual, such as the young waiter in the restaurant car, when he was travelling from London to Liverpool with his father to visit some of their relatives. Ackerley immediately recognized the waiter as a 'queer'. What happened then is best recounted in his own words:

> While my father studied the menu I exchanged smiles and winks with this youth. Towards the end of the meal, when the business of serving it was over, he passed me with a meaning look and backward glance and disappeared down the corridor. Excusing myself to my father for a natural need I followed him. He was waiting for me by the door of the toilet. We entered together, quickly unbuttoned and pleasured each other. Then I returned to finish my coffee. I had scribbled down my address for this amusing youth, but never heard from him again.

Ackerley's lively account of his various guardsmen associations is also worth quoting:

> In the 'thirties I found myself concentrating my attention more and more upon a particular society of young men in the metropolis which I had tapped before and which, it seemed to me, might yield, without further loss of time, what I required. His Majesty's Brigade of Guards had a long history in homosexual prostitution. Perpetually short of cash, beer, and leisure occupations, they were easily to be found of an evening in their red tunics standing about in the various pubs they frequented, over the only half-pint they could afford or some 'quids-in' mate had stood them, in Knightsbridge, Victoria, the Edgware Road, and elsewhere, or hanging about Hyde Park and the Marble Arch, with nothing to do and nothing to spend, whistling therefore in vain to the passing 'prossies',

whom they contemptuously called 'bags' (something into which something is put), and alert to the possibility that some kind gentleman might appear and stand them a few pints, in return for which and the subsequent traditional tip—a pound was the recognised tariff for the Foot Guards then, the Horse Guards cost rather more—they were perfectly agreeable to, indeed often eager for, a 'bit of fun'. In their availability and for other reasons they suited my book, though generally larger than I liked, they were young, they were normal, they were working-class, they were drilled to obedience; though not innocent for long, the new recruit might be found before someone else got at him; if grubby they could be bathed, and if civility and consideration, with which they did not always meet in their liaisons, were extended to them, one might gain their affection.

Evening after evening, for many years, when I was free I prowled Marble Arch, the Monkey Walk and Hyde Park Corner, or hastened from pub to pub as one unrewarding scene replaced another. Seaport towns also (sailors too were jolly and short of cash) were often combed at weekends. The taint of prostitution in these proceedings nevertheless displeased me and must, I thought, be disagreeable to the boys themselves, accept it though they did. I therefore developed mutually face-saving techniques to avoid it, such as standing drinks and giving cash at once and, without any suggestive conversation, leaving the boy free to return home with me if he wished, out of sexual desire or gratitude, for he was pretty sure to know what I was after. This, I suppose, was akin to my father's technique of bribery in advance for special restaurant service, for of course I too hoped for responsiveness to generosity and was annoyed if I did not get it. A similar but more self-restrained and hazardous form of procedure was to treat the soldier, if he was particularly attractive, to a pleasant evening's entertainment—cinema, supper—give him a present at the end of it when he had to return to barracks, and leave it to him to ask, 'When can I see you again?' Thus, by implying that it was more his society than his body that interested me, did I hope to distinguish myself from the other 'twanks' (as guardsmen called people like myself) and gain his respect. If he did not turn up to his future appointment I was upset and would loiter about his barracks for days. These methods had another advantage: they disarmed, or could be hoped to disarm, any tendency the guardsman might have to robbery or violence. Such incidents were not frequent but they occurred, sometimes brutal (the homosexual who was found murdered, his penis severed and stuck into his own mouth), sometimes jolly (the Hammersmith quean, who, robbed by a guardsman of his fur coat, flew out in a rage and found a police-man, who quickly recovered the conspicuous garment and went to bed with the grateful owner himself). Cautious and nervous as I was, I myself did not get through without a few episodes of extortion and theft, in France of actual violence, so repugnant to my mind that I noticed in course of time that the boys I picked up were almost always mild and character-less, as perhaps they had been from the very beginning; charac-ter tended to be difficult, and it was as though some instinct for safety within me recognised and selected boys with no character whatever.[1]

Another autobiography of a homosexual and contemporary of Ackerley is that of Michael Davidson. By contrast with Ackerley, who stuck to his job with the B.B.C. throughout, Davidson was very much of a rolling stone, being at various stages of his career a subaltern in the Regular Army, tally-clerk in the Durban docks, cattle farmer in Zululand, unofficial spy in the Second World War, and journalist covering most of the countries between Morocco and Japan, as well as a convicted pederast in Worm-wood Scrubs prison. 'This is the life-history of a lover of boys,' so he begins. 'It's a first-hand report, therefore, on that heresy which, in England especially, is reprobated above all others.' As a young man in the 1920s he visited the octogenarian Edward Carpenter at his house near Guildford, 'where, as one's great-aunts used to recall being patted on the head by the Duke of Wellington, I can say I was pinched on the bum by England's Walt Whitman'. In 1936, Davidson pleaded guilty to an offence with a youth and somewhat surprisingly for a first offender got four months with 'hard labour' from the magistrate. (By this date the only residue of 'hard labour' was having to sleep for the first two weeks of one's sentence on bare boards. 'The object of the plank bed is to produce insomnia,' wrote Oscar Wilde after his first experience of it. 'There is no other object in it, and it invariably succeeds. . . . It is a revolting and ignorant punishment.') In passing sentence the magistrate told Davidson that when he was in prison he would receive 'psychological treatment'. The treatment consisted of one or two talks with a young psychologist,

[1] J. R. Ackerley. *My Father and Myself* (1968), 124, 134–7.

but the advice which the prisoner received was hardly what the magistrate had in mind. 'I was sorry I had with him so few talks,' wrote Davidson afterwards of this particular psychologist. 'The upshot of my treatment, really was that he urged me to raise, so to speak, my 'age of consent'; couldn't I, he asked in effect, persuade myself to be attracted by people much older—above the age, at least of 18? The risk then, he pointed out, would be less.'[1]

[6]

A significant landmark in the London homosexual scene between the two World Wars, now almost entirely vanished, was afforded by the old-fashioned urinal. This form of public convenience, resembling in some ways the French *vespasienne*, dated from late Victorian and Edwardian times and was constructed of iron work, usually painted green, the design sometimes including tiny holes or lattice tracery through which those inside could see whether anyone was approaching from without who might disturb their pleasure. Above each 'stall' was the printed legend: 'Adjust your dress before leaving.'

An elderly homosexual has recorded the following hitherto unpublished reminiscence of this interesting architectural feature of the pre-war metropolis:

These small unobtrusive urinals were, in many ways, the most important meeting places for homosexuals of all and every kind. Always open, usually unattended, and consisting of a small number of stalls, over the sides of which it was quite easy to spy and get a sight of one's neighbour's cock, they were ideally built for the gratification of the voyeur's sexual itch. Very frequently the sides of the stall were covered with graffiti and randy writing, which served to excite the urinating frequenter. It was pleasant indeed to add to the writing and suggest meeting someone for sexual purposes and, in due course, see if someone had added to one's own writing and suggested a meeting.

When one considers the numbers of men, not by any means all homosexuals, who used these small urinals, it is almost certain these graffiti and suggestive writings and appointments introduced hundreds of so-called 'normal' men to the pleasures of homosexual gratification, and to an easy way of making a

[1] Michael Davidson. *The World, the Flesh and Myself* (1962), 1, 66, 168–70, 176. *The Letters of Oscar Wilde*, 723–4.

few extra pounds to add to their wage packets. In fact these urinals were a very important part of the social life and scene of those days. And, when one remembers the vast amount of homosexuality indulged in in these small 'conveniences', it is somewhat surprising they were permitted to remain *in situ* and free from all attention of the authorities for as long as they did. Many homosexuals spent hours going from one of these places to the next, spying, feeling and indulging in all forms of homosexual pleasure in each of them. . . .

Frequently there would be several men in these places and they would take turns to keep a watch out against anyone coming in suddenly and disturbing the remaining others while they gratified themselves. . . . This keeping 'a watch out' was very often easy, as there were perforations in the iron walls of the urinal—which allowed the watcher to see anyone coming suddenly on the scene. And in some cases the 'watching out' was even easier in the case of there being only one entrance to the place. They were generally so dimly lit that anyone coming in out of the more brightly lighted street was unable to see distinctly for a moment or two exactly what was happening, which would give the actors time to set themselves more or less to rights.

The most famous or rather notorious of these urinals in the West End was situated in Dansey Place, off Wardour Street, and within a stone's throw of Leicester Square, known popularly as 'Clarkson's Cottage' from its close proximity to Willie Clarkson's theatrical costume shop. It had two entrances and contained four or five 'stalls', was quite large and high, usually well lighted, while its grey iron work had no perforations in its construction. If it had certain disadvantages for the visiting homosexual compared with the more dimly lit one-entrance structures elsewhere in London, on the other hand 'for meeting all and sundry of the West End "fraternity" it was marvellously placed and frequented'. Visitors from as far afield as Australia and Tasmania are said to have spoken of 'Clarkson's Cottage' with nostalgia. Its disappearance shortly after the Second World War was occasioned by its sale to a wealthy American, allegedly on account of its architectural interest, for re-erection in the large grounds of his country house outside New York. There it was 'done up', the running water put in order, and the restored edifice treated as a show place. 'I was surprised that the Westminster Council permitted this "cottage" to be sold,' my elderly homosexual informant remarked to me, 'as they must have realized exactly why this place was being treated in this regal way!'

Besides the small iron urinals there were the larger public lavatories, which were furnished with W.C.s as well as urinals, particularly in the London Underground and Tube stations.

Up to about 1925, when many Tube stations started to be 'cleaned up', they were really fantastic for indulging in all sorts of homosexual practices. Very many were without an attendant and in the cases where some attendant was provided he seemed utterly uninterested in what went on in the urinal and more especially in the W.C.'s . . .

Today with hardly a single lavatory unattended, it will seem unbelievable that one could move freely from one to another without exciting any remark. Leicester Square and Piccadilly Tube stations before they were 'improved' were, of course, extremely well frequented, but very often the W.C.'s were occupied for such a length of time it seemed more profitable to go elsewhere. A rather more secluded Tube station was Down Street—very suitable should one happen to 'strike lucky' with one's neighbour in the adjoining W.C., as one could remain quite undisturbed for a long time, and without running any great risk one could go into his W.C. for complete enjoyment.

Down Street Tube station, with its convenient 'convenience', has long since been closed, although the trains still run through where it used to be.

The larger main line railway termini, such as Waterloo, Victoria, Charing Cross and Paddington, also had their uses, particularly at week-ends when bluejackets used to come up from their Royal Naval bases or ships for short leave.

On arrival of the train there would be scores of young sailors tumbling out of the train, all it seemed in violent need of a good piss. They ran helter-skelter into the large lavatory on the platform, and, pulling down the flap of their trousers, pissed for all they were worth. . . . If they happened to note some eager looker, they would exclaim 'He's a beauty, isn't he? Like him up your bum, chum?' This sally would be followed by gales of laughter from the other pissing fellows. If the pubs were still open and one were wise, one at once said: 'Come along for another one, Jack, before the boozers shut.' And, once safely behind a pint at the bar, as often as not one succeeded in dragging him back to one's rooms. . . .

On the other hand, guardsmen were rarely encountered in these 'conveniences'.

There was no need for a Guardee in uniform to go into a piss place to meet a queer. All they had to do, if they wished to make contact with one, was to walk along the street or hang around Hyde Park, and it was certain some queer would speak to them or give them 'the look'. Another reason, no doubt, why the Guardee didn't frequent these urinals was that he was pretty sure, if he did, some queer would manage to get a good look at his prick, free of charge and without necessarily arranging to take him for a drink and probably for a stroll, or back to his rooms for full enjoyment and payment.

A favourite urinal with my informant was a small three-stalled affair down a steep flight of steps outside the Yorkshire Stingo public house beside Queen Charlotte's Hospital in the Marylebone Road. Because of the steep approach it was impossible to be surprised there by the unwanted intruder.

Another interesting urinal in this neighbourhood was the tiny one down a passage off Norfolk Street, Paddington, which provided excellent opportunities for spying on any men who happened to come in, as the stalls being very 'shallow' and low it was impossible for anyone to hide his fascinating appendage from the sly gaze of a randy queer. A well-known member of the C—— family lived *en pension* at the Norfolk Hotel almost opposite this urinal. He used to take up his stand in one of the stalls in this pee place, place his umbrella— he invariably carried a brolly even in high midsummer—on the ledge at the back of the stall and stay there for hours and hours. I never saw him speak to anyone or attempt to handle any fellow urinator's prick. But he was virtually a fixture there once he had installed himself in this 'cottage'. I noticed just after the end of the last war this urinal was still functioning, though a gate had been attached to it; it closed down when the pub nearby shut.

These unique iron structures, widely scattered over London, were not without risk for the frequenter, particularly late at night. The small urinal in Hill Place off Berkeley Square had a bad name for 'toffs' being assaulted and robbed by gangs of roughs who hunted about for this purpose. Anyone in evening dress was an obvious target for attack. Blackmailers too plied their loathsome trade. A blackmailing gang, which was broken

up shortly after the First World War, operated in the neighbourhood of 'Clarkson's Cottage', where they entrapped their victims;
one ruffian named Arthur Taylor, subsequently caught and
sentenced to a long term of penal servitude, is said to have
extorted £100,000 from a wealthy homosexual. Occasionally the
police officers in uniform would visit the urinals and pick up
delinquents caught in the act, but these raids were quite open
affairs, and the police were not then in the habit of employing
good-looking young detectives in plain clothes to act as *agents
provocateurs*, as they later did. This detestable practice, which
began after the last war, reached its height in the anti-homosexual
drive instigated by the authorities in the early nineteen-fifties.

A typical example was witnessed by Peter Wildeblood, the
journalist, who was shortly afterwards involved in the celebrated
Montagu case, which is described in the following chapter. One
night, when he had been working late at his office, Wildeblood
was walking along Brompton Road towards his flat. He noticed
two men loitering in an alleyway. Then a man, aged about
seventy, with white hair, walked past them and went into a
lavatory at the side of a public house which had closed. He was
followed in by the younger of the two men. Almost immediately
there was a sound of scuffling and shouting, and the older of the
two also ran into the lavatory. He and his companion dragged the
old man out, each holding him by an arm. He was struggling
and crying. Wildeblood, whose first thought was that they must
be local roughs trying to rob the old man, went up to them and
shouted at them to let him go, or he would call the police. 'We
are police officers,' the younger man replied.

By this time a woman had appeared at the street corner. She
asked what the old man had done, and received the reply that he
had been 'making a nuisance of himself'. He had now begun to
struggle violently and the two detectives pushed him up against
the railings of the Cancer Hospital outside which they were
standing. His head became wedged between two iron spikes and
he started to scream. The detectives asked if one of them would
ring up Chelsea Police Station and ask for a van to be sent.

'Just tell them we're at the top of Dovehouse Street, they'll
know what it's about.'

'You can do your own dirty work, damn you,' said the woman.

It seemed to Wildeblood, however, that the old man might be
seriously injured if he continued to struggle; so he went into a
telephone box a few yards away and called the police station. The
duty sergeant was evidently expecting the message, as the van

arrived almost immediately. The old man, who by this time was lying on the pavement in a pool of blood, was picked up and taken away. It was quite obvious to Wildeblood what had happened.

The younger and better-looking of the two policemen had been sent into the lavatory for the purpose of acting as an *agent provocateur*. It was his duty to behave in such a way that some homosexual would make advances to him. The old man had fallen into the trap and he would now be prosecuted and perhaps imprisoned. The young policeman, having behaved like a male prostitute, would probably be commended for his night's work. And tomorrow night, he would be back there again.

No wonder Peter Wildeblood was 'deeply shocked and angered' by this incident, which was only too common at this period. Yet when I asked the Home Secretary in a parliamentary question—I was a member of the House of Commons at the time—whether, in view of the judge's findings in a similar case, he would issue instructions to the Metropolitan Police 'to discontinue the practice of frequenting public lavatories in plain clothes for the purpose of acting as *agents provocateurs* towards suspected homosexuals', I received the astonishing reply that the Home Secretary 'completely rejects the suggestion that it is the practice of members of the Metropolitan Police to act as *agents provocateurs* in carrying out duties which, though distasteful, are essential to the preservation of public order and decency'.

One of my House of Commons colleagues had recently walked into such a trap. 'It is an unsavoury kind of police action and many people have an uneasy conscience about it,' I wrote at the time. 'There is always the danger too that it may open the door to police corruption, since it provides the unscrupulous police officer with an easy opportunity for "framing" the author of an innocent smile or harmless remark.' The case I had in mind when I asked my parliamentary question concerned a twenty-eight-year-old British subject from Singapore named Weng Kee Sam, who was arrested by two railway police in the lavatory of Gloucester Road Underground Station in West London on a charge of 'committing an act of gross indecency' with a man named Frederick Charles Beauchamp, twenty years older than Sam. The two police had been keeping watch in one of the W.Cs. and made their alleged discovery while peeping through a crack in the wooden partition. The young man from Singapore, who had never been in any kind of trouble before, swore that he was adjusting his clothing in one of the stalls when Beauchamp arrived and stood in the stall beside him and smiled at him. Sam thereupon stepped back and to his amazement Beauchamp, whom he had never seen in his life before, came up to him and kissed him and put his hand down towards where Sam was buttoning up his trousers. Sam pushed the other man's hand away, saying 'Don't be silly!' The police then emerged from their hiding place and took Sam to Kensington Police Station, where they kept him in a cell for an hour and a half before formally charging him. They also arrested Beauchamp, who committed suicide before he could be brought to trial.

At Sam's trial both policemen testified that the kiss they saw on his part was not the sudden unexpected kiss which the accused had described but a homosexual 'kiss of mutual affection'. This was extremely unlikely, because, as Sam said in evidence, 'in my country men do not kiss—there is never any kissing even between male and female'. In the result Weng Kee Sam was acquitted. He then sued the police and the railway for false imprisonment, malicious prosecution and conspiracy to give perjured evidence against him. The judge held on the jury's findings that the police did not have 'reasonable cause' for making the arrest, and the jury awarded Mr Sam damages in the substantial sum of £1,950.

To return to the iron green-painted urinals. One of the most notorious was beside the Lyric Theatre in Hammersmith, 'chock-a-block from dusk to dawn the following morning and all the occupants indulging in every form of debauchery'. The urinals which survived the German bombing of London in the Second World War were mostly replaced by brick buildings, which lacked both the charm and the facility for the itinerant homosexual to enjoy himself compared with the old unattended *pissoir*. A few of the iron structures lingered outside London.

One of the last of the unattended urinals to be closed was in Black Lion Street, Brighton, described by a local town councillor as a 'hot bed of male prostitution'. If its patrons did not come from so far afield as those of 'Clarkson's Cottage', nevertheless those who were unfortunate enough to be arrested in the Brighton urinal in recent years gave their home addresses in such widely separated centres as Nuneaton, Caterham, Ilkeston, Swindon and Tunbridge Wells.

'I fancy, until these urinals were "cleaned up", London must

have been about the most secretly homosexual city in existence,'
remarked my informant. 'The Blitz on London, of course,
precipitated the total disappearance of these exciting landmarks,
together with the ever-increasing knowledge that male homosexuality was practised, very largely, in these small, unobtrusive,
green-painted, iron, unattended urinals.'[1]

[7]

During a period of some fifteen years covered by the Second
World War and its immediate aftermath, homosexual offences
of an indictable character increased between fourfold and five-
fold. Only one socially prominent individual, however, was
prosecuted in the war. This was Sir Paul Latham, thirty-six-
year-old millionaire baronet, old Etonian and Conservative M.P.,
whose wife was a daughter of the Earl of Drogheda. He was tried
by court martial in 1941 on charges of improper conduct with
three gunners and a civilian while he was serving as an officer
with the 70th Searchlight Regiment, Royal Artillery, in Sussex.
There was a further charge of attempted suicide, since he had
thrown himself off his motor-cycle (and as a result was seriously
though not fatally injured) on learning that a letter from one of
the gunners containing allegations against him had been seen
by the military authorities. It was a particularly tragic case
involving the ruin of a most promising career, since he had
joined the army of his own accord at the beginning of the war
and he could easily have been excused service in the armed
forces through being an M.P.; he had of course now to resign
his seat in the House of Commons. 'I imagine that whatever your
decision is in this case,' his defending counsel told the court,
'Sir Paul's life is now pretty well damned'. In fact, he was found
guilty on ten out of thirteen charges and was sentenced to be
cashiered and also to two years' imprisonment.[2] His wife divorced
him while he was still in prison, and he died a broken man a few
years after his release.

In 1938 there were 134 cases of sodomy and bestiality known
to the police in England and Wales. The number in 1952 was
670. During the same period the number of attempts to commit

---

[1] Private information. Peter Wildeblood. *Against the Law* (1955), 42–3.
H. Montgomery Hyde. *United in Crime* (1955) xvii. Hansard. *Commons Debates*,
Vol. 548. Col. 2525 (February 16, 1956). *Sam* v. *Cluny: The Times*, February 3,
1956. *Brighton Gazette*, April, 1965.
[2] *The Times*, September 5, 6, 24, 1941.

'unnatural offences', including indecent assaults, increased from 822 to 3,087. Offences of gross indecency between males went up from 320 to 1,686. Importuning also increased substantially, 373 cases of proceedings in London alone being reported in 1952. In commenting on these figures in the House of Commons, the Under-Secretary for Home Affairs (Sir Hugh Lucas-Tooth) admitted he was baffled. 'I cannot give the House any opinion for the reason for that increase, and I think I can say with complete truth that the reasons are simply not known,' he declared. 'Quite clearly, this is a problem which calls for very careful consideration on the part of those responsible for the welfare of the nation.'[1]

The reasons may not have been known to the minister, but to anyone such as the present writer who has studied the matter, particularly in his capacity of a Member of Parliament, which he was at the time, they are demonstrably attributable, at least in great part, to an excess of zeal on the part of the police. Promotion in the junior ranks of the force has always depended to a considerable extent upon the number of convictions a particular officer has been able to secure, and when the news filters down to the lower ranks that the authorities are interested in a particular type of offender the inference is obvious, especially as in this instance it was easier and incidentally safer and less troublesome for a police officer to catch a homosexual than a burglar. The stepping-up process may be said to have begun with the appointment of Sir Theobald Mathew, a devout and conscientious Catholic, as Director of Public Prosecutions in 1944. The war was thought to have been responsible for an increase in homosexual behaviour and Mathew with the support of the then Home Secretary, Herbert Morrison, whose father had been a policeman, believed that the trend should be halted. The drive against homosexuals proceeded on a relatively minor scale until 1951, when it suddenly began to be intensified as the result of an incident of international proportions which occurred in March of that year. This was the flight of the two British diplomats Guy Burgess and Donald Maclean in March 1951 and their defection to the Soviet Union. Both men were homosexuals, and when Maclean was serving in a senior position in the British Embassy in Washington in the immediate post-war years there is reason to believe that he was blackmailed by Burgess and the master-spy 'Kim' Philby into handing over top-secret information to which he had access from American sources to the Russians. After Maclean's dramatic disappearance with Burgess, the result of a 'tip-off' from Philby

[1] Hansard. *House of Commons Debates*, Vol. 526. col. 1753 (April 28, 1954).

('the third man'), the Americans were naturally most concerned
at a security leak of such magnitude, and they made representations
to the British to weed out all known homosexuals from Government service as bad security risks, as was already being done in
Washington.[1]

Steps to this end were taken by Herbert Morrison, and when
the Conservatives were returned to office later in the same year
they were continued by the new Home Secretary, Sir David
Maxwell Fyfe (later Lord Kilmuir), who was to extend the campaign to the pursuit of all homosexuals, whether they were in
Government employment or not. The McCarthy witch-hunt
against suspected Communist sympathizers and homosexuals in
official positions in the United States was already in full swing,
and a senior officer from Scotland Yard was sent over to America
to confer with the Federal Bureau of Investigation in Washington.
In Britain the campaign reached its height in the latter part of
1953 and the early months of 1954, receiving a big fillip from the
appointment as Metropolitan Police Commissioner of Sir John
Nott-Bower, who, according to one report, 'swore he would rip
the cover off all London's filth spots'. In October 1953 it was
reported that the Home Office had instructed the police to
institute 'a new drive against male vice'. Mr Donald Horne, the
London correspondent of the *Sydney Morning Telegraph*,
elaborated on this theme in an informative despatch which
appeared on October 25, 1953.

> Sir John swung into action on a nation-wide scale. He
> enlisted the support of local police throughout England to
> step up the number of arrests for homosexual offences. For
> many years past the police had turned a blind eye to male vice.
> They made arrests only when definite complaints were made
> from innocent people, or where homosexuality had encouraged
> other crimes. . . . Now, meeting Sir John's demands, they are
> making it a priority job to increase the number of arrests.

The new Metropolitan Police Commissioner was a man after
the Home Secretary's heart, and together with Sir Theobald
Mathew, who still held the office of Director of Public Prosecutions, they set the stage for the full-scale harrying of male homo-

---

[1] The process began in Washington in 1950. Between January 1, 1947, and
April 1, 1950, only 192 cases of homosexuals and other perverts were handled
by the U.S. Government departments, but in the succeeding seven months 382
such cases were handled: see U.S. Congress *Employment of Homosexuals and Other
Sex Perverts in Government*. Senate Resolution 290, 81st Congress, 2nd Session.
Document 241, December 14, 1950.

sexuals which was to take place during the succeeding months. Sir David Maxwell Fyfe made it clear that they must expect no mercy. Displeased by the 'widely different sentences which have been passed in London Courts on male perverts', he bluntly told the metropolitan magistrates to make their sentences uniform and stiffer. As a result the magistrate of the West London Court stated publicly that he was coming to the view that homosexuals convicted of importuning 'should all be sent to prison as they were in the old days'. Sir David also told the House of Commons:

> Homosexuals, in general, are exhibitionists and proselytizers, and a danger to others, especially the young. So long as I hold the office of Home Secretary, I shall give no countenance to the view that they should not be prevented from being such a danger.[1]

In the resulting wave of prosecutions, several objectionable methods were employed to secure convictions. In particular, extended use was made of police *agents provocateurs* in plain clothes to entice and entrap homosexuals in public lavatories and the like, while every effort was made to persuade accomplices to come forward and 'turn Queen's evidence' in return for a pledge of immunity from criminal proceedings against themselves. Most objectionable of all was the revival of the conspiracy charge, counts under this head being added to the indictment, thus making the words and acts of each of the defendants accused jointly admissible in evidence against all the others. This practice had been severely condemned by the Court of Criminal Appeal in 1948, when Mr Justice Humphreys, the most distinguished British criminal judge of the time, had remarked in language similar to that used by the Lord Chief Justice Cockburn in the case of Boulton and Park:

> There is a growing tendency to charge persons with criminal conspiracy rather than with the specific offences which the evidence shows them to have committed. It is not to be encouraged.
> . . . if the law of criminal conspiracy is to be invoked, then each count of the indictment should be framed as to enable the jury to put their fingers on the specific part of the conspiracy as to which they are satisfied that the particular defendant is proved to have been implicated and to convict him of that offence only. It is an essential feature of the criminal law

[1] Hansard. *House of Commons Debates*, Vol. 251, col. 1298 (December 3. 1953).

that the accused person should be able to tell from the indictment the precise nature of the charge or charges against him
so as to be in a position to put forward his defence and to
direct his evidence to meet them.[1]

This opinion was confirmed by Mr Justice Jackson in the
United States Supreme Court a year later. 'A co-defendant in a
conspiracy trial occupies an uneasy seat,' said Justice Jackson in
the United States Supreme Court in 1949. 'There generally will
be evidence of wrongdoing by somebody. It is difficult for the
individual to make his own case stand on its merits in the minds
of jurors who are ready to believe that birds of a feather are
flocked together. If he is silent he is taken to admit it and if, as
often happens, co-defendants can be prodded into accusing or
contradicting each other, they convict each other.'[2]

Finally, the police in making arrests adopted the habit of
searching the premises of the accused without previously having
obtained a separate search warrant, a process of doubtful legality,
to say the least. The purpose of this exercise was the expectation
of finding compromising letters or other documents which could
be used to corroborate the evidence of an accomplice who had
agreed to testify for the prosecution. Where the owner or occu-
pant of the premises was suspected of concealing stolen property
there was a colour of legal justification for such a search under
the powers conferred on the police by the Larceny Act, but in no
other instance. This practice of ransacking the premises of alleged
homosexual offenders contributed strongly to the public revulsion which set in against the official persecution of homosexuals
and which was to lead directly to the setting up of the Wolfenden
Committee.

[8]

The police drive in the autumn and winter of 1953–4 culmi-
nated in the prosecution of four individuals whose trials made
news headlines for many weeks. The accused were an author, a
peer, a country landowner, and the diplomatic correspondent of
a popular daily paper; their names were respectively Rupert
Croft-Cooke, Lord Montagu of Beaulieu, Michael Pitt-Rivers,
and Peter Wildeblood. The resulting trials showed up the police
in a highly unfavourable light.

[1] *Rex* v. *West* [1948] 1 All E.R. (C.C.A.) 718, at p. 723.
[2] Cited in *New Statesman*, April 10, 1956.

Rupert Croft-Cooke, then aged fifty, was widely known as a novelist, playwright, biographer and travel writer, as well as book critic of *The Sketch*. After the Second World War, in which he served with distinction in the Madagascar campaign and India, he bought a house in a Sussex village, where he lived quietly with his Indian secretary, Joseph Alexander, carrying on with his writing and cultivating his garden. Like other novelists who drew their characters to some extent from real life, he would talk to all and sundry in pubs and elsewhere and had a wide circle of friends and acquaintances from peers to dustmen, whom on occasion he would invite down from London for the week-end. Admittedly his social behaviour was unconventional and he was not popular with the local gentry and their ladies, particularly after he had published a book called *The Life for Me* early in 1953, in which he described their 'determined gentility' as 'pretentious and unattractive'. A friend who was a magistrate in another part of England warned him of the risks he was running and that he would 'simply not be allowed to live' as he wished. This Croft-Cooke could scarcely believe. 'My dear chap, the police force, like everything else, has changed,' said his friend. 'I know nothing about your local men but I do know how nearly all policemen work and think and behave in other rural districts. . . . They are always on the look-out for a well-publicised conviction which may mean a pat on the shoulder from a higher official. That's largely true of the superintendents and inspectors, too. They're out to make a name for themselves.'

A month or two later Croft-Cooke was to realize how right his magistrate friend had been. His undoing was the result of a spontaneous act of kindness. He had driven up to London for dinner one Friday with Joseph, whom he arranged to meet with another friend in a pub near Oxford Street after keeping his dinner engagement. While Croft-Cooke was talking to the other friend, his secretary got into conversation with two young men at the bar who turned out to be Royal Navy cooks on forty-eight hours' leave from Chatham. Joseph, who possessed what his employer called a most responsive and trusting nature, took a liking to them at once, and when they said they were looking for somewhere to spend the week-end he came over and asked Croft-Cooke if he could invite them down. The result was that within half-an-hour the two naval cooks were in the car with Croft-Cooke and Joseph on their way to the country.

At his subsequent trial on charges of committing 'acts of gross indecency' with the two navy men, whose names were Altoft and

Dennis, Croft-Cooke was asked by the judge, 'Have you ever before picked up any ordinary person, any Tom, Dick or Harry, that you have met in a public house in the West End of London, to come to your place for the week-end?' Croft-Cooke replied that he had not, at the same time adding that he saw nothing in the least extraordinary about his action.

Afterwards, looking back on what happened, he wrote:

> It still seems to me a friendly, natural thing to do and one which I might have done at any time. I have made many spontaneous invitations on other occasions which have been extended to tramps on the road or acquaintances of less than an hour, and have never had cause to regret it. It was the *circumstances* in which the two men were invited to my house which were later quoted as 'corroborative evidence', indeed which provided the only corroborative evidence of the prosecution, yet these circumstances seems to me the most innocent imaginable. When they are seen with eyes accustomed to evil, perhaps, or when they are described to serious-minded jurymen as 'picking-up', they take on a muddier colour.[1]

According to Croft-Cooke, the week-end was in no way extraordinary. 'The two young men did as other guests have done, helped with the housework, lounged in the garden, talked, played darts at the pub across the road and, as they told a number of people and later admitted in court, passed what they considered the best week-end in their lives.' Their host did not see a great deal of them because he was working, leaving them to entertain themselves, which they were capable of doing quite happily. 'So far as I remember I quite liked them,' Croft-Cooke wrote afterwards, 'but they did not make any great impression on me'.

On the Sunday evening Croft-Cooke had intended to drive the two men to Hawkhurst, where they could catch a direct bus connection to Chatham. But at the last moment he discovered that his car had a broken spring. He therefore saw Altoft and Dennis on to the village bus, giving them a pound to pay their fares.

Unfortunately the two men missed their connection at Hawkhurst. After spending some time and money in a pub there, they proceeded to assault a roadmender, whose bicycle they tried to steal; and they also came to blows with a policeman who appeared on the scene. As a result they were taken into custody on a charge of assault. Under police questioning they admitted where they

---

[1] Rupert Croft-Cooke. *The Verdict of You All* (1955), 13–15.

had spent the week-end, adding in response to further probing that they had committed indecencies with both Croft-Cooke and his secretary. 'We were told you would never know what we said,' Altoft afterwards confessed to Croft-Cooke. 'It was only for the files.' This was later confirmed in court by Dennis, who identified the police officer who had questioned them as being from the Sussex constabulary and as having said that if they 'cared to make a statement' about Croft-Cooke and Joseph 'it would probably help us in the assault case'. They subsequently informed the Legal Aid Officer at the Royal Naval Barracks at Chatham that the statements they had made were completely untrue and that the incidents alleged never took place. However, under further police pressure they retracted this, and agreed to testify for the prosecution at Croft-Cooke's trial.

Croft-Cooke and his secretary were arrested in the middle of the night. Although the police making the arrests had no search warrants, they spent several hours opening drawers, examining letters and pulling the beds to pieces. However, they found nothing that could be produced in any of the proceedings which followed. But they did find two bamboo canes in a cupboard, and were disappointed that they had been merely used to tie up indoor plants. 'Have you ever seen Mr Croft-Cooke with a cane in his hand?' a detective subsequently asked another man who had stayed in the house. 'I find that worth recording,' Croft-Cooke noted afterwards, 'since it shows only too plainly the state of mind of men employed by the State to dig in dark places.'

Two of Croft-Cooke's friends well known in the literary profession, Sir Compton Mackenzie and Lord Kinross, gave evidence at the trial of his exemplary character. Both said they had known him for twenty years. 'His reputation for decency and cleanness of living was very high,' said Lord Kinross, who added that personal contact with him 'confirmed that entirely'.[1] In spite of their eulogies and the fact that his previous record was entirely unblemished, Rupert Croft-Cooke was convicted on the virtually uncorroborated testimony of the two naval ratings whom the Legal Aid Officer at Chatham had described as 'completely wayward and thoroughly irresponsible in every way'. He was sentenced to nine months' imprisonment. His secretary, who was tried after him, got three months. Though urged to appeal by his lawyers, Croft-Cooke on careful reflection decided that it was not worth while going through a further period of suspense and spending a further £500 on top of the £1,000 which his

[1] *The Times*, October 10, 1953.

defence had already cost. Accordingly he served his time in
Wormwood Scrubs, the prison reserved for first offenders,
gaining full remission for good conduct.

A few days after his release, a man called on him at the house
where he was staying in London and asked whether he could
speak to him for a few minutes as he had been 'following his case'.
He did not reveal his identity and when Croft-Cooke eventually
asked him for his name refused to give it. After a few apparently
sympathetic generalities, the visitor, clearly a plain clothes
detective from Scotland Yard, said what he had evidently been
sent to say.

'I hear you're going to write a book about all this. Are you
going to give details of how your conviction was brought about?'

'Of course,' Croft-Cooke told him.

'I shouldn't do that, if I were you. It won't do you any good
and it might do you irreparable harm. If mistakes were made by
anyone—if anyone went too far, I mean—it's best forgotten now.'

Croft-Cooke replied that he did not agree at all, and that in any
event there were other people to consider. 'This filthy witch-
hunt is still going on.'

'That's what I mean,' he said smiling. 'It is. And you know,
a second conviction is very much more easily obtained than
a first, especially when the first has been well publicised. It
needs only the word of one person, a policeman perhaps or
someone who has been given an interest in the matter. If you
weren't believed before, you are scarcely likely to be believed
again, are you? No, I don't think you should rake up the
story now. Write about prison by all means, but the other
things . . . well, you wouldn't like another term, would you?
I mean it would be Wandsworth this time. Not nearly so
comfortable as the Scrubs. You think it over.'

Croft-Cooke did think it over, and as a result removed himself
to the comparative safety of Morocco, where he was free to go
ahead and publish his book in the form he had planned it without
fear of the consequences which his anonymous caller had indicated. 'I showed him the door,' Croft-Cooke wrote recalling this
unpleasant visit, 'and he left as unruffled as he came, apparently
pleased to have delivered his ultimatum. I hope I have shown
what I think of it.' He has done so in *The Verdict of You All*,
a vivid exposure of police and penal methods during the period
of the homosexual witch-hunt in the England of the early 1950s.

The most socially conspicuous victim of the witch-hunt was

twenty-seven-year-old Edward John Barrington Douglas-Scott-Montagu, third Baron Montagu of Beaulieu, an old Etonian and ex-Grenadier Guards Officer, who was best known for the vintage car museum which he had formed in the grounds of his historic Hampshire home. In his way Lord Montagu was as eccentric and unconventional as Rupert Croft-Cooke, 'rejecting the class-system which so many of his friends and neighbours held sacred', to quote his friend Peter Wildeblood.

His guests, both at Beaulieu and in his London flat, formed an extraordinary assortment of conflicting types: business men and writers, Duchesses and model-girls, restaurateurs and politicians and musical comedy actresses and Guards officers and Americans wearing hand-painted ties. He was always intensely busy and often merely used to introduce his guests to each other and then disappear. . . . Trivial though it may seem, this kind of behaviour enraged some people who took themselves extremely seriously and expected Lord Montagu to do the same. He made enemies, as well as friends.

Among the former could be reckoned the Hampshire County Constabulary.

Members of the local troop of Boy Scouts used to act as guides at Palace House, the Montagu property at Beaulieu, on the days it was open to the public. During the August Bank Holiday week-end in 1953 Montagu and one of his house guests, a film director named Kenneth Hume, took two of the scouts to a beach-hut he owned for a bathe. According to Montagu, the purpose of the visit was to find a camera which had been left there on a previous visit, and the bathe was only incidental. He reported the loss to the police; but when the police came to see him, they showed much more interest in him and his friend Hume than in the camera. Under questioning, the scouts now accused Montagu and Hume of having indecently assaulted them in the beach-hut. On the face of it, this story was most unlikely. Had there been any substance in it, Montagu would hardly have complained to the police in the first instance and asked them to make inquiries. What made the tale even less plausible was that he had only a week or two previously announced his engagement to a charming girl with whom he was obviously very much in love. (The engagement was subsequently broken off.)

While the police inquiries were still proceeding, Montagu went to France and from there directly to America. On learning that a warrant had been issued for his arrest, he immediately returned to England and surrendered to the authorities, at the same time handing over his passport. At his trial, which took place at Winchester Assizes in December 1953, on charges of committing an unnatural offence and an indecent assault, the prosecution sought to prove that instead of flying direct from Paris to New York on September 25, as he swore in his evidence he had done, he had returned to England for a brief visit of a couple of days and had flown to America from England on September 25. In support of this the prosecution pointed to an entry in his passport which seemed to indicate that he had been stamped out of Boulogne by the French passport authorities on September 23. Montagu denied this vigorously, saying he had not been in Boulogne for several years, and on examining the passport the judge pronounced that the date had been altered, the figure '5' having been apparently changed from '4'. The obvious inference was that the passport, which had been in the possession of the police ever since Montagu had given it up, had been tampered with to show that Montagu was a liar, and that if the jury could be convinced that he was lying about his movements, they might naturally conclude that his other evidence was not to be believed. It was never proved that the police were responsible for the passport forgery, neither was any official explanation of the forged entry ever forthcoming. As things turned out, Montagu was acquitted on the more serious charge of committing an unnatural offence, but on the lesser charge of indecent assault the jury disagreed, and the Director of Public Prosecutions decided that he and Hume should be tried again on this charge at the next sessions.[1]

The arrests of Pitt-Rivers and Wildeblood took place three weeks later, their premises being searched without a warrant, as had happened with Croft-Cooke. In addition to several specific indecency charges they were also accused of conspiring with Lord Montagu to commit them. The addition of the conspiracy charge in Montagu's case was most unfair and calculated to prejudice gravely his chances of acquittal at his retrial. Peter Wildeblood, who was diplomatic correspondent of the *Daily Mail* at the time of his arrest, and Michael Pitt-Rivers, a cousin of Lord Montagu's, were specifically accused, besides conspiracy, of offences with two R.A.F. men named Edward McNally and John Reynolds at the beach-hut near Beaulieu and also at the Pitt-Rivers estate in Dorset. Wildeblood had borrowed the beach-hut for a holiday in 1952, and there was a small party there on the first night

[1] *The Times*, December 15, 16, 17, 1953.

attended by Montagu and some of his house guests from Beaulieu. The prosecution was to suggest that it developed into a Bacchanalian orgy of the most revolting character. Actually it was a rather tame affair, there being no dancing between males or anything of that kind. As a matter of fact, throughout the evening the hut was encircled by Girl Guides, apparently engaged in bird-watching—a fact which, as Wildeblood observed afterwards, did not suggest that anything very lascivious was taking place.

Montagu, Pitt-Rivers and Wildeblood were tried together at Winchester Assizes in March, 1954. The charges in respect of the boy scouts on which the jury had disagreed at Montagu's previous trial were not included in the indictment, since neither Pitt-Rivers not Wildeblood had anything to do with these. But, of course, the extensive publicity which the previous trial had received was bound to prejudice Montagu in the eyes of the jury and in the circumstances to militate against his having a fair trial on the second occasion that he stood in the dock. The principal witnesses against the three defendants were the two airmen.

Reynolds and McNally are put forward as perverts, men of the lowest possible character [said counsel in opening the case for the prosecution], men who were corrupted, who apparently cheerfully accepted corruption, long before they met the three defendants. It is not to be laid at the door of the defendants that they were a party to this corruption at all.

These are witnesses whom we, in law, know as accomplices. They were willing parties to these unnatural offences, although, of course, they were committed under the seductive influence of lavish hospitality from these men, who were so infinitely their social superiors.

It came out in the course of the trial that the hospitality which the airmen received was quite the reverse of lavish, consisting for the most part of bottles of cider and simply cooked meals on the stove in the hall of Wildeblood's Kensington flat. It also came out that Reynolds was interrogated by the police for a total of eighteen hours and that McNally had been persuaded to 'confess' on being told that Reynolds had already 'squealed'. The airmen were further shown to have been involved in twenty-four other homosexual affairs, as a result of which neither they nor any of the others were ever prosecuted. McNally had a friend named Gerry, a male nurse, whom he described as 'my husband', and a receipt produced by the defence from the Regent Palace

Hotel in London showed that they had shared a room there together. 'The fact that neither of them was charged with an offence,' Wildeblood afterwards wrote, 'proves, I think, conclusively that the Crown in this case was not even concerned with the administration of the law as it stood. It was simply out to put Lord Montagu behind bars.'[1]

The Montagu trial, which lasted for eight days, was so well publicized on both sides of the Atlantic that it is unnecessary to go into it in any further detail here beyond emphasizing the atmosphere of heavy prejudice which characterized it throughout. The conspiracy counts bore heavily on all the accused, particularly Montagu, as well as the admission by Wildeblood, frankly and honestly made under cross-examination, that he was an invert. It may be added that Sir Theobald Mathew, the Director of Public Prosecutions, took the liveliest personal interest in the case. Not only did he give the assurance that Reynolds and McNally, no matter how many offences they might admit, would never in any circumstances be prosecuted, but he took the trouble to come down from London to Winchester and be present in court when the sentences were passed after the three defendants had all been convicted—18 months in the case of Pitt-Rivers and Wildeblood, and 12 months in the case of Lord Montagu. 'To punish a man at the age of twenty-seven for what was alleged against him at twenty-five must be a difficult task,' said Montagu's counsel in his plea of mitigation to the judge. 'If it had not been for recent events, Lord Montagu today would be a happily married man. That must be a devastating thought. He is a useful member of the House of Lords and a kindly landowner; he is faced with a bitter future.'[2]

[9]

In its next issue following the convictions at Winchester, the *Sunday Times*, which some months previously had drawn attention to the 'social problem' posed by the homosexual offender, claiming to be possibly the first national newspaper of standing to devote its whole leading article to this subject, came out with an even stronger leader under the heading 'Law and Hypocrisy'. It began by attacking the procedure by which homosexuals were convicted and sent to prison on the tainted evidence

[1] Peter Wildeblood. *Against the Law* (1955), 36–7, 48–50, 61, 69.
[2] *The Times*, March 16, 17, 18, 19, 20, 23, 24, 25, 1954.

of accomplices, often blackmailers and already themselves corrupted, 'for the witness is by confession "queer" and being queer he is liable to be activated by powerful motives other than respect for truth—jealousy, delusion, fear'. After showing how homosexuality was 'rich pasture for the blackmailer', the article continued:

> One may well ask whether, in regard to consenting acts between male adults, the real offence is to be found out. Notorious inverts occupy eminent places, and few people of wide acquaintance would be prepared to say that they know no one whom they could suspect of conduct which—if found out—would bring legal punishment and social disgrace. In all this matter, our society is riddled with hypocrisy.
>
> The law, it would seem, is not in accord with a large mass of public opinion. That condition always brings evil in its train: contempt for law, inequity between one offender and another, the risk of corruption of the police. In this instance, the law was imposed, and is applied, by the normal majority, who of their nature cannot experience any temptation to break it, and find it hard to understand the minds of those who do. . . .
>
> The case for a reform of the law as to acts committed in private between adults is very strong. . . . The case for authoritative inquiry into it is overwhelming.[1]

This was followed, among other press attacks, by an equally powerful article in the *New Statesman* on 'The Police and the Montagu Case'.

> On a careful consideration of the trial of Lord Montagu and his co-defendants at Winchester Assizes, several major abuses in police and penal policy become strikingly apparent. If they are allowed to go unredressed, it will be a fresh victory for the public apathy and gullibility that have always nourished the most illiberal tendencies among those in authority.

After enumerating these abuses, including the use of the conspiracy charge, which it stigmatized as 'the cruellest trap that the law ever contrived, an invention of the Star Chamber and a weapon of political oppression for centuries', the article concluded as follows:

> Regardless of the guilt or innocence of the defendants, of their social status, and of the humanity of the law relating to homosexuality, the Winchester trial provides, by itself,

[1] *Sunday Times*, March 28, 1954.

ample reason for an inquiry into the present methods of the Director of Public Prosecutions and the police. It also makes abundantly clear the need for a permanent committee . . . to review and as occasion demands to recommend reforms in the whole of our criminal law and procedure.[1]

While the charges in the Montagu trial were pending, another plea for the reform of the law relating to homosexual offences had been put forward in an interim report issued for private circulation by a group of Anglican clergy and doctors through the Church of England Moral Welfare Council. It expressed the hope that the facts it revealed about blackmail, the suicide of homosexuals, and police behaviour might be 'regarded as of sufficient importance to deserve a full official inquiry'. In changing the law, it recommended the fixing of an 'age of consent' as twenty-one, 'thus protecting the young National Serviceman who is compelled to live for two years in a predominantly male community and faces rather special risks of mixing with homosexuals'.

The Government eventually bowed to the storm of criticism. Just a month after the Montagu trial the Home Secretary, along with the Secretary of State for Scotland, agreed to the appointment of a Departmental Committee to examine and report on the law of homosexual offences and the 'parallel' problem of the law relating to prostitution.

The official announcement was made in the House of Commons on April 18, 1964, by the Joint Parliamentary Under-Secretary at the Home Office, Sir Hugh Lucas-Tooth, M.P., at the end of a short debate on the adjournment in which a Labour backbencher, Mr Desmond Donnelly, had pressed for the appointment of a Royal Commission 'to investigate the law relating to and the medical treatment of homosexuality'. In his speech Mr Donnelly read out passages from what he called the 'very interesting preface by Sir Travers Humphreys' to my book *The Trials of Oscar Wilde* on the blackmail aspect quoted above in Chapter 5. Mr Donnelly was supported from the Conservative back benches by Sir Robert Boothby (as Lord Boothby then was), who referred to 'recent cases which have caused distress to the country as a whole' and 'recent discussion in responsible newspapers' on the subject. Boothby added:

The duty of the State, as I see it, is to protect youth from corruption and the public from indecency and nuisance. What

[1] *New Statesman and Nation*, April 10, 1954.

consenting adults do in privacy may be a moral issue between them and their Maker, but in my submission it is not a legal issue between them and the State. The law must make adequate provision for the appropriate punishment of seduction or attempted seduction of youth—perhaps more appropriate punishment than exists today—of violence in any shape or form, of importuning and of acts of indecency committed in public. But there, in my opinion, the law should stop; and I believe that if it did, we would at once get a vast improvement in the existing situation, which to anyone who knows anything about it must give cause for the gravest anxiety and apprehension.

In making his announcement Sir Hugh stated that the Home Secretary felt that a Departmental Committee would be more appropriate than a Royal Commission, which was quasi-judicial in character. 'But he is anxious to secure the services of able and experienced men and women to serve upon this committee,' the minister reassured the House, 'and, therefore, it may be some little time before he is in a position to announce its membership and terms of reference'.[1]

While the Home Secretary was looking round for a body of suitable persons to serve on the committee, the septuagenarian Conservative peer, Earl Winterton, initiated a debate in the House of Lords on what he called 'the incidence of homosexual crime in Britain'. In a most reactionary speech, which he prefaced with an apology for bringing forward 'this nauseating subject', Lord Winterton castigated the Church of England for publishing the report of its Moral Welfare Council and praised the police for their recent actions, harking back to Wilde. 'It may well be said that the Oscar Wilde case was a moral purge,' he declared, 'and it may be that certain recent cases will have the same effect. If this be so, the whispering campaign against the police, which is going on very strongly, and sometimes in circles which ought to know better, should cease. In any event, I believe it to be unjustified, and I stand here to say that the police have been fully justified in the action they have taken in all the recent cases.' When he was young, Lord Winterton went on, 'this thing was never mentioned in decent mixed society', but now, to his disgust 'you hear young ladies, themselves of irreproachable morality, say, half-pityingly, half-facetiously, "Of course, he is a pansy: he cannot help it".' Finally, he referred to the great

[1] *Commons Debates*, Vol. 526, cols. 1745–56 (April 28, 1954).

actors like Sir Herbert Beerbohm Tree, whom he had known in the early days of the century. 'We were members of the same club,' he said. 'It is inconceivable that they would have been guilty of the disgusting offence of importuning or that the theatrical public in those days would have treated the offence with the leniency accorded to a well-known actor of the present day.' (The actor was Sir John Gielgud, who had been convicted in 1953 of 'persistently importuning for immoral purposes' and fined £10.)

Lord Winterton concluded this remarkable speech with these words:

> I am convinced that the majority of British people agree with me that few things lower the moral fibre and injure the physique of a nation more than tolerated and widespread homosexualism (*sic*). I hope and believe that we have not reached that point and never shall. If we did—and here I think I should have the support of everyone in this House— we should lose our influence for good in the world, and we should go the way of other countries in the past, who were once great but became decadent through corrosive and corrupting immorality.[1]

One wonders how the noble lord would have reacted when the House of Lords passed the Bill legalizing homosexual conduct between adult males in private, as it did thirteen years later. Fortunately he did not live to see what would have been for him a most terrible day.

This legislative achievement can be traced to the appointment by the Home Secretary of the Wolfenden Committee and the official announcement of its composition on August 26, 1954.

[1] Hansard. *House of Lords Debates*. Vol. 187, cols. 737–45. (May 19, 1954).

CHAPTER SEVEN

The Struggle for Reform

[1]

The Departmental Committee appointed in 1954 to consider the law and practice relating to homosexual offences and prostitution, under the chairmanship of Sir John Wolfenden, consisted of fifteen members who were drawn from Parliament, local government, education, law, prison administration, medicine and the Churches. During the three years which it took to produce its Report, the committee held sixty-two meetings and received evidence from over two hundred witnesses, both individuals and societies, most of them experts in their own particular fields.

So far as existing homosexual offences were concerned, the Report began with the following premise:

> We do not think that it is proper for the law to concern itself with what a man does in private unless it can be shown to be contrary to the public good that the law ought to intervene in its function of the guardian of the public good.

The committee then proceeded to examine and controvert the arguments for retaining the existing law, on the grounds that homosexual behaviour between adult males, in private no less than in public, was contrary to the public good, in so far as:

(i) it menaced the health of society;
(ii) it has damaging effects on family life and
(iii) a man who indulged in these practices with another man might turn his attention to boys.

Advocates of the first of these arguments held that homosexual behaviour was a cause of the demoralization and decay of civilizations, and that in Britain such conduct should be stopped by every possible means if the nation was not to degenerate and decay. 'We have found no evidence in support of this view,' said the committee, 'and we cannot feel it right to frame the laws which should govern this country in the present age by reference to hypothetical explanations of the history of other peoples in ages different in time and different in circumstances from our own.' As for the view that, if such men were employed in certain professions or certain branches of the public service, their private habits might render them liable to threats of blackmail or to other pressures which might make them 'bad security risks', the committee argued that this might be just as true of other categories of person such as drunkards, gamblers and those who became involved in compromising situations of a heterosexual kind. 'While it may be a valid ground for excluding from certain forms of employment men who indulge in homosexual behaviour, it does not, in our view, constitute a sufficient reason for making their private sexual behaviour an offence in itself.'

While generally admitting the truth of the second contention and deploring the damage capable of being caused to the basic family unit of society by a homosexual husband, the committee pointed out that cases were also 'frequently encountered' in which a marriage had been broken up by homosexual behaviour on the part of the wife.

> We have had no reasons shown to us which would lead us to believe that homosexual behaviour between males inflicts any greater damage on family life than adultery, fornication and lesbian behaviour. These practices are all reprehensible from the point of view of harm to the family, but it is difficult to see why on this ground male homosexual behaviour alone among them should be a criminal offence. This argument is not to be taken as saying that society should condone or approve male homosexual behaviour. But where adultery, fornication and lesbian behaviour are not criminal offences there seems to us to be no valid ground, on the basis of damage to the family, for so regarding homosexual behaviour between men.

Moreover, as the committee went on to argue, it had to be recognized that the mere existence of a condition of homosexuality in one of the partners could result in an unsatisfactory marriage, so that for a homosexual to marry for the sake of conformity with the existing structure of society or in the hope of changing his condition might well result in disaster.

As regards the third argument in favour of retaining the existing law, the committee did not think that the legalization of homosexual acts between adults would lead to similar acts with boys; on the contrary, the committee felt that such a change in the law would protect boys rather than endanger them.

> With the law as it is there may be some men who would prefer an adult partner but who at present turn their attention to

boys because they consider that this course is less likely to lay them open to prosecution or to blackmail than if they sought other adults as their partners. If the law were changed in the way we suggest, it is at least possible that such men would prefer to seek relations with older persons which would not render them liable to prosecution.

Confirmation of this view was received from the police authorities in Holland in the shape of information which suggested that homosexuals in that country were to some extent turning from those practices which were punishable under the Dutch criminal law to those which were not, e.g. as between adults over 21 and as between minors from sixteen to twenty-one.

The committee further sought to meet the more general argument that a change in the law would 'open the floodgates' and result in unbridled licence.

This expectation seems to us to exaggerate the effect of the law on human behaviour. It may well be true that the present law deters from homosexual acts some who would otherwise commit them, and to that extent an increase in homosexual behaviour can be expected. But it is no less true that if the amount of homosexual behaviour has increased in recent years, then the law has failed to act as an effective deterrent.

It seems to us that the law itself probably makes little difference to the amount of homosexual behaviour which actually occurs; whatever the law may be there will always be strong social forces opposed to homosexual behaviour. It is highly improbable that the man to whom homosexual behaviour is repugnant would find it any less repugnant because the law permitted it in certain circumstances; so that even if, as has been suggested to us, homosexuals tend to proselytize, there is no valid reason for supposing that any considerable number of conversions would follow the change in the law.

The final counter-argument which the committee advanced was 'the importance which society and the law ought to give to individual freedom of choice and action in matters of private morality'. This the committee believed to be decisive.

Unless a deliberate attempt is made by society, acting through the agency of the law, to equate the sphere of crime with that of sin, there must remain a realm of private morality and immorality which is, in brief and crude terms, not the law's business. To say this is not to condone or encourage private immorality. On the contrary, to emphasize the personal and private nature of moral or immoral conduct is to emphasize the personal and private responsibility of the individual for his own actions, and that is a responsibility which a mature agent can properly be expected to carry for himself without the threat of punishment from the law.

Such in brief were the arguments and counter-arguments which led the Wolfenden Committee (with one member dissenting) to make its revolutionary recommendation that homosexual behaviour of whatever kind between consenting adults in private should no longer be a criminal offence.

For the purposes of the proposed change in the law the committee recommended that the age of 'adulthood' should be fixed at twenty-one. The Report also included other proposals of a more detailed nature, designed to make the remaining law fairer and more logical; for example, that no proceedings should be taken in respect of any homosexual act (other than an indecent assault) committed in private by a person under twenty-one, except by the Director of Public Prosecutions or with the sanction of the Attorney-General; that, except for some grave reason, proceedings should not be brought in respect of homosexual offences incidentally revealed in the course of investigating allegations of blackmail, and that except for indecent assaults, the prosecution of any homosexual offence more than twelve months old should be barred by statute. ('We do not think that any public interest is served by pursuing stale offences.') On the other hand, an increased maximum penalty for homosexual acts between adults and consenting partners between the ages of sixteen and twenty-one was recommended. 'This was because the danger of emotional or psychological damage is . . . dependent more on the surrounding circumstances than on the specific nature of the act committed.'

> Even where no resistance is offered and no physical harm ensues, there may be considerable damage to the moral and emotional development of the victim. For example, a boy or youth who is induced by means of gifts, whether in money or in kind, to participate in homosexual behaviour, may come to regard such behaviour as a source of easy money or as a means of enjoying material comforts or other pleasures beyond those which he could expect by decent behaviour, and we have encountered cases where this has happened. Indeed, it is our opinion that this sort of corruption is a more likely consequence

than the possible conversion of the victim to a condition of homosexuality.

It is a view widely held, and one which found favour among our police and legal witnesses, that seduction in youth is the decisive factor in the production of homosexuality as a condition, and we are aware that this view has done much to alarm parents and teachers. *We have found no convincing evidence in support of this contention.* Our medical witnesses unanimously hold that seduction has little effect in inducing a settled pattern of homosexual behaviour, and we have been given no grounds from other sources which contradict their judgment. Moreover, it has been suggested to us that the fact of being seduced often does less harm to the victim than the publicity which attends the criminal proceedings against the offender and the distress which undue alarm sometimes leads parents to show. [My italics.]

Further recommendations covered the need for psychiatric reports before sentence and medical treatment in prison.[1]

Such a positive call for reform of the existing law might have been expected to produce a strong outburst of public indignation. But did not. On the contrary, the Wolfenden Report, certainly as regards Part II which dealt with homosexual offences, received a very largely favourable press, and was welcomed by practically every organization which had submitted evidence to it, as well as by leading spokesmen of most of the Christian denominations. It received the widest publicity both in Britain and overseas, much of it centred on the person of the chairman, who was believed to have written the greater part of it. Indeed Sir John Wolfenden was surprised by the nature of its reception; he was generally complimented and he stated, no doubt in jest, that he had even received an offer from America for the film rights. Opinion polls taken shortly after the Report's publication indicated that over 40 per cent of the community accepted its findings, while just over 50 per cent were opposed to them. Nevertheless, it soon became clear that the Conservative Government and in particular the Home Secretary, Mr R. A. Butler (as he then was) were in no hurry to implement any of the recommendations of the committee which a previous Conservative Government had initially set up.

This did not prevent a prominent parliamentary Labour front bencher, Lord Pakenham (later Earl of Longford), from raising

[1] *Report of the Committee on Homosexual Offences and Prostitution* (1957) paras. 52–63, 71, 72, 92, 97, 98, 135, 187, 211.

the matter in the Upper House, where he opened a debate on the Wolfenden Report just three months after its publication but did not press his motion to a division. Lord Pakenham, who favoured the committee's principal recommendation, was supported by speeches from nine fellow peers, including the Archbishop of Canterbury. On the other hand, eight peers spoke against this controversial recommendation, among them the Lord Chancellor (Lord Kilmuir, formerly Sir David Maxwell Fyfe) and the die-hard Earl Winterton. One of the most sincere and moving speeches was made in favour of the recommendation by Lord Brabazon of Tara, who, it will be remembered, had as a Member of the House of Commons in 1921 spoken against the proposal to make lesbian acts criminal.

When we speak about the repugnance and disgust of the [homosexual] act, we have to face the fact that all sexual intercourse, be it heterosexual or homosexual, if it is looked at anatomically and physiologically, is not very attractive. But along comes the glamour of love; and that is a mystical, creative, Divine force which comes over two people and makes all things seem natural and normal. And what we have to get into our heads, although it is difficult, is that that glamour of love, odd as it may sound, is just as much present between two homosexuals as it is between a man and a woman. Perhaps that is a terrible thing, but it exists and we cannot get away from it. We are all born not all the same. We may be right-handed or left-handed, intelligent or not intelligent, but we ought to thank our Maker that we are not born warped as to sex, because no more terrible affliction can be imposed on anyone.

These people are self-eliminating. They do not breed. They do very little harm if left to themselves. I feel myself that to have on the Statute Book of this great country imprisonment for life for one act of homosexuality between men is almost going back to the time when people were hanged for stealing five shillings. Because we do not understand the mysteries of sex; because we do not understand the terrible handicap of an invert, it should surely not be in our traditions to beat our breasts, and say 'We are holier than thou', and persecute. . . .

Sometimes, my Lords, great wisdom reposes in the sayings of the man in the street, and I should like to quote a saying that is known so well, when somebody is referred to as 'the poor bugger'. In those three words is a wealth of human understanding and charity towards a member of our race who has not been given the advantages of others—'the poor bugger'. We must not laugh at India, with their untouchables; we have our untouchables here in these poor people who are inverts. If there is one thing that I deplore more than anything else, it is the inclination in some quarters to indulge in witch hunts.[1]

No doubt when he uttered the last sentence above, Lord Brabazon was thinking in particular of the Montagu case. He had shown considerable sympathy for his unfortunate fellow peer, with whose father Brabazon had been a pioneer of British motoring and whose enthusiasm for vintage motor vehicles he shared. In the previous year Montagu had founded the world's first motor cycle museum, as an addition to his motor car museum at Beaulieu. At that time, having only recently been released from prison, he was still very much ostracized by society. This fact was not lost upon Brabazon, who made a point of coming down to Beaulieu for the opening ceremony and taking a conspicuous part in the proceedings. Brabazon was one of the earliest and most courageous advocates of homosexual law reform; he was unfortunately not to live to witness its achievement in Parliament. (He died in 1964.)

As the months passed, it looked more and more as if the Wolfenden Report would be quietly shelved, while at the same time homosexuals continued to be rounded up and prosecuted by the same old objectionable methods as had characterized the Montagu case. Hence two young Cambridge graduates decided that they would do something in order to bring pressure to bear on the Government, which had shown no signs of providing any time for the Report to be discussed in the House of Commons. The two men, Mr A. E. Dyson, then Lecturer in English Literature at the University of Wales, and the Rev. Andrew Hallidie Smith, an Anglican clergyman, were old college friends, who shared unhappy memories of the suicide of an undergraduate at the same Cambridge college. Together they took the initiative in forming the Homosexual Law Reform Society with the object of pressing for the necessary legislation. Kenneth Macfarlane Walker, a distinguished surgeon, psychotherapist and authority on sexology, who was Medical Secretary of the British Social Hygiene Council, became the society's chairman. He was a natural choice, since he was also chairman of the research com-

[1] *Lords Debates*, Vol. 206, cols. 733–832 (December 4, 1957).

mittee of the British Social Biology Council which, while the Wolfenden Committee was still sitting, had instituted the research project, the first of its kind in this country, which was undertaken by Gordon Westwood (Michael Schofield) into the lives of more than a hundred male homosexuals in Great Britain. With A. E. Dyson as vice-chairman and Hallidie Smith as the society's secretary, a campaign for the reform of the law was quickly launched.[1]

The first move was to enlist the support of a number of well-known public figures. This was done, and in due course a letter appeared in *The Times* (March 7, 1958) above thirty-three distinguished signatures. They included those of the ex-Labour Prime Minister, Lord Attlee, the Bishops of Birmingham and Exeter, Professors A. J. Ayer, Isaiah Berlin, and Julian Huxley, Sir Robert Boothby, M.P. (later Lord Boothby), J. B. Priestley, Bertrand (Earl) Russell, and Barbara Wootton (later Baroness Wootton of Abinger).

The present law is clearly no longer representative of either Christian or liberal opinion in this country, and now that there are widespread doubts about both its justice and its efficacy, we believe that its continued enforcement will do more harm than good to the health of the community as a whole.

The case for reform has already been accepted by most of the responsible newspapers and journals, by the two Archbishops, the Church Assembly, a Roman Catholic committee, a number of Non-Conformist spokesmen, and many other organs of informed public opinion.

In view of this, and of the conclusions which the Wolfenden Committee itself agreed upon after a prolonged study of the evidence, we should like to see the Government introduce legislation to give effect to the proposed reform at an early date and are confident that if it does it will deserve the widest support from humane men of all parties.[2]

This outspoken plea naturally produced a number of replies for and against. The latter included Lord Winterton, who had delivered such a reactionary speech four years previously. His contribution was to a great extent offset by a letter signed by

---

[1] Kenneth Walker. *Sexual Behaviour Creative and Destructive* (1966), 242. Walker, who died in 1966, retired in 1964 and was replaced by C. H. Rolph (Cecil R. Hewitt) as chairman, while Mr Antony Grey (A. E. G. Wright), a barrister and journalist, became secretary in the same year. Professor A. J. Ayer was the society's president.
[2] *The Times.* March 7, 1958.

Lady Adrian, wife of the Vice-Chancellor of Cambridge University, and fourteen other eminent married women urging the Government to implement the Wolfenden findings.

However, the Government continued to take its leisurely time, and Parliament was allowed to disperse for the long summer recess without any action being taken on the Report. Eventually, over a year after its publication, after some prodding at the beginning of the new session, the Government put down a motion in the Commons 'that this House takes note of the Report', an ineffective and inconclusive motion expressly designed to avoid a vote. It was moved in a fairly full chamber by Mr Butler, the Home Secretary, on November 26, 1958.

[2]

So far as Part II of the Wolfenden Report went, Mr Butler indicated in the debate that the Government did not feel justified in the present state of public opinion in proposing legislation to carry out the committee's recommendations. 'What is clear,' he said, 'after taking his time to think it over and to receive all the impressions and consider the perplexities of this problem, is that there is at present a very large section of the population who strongly repudiate homosexual conduct and whose moral sense would be offended by an alteration of the law which would seem to imply approval or tolerance of what they regard as a great social evil.' At the same time, he admitted that he was aware that 'much human suffering derives from the operation of the present law', particularly in offering scope for the blackmailer. He hoped that the debate would do something to 'educate public opinion' towards the type of reform 'which may be generally accepted', and he stressed the need for more knowledge of the subject. 'We know little of the causes or extent of homosexual conduct,' he added, 'and in the absence of knowledge we cannot adequately judge the consequences of any action we might take'.

Mr Anthony Greenwood, vice-chairman of the Labour Party Parliamentary Committee, made the opening speech from the Opposition Front Bench. However, he spoke solely in a personal capacity and did not seek in any way to commit his party. But he did make it clear where his own sympathies lay. On the question of treatment he thought that one was as likely to cure homosexuals by sending them to an all-male prison as one was likely to cure a drunkard by incarcerating him in a brewery. 'I believe that, ultimately, this reform will come,' he said. 'I am only saddened by the fact that it should come only after a still greater toll of human misery has been exacted by society.'

In the previous parliamentary session I had tried to initiate a debate on the Report through a Private Member's motion, but I did not draw a high enough place in the ballot to make this possible. It was therefore some consolation when I managed to catch the Speaker's eye immediately after Mr Greenwood had sat down, with the result that I was called third in the debate. In my speech, which was strongly in favour of the Wolfenden proposals, I quoted a pathetic letter which I had received a few days previously from a homosexual when he had heard that the Report was to be debated in the House of Commons. He was a 'consenting adult' who had been convicted some years before on the evidence of an accomplice for an act committed in private, as a result of which he served a term of imprisonment. On his release from prison he got a job as a clerk in a solicitor's office. He filled that job with complete satisfaction to his employers for several years; then someone wrote to the firm sending a press cutting with an account of his trial and conviction. The result was that he was promptly dismissed and it was impossible for him to find another job in the same neighbourhood where he lived.

I don't wish to pretend I'm good—but I am like many of the homosexuals, cursed with the thing from the beginning. God in heaven only knows the fights I have put up against it—and I'm sure I'm one of many—and have lost each time. It seems so utterly ridiculous for two men, who wish to live together in their own home, to be classed as criminals and 'sex maniacs'. I know men and women who have committed far, far worse acts than homosexuals look upon us as worse than if we were murderers.

I do so want to try and make you people look upon this coming debate with kindness and sympathetic consideration and think 'There but for the grace of God go I.' It is all right for people to condemn us so much, but they have no idea of the life of fear and dread we live all the time, in case our friends find out or we are caught. I know I did, and I know the hell I lived in when the police came to me, and I'm still living in hell now! You seem to be 'cut off' from everything, and can get no employment. Just because I was cursed with the homosexual trait, I was no more able to get rid of it than

a man could get rid of cancer. It's in you from birth—I feel
sure of that. I have studied so many cases and men I have met.
When you understand, you feel terribly sorry.

'I do not think,' I commented, 'having read a letter of that kind,
that there is anyone who cannot feel the same spirit of sympathy.'
Certainly no voice was raised in disssent.

Some ignorant prejudices were expressed, particularly by one
Conservative backbencher who was convinced that the condoning
of homosexual behaviour led to the downfall of Nazi Germany.
But on the whole the debate was conducted on a remarkably high
level. Much of it was concerned with the prostitution side of the
Report, but it did show that a subject as emotive as homosexuality,
apart from one Conservative backbencher's ludicrous argument,
could be discussed sensibly and sympathetically in the Commons.
Somewhat surprisingly the only two professional psychiatrists in
the House both came down on the side of retaining the existing
law. Although a number of Labour Members voiced their opposition to the proposals in Part II just as a number of Conservatives, including the present writer, supported them, it was apparent
that the Conservatives were generally opposed, just as Labour
as a whole tended to be in favour. Indeed this was indicated by
Mr David Renton, the Under-Secretary for Home Affairs, in
winding up the debate for the Government, when he went rather
further than Mr Butler had gone in opening it and said: 'We
believe it is the instinct of most members of the public and most
Members of both Houses of Parliament to decline the Wolfenden
proposal.'[1]

It was clear from this that a long and arduous fight lay ahead
for the reformers. For a small and slenderly financed organization
such as the Homosexual Law Reform Society, 'to educate public
opinion' was a formidable task if the Wolfenden proposals were
to be made palatable to the majority of M.P.s who feared, not
without good reason, a constituency backlash from the ignorant
and prejudiced. Incidentally, my own constituency association's
refusal to readopt me as their official party candidate at the
General Election in 1959 was directly due to my outspoken
support of Wolfenden. ('We cannot have as our Member one who
condones unnatural vice.') Meanwhile the society pressed ahead
with its policy of distributing informative literature and initiating
discussions at meetings of professional and business groups,
debating societies, Rotary Clubs and the like, besides continually

[1] Hansard. *House of Commons Debates*, Vol. 596, cols. 365–508 (November 26,
1958).

lobbying the politicians. Its arguments were crystallized in an
early progress report in the following words:

> Homosexuality is the problem of a minority, but not of an
> insignificant minority. The lowest reliable estimate is that there
> are at least a million each of men and women who are capable
> of sexual feeling only towards members of their own sex. Thus
> in terms of numbers alone, there are four times as many
> homosexuals as unemployed, and every section of society is
> affected by the problem. It is intolerable that a million men
> should continue to live in fear of the criminal law, and should
> be denied that freedom to make the choices for good or ill
> about their personal relationships which is given to all hetero-
> sexuals and to homosexual women. And if Kinsey's figures
> have any relevance to this country, over a third of the male
> population have had some homosexual experience at some
> time in their lives, which means that under the present law
> they are technically criminals. The absurdity of retaining this
> law is becoming increasingly apparent and needs to be con-
> tinually pointed out.[1]

An opportunity for pointing it out was at a large public
meeting which the Homosexual Law Reform Society held in
Caxton Hall, Westminster, on May 12, 1960, the second anniversary of the society's foundation. Mr Kenneth Walker acted as
chairman and the speakers included the Bishop of Exeter, Dr
Lindesay Neustatter, a well-known psychiatrist, Mrs Anne Allen,
equally well known as a magistrate and social worker, and Mr
Kingsley Martin, editor of the *New Statesman*. About a thousand
people turned up, so many that there had to be an 'overflow'
meeting in an adjacent hall. The bishop's description of the
present law as a 'monstrous injustice' summed up the general
feeling.

The chairman in his speech related a pathetic story of a
young man who had been rounded up in one of the periodic
police raids, and was brought by his parents from the north of
England to see Mr Walker. This is what happened:

> I had a talk with this young man—a very decent young
> man—and I said: 'Well, I don't know if I can do anything.
> At any rate I'll write a letter for your attorney to take [to
> court].' And I wrote a letter, a very strong letter, saying
> that this boy would be ruined if he were sent to prison, that

[1] Homosexual Law Reform Society. *Progress Report* (April, 1959).

there was a chance for him if he were treated, and that he could be helped. He was sent to prison.

Eight years later a strange patient, a young man, came into my consulting-room. He said 'Don't you remember me?' And there I saw in this now neurotic young man, who could only come to face me by priming himself with alcohol, the young man, I don't say of promise, but of possibilities whom I had seen eight years before. He had been confined in the usual crowded prison. Homosexual practices had taken place; even a warder had availed himself of the chances. He was complete neurotic, in the hands of a psychiatrist in the north of England who was going to give him shock therapy. He had come to me, this boy, to see what I could do. I had to say, 'He's beyond my help'.

And that was completely produced by this outrageous, this barbaric law.

Mr Kingsley Martin, who moved the resolution which was passed unanimously calling on the Government to implement the Wolfenden Committee's findings 'without further delay', referred to what had been said to the effect that the Wolfenden Report had already done something to improve the situation. 'The police are said to be more careful,' he remarked. 'Now I find that a bit trying myself. I think it means that they are more choosey, in the sense that they choose people who are less likely to make a fuss. I think it means that the working-class man, the person whose reputation is not very high or distinguished or something, is picked on, and that the son of Lord So-and-So and So-and-So is given a hint that he'd better go and live abroad and is not noticed at all. I find this singularly repulsive myself. And I find it repulsive that our political parties should all be frightened: not sure, that is, that they could benefit by taking this off the Statute Book.' In short, the Home Secretary had to face up to it. 'Either this is a law which he believes in and should enforce, or it's a law which he knows with all of us is archaic, inhumane, bad, cruel, and ought to be abolished.'

Shortly before this meeting, Mr Butler, who had been re-appointed Home Secretary after the 1959 General Election, had received a deputation from the society and had informed its members that, since 'the public had not shown its feelings in the matter', it would be premature for the Government to introduce legislation. Evidence of the successful meeting was now sent to Mr Butler together with particulars of the favourable reception with which the Society's campaign had been meeting throughout the country. In his reply, Mr Butler contented himself with repeating his view that the proposed legislation would be premature, reserving a more detailed opinion for the next Commons debate on the subject due to take place in the following month.

Mr Kenneth Robinson, a Labour M.P. and future Minister of Health, who was also a member of the society's executive committee, had been lucky in the ballot, and so was able to introduce a motion calling on the Government 'to take early action' on the recommendations in Part II of the Wolfenden Report. With one exception, every Labour speaker supported Mr Robinson's motion, and every Conservative speaker, without exception, opposed it. The more extreme Conservative view was expressed by a backbencher, Mr Godfrey Lagden, recalling the arguments for the burning of witches in an earlier age. 'Especially should people be punished,' said Mr Lagden, 'if their actions, which I contend are evil, have physical and mental danger to those with whom they come in contact. . . . In my opinion, in the general run the homosexual is a dirty-minded danger to the virile manhood of this country.' This observation produced a loud laugh from the Labour front-bench member and doctor, Edith Summerskill, which considerably annoyed Mr Lagden, who listed his recreations in *Who's Who* as cricket, water polo, boxing, and dog breeding. 'It is important for any country to have a virile manhood,' he continued with an angry glance at Dr Summerskill, 'and to see that it is not corrupted by such men as these. . . . I am sure that if many Honourable Members had seen the mental and physical state to which some young men have been reduced by being corrupted by these homosexuals they would know what was their duty tonight.' On the other hand, several more enlightened Conservatives went so far as to suggest that a change of law was inevitable, perhaps even desirable, but they boggled at the word 'early' in the call for Government action. Why reform, if it was right in principle, was better delayed was never made clear, but it was suggested somehow that the moral climate of the day made such a change inappropriate just then.

When he came to reply for the Government, Mr Butler made a temporizing speech, similar to what he had said in the previous debate, and he seemed to find as great a difference of opinion as there was on that occasion. 'I do not believe that the full case for a change has yet been made,' he said, 'nor am I convinced that we are yet in a position to take the final decision on what the precise nature of the change should be. We need more information and we are trying to get it. We need more time to discuss the very fundamental issues which arise in this matter of the relationship between law and morals and more time to weigh the possible, and necessarily speculative, consequences of modifying that relationship.'

Looking back afterwards on this debate and the free vote with which it terminated, Mr Robinson said:

> To anyone who believed that the Government *had* modified its view, or was at least content to take a neutral stance, Mr Butler's speech was a cold douche. After this strong indication of the official view, it was clear, despite the fact that Members enjoyed the rare privilege of a free vote, that the motion would be lost. In fact nearly half the House voted in the division lobbies—a very high proportion for a Private Member's Motion. Of the 300-odd who were absent, some abstained either for tactical reasons or because they were genuinely unable to make up their minds. I think most of them probably stayed away simply because, with the Whips off, there was no incentive to remain.

The result of the division was: for the motion 101, against the motion 215, so that the motion was defeated by more than two to one. The minority comprised 75 Labour Members, 22 Conservatives and 4 Liberals. The majority against the motion was made up of 178 Conservatives and 37 Labour. It is worth noting that the small Conservative minority for Wolfenden included Mr Enoch Powell, a future Minister of Health, later to become celebrated for his stand on the coloured immigration question.[1]

There the matter rested for nearly two years. Then in March 1962 another Labour Member, Mr Leo Abse, who had been successful in the sessional ballot for Private Members' Bills, introduced his Sexual Offences Bill in the Commons. This had three main objects: (1) in order to establish some degree of uniformity in the application of the law, all prosecutions for offences in private between consenting adults should be authorized, if at all, by the Director of Public Prosecutions; (2) in order to minimize the opportunities for blackmail by eliminating 'stale' prosecutions, proceedings in respect of such offences should only be commenced within twelve months of the alleged offence; and (3) it should be mandatory upon the courts to obtain a

[1] Hansard. *House of Commons Debates.* Vol. 625, cols. 1453–1514 (June 29, 1960).

psychiatrist's report with respect to all first offenders. However, even this modest measure designed to remedy some of the lesser evils of the homosexuality laws without including the major issue did not commend itself to the Conservative majority. Unfortunately, the debate on the immediately preceding Bill on shop front advertising, was unnecessarily and perhaps with unofficial Government blessing deliberately prolonged, with the result that there was less than an hour left at the end of the day for the consideration of Mr Abse's Bill, which was consequently 'talked out' under the procedural rules of the House. The Under-Secretary for Home Affairs, Mr Charles Fletcher-Cooke, who represented the Government during the debate, was, no doubt happily for him, not called upon to express the official view, since he had supported the Wolfenden proposals as a back-bencher two years before, and all the indications were that the official view continued to be unfavourable.[1]

Afterwards Mr Abse wrote about the fate of his Bill and advanced an interesting reason for its rejection.

> Yet no one examined this mild reform in any detail. The reaction was exactly the same as if one had attempted to implement the whole of the Wolfenden Report. That the Bill had the support of people such as the present Solicitor-General (Sir Peter Rawlinson) had no relevance. The arguments deployed were the same arguments as were deployed against the recommendations of the Wolfenden Report.
>
> Why? Is it that people who have not dealt with their own homosexual component are frightened of anything which would permit a more permissive law relating to homosexuality? If you get a community of men who in fact have not come to terms with their own homosexuality, who in fact are frightened of it, they are precisely the group of people who will insist upon legislation of a most repressive character. It is inescapable that every man must at some time, one way or another, come to terms with his own homosexual component. For those who are fortunate enough to be able to work through it and have the benefit of a stable family life there is the benefit of having a family happiness. But there are others who, largely because of accidents of fate within their early familial upbringing, have not come to terms with it and have consequently a reaction of fear. It is not a question of lack of sympathy—it is fear. It is fear that if you alter the law, that if you do not have the

[1] Hansard. *House of Commons Debates*, Vol. 655, cols. 843–60 (March 9, 1962).

external tabu against it, they will perhaps not be able to control their own emotions.

'Perhaps the most encouraging aspect of these very disappointing debates,' Mr Kenneth Robinson remarked later the same year, 'was the widespread recognition that reform must come, and the absence of any serious attempt to justify the existing state of the law. There was a transparency about the excuses for delay. . . . Whenever it does come, there is almost certain to be a short, sharp outcry: but I think this will soon die away, and the new situation will be as readily accepted as the present one. The essential work of public education has been done—it has been done by the Wolfenden Committee itself, in exposing for all who wish to see, the injustice, the ineffectiveness, and the hypocrisy inherent in the law as it stands. Parliamentary and outside pressure will continue until we have a Government and a Home Secretary willing to risk the brief storm—unlikely to be a very violent one— which reform of this law may provoke.'[1]

[3]

Three years were to elapse before the matter was again discussed in Parliament, by which date a Labour Government had come into power, and there had been a noticeable change in public opinion, thanks in great part to the activities of the Reform Society. In the meantime, the subject was constantly in the public eye, notably later in 1962 when it was officially stated that a homosexual civil servant employed in the Admiralty had been entrapped by the Russians and had as a result of the pressure put upon him been spying for the Kremlin for the past seven years.

Of course there was nothing new about this Soviet technique, which had been carried over from Tzarist times. In 1913, there was the sensational case of Colonel Alfred Redl, a senior intelligence officer in the Austro-Hungarian army, who had been blackmailed by the Russians for years into turning over valuable military secrets to them and then had blown out his brains in a Vienna hotel bedroom after a chance incident had led to his discovery.[2] Similar methods were stated to have been used in 1955 with thirty-one-year-old William John Christopher Vassall,

---

[1] Albany Trust. *Winter Talks 1962–63 Series* (1963), 37; *Man and Society* No. 8 (Spring, 1965), 4–5.
[2] Robert B. Aspry. *Feasting with Panthers* (1939).

then working in the Naval Attaché's office in the British Embassy in Moscow.

Unlike Burgess and Maclean, John Vassall was no 'pampered child of the Establishment', to quote Rebecca West. 'True, he had a grand-uncle who was a senior housemaster at Harrow, and another who taught at Repton, but the old school tie hardly stretches as far as that.'[1] In fact, his father was an impoverished Church of England parson, who could not afford to keep him at his grammar school beyond the age of sixteen. The elder Vassall, however, had enough influence to get his son into the Admiralty as a temporary clerk, a position made permanent after the war, during which young Vassall had served as a photographer in the R.A.F. Whatever his use to the Russians as a spy, he does not seem to have been particularly good at his work in the Admiralty, possibly because he devoted too much energy to his private life. A slightly effeminate manner emphasized that he was 'queer', and indeed he boasted afterwards that men had told him that he had 'come to bed' eyes. A journalist who visited his flat in Dolphin Square after his arrest was surprised by its elegance and luxurious furnishings, and by Vassall's expensive suits, perfumes, catalogues of women's corsets, and pictures of hirsute French rugby players. 'On my dressing table stood a miniature toy white poodle and other furry objects, and on my bed my favourite friend, a cuddly white cheetah,' he wrote in his life story which he sold to a Sunday newspaper at the time of his trial. 'I had a photograph specially taken in colour of me and my cheetah. I wish I had it with me now.'

Amongst the locally recruited staff in the Moscow Embassy was a Polish homosexual named Sigmund Mikhailski, who had been planted there by the Russians. A report from Mikhailski to his superiors that Vassall had the makings of a potential traitor led to a series of parties culminating in a dinner at which the unfortunate Vassall, according to his subsequent confession, became drunk, removed most of his clothes, and was photographed on a couch alongside a naked Russian. Another photograph, with which his Russian hosts subsequently confronted him, showed him grinning sheepishly and holding up a pair of men's briefs. To make sure that he should not escape from their net, it was said that the Russians later interrupted Vassall again, partly undressed and in the middle of a sex act with a handsome military officer who had likewise been planted on him, threatening him that if he did not agree to spy for them they would show the photographs

[1] Dame Rebecca West. *The Vassall Affair* (1963), 7.

to senior members of the British Embassy staff and 'would make an international incident of the matter'.

Sir William Hayter, who was the Ambassador at the time, has recalled in his memoirs that Vassall was 'very amusing' in a small part in an Embassy production of Terence Rattigan's *Harlequinade*. 'I remember him dimly as an obliging little figure who was useful at tea parties,' Sir William added. 'There was no excuse for him. If he had come to me or to the Naval Attaché and told us that he was being blackmailed by the Russians he could have been sent home at once without any opposition from the Soviet authorities. One or two similar cases occurred during my time, and in none of them was there any difficulty about exit visas.'[1]

In her study of treason, Dame Rebecca West has suggested with some plausibility that Vassall's failure to disclose the blackmailing story to the Embassy was because he had become a professional spy of his own accord, and that the Russians had engineered the allegedly compromising incidents to provide him with an excuse for his treachery in the event of his being caught. However, the blackmailing story was repeated by the prosecution and judge at Vassall's trial and was subsequently accepted by the press and Parliament. This in turn gave rise to the impression that Vassall was a weak, vain creature of inferior intellect. Vain he may well have been, but otherwise this was unlikely to be the correct view of a man who for seven years had carried on an occupation demanding unremitting industry in a skilled craft conducted in clandestine conditions, an endless capacity for dissimulation, and sustained contempt for personal danger.[2]

It is significant that the Tribunal, subsequently appointed by Parliament to inquire into the circumstances of Vassall's treachery, attributed this to his homosexuality, in reporting on his Moscow appointment.

> The selection of Vassall, a weak, vain individual and a practising homosexual . . . can now be seen to be the decisive mistake in the history of this case. It exposed him to the attention of the Russian Intelligence Service in conditions in which they were most readily able to identify him for what he was and to compromise him.
>
> This is not to say that his selection was a mistake for which there must necessarily be blame. His weaknesses were not readily apparent and the Admiralty method of selection of

[1] Sir William Hayter. *The Kremlin and the Embassy* (1966), 44
[2] Rebecca West. *The Meaning of Treason* (1965), 368.

staff for appointment of Naval Attaché's clerks was ill-adapted
for assessing strength of character and freedom from those
defects which the Russians might exploit.

Personally I am inclined to agree with Dame Rebecca West that
the Russians exploited the fact of Vassall's homosexuality, but in
quite a different sense from what has been generally believed.

Vassall returned to the Admiralty in 1956, after completing
two years' tour of duty in Moscow, and continued to work for the
Russians until his arrest in September, 1962. For part of this
time he acted as assistant private secretary to Mr T. G. D.
Galbraith, M.P., Civil Lord of the Admiralty. The precise nature
of the information which he imparted to the Russians was not
revealed at his trial. The Attorney-General described it as 'of the
highest importance', while the Lord Chief Justice, Lord Parker,
referred to the classification of some of the documents which he
passed on to his spy masters as 'Top Secret'. That his espionage
work was appreciated by the Russians may be gauged from the
fact that they rewarded him handsomely. Vassall's Admiralty pay
was only £700 a year, whereas in a single year he paid £3,000
into his bank account. What put the authorities on to his track
in the first instance did not emerge from his trial, but it is
probable that it was his extravagant mode of living, frequenting
expensive restaurants and night clubs in the West End of London,
that first attracted attention and led to his being watched by
security service agents. At the Old Bailey he pleaded guilty and
was sentenced to eighteen years by the Lord Chief Justice. ('I
take the view that one of the compelling reasons for what you
did was pure selfish greed.')

The discovery in Vassall's flat of several photographs of
Mr Galbraith and a number of letters from him to Vassall gave rise
to rumours that there was or had been a homosexual relationship
between the two men. However, the contents of the letters were
seen to be quite trivial and innocuous when the Prime Minister,
Mr Macmillan, authorized their publication, no more intimate
than one would normally expect as from a minister to a confidential clerk, who was acting as his secretary. Mr Galbraith's reputation was completely cleared by the Tribunal of Inquiry, although
the incident of the letters can hardly be said to have contributed
much to the advancement of his political career. Vassall's evidence
before the Tribunal confirmed that of Mr Galbraith as to the
nature of their relationship. Vassall was brought from prison and
questioned by the Attorney-General (Sir John Hobson).

It is plain, Vassall, that you had conceived an admiration at least for Mr Galbraith?—Yes.

Anything more?—I just liked him very much.

What do you think his view of you was?—I think he liked me and appreciated what I did in my own way for him and for Mrs Galbraith.

You, of course, had met a great number of men in the course of your life?—Yes.

And you know that we know that with many of them you have established a homosexual relationship?—With some people, yes.

You know quite well when another man has conceived a homosexual affection or regard for you?—Yes. Sometimes I did not know what it was to start with.

But you found out fairly quickly?—Sometimes.

Was there anything in Mr Galbraith's attitude towards you that led you to believe that he had formed a homosexual attraction or admiration for you?—Not a physical homosexual attraction, no.

Anything else?—Not that I can think of.

Was there any sex of any sort discussed between you and him at any stage?—No. We never discussed sexual matters.

Or any display of physical affection, however slight between you and him?—No.

Are you sure of that?—Yes.[1]

The Vassall affair had the effect of drawing general attention to the 'security risk' aspect of homosexuality and incidentally to the fact that the 'risk' was very largely the result of the existing state of the law. Some Labour politicians criticized Mr Galbraith for not having cottoned on earlier to the fact of Vassall's homosexuality; but here they were really getting their own back on the Conservatives for their criticism of Mr Hector McNeil, when he was Labour Minister of State at the Foreign Office in 1951, for having so long tolerated the much more blatant homosexual Guy Burgess as his assistant private secretary. Mr Donald Maclachlan, a former naval intelligence officer who was editor of the *Sunday Telegraph* at the time of the Vassall affair, gave as one of the reasons for official failure to detect Vassall's 'character defects' as being connected with society's growing tolerance of the homosexual character. 'To the Whitehall of 1962 he is in the category that a Jacobite was in 1745 or a Catholic in the days of the Spanish

[1] Cited Rebecca West, 67.

Armada: unreliable because he cannot altogether help it: a potential traitor because he has a guilty secret: a colleague with a weakness which cannot be condoned but whom it is distasteful to persecute.'[1] In its report, which was published some months later, the Tribunal of Inquiry admitted that it knew enough about Vassall to say that 'he was already committed to homosexual practices' before he was posted to Moscow, but that the fact of Vassall's homosexual behaviour was 'a private matter, and in any event information about homosexuals in general is not collected and recorded by the Security Service'. The omission, it is not unreasonable to assume, was speedily rectified.

Towards the end of 1963 Mr Macmillan resigned as Prime Minister. He was in poor health and no doubt much disheartened by the series of espionage scandals which had marred the last two years of his government—Vassall had been preceded by the case of the Soviet spy Gordon Lonsdale and followed by that of another Russian, the Soviet embassy attaché Ivanov Yevgeny, indirectly involving the British War Minister, John Profumo, through his association with Ivanov's mistress Christine Keeler. Contrary to the general expectation, Mr Macmillan did not hand over the reins of office to Mr Butler, the Home Secretary, but advised the Queen to send for the Foreign Secretary, Sir Alec Douglas-Home, who duly moved in to No. 10 Downing Street.

A few weeks later, the Earl of Arran, a Liberal peer and an enterprising and lively professional journalist, who strongly supported the aims of the Homosexual Law Reform Society, wrote to the new Prime Minister, asking for government support if he were to raise the subject in the House of Lords either by putting down a motion or by introducing a Private Member's Bill to implement the main recommendations of Part II of the Wolfenden Report.

January 29, 1964.

I have long felt that action towards this end would not only be human, but the sensible thing to do. And I also feel that public opinion is now ready for this step forward. It is difficult to give valid reasons for saying this: who can ever say for certain what people are thinking? But the changed attitude of the more serious newspapers, and the forthright views expressed on television and the radio which go unchallenged

---

[1] Donald Maclachlan. ('Who's to Blame for Vassall?') *Sunday Telegraph* November 11, 1962.

seem to indicate that the violent 'antis' are now a minority, though admittedly a vocal minority.

Moreover the attitude of the schoolmasters and school-mistresses (leaving out the public schoolmasters who remain pathologically 'anti') seems much more tolerant than in the past. And this, of course, reflects itself in the attitude of the younger generation itself. I know this because I go to quite a number of schools these days, presenting prizes, etc.

Finally, and most pragmatically of all, those Peers who feel most deeply about, and spoke most strongly against Wolfenden Part II, have now been removed from their Lordships' House either through Divine intervention or through other causes, and I think we stand a reasonable chance of getting a majority vote.

Lord Arran went on to express the view that in the event of a Labour Government being returned at the next General Election, it would either introduce legislation on the lines of the Wolfenden Report or else 'give a fair wind' to a Private Member's Bill. 'But might it not be better if the change were brought about under a Tory Government?' he asked. 'Many people tend to regard the Labour and Liberal Parties as the parties of compassion, and it would be useful, I feel, if the Tories were to give their blessing to this major piece of social legislation.'

The Prime Minister's reply, which it took him five weeks to compose, was not encouraging. 'I don't really share your confidence that the balance of Parliamentary and public opinion is now in favour of amending the law,' Sir Alec wrote from Downing Street on March 4, in the light of the motion which had been 'heavily defeated' in the Commons in 1960. 'I have no reason to think that there has been a significant change in the balance of opinion since that time, and I know that the Home Secretary, who has been keeping the matter under review, agrees with me.'

I am sorry to be discouraging, but I cannot feel that amend-ing legislation would have much prospect of success in the present Parliament, nor can I give any undertaking about the Government's attitude to a Bill or motion on this subject.

Anyhow I should leave it over to the next Parliament and see what you think of the chances then.

A few weeks later, Mr Henry Brooke, who had replaced Mr Butler as Home Secretary, repeated in the House of Commons that he had 'no evidence' that there had been any 'material change in the balance of opinion' since the debate four years previously.[1]

[4]

Throughout 1963 and 1964 homosexual offenders continued to be treated with considerable severity by the courts. In one case, in June, 1963, the Lord Chief Justice sentenced a twenty-two-year-old labourer and a twenty-four-year-old coloured U.S. airman to three years for offences of buggery and indecency. 'Whilst there is no question of corruption, both prisoners being grown-up men,' said the judge, 'I am not going to condone such action between consenting adults.' The sentence was much criticized at the time as being disproportionately severe, particularly when it appeared that the labourer was feeble-minded. In another case, involving a twenty-four-year-old labourer, described by the prosecution as 'of low intelligence', police questioning of this man about a minor non-homosexual offence led to the conviction of seven other men, all of whom pleaded guilty to homosexual offences, mostly committed in private. At the same time a considerable amount of police effort went into the ferreting out of some old and stale offences, one of which, for example, concerned an act of indecency committed by the accused nine years previously when he was sixteen.

Meanwhile the Law Reform Society's charitable counterpart, the Albany Trust, was developing a counselling and advice service for homosexuals and others with sexual difficulties, referring them to appropriate medical or spiritual help where this was available, which was by no means always the case. The following example in 1964 concerned a young rating in the Royal Navy, who was court-martialled on an indecency charge and sentenced to nine months in a military prison, besides being dismissed from the navy. While he was serving his sentence, he wrote to *The People* newspaper asking for help on his release and the editor put him in touch with the Trust.

I'm very much ashamed to say that I'm a homosexual. I am 24 years old and until now I have managed to keep this terrible disease secret. But the inevitable occurred and I must pay my debt to society for being born like this.

The real reason I'm writing is because my whole life has collapsed to the ground and I have nobody to turn to for help.

[1] Hansard. *House of Commons Debates*, Vol. 693, col. 587, (April 16, 1964).

I have been in the Navy for nearly 7 years as an Officer's
Steward and according to my service documents I was a
complete success until this unfortunate episode. The thing
that is worrying me is when I'm released from here I have no
job to go to, and who will employ a convicted homosexual?
The only job I know is what the Navy has taught me and a
job I really enjoyed doing. . . .

Another thing that is worrying me. Is there really a cure for
this, or is it a thing I've just got to live with?

Fortunately the Albany Trust was able to put the ex-naval
rating in touch with an agency which secured him a post in
domestic service, where he settled down quite happily. But by
no means every convicted homosexual was as fortunate as this
young man when he left prison. Incidentally, his letter is of
additional interest as an example of the mistaken impression,
often held by homosexuals themselves, including Oscar Wilde,
that homosexuality is a 'disease' capable of being 'cured'.

In July 1964, following on the appointment of a new Director
of Public Prosecutions, it was widely reported in the press that
the Director had requested Chief Constables to consult him before
commencing proceedings in respect of consenting homosexual
adults in private, and it was hopefully, though as it subsequently
turned out mistakenly, assumed that this would in practice mean
the end of such proceedings. The Home Secretary made it clear
in Parliament that there was no question of the Director's consent being required or of otherwise restricting the police in
bringing prosecutions, merely that it was 'thought better, for the
purpose of uniformity throughout the country, that the Director
should be consulted, although Chief Constables will remain the
prosecuting authority in each case'.[1] Indeed, it appeared that
the official view was that 'some authorities are too lax in ad-
ministering the present law about consenting males committing
an offence in private, not that others are too severe'.[2] So the
prosecutions went on, stale cases continued to be raked up, and
the quota of tragic blackmailing and suicides proceeded as before.
A disturbing feature of these cases was that in many instances
they were 'group' prosecutions where several men were accused
usually as the result of inquiries set in motion by a statement
obtained from one of them who had been arrested for importuning
and sometimes, as has already been seen, for a completely different
type of offence altogether.

[1] Hansard. *Commons Debates*. Vol. 699, cols. 1207–11 (July 28, 1964).
[2] James Margach, political correspondent, *Sunday Times*, July 19, 1964.

'It's easier than breaking and entering,' the teen-age leader of a blackmailing gang admitted at this period. 'We pretend we're queer, then let them take us back home, then rob them of everything. They're too scared of the police to do anything.' This young scoundrel added that he knew a boy who got £350 'straight off that way, just by threatening the queer'. In one case, reported to the Homosexual Law Reform Society by the victim, a man was on the point of opening the front door of his flat in south-east London one night when two youngsters emerged from the shadows, pushed him inside, and after threatening to reveal publicly that he was a homosexual if he resisted them, ransacked the flat and escaped with belongings to the value of £100. The man complained to the police and was told there had been a dozen similar cases reported to them within the previous month or so. In other contemporary cases from the society's files, the victims were too frightened to go to the police. They included a university undergraduate who was asked to 'purchase' a tape recording which had been made at a party which he attended, a man who was violently robbed in his office by two youths who threatened to accuse him of making homosexual advances, and another man who had £50 stolen from him by a soldier who had spent the night at his flat. In sentencing a young blackmailer who had been caught, the judge said: 'There are far too many of these cases where homosexuals are regarded by men of natural habits as victims they can knock about and rob.'

Besides these victims of robbery with violence, there was the unfortunate man who was systematically and ruthlessly bled white by the blackmailer over a period. He usually paid up under threats of exposure to his boss or his wife or the police. Sometimes the victim committed suicide when he could stand the pressure no longer. Occasionally he would go to the police, as happened with the retired army captain who was stopped one day by a West Indian in the Charing Cross Road with a hard luck story. A minor act of impropriety followed and the man from Trinidad was given a small sum of money. After this encounter the Trinidadian constantly pestered Captain 'X' for more money. Seldom a week passed without his asking for something. The result was that over a period of three years the victim parted with nearly £9,000, amounting to most of his life's savings. Finally Captain 'X' went to the police and the Trinidadian was arrested, convicted at the Old Bailey of extorting money with menaces, and sent to prison for seven years. He pleaded in the dock for mercy, but the judge very rightly cut him short with the words, 'Let me ask how much mercy you showed.'

Sometimes the blackmailer was a police officer. A case of this kind happened in 1964 when a constable was convicted of the attempted blackmail of a man he had met in a public convenience in Westminster. According to the evidence, the policeman, who was in plain clothes, exposed himself and then told the man that he must arrest him for importuning. On their way to the police station, the constable said to the man: 'This is a serious matter. You will appear in court tomorrow morning, and it will mean at least a £30 fine. You will probably lose your job and be shown up in the papers.'

The intended victim in this case, who was a chauffeur, replied that he had not been misbehaving himself in any way and that he would strenuously resist the charge. The policeman then told him that a payment of £25 to the Police Orphans Fund 'would settle the matter'. The chauffeur said that he did not have that much money on him, and they consequently arranged to meet the following afternoon outside a bank in Piccadilly. After they had separated, the chauffeur saw the policeman go back to the lavatory and then into a public house. He then telephoned Scotland Yard, and the plain clothes police officer was arrested at the Piccadilly rendezvous next day. He was subsequently tried at the Old Bailey, found guilty and got three years.

In October 1963 the Home Secretary informed the House of Commons in answer to a parliamentary question that homosexual victims of blackmail who complained to the police would not themselves be prosecuted save 'in grave or exceptional cases'. Unfortunately subsequent cases did not bear out this assurance, such as the case concerning a twenty-one-year-old motor fitter named Kenneth and a thirty-three-year-old clerk named Percy.

The two men, who met casually, went off together in Kenneth's car and had sex. Afterwards Kenneth asked Percy for some money towards the petrol. Percy offered him two shillings, but Kenneth insisted that he wanted more. He eventually accepted £1. Percy then tried to get out of the car, but Kenneth accelerated, and when the older man tried to interfere with the gears, the other stopped the vehicle, picked up a large iron file and threatened to smash Percy's face in unless he gave him more money. Percy, who was now thoroughly frightened, agreed to fetch another £1 from his house. When they arrived there, Kenneth took Percy's wallet and brief case which he said he would keep as security if he failed to return with the money. As soon as he got inside the

house, Percy telephoned the police, who soon appeared on the
scene and arrested both men. In due course both were charged
and subsequently convicted of private indecency, and in addition
Kenneth was found guilty of attempted blackmail. 'You are a
nasty, sefish young man,' said the judge in sentencing Kenneth
to 18 months. Percy, on the other hand, was put on probation
for a month. Although Percy was thus bound over, nevertheless
he was convicted of a homosexual offence and his conviction
remains on the court record.

If a greater measure of uniformity in prosecutions was achieved
as a result of the Home Secretary's announcement in July 1964,
there was in practice no alteration of the law by administrative
action and no let-up in the prosecution of 'consenting adults'.
Indeed, during the succeeding eighteen months, that is until the
end of 1965, eighty-one 'consenting adult' cases were reported
by the police, an average of over one a week, though not all
these were prosecuted to conviction. A particularly objectionable
feature of police methods which came to light at this time was
the assurance given in the course of questioning men who were
subsequently charged with homosexual offences that it was safe
to speak freely 'because the authorities take a lenient view of this
sort of thing nowadays', or, 'do you know that we have had a
letter from London telling the Chief Constable to be easy on
people like you?' For example, a twenty-three-year-old man
pleaded guilty to a homosexual charge at Winchester Assizes on
the advice of the police who told him that 'this would help him'.
It was his first offence. After hearing a medical report that no
treatment would be likely to change his homosexual inclinations,
the court sentenced him to eighteen months' imprisonment. His
forty-six-year-old partner, on the other hand, a married man
with two teen-age daughters who said he also enjoyed normal sex
relations with his wife, was merely bound over in the sum of £50
for twelve months.

[5]

A curious sidelight on the current police attitude to the homosexual underworld of London was provided at this time by the
action taken over an outbreak of 'Jack the Ripper' type of murders
of prostitutes. The speed with which detectives combed certain
pubs and clubs in Soho made it clear that Scotland Yard was
under no illusion about the nature of these establishments,

preferring to keep them under observation rather than closing them down and thus encouraging them to open surreptitiously elsewhere. This led to the paradoxical situation that a promiscuous and sometimes vicious homosexual who toured the Soho and Paddington clubs and bars where 'queers' forgathered nightly had usually less to fear from the police than someone with no experience of the 'gay' world who picked the wrong person for his fumbling advances in the suburbs or provinces.

Nevertheless the feeling was growing that a change in the law could not be long delayed. During the last months of the 1959–64 Parliament, the *Daily Telegraph*, the most widely read and influential Conservative daily newspaper in the country, joined the *Sunday Times* on the side of reform. 'There can no longer be any doubt', wrote the *Daily Telegraph* in a leading article, 'that the moral corruption which follows from the attempt to punish homosexual vice between consenting adults is greater than that which would follow from the abolition of this law. It should be abolished.'[1]

It is likely that the *Daily Telegraph* leader was inspired by an extraordinary news story which had appeared in the pages of another newspaper a few days previously. According to the *Sunday Mirror*, a top level Scotland Yard investigation into the alleged homosexual relationship between a prominent peer and a leading thug in the London underworld had been ordered by the Metropolitan Police Commissioner, Sir Joseph Simpson.[2] 'The peer concerned is a household name,' so the story went, 'and detectives are inquiring into allegations that he has a "relationship" with a man who has criminal convictions and is alleged to be involved in a West End protection racket.'[3] Two days later a statement was issued from Scotland Yard denying that any such investigation had been ordered. But by this time Parliament, Fleet Street and other informed quarters were seething with rumours that the peer had been to all-male parties with the thug in Mayfair, that he had been photographed with him in a compromising position on a sofa, that a homosexual relationship existed between him and some East End gangsters and a number of clergymen in Brighton, that some people who knew of these relationships were being blackmailed, and that Scotland Yard had for months been watching meetings between the peer and the underworld thug and had investigated all these matters and reported them to the Metropolitan Police Commissioner.

[1] July 20, 1964.
[2] Sir Joseph Simpson had succeeded Sir John Nott-Bower in 1958.
[3] *Sunday Mirror*, July 12, 1964.

The peer in question was not mentioned by name in any of the newspaper accounts, but he was easily identifiable as Lord Boothby, who was at this time widely known for his appearances on radio and television. He was not a homosexual, and it is scarcely necessary to add that there was not a word of truth in the story. On the other hand, Lord Boothby was known to be a strong supporter of homosexual law reform; he had spoken in favour of Lord Arran's Bill, and when he was a Member of the House of Commons he had been instrumental, along with the Labour M.P. Mr Desmond Donnelly, in persuading the Government to appoint the Wolfenden Committee. The alleged underworld thug was thirty-one-year-old Ronald Kray, who with his twin brother Reginald ran a number of clubs in the West End of London. Ronald Kray had at his own request met Lord Boothby on three occasions in the latter's flat, when others were present, in an attempt to interest him in a business proposition in West Africa, which Lord Boothby eventually turned down. On one of these visits Lord Boothby permitted a photographer supplied by Ronald Kray to take a perfectly innocuous picture of himself and the Kray brothers in the flat, and a print of this photograph found its way into the possession of the *Sunday Mirror*.

At this time Lord Boothby was undergoing a health cure, along with Sir Colin Coote, a former editor of the *Daily Telegraph*, at Vittel in eastern France. Airmail editions of newspapers referring to the story reached the spa and were read by Lord Boothby and Sir Colin. 'We had no idea who the peer was,' Lord Boothby said afterwards. 'We had guessing games about it, but it never occurred to me that I was the man.' He only discovered it after returning to London on July 17, when he learned the news from a Labour M.P. who telephoned him about it. This was confirmed by three Conservative M.P.s who called on him at one o'clock in the morning with a copy of the German magazine *Stern*, which mentioned him and Ronald Kray by name. Lord Boothby thereupon consulted his lawyers with a view to taking legal proceedings against the publishers of the *Sunday Mirror* and its sister journal the *Daily Mirror*. He also wrote a letter from the House of Lords to *The Times* categorically denying the whole story. 'It had to come out in the open,' he said. 'My name and Mr Kray's had appeared in the German magazine *Stern*, and wild rumours were flying about.'

I am satisfied that the source of all these rumours is the *Sunday Mirror* and the *Daily Mirror*. I am not a homosexual.

I have not been to a Mayfair party of any kind for more than twenty years. I have met the man who is alleged to be a 'king of the underworld' only three times, on business matters, and then by appointment, at his request, and in the company of other people.

I have never been to a party in Brighton with gangsters—still less clergymen. No one has ever tried to blackmail me. The police say that they have not watched any meetings or conducted any investigations, or made any request to the Home Secretary connected with me. In short, the whole affair is a tissue of atrocious lies.

It was intolerable, Lord Boothby continued, that any man should be put into the cruel dilemma of having either to remain silent while such rumours spread, or considerably to increase the circulation of the newspapers mentioned by publicly denying them. Accordingly he challenged the papers in question, if they had 'a shred of evidence' against him, either documentary or photographic, 'to print it and take the consequences'.[1]

The newspapers made no attempt to do so. A few days later, it was announced that the International Publishing Corporation, which owned the *Sunday Mirror* and the *Daily Mirror*, had paid Lord Boothby the sum of £40,000 'as compensation' for injury to his reputation. This was accompanied by a public apology from Mr Cecil King, the chairman of I.P.C. 'I am satisfied', stated Mr King, 'that any imputation of an improper nature against Lord Boothby is completely unjustified.'[2]

The alleged 'king of the underworld' also got an apology from the newspapers—but no money. Five years later—in March, 1969—he and his twin brother were convicted of murdering a fellow gangster and sentenced to thirty years.

[6]

The General Election, which took place in October 1964, wiped out the 100-strong Conservative majority in the House of Commons, and returned a Labour Government to power after thirteen years in Opposition. But Mr Wilson, who took office as Prime Minister, only had a tiny majority of five with which to govern, and in these circumstances the new Parliament was likely to be a comparatively short one. Nevertheless the reformers felt

it was worth while putting opinion to the test in the new Parliament, and Lord Arran was quickly off the mark in the Upper
House. With the help of the Reform Society, he put down a
motion 'to call attention to the recommendations of the Wolfenden Committee on homosexual offences, and to move for Papers',
for debate on May 12, 1965. This was the traditional preliminary
to the initiation of legislation by a Private Member of the House
of Lords. Its counterpart in the Commons was to seek leave
to introduce a Private Member's Bill under the 'ten minute rule',
by which the speeches of the mover and opposer of the measure
are limited to ten minutes duration. Mr Leo Abse, M.P., who
had replaced Kenneth Robinson on the Law Reform Society's
Executive Committee upon the latter's appointment as Minister
of Health following the General Election, gave notice that he
would seek leave to introduce such a bill under the 'ten minute
rule' after Lord Arran's motion had been debated by the Peers.

An unfortunate incident occurred at this time affecting a
member of the Upper House and ending in tragedy. The peer
concerned was the fifty-eight-year-old Patrick Lord Moynihan,
a stockbroker by occupation, whose father had been a famous
surgeon. Married twice, he had children by both wives. Besides
his City interests, the second Lord Moynihan was active in public
life, a former chairman of the Liberal Party Executive, a supporter
of penal reform and the remedial treatment of offenders, and
he had already raised his voice in the House of Lords in favour of
the Wolfenden Committee's recommendations. He intended to
speak in the debate to be initiated by Lord Arran, and with this
object he set about collecting material for the speech which he
hoped to make. His researches took him to the public lavatory
at Piccadilly Underground Station so that he could observe at
first hand any importuning which may have been taking place
there. Unfortunately his 'loitering' for this purpose aroused the
suspicions of the plain clothes police who constantly patrol the
lavatory and its immediate neighbourhood, and he suddenly
found himself arrested and charged with 'persistently importuning for an immoral purpose'. The magistrate remanded him
for a week on bail of £25, but he was too ill to appear in court
again. His arrest had been such a shock to his system that it
brought on an apoplectic stroke from which he died a few days
later. The solicitor whom he had instructed for his defence
thereupon applied to the court to dismiss the charge on account
of the defendant's death and to mark the register accordingly.
But the magistrate felt that he could not depart from the usual

procedure in such cases which was simply to mark the register, 'No appearance—Defendant dead', although the solicitor had made it clear that if Lord Moynihan had lived the charge would have been vigorously contested. 'In my submission,' said the solicitor, 'it is wrong, where a charge cannot be proceeded with, that it should stand against the memory of a man who has done memorable service to his country.'[1]

On the eve of the Lords debate, an important letter appeared in *The Times* over the signature of eight influential peers, five being 'spiritual' and three 'temporal'. The former were the Bishops of Birmingham, Bristol, Exeter, London and St Albans; the latter were leading figures in the fields of medicine (Lord Brain), law (Lord Devlin) and education (Lord Robbins).

> Seven years ago a distinguished list of 33 signatories wrote in your columns that the existing law clearly no longer represented either Christian or liberal opinion in this country, and that its continued enforcement would do more harm than good to the community as a whole.
>
> In our view, the passage of time has only served to confirm this judgment, and we hope as a result of the Motion . . . which Lord Arran is to move in the House of Lords on the 12th May, Her Majesty's Government will recognise that the time for this reform is overdue, and will introduce the necessary legislation with the minimum of delay.

Lord Devlin's signature to this letter was especially interesting, since he had emerged in his 1959 Maccabean Lecture on 'The Enforcement of Morals' as the leading theoretical opponent of the doctrine of John Stuart Mill, substantially adopted by the Wolfenden Committee, that the law has no right to interfere with the adult citizen's private moral choice.

In introducing his motion, Lord Arran made a simple, straightforward speech 'as an ordinary man, who is privileged to be a Member of your Lordships' House, and as a Christian'. He spoke for half an hour. 'I have read much on this subject,' he said, 'so much, indeed, that at times the issues became blurred, and I no longer knew what it was all about. But, in the end, having read all, or most, of the books, and absorbed to the best of my ability all the clever arguments and counter-arguments, I found myself back where I started, and with these conclusions: that, in accepting the law on homosexual practices as it now stands, we are persecuting a minority and we are being unjust. And these

[1] *The Times*, April 21, 28, May 4, 1965.

things, I think, are unbecoming to our country.' In the ensuing debate, sixteen peers, including the Archbishops of Canterbury and York spoke in favour of implementing the main recommendations of the Wolfenden Committee, and only three against, with the Government spokesman, Lord Stonham, adopting a neutral position. Fortified by this impressive demonstration of opinion, Lord Arran withdrew his motion at the end of the debate and announced that he would bring in a Private Member's Bill on the subject at the earliest opportunity.[1] Twelve days later, after it had received a formal First Reading, he moved the Second Reading of his Sexual Offences Bill, a simple one-clause measure designed to protect consenting adults.

On this occasion, the opposition was more vocal. It was led by Field Marshal Viscount Montgomery of Alamein, who said that he could not reconcile with his beliefs what was said by the prelates in the previous debate, which incidentally he had not attended. 'To condone unnatural offences in male persons over twenty-one, or indeed, in male persons of any age, seems to me utterly wrong,' the gallant field marshal proclaimed. 'I am against any suggestion that we should weaken the law as it stands at present. My main reason is that a weakening of the law will strike a blow at all those devoted people who are working to improve the moral fibre of the youth of this country. And heaven knows, it wants improving!' Adopting a metaphor from the peculiarly English game of cricket, Lord Montgomery besought his fellow peers, when the time came to vote, to go with him into the opposition lobby and 'knock this Bill for six right out of the House'. He was supported in the debate by among others two Conservative ex-Lord Chancellors (Kilmuir and Dilhorne), a former Lord Chief Justice (Goddard), and the recent head of the Boy Scouts in the British Commonwealth (Rowallan). In particular, Kilmuir spoke of the 'proselytization which goes out from sodomitic societies and buggery clubs which everyone knows exists', while Goddard expressed the conviction that if Arran's Bill were passed it would be 'a charter for these buggers' clubs' and they would consequently be able 'to spring up all over the place'. The eighty-eight-year-old ex-Lord Chief Justice recalled that once when he was on circuit in Suffolk sixteen people stood before him in the dock at the same time, and that none of these people would be guilty of any offence if Arran's Bill went through. It is noteworthy that neither of these two distinguished lawyers produced any evidence of the existence

[1] *Lords Debates*, Vol. 266, cols. 71–172 (May 12, 1965).

of the so-called buggers' clubs, and when subsequently tackled by the Homosexual Law Reform Society declined or were unable to do so. Nor for that matter did any other peer who spoke in the debate with the exception of Dean Farrar's grandson, the Earl of Iddesleigh, who informed the House that when he was a young man about the end of the First World War he once walked through Soho with a knowledgeable journalist friend who pointed out to him the door of a well-known buggery club. 'It is obvious that if we pass this Bill, we shall have an increase of these clubs,' said Lord Iddesleigh, 'and we shall have to consider the question whether the club in which men dance with male partners and see the kind of cabarets that homosexuals want to see is, or is not, a private place.' It was this argument which in the final version of the Bill restricted immunity from the criminal law to occasions where not more than two consenting persons aged twenty-one or over were present when the homosexual act took place—an amendment which had been carried and incorporated in Lord Arran's first Bill by its opponents led by Lord Dilhorne, whose numerous supporters in the debates were implacably hostile to any amelioration of the full rigours of the old law. On the other hand, the Marquess of Queensberry, thirty-five-year-old great-grandson of Oscar Wilde's determined persecutor, pleaded for toleration in a maiden speech which was acclaimed from every side of the House. 'I believe these laws will be changed,' he said, 'and that when my children are grown up they will be amazed that laws of this sort could have existed in the middle of the twentieth century.'[1]

When the division took place at the end of the debate, Lord Arran's majority for his Bill was nearly two to one, the figures being 94 in favour and 49 against. Although the Government could not officially take over the Bill, Lord Arran was offered the help of the official parliamentary draftsman so as to enable him to incorporate more of the Wolfenden recommendations in his measure while it was being considered in detail.

In the Commons Mr Abse was less successful, although the result was by no means wholly discouraging. He was refused leave to bring in a similar Bill to Lord Arran's by 178 votes to 159, but the size of the opposing majority—only 19 votes compared with 114 when Mr Robinson's motion was defeated five years previously—showed that parliamentary opinion in the elected Lower House had changed considerably since 1960.[2]

---

[1] *Lords Debates.* Vol. 266, cols. 631–711 (May 24, 1965).
[2] *Commons Debates.* Vol. 713, cols. 611–20 (May 26, 1965).

Opinion had also been moving in the direction of reform in the constituencies, as shown by a National Opinion Poll and a Gallup Poll taken later in the same year. There the figures—as it happened, identical—indicated 63 per cent in agreement with the Wolfenden proposals and 36 against.

Meanwhile Lord Arran's Bill slowly progressed in the Lords, where numerous amendments were moved, some friendly and others hostile, in the course of the Committee and Report stages, which occupied twenty-seven hours, during which eighty-two speeches were delivered. One amendment which was designed to retain buggery between consenting adults as a crime apart from 'gross indecency' was quite rightly rejected, since its effect would have been to place an impossible burden upon the police in deciding whether or not to make an arrest. Serving officers and men in the armed services were exempted from the proposed measure to meet the complaint loudly voiced from the opposition that to have included them within its scope would undermine discipline. Throughout the lengthy discussions, Lord Arran handled all the amendments and interjections with the utmost patience and imperturbable good humour. The Third Reading was carried on October 28 by 116 votes to 46.[1]

In moving the final passage of his Bill, Lord Arran read a letter which he had received from the father of an adult homosexual.

> We—that is my wife and I—are particularly anxious that this Bill shall become law because our son is, most unfortunately, a homosexual. Naturally we are very concerned, worried and terrified lest he gets into serious trouble as a result. Recently I had a friendly talk with him on his behaviour and the appalling consequences should he get found out. To my horror he replied, 'Don't worry, Dad, if we get found out there will be no disgrace, I shall quietly snuff it.' Understandably I have not told my wife this, but I assure you I live in a world of perpetual fear and anxiety lest one of his contacts, who are unknown to me, should in some way expose him.

'By "snuff it" presumably the fellow means that he would kill himself,' was Lord Arran's comment. 'That letter seems to me to epitomize the situation and show what it is all about.'

There was now no chance of the Bill reaching the Statute Book in that session, since there was insufficient time available for its passage through the Commons, even if a sponsor could have been found among the M.P.s on the backbenches there. Lord Arran

[1] *Lords Debates*, Vol. 269, cols. 677–730 (October 28, 1965).

therefore reintroduced it in the Lords immediately after the start of the new session in November, when it was given a formal First Reading on November 10. Meanwhile in the Lower House, a Conservative M.P., Mr Humphry Berkeley, who drew second place in the sessional ballot for Private Members' Bills, announced his intention of introducing a measure identical with Lord Arran's. He duly did so and moved the Second Reading on February 11, 1966. This was carried by 166 votes to 109 on a free vote, a majority of 57 for the Bill. The Prime Minister, Mr Wilson, did not vote, but no less than thirteen members of his Cabinet did so in favour of the measure. They included the Home Secretary, Mr Roy Jenkins, who also made an impressive speech, in which he recalled that his Conservative predecessor, who had since become Lord Butler, had argued for more time for research and the education of public opinion. 'Well, we have had more time,' said Mr Jenkins. 'Just as Lord Butler believed that public opinion would continue to be educated, so I believe that to a substantial extent it has now been educated. It is for the House to decide, but I do not think we shall gain by further postponement, that an easier time for decision will arise, or that Parliament will get a better Bill on which to face this difficult issue.'[1]

Mr Berkeley's Bill was committed to a Standing Committee and all seemed set for its further progress when the Prime Minister decided to call a General Election and Parliament was dissolved in March. In Lord Arran's words 'once again the Bill went into limbo. It was then necessary to start all over again from, if you like, square one, but what I call square nought.' Unfortunately Mr Berkeley lost his seat at the Election, and it was suggested in some quarters that this was due to his forthright championing of the cause of homosexual law reform. But this was doubtful, since Mr William Shepherd, the Berkeley Bill's principal opponent in the Commons, was also defeated as well as twenty other M.P.s who had voted against the Bill. The truth was that there was a decided swing towards Labour, which came back with an overall majority of 99, and the Labour gains in marginal Conservative constituencies were made irrespective of the candidates' records on the homosexual issue.

Lord Arran would have preferred that the matter should have been put in train afresh in the Commons, but it appeared that there was to be no ballot there for Private Members' Bills until November, besides which there was no certainty that any M.P. in the new House would be prepared to take on the Bill again.

[1] *Commons Debates.* Vol. 724, cols. 782–874 (February 11, 1966).

So for the third time he introduced it in the Lords, where the Second Reading was carried on May 10, 1968, by 70 votes to 29. 'I know that there are dangers in this Bill,' Lord Arran said on this occasion. 'There are dangers in all reform. I suppose there was a danger in the Bills for the abolition of hanging for sheep stealing and for slavery. These things seemed to a number of wise people at the time to be wrong; but they were done, and Britain survived and was the better for it.'[1] Although a field marshal (Lord Montgomery) continued to oppose it, Lord Arran was very glad to be able to inform the House that Admiral of the Fleet Earl Mountbatten of Burma 'approves most strongly of homosexual law reform'. (So did the Lord Chief Justice, Lord Parker.) The remaining stages were passed quickly, although on the occasion of the Third Reading, which took place on June 16, the majority for the Bill fell to 18, the lowest yet.

Three weeks later, Mr Leo Abse asked leave to introduce a similar Bill in the Commons under the ten-minute rule. On this occasion the result was a pleasant surprise for him and his followers. Mr Abse was given leave by a majority of 144, the voting being 246 to 102.[2] As usual, the Northern Ireland Members, including my successor, went into the Noe lobby against the Bill, which was automatically given its First Reading immediately afterwards. For procedural reasons, the next debate did not take place until the new session in December, when the Bill, which was identical with Lord Arran's measure, was given an unopposed Second Reading; but its safety was now assured, since the Government agreed to provide such additional time as might be necessary for its further stages.[3] It was duly committed to a Standing Committee, which passed a significant amendment exempting merchant seamen from its provisions. But it required an all-night sitting to get the Bill through its remaining stages in the Commons. This was by no means plain sailing for Mr Abse, since by the rules of the House he had to have not less than 100 supporters available to vote in case the closure should be moved; if he should fail to muster less than that figure, the proceedings would be automatically adjourned and being so near the end of the session the Bill would in all probability be lost. In fact, seven divisions were called in the course of the night before the vote on the Third Reading was taken, and Mr Abse must have had some anxious moments, particularly

---

[1] *Lords Debates.* Vol. 274, cols. 605–52 (May 10, 1966).
[2] *Commons Debates.* Vol. 731, cols. 259–68. (July 5, 1966).
[3] *Commons Debates.* Vol. 738, cols. 1068–1148 (December 20, 1966).

when the majority in one of the divisions fell to 103. However, all came right in the end and as the first rays of the rising sun were seen over Westminster Bridge in the morning of July, 4, 1967, the Bill passed its Third Reading by 85 votes. The last member to speak in the debate was Sir Edward Boyle, a former Conservative Minister of Education, who voted for the Third Reading. 'I believe that, rightly, the Bill humanizes our criminal law,' said Sir Edward, 'and I do not think that we need worry that other people will take it as a sign of Britain's degeneracy. I am not greatly concerned about what opinion overseas will think of it. The House of Commons is right to do what we think is proper and to pursue what we think are the right ideals for British society.'[1]

As it was necessary for the Bill to pass through all its stages in each House during a single session in order to become law, it had now to be introduced yet again in the Lords. This task Lord Arran performed with his customary *bonhomie*, while the ex-Conservative Lord Chancellor Viscount Dilhorne fought a stubborn rearguard action on behalf of the Bill's diehard opponents.

Among other features the debate was noteworthy for intelligent contributions from two peeresses. One of these was Lady Gaitskell, widow of the Labour leader Hugh Gaitskell. 'As a society,' she said, 'we gloss over many perversions between men and women in private. The law, and society, are very tolerant towards these and turn a very blind eye. Those men who are born, conditioned or tempted irrevocably into homosexuality should have extended to them the same degree of tolerance as is extended to any other so-called perversion between men and women. I do not believe, my Lords, that intolerance towards homosexuals is a hallmark of virtue.'

Lady Wootton had not intended to intervene, but she could not resist doing so with a characteristic impromptu utterance after she had listened to Lord Dilhorne for the third time and had come to the conclusion that the gulf between them was completely unbridgeable. 'What are the opponents of this Bill afraid of?' she asked.

They cannot be afraid that these disgusting practices will be thrown upon their attention, because these acts are legalised only if they are performed in private. They cannot be afraid that there will be a corruption of youth, because these acts will be legalised only if they are performed between consenting adults. And obviously, they cannot be afraid, as they might be

[1] *Commons Debates.* Vol. 749, cols. 1403–1516 (July 3, 4, 1967).

afraid in the case of illicit heterosexual intercourse, that such action will result in irresponsible procreation. I can only suppose that the opponents of this Bill will be afraid that their imagination will be tormented by visions of what will be going on elsewhere. Surely, if that is so, that is their own private misfortune, and no reason for imposing their personal standards of taste and morality on the minority of their fellow citizens who can find sexual satisfaction only in relations with their own sex.

The Second Reading was secured by a majority of 63 on July 13, and a few days later the Bill passed through all its remaining stages without a division.[1] In moving that 'this Bill do now pass', Lord Arran said:

When we first debated these affairs—and how long ago it seems!—I said that your Lordships had it in your power to remove fear from the hearts of men. This you have done. It was this House that gave the lead. Because of the Bill now to be enacted, perhaps a million human beings will be able to live in greater peace. I find this an awesome and marvellous thing. . . . My Lords, Mr Wilde was right: the road has been long and the martyrdoms many, monstrous and bloody. Today, please God! sees the end of that road.

Lest the opponents of the Bill think that a new freedom, a new privileged class, has been created, let me remind them that no amount of legislation will prevent homosexuals from being the subject of dislike and derision or at best of pity. We shall always, I fear, resent the odd man out. That is their burden for all time, and they must shoulder it like men—for men they are.

Lord Arran concluded by paying a well-deserved tribute to four individuals for their help—Lord Stonham, the Under-Secretary at the Home Office; Lord Gardiner, the Lord Chancellor; Mr Antony Grey, Secretary of the Homosexual Law Reform Society, 'who has done more than any single man to bring this social problem to the notice of the public'; and Sir John Wolfenden, 'that great man whose name has been mentioned more often than any other in these long debates'.

The Sexual Offences Act received the Royal Assent on July 27, 1967, and immediately became law throughout England and Wales. It did not apply to Scotland and Northern Ireland, where the old law still prevails.

[1] *Lords Debates.* Vol. 284, cols. 1283–1324 (July 13, 1967), Vol. 285, cols. 522–6 (July 21, 1967).

CHAPTER EIGHT

Whither Now?

[I]

The 1967 Act, which legalized homosexual acts between consenting adults in private, had the immediate effect of
encouraging a measure of permissiveness, certainly as regards
public discussion, the theatre, radio and television, of which
there were already some signs during the decade following the
publication of the Wolfenden Report. On the other hand, the
fear that such permissiveness would lead to more offences in
public and against young persons has not been supported by the
known facts. In fact convictions for homosexual crime have
actually decreased from about 2,000 annually to below 1,600,
whereas almost all other crimes have shown a substantial increase.
Following the passing of the Act the number of convictions for
importuning fell even more sharply. Of course, one ought not to
make too much of these statistics, which may well reflect the
intensity of police activity rather than a change in the habits of
male homosexuals, but at least they suggest that there has been
no opening of the flood gates as the Act's more vocal opponents
feared.

Criticism of the Act has been concentrated on the fixing of the
age of consent at 21. For instance, consenting 20-year-olds can
still be sent to prison for two years, even if the homosexual act
takes place in private, while a man over 21 who behaves in similar
circumstances with a youth between the ages of 16 and 21 can
now be sentenced to a maximum of five years instead of two as
formerly. Problems are also posed by the exclusion of the armed
forces and the merchant navy from the operation of the consenting adult clause, as well as by the extent to which social
organizations for homosexuals may exist without falling foul of
the criminal law.

Thus, any homosexual behaviour by a member of the armed
services, even with another consenting adult in private, remains
an offence against service discipline. A case involving two Royal
Air Force officers, apparently the first of its kind since the passing
of the Act, came before a court martial at a R.A.F. station in

Norfolk early in 1969. A flying officer was accused of having a homosexual relationship with a pilot officer. It was not suggested by the prosecution that the relationship had adversely affected the flying officer's efficiency. On the contrary, he appeared from the evidence to have been an outstanding officer, who had discovered a method of preventing ejection equipment on certain aircraft from jamming and also preventing the vibration from rupturing a fuel pipe and thereby causing loss of fuel to one of the engines. The two officers had a common interest in sailing and the affair between them had begun some months previously during a trip on the Norfolk Broads. Something about the behaviour of the two officers had aroused the suspicions of the station security officer, and in an interview with the flying officer he told him that he had reason to believe that the flying officer was having a homosexual relationship with the pilot officer. The flying officer might well have denied it, but he admitted that this was so. 'Yes,' he was stated to have said. 'It is basically homosexual. It is homosexual physically and mentally.' In due course he pleaded guilty to the charge.

'We are dealing with a test case,' said his defence counsel. 'If today in this case a decision is made to dishonourably discharge him, well, in my submission, the matter can be taken no further because in a sense there is no worse punishment. But in my submission there will be far worse cases. If this man is cashiered, then it puts a barrier to future confessions, voluntary confessions to homosexual behaviour, because I have emphasized the conduct of this officer was at all times to confess. We stand on the watershed of a crucial and important decision of policy. I can only respectfully plead that this man's resignation lies on the table.' Counsel added that the accused man had 'faced up to his responsibilities in that he had given honest and candid replies to the questions that were put to him'.

This plea was made in the hopes that the court would accept the officer's resignation and leave it at that. But, as no doubt was inevitable, the matter had gone so far that the court was unable to do this, and although it did not send him to prison it did dismiss him ignominiously from the service.[1]

Shortly after the 1967 Act reached the statute book, the Special Branch at Scotland Yard began an extensive investigation into allegations of the procuring of guardsmen and troopers—'the Curzon Street Cowboys', as they were popularly known from their habit of frequenting this part of Mayfair—by certain

[1] *Eastern Daily Press* (Norwich), February 12, 1969.

wealthy homosexuals. Of course, there was nothing new about this. The picking up and prostitution of private soldiers and N.C.O.s in the Household Cavalry and the Brigade of Guards had been going on for at least 250 years, since the time of Lord Leicester and the Bishop of Clogher. The late J. R. Ackerley's account of his experiences with the Brigade of Guards between the two world wars has already been quoted. That the pattern had not changed in the 1950s and early '60s has been confirmed by Simon Raven, a journalist who conducted a private investigation a few years ago into male prostitution in London. Mr Raven has recorded how soldiers, and sailors too, particularly those on shore leave, would be told by friends or bar acquaintances to ring up 'So-and-So', who said 'to send my mates' to him. 'He's very rich with a smashing flat, and he'll give you a fair old time if you don't mind being fiddled with now and again.' One guardsman told Raven that when he was hard up and needed some money to take his girl out, he would go with men and during the homosexual act would close his eyes and think of 'girls and things', while his partner provided the necessary mechanical stimulus. Others quite enjoyed themselves on these occasions. 'Some of us get quite fond of the blokes we see regularly,' a young lance-sergeant in the Brigade confessed to Raven. 'You go to their flats and have some drinks and talk a bit—they're nice fellows, some of them, and interesting to listen to. And as for the sex bit, well, some of the younger ones aren't bad looking and I've had some real thrills off them in my time....'[1]

It is possible that the renewed police drive in 1967 was not a deliberate act following upon the immunity conferred on consenting adult homosexuals which led the police to transfer their attentions to the guards regiments. It has been said that the whole business began with an incident at a cocktail party in Chelsea, where a guards officer was approached by a middle-aged homosexual and asked to get him an invitation to a party where members of the Royal Family were present so that he could meet some of them personally. 'If you don't fix it,' the civilian went on after the officer had ignored his request, 'I will reveal a scandal about your men.' He then proceeded to mention a number of names which the officer recognized as those of men in his regiment, and referred to specific occasions when the men had acted as male prostitutes.

Inquiries which the officer set in motion led to Scotland Yard being called in to assist. Detectives interviewed more than sixty

[1] Simon Raven. 'Boys will be Boys' in *Encounter* (November 1960), 20.

N.C.O.s and private soldiers and their investigations led them to country houses outside London, to Jersey and the south of France, where two rich 'queers' were traced as having had relations with guardsmen. One of the 'queers' was Lawrence Gardner Bell, who lived at Sunningdale and had married the Yardley perfume and cosmetics heiress; the other was Oliver Ford, a 42-year-old furniture and fabrics designer, with a £35,000 manor house, also in Berkshire, who was said to have done interior decoration for the Queen Mother at Royal Lodge, Windsor. Gardner, Bell and some others fled abroad to avoid investigation, but Ford and three soldiers were arrested on charges of conspiring to procure other soldiers to commit indecencies with Bell and Ford. The fact that more arrests were not made was due to the clause in the 1967 Act which requires prosecutions to be brought within twelve months of the alleged offences. 'Maybe some soldiers in Knightsbridge barracks might wonder why they have not been called for the prosecution or wonder why they are lucky not to be charged,' said prosecuting counsel at the trial of Ford and two of the guardsmen. 'Others who may well have been in the dock only escape for that reason.' According to a detective inspector, who gave evidence for the Crown, another 30 to 40 troopers had been engaged in indecent acts besides the two men charged with Ford.

The evidence on which the trooper had been arrested for offences in connection with Bell, whom he had met in a public house at Sunningdale, was held to be inadmissible and the trooper was discharged. But Trooper Barry Brooks, aged 21, and Corporal Jeffrey Sheffield, 27, both pleaded guilty to the conspiracy charges, as also did Ford; one of the charges incidentally involved a 19-year-old guardsman. Said Trooper Brooks: 'I heard in the barrack room that if you wanted to make a few bob you went to Tattersall's Tavern opposite the barracks and met the queers.' The detective inspector agreed with defending counsel that it had become almost a habit among some of the troopers to take money for committing acts of indecency with homosexuals. 'Trooper Brooks was no worse than perhaps 30 or 40 other troopers who had been indulging in the same sort of thing.' It was in the 'notorious' Tattersall's that Corporal Sheffield met the man who introduced him into the homosexual circle; this was a senior N.C.O. who was later put in charge of recruits at the Guards depot at Pirbright. 'Many troopers boast how much they get out of the homosexuals,' Sheffield declared. 'I myself have only ever done it for money.' For introducing soldiers to Ford, he admitted that he had received £180, a sum which his defending counsel described as 'veritable riches' for someone on service pay of £8 a week, working out at about £10 a guardsman. 'I realize I have been very foolish and stupid,' Ford had said when the police eventually caught up with him. 'About three months ago I consulted my doctor about my bi-sexual feelings.'

'In this case, the least said soonest mended,' pleaded Ford's counsel. 'Everything between Mr Ford and the guardsmen was in private and with discretion. His attitude now is one of shame and distress.' The judge took a relatively lenient view and fined Ford £700 with the alternative of eight months' imprisonment. 'I accept that no one was seduced or corrupted by these acts of yours,' he told Ford in passing sentence. At the same time the judge spoke sternly to the two guardsmen, whom he discharged conditionally since they were being dismissed with ignominy from the army. 'You were simply acting as male prostitutes,' he told them. 'I do not think it would be right to send you to prison bearing in mind that other people, possibly senior to you in the Service, and possibly as many as 30 or 40 others have escaped standing in that dock.'[1]

On the subject of prostitution, a man or a woman 'who know-ingly lives wholly or in part' on the earnings of a male prostitute is still liable on conviction by magistrates of up to six months' imprisonment (as under the old law), but he or she may get anything up to seven years on conviction by a jury (two years under the old law). Also, premises which would in law be regarded as a brothel for heterosexual purposes are likewise treated as a brothel 'if people resort to it for the purpose of lewd homosexual practices'. Incidentally the use of the word 'lewd' in the new Act (section 6) is like that of 'gross' in relation to indecency under the Act of 1885. It is doubtful whether there is any distinction in law between homosexual acts which are 'lewd' and those which are not.

A man who 'procures' the commission of a homosexual act between two other men which is not in itself an offence (i.e. because they are two consenting adults in private) is liable if convicted by a jury to a maximum of two years' imprisonment, or six months if tried by a magistrate. It is worth noting that it is no longer an offence for a man to 'procure' another man to commit 'an act of gross indecency' *with himself* with consent and in private if both are over the age of twenty-one, but it remains an offence

[1] *The Times, Daily Telegraph, Daily Express,* May 7, 8, 1968.

(punishable with up to two years if tried before a jury or six months if tried by magistrates) for a man to 'procure' another man to commit either indecency or buggery with a third man, or apparently buggery with himself. The essential ingredient of the offence of 'procuring' is an element of solicitation or persuasion that a homosexual act shall be committed by two men brought together for this purpose, whatever the circumstances, and is not restricted to situations connected with prostitution or to introductions performed for financial or other material reward.

No doubt the biggest problem reflected in the aftermath of the 1967 Act is caused by teen-agers and their relations with each other as well as adults over 21, as has been briefly indicated in the first chapter of this book. This in turn is bound up with the complex question of social meeting places for homosexuals and their counselling by such institutions as the Albany Trust. Lord Arran, who piloted the Act through the House of Lords, regards it 'merely as a holding measure', particularly in view of the lowering of the age of adulthood from 21 to 18 so as to enfranchise the lower age groups. Also, if heterosexual relationships are legal at 16, why should not the age of consent as between homosexuals be the same?

[2]

'I ask one thing and I ask it earnestly,' said Lord Arran when moving the passage of the Sexual Offences Act in the House of Lords in July 1967. 'I ask those who have, as it were, been in bondage and for whom the prison doors are now open to show their thanks by comporting themselves quietly with dignity. This is no occasion for jubilation; certainly not for celebration. Any form of ostentatious behaviour now or in the future, any form of public flaunting, would be utterly distasteful and would, I believe, make the sponsors of the Bill regret that they have done what they have done.' One of the reactions to this admonitory request has been a considerable volume of mail addressed to the Albany Trust, begging the Trust to sponsor properly run social clubs for homosexuals such as exist in Holland and Denmark. By reason of the eminent names on its council and its good relations with the Home Office, the Trust has had of necessity to tread warily in this matter. 'Hasten slowly' has been its advice to prospective club founders, since there are many pitfalls for the unwary.

Prior to the change in the law, the main public social meeting places for male homosexuals were, and still are, certain public houses and a number of private drinking clubs—at least twenty in the West End of London—the clientele of which is largely or entirely homosexual. This fact is not, of course, explicitly admitted. A number of them have existed for ten or more years as tacitly accepted features of the social landscape. The age limit for membership of such clubs is normally eighteen, in accordance with the licensing laws. Such a tacit arrangement has its advantages and its disadvantages: what may seem discreet to some appears furtive to others, and a measure of semi-official toleration by the police may be accompanied by 'protection' or worse evils. Certainly most of those who frequent these pubs and clubs still do not find it easy to relax with the same degree of openness as heterosexuals do in similar surroundings.

In 1965, the licensee of the Kent Arms public house in North Woolwich was convicted of keeping a disorderly house and was fined £35 with 50 guineas costs. 'Conduct seen in the gentlemen's toilet,' said prosecuting counsel 'made it almost impossible for any decent person to go into there.' Evidence was given that men frequenting the pub were painted and powdered, wore earrings, carried handbags and kissed when they met. They also danced together and sang obscene versions of popular songs.[1]

Homosexuals continue to pose a problem for pub landlords or licensed victuallers, to give them their trade name. A spokesman for the Licensed Victuallers Association was recently quoted as saying:

> We were very worried when the Sexual Offences Act was passed because it looked as though some pubs, particularly in the West End of London, would become meeting places for more and more homosexuals. It has not happened as much as was feared. But then many of the queers are difficult to detect. It is even more difficult to bar them when they cause no trouble.
>
> Our problem is financial. Though queers are often good customers themselves, they tend to drive ordinary customers away if they become too numerous. It gives the landlord a real problem. If he asked them politely to drink up and leave, he sometimes gets a glass smashed in his face. There has been a big increase in this sort of assault recently, though, of course, they are not all committed by homosexuals.

[1] *Stratford Express.* August 13, 23, 1965.

If a customer refuses to leave, the landlord can call in the police to remove him. Most landlords hesitate to do this for several reasons. One is that the presence of police in a pub upsets the customers and is inclined to give the house a bad name. Another is that the police don't like being called in to settle a landlord's problems. They tend to keep a special eye on the pub afterwards as a possible hangout for bad characters.

Most landlords are specially wary of this situation because of a case several years ago. A landlord in the West End became worried as literally hundreds of homosexuals were using his bars as a meeting place. The situation became out of hand and he decided to call in the police. The result? He received a summons for harbouring homosexuals. Though he was acquitted, he was so disgusted that he packed up the pub business.[1]

To some extent the needs of the teen-age homosexual are met by the coffee-bar and similar non-alcoholic establishments. Unlike the pubs and drinking clubs, the coffee-bars, which are a phenomenon of comparatively recent growth, have no lower age limit, although some of the coffee-bars impose a more or less flexible upper limit of from 30 to 35. Unfortunately some of these coffee-bars, which the police know are frequented by young homosexuals, are also venues for drug-peddling, and those who operate and use them often do so at considerable personal risk by reason of the drugs as well as the age factor.

In 1966 a coffee-bar called 'The Other Place' in Chelsea, was raided by the police, and the owner sentenced to nine months imprisonment for keeping a disorderly house. According to the police evidence, about two hundred men were there trying to dance on the night of the raid. 'Some were kissing passionately and fondling each other in an indecent way. They were also indulging in unnatural sexual practices and while they kept observation the police officers themselves were subjected to indecency on several occasions. Most of the men there were of an effeminate kind and obviously homosexual.'[2]

There are also some 'pen-pal' correspondence clubs and magazines with advertisement sections which helps to put homosexuals in touch with one another. Some of these are quite genuine and sincere attempts at relieving homosexual loneliness, but of course the bridge between that laudable object and the deliberate promotion of homosexual practices is narrow. A

---

[1] *Tit-Bits*, November 2, 1968.
[2] *Chelsea News*, December 2, 1966.

nationally advertised male fashion magazine recently announced its intention to open a residential club and hotel in London, but this project—if it ever gets off the ground—could easily fall foul of the law. In the matter of advertising, the permissiveness which was encouraged by the Sexual Offences Act, naturally led to a certain amount of licence or rather licentiousness typified in the magazines of the 'poove and perve' variety, mostly originating in Soho. Such a production is *Camp*, published by 'Cottage Productions' expressly 'for the consenting adult', and consisting of eight duplicated pages of small ads costing 10*s.* 6*d.* A typical ad in *Camp* runs:

> London area. Well educated young man, 34, car owner, wishes to meet riding master who is strict. Interested in leather and domestic correction.

The ads in *International Times* are equally inviting, though less 'kinky' in character:

> LONELY young man seeks friends (20's), also introduction. Photos appreciated. All letters answered.
> GAY London bachelor (36) offers free overnight or weekend accommodation to young males. No 'hippies' please. All letters answered promptly. Photo helps.[1]

Electrical terminology is a convenient form of slang in these ads—DC (direct current) meaning homosexual, AC (alternating current) heterosexual, and AC/DC bisexual. Women also figure amongst the advertisers, such as the one describing herself in a magazine called *Way Out* as a 'young (25) AC/DC housewife' from County Durham who 'wishes to correspond/meet similar age AC/DC girls or straight Lesbian. One good figure would also interest my husband. No ties barred, photos exchanged.'

In 1963, a North-West Homosexual Law Reform Committee was founded by a Labour councillor in Nelson named Allan Horsfall under the chairmanship of Mr Colin Harvey, Senior Social Worker with the Manchester Diocesan Board for Social Responsibility (formerly the Church of England Moral Welfare Council). A prime mover on the committee was the owner of the Rockingham Club in Manchester, along with a sprinkling of shop assistants, students, clerks, doctors, engineers and other professional people. Unlike the London society, with which it was affiliated, the committee was largely composed of homosexuals.

[1] Cited by Ray Gosling in 'Homosexuals Now', *New Society*. August 29, 1968.

After the passing of the 1967 Act, the committee promoted a company, Esquire Clubs Ltd., for the purpose of taking over the Manchester club and opening similar clubs in other towns in the north-west. A chain of breweries offered to help with finance if sufficient members were forthcoming. Mr Horsfall, who became the company's secretary, made it clear from the outset that the clubs would be strictly controlled, there would be no bedrooms, no gambling and no indecencies permitted. 'We hope the clubs will be such that members will bring their sisters and heterosexual friends along,' he said. 'For too long now homosexuals have been forced to meet in seedy bars and public lavatories.'[1]

In spite of having two respectable clergymen as vice-presidents, all has not been plain sailing for the Esquire Clubs. To begin with they were publicly denounced by Lord Arran and Mr Abse, the principal sponsors of the 1967 Act. 'The setting up of these clubs is an open flaunting of the new and legal freedom of outlet,' said Lord Arran in his column in the London *Evening News*. 'Moreover the organisers of the proposed clubs, though I am sure they would be most respectably run, would do well to remember the clause which provides that a homosexual act in the presence of a third party is a crime. I imagine that they have obtained permission of the police and Home Office. If not, they would be wise to do so.'[2] Point was given to Lord Arran's remarks a few days later when the Manchester city magistrates fined the owner of the Baton Rouge club there for having allowed men to dance together on the premises. Evidence was given by the police who had visited the club in plain clothes that it was 'a haunt of homosexuals'.

The condition under which a music licence had been granted to the club laid it down that no dancing would be permitted which was 'indecent, improper, or of such a nature as would be likely to cause a breach of the peace', and prosecuting counsel argued that this condition had been violated. One police witness said that throughout the evening there had been a constant procession of men to the dance floor. 'They were seen to kiss and hold each other in passionate embraces.' No restriction had been imposed on this kind of dancing by the management. 'On the first visit,' counsel added, 'the observing officer became so conspicuous because he was not engaging in this kind of behaviour that when he was approached by a homosexual he was obliged

---

[1] *Burnley Evening Star*, September 9, 1968.
[2] *Evening News*, September 4, 1968.

to dance with him or risk being singled out and having to discontinue his observations.' Answering the prosecution's suggestion that the club was frequented by homosexuals, defending counsel pleaded that 'it was better to have these types concentrated in one club rather than spread them over all the clubs in the city.' The manager, who was also convicted of supplying intoxicating liquor after the permitted hours, pleaded guilty to the charge of permitting dancing of such a nature as would be likely to cause a breach of the peace. He was ordered to pay a fine of £30 together with five guineas costs. He was also dismissed from the management of the club and the club's licence was revoked.[1]

The idea of clubs for homosexuals also alarmed Mr Abse. In his view they would give those hostile to the recent liberalization of the law ample grounds for saying that their worst fears were being realized. 'Certainly the admission of those aged under twenty-one combined with the provision of dancing could be interpreted as a defiance of the law,' he told the committee of the Albany Trust. He regarded the clubs as highly undesirable. The whole idea of separation was wrong, and contrary to what the sponsors of the recent Act had set out to do. 'They did not wish to see the creation of homosexual ghetto communities.'

Naturally the chairman and secretary of the Esquire Clubs leaped to the defence of their pet project. The clubs were 'overdue', said Colin Harvey, 'as is the provision of a counselling service and the effective liaison at local level with social and educational agencies which are also aims of Esquire'. Allan Horsfall was similarly convinced that Lord Arran was wrong, and he told his paper so.[2]

> We at Esquire Clubs regret that it is necessary for minorities to be organised in this way, but homosexuals at the moment are misunderstood and misrepresented to an extent that they *need* the particular support and protection that only the proposed clubs can give them.
>
> We will continue to work and pray for the time when the clubs are no longer needed and when the homosexual can take his place in the wider community, but for the present we are simply not prepared to sacrifice this generation for the sake of the next.

Attempts to start homosexual clubs in other parts of England have also encountered difficulties. In Coventry, for example, a

[1] *Manchester Evening News*, September 9, 1968.
[2] *Evening News* (London), September 19, 1968.

well-meant attempt by a cathedral canon and a psychiatric social
worker to provide social facilities for lonely homosexuals in
addition to a counselling service caused something of a press
sensation. ('Special "Clinic" for Homosexuals at a Cathedral'
was a headline of the *Daily Mirror*.) 'We want to set up quite
informally, a centre where homosexuals can meet and feel free
to talk,' said Canon Stephen Verney. 'We want to provide them
with somewhere where they will feel welcome as people.' However, the Provost of Coventry immediately stepped in and
announced that there would be no 'club' for homosexuals at the
Cathedral so long as he was in charge.[1] Consequently all that
Mr Tom Frost, the social worker, has been able to do has been
to provide a telephone number, an answering service and a room
over a local pub for interviews.

In another Midlands town, Wolverhampton, a nineteen-year-
old accounts clerk named John Holland, who was living with his
parents and brother in an old council housing estate, founded a
group with the impressive title of The Male and Female Homosexual Association of Great Britain (MANDFHAB), along with
a twenty-eight-year-old lesbian named Elizabeth Cooke, who
admitted to a *News of the World* reporter that she had been
involved in physical love affairs with other women. 'I first noticed
I was different when I was still at school,' said John Holland. 'I
got crushes on other boys and wasn't the least bit interested in
girls. I got sneered at and taunted.' Somewhat unwisely, he
fixed the minimum age for joining at sixteen, although begged
by the Albany Trust's secretary to make it higher. 'Some of us
are prepared to parade with banners proclaiming our homosexuality if it will help,' this determined but naïve crusader
declared. 'We are in the position of the old suffragettes, struggling
for our democratic rights.' The founder of MANDFHAB went
on to make the extravagant claim that homosexuals had in the
town's Flamingo Club 'the best social club in Europe', with 550
members drawn from all over the country. It was certainly too
'gay' for the Wolverhampton police, who raided it shortly afterwards, subsequently bringing a number of charges including one
in respect of 'obscene and indecent acts committed on the
premises'—apparently men dancing together. The raid occurred
a few days after an article had appeared in a popular Sunday
newspaper describing a visit paid by a reporter to a certain pub
in Leeds. 'I saw men *dancing cheek to cheek, kissing passionately,
holding hands, petting and embracing* ... men in women's clothes ..
.

[1] *Daily Mirror*, January 12, *Coventry Evening Telegraph*, January 17, 1968.

a strip show . . . it is about time that the police put a stop to the odd goings on there.'¹ One result of the raid on the Flamingo Club was that the police visited several of the club members in their homes and questioned them with a view to obtaining details of alleged teen-age homosexual relationships in the area.

'We danced together—I admit this,' said a member of a homosexual club describing what went on there before it was closed down as the result of police action. 'If I dance with a person I enjoy the person that I dance with. We can't go into the normal pubs; they abuse us, they take the mickey out of us. We went to this club and we let ourselves go. We enjoyed ourselves, we enjoyed our own company. A normal person doesn't recognize a third sex. We do.'

The Albany Trust's attitude to the question of clubs has already been indicated. Mr Antony Grey, the Trust's secretary, has pointed out that clubs can undoubtedly help in bringing the homosexual 'to a full personal understanding of him or herself as a homosexual person . . . but only if the provision of a physical meeting place is not regarded as the be-all and end-all'.

> Much more immediately important is the need to build up new personal and community attitudes, which will replace the too common cynicism and loneliness of the sexually different with a new sincerity of comradeship and concern for one another.
>
> It is because we at the Albany Trust are so acutely aware that individuals' problems must be resolved through constructive social welfare action, at as many different levels as possible, that we hope the energies of others who are concerned to improve the lot of the homosexual in society will not be confined to a premature demand for the establishing of clubs which—with or without drinking, dancing and dating—may unnecessarily arouse groundless public alarm.²

[3]

Lesbians cannot be left out of any consideration of the homosexual problem. In England, they have never suffered from the same degree of legal and social discrimination that male homosexuals have experienced even under the revised law, although

---

¹ *News of the World*, January 21; *The People*, March 24, 1968.
² 'World This Weekend' B.B.C. transmission, September 1; *New Society*, September 5, 1968.

they have on occasion been discriminated against. They too have their drinking clubs in London and elsewhere, relatively few in number compared with the men's, while a lesbian brothel is a rarity, at least in this country, as indeed is a lesbian prostitute. As has already been indicated, lesbians, like male homosexuals, are found in all walks and conditions of life, and except for a tiny minority who deliberately draw attention to themselves by their manners and behaviour are outwardly indistinguishable from their normally sexed neighbours. There was a period in England shortly after the First World War when some lesbians cut their hair short and wore men's clothes, a habit which was designed to emphasize the masculine role in their relationships with other lesbian women. But this distinguishing feature has virtually disappeared today, when so many women do jobs formerly reserved for men, such as factory charge hands, bus conductresses and so on, and they dress accordingly.

However, the differences between the two genders of homosexual are no doubt greater than the similarities. For one thing, the women are by and large much less promiscuous and more discreet than the men. They do not as a rule pick up partners in the streets or bars of pubs or in hanging round public lavatories. Their relationships with other like-minded women tend to be firmer and more lasting than is the case between homosexual men. They seem more inclined to settle down and make a home with one person, and it is probably true to say that, generally speaking, they are more affectionate and faithful to each other than the men. Also, while they indulge plentifully in kissing and caressing, they are often apt to stop short of full physical expression. The most serious problem facing the average lesbian is loneliness and a sense of being cut off from the rest of the community. 'I am suffering from isolation,' one lesbian wrote recently. 'I've been chucked out of my job. Though the reason wasn't given that I'm a lesbian, I was forced to resign.'

Some normally-sexed English men and women regard lesbianism with more horror and disgust than male homosexuality. To some extent no doubt this feeling is subconscious, since they inwardly resent a way of life on the part of women which denies their biological function in the procreation of children, though lesbian mothers are by no means unknown. (Oscar Wilde's mother, for instance, was a pronounced lesbian, as also was Cecil Rhodes's sister.) Of course, ignorance of the subject goes hand in hand with prejudice. This was strongly brought out in a recent survey of homosexuality carried out by a team of students in

Edinburgh University. The team reported that attitudes varied widely, from a science student who recommended that all male 'queers' should be castrated, to a law student who was eager to see the establishment of homosexual clubs in Britain like those in Amsterdam and Copenhagen. In spite of one or two conspicuous exceptions, the women students were more tolerant than the men, many confessing that they were uninformed on the subject.

An interesting point was that most of those questioned—and this applied to both sexes—found lesbianism more repugnant than male homosexuality. Terms such as 'absolutely revolting', 'distasteful', and 'thoroughly disgusting' were used to describe lesbian associations. The more intelligent students, asked to account for the average lesbian's 'revolting' conduct, gave a variety of 'explanations'. Some put it down to a 'schoolgirl crush' hangover, some to the inadequacy of Britons as husbands and lovers, and others to the need for 'unattractive or shy girls' to resort to each other for friendship. One arts student (female) said she would like to see all lesbians 'confined to institutions'. No doubt some lesbians would like this, since it would give them an uninhibited freedom and range of choice of a partner which the ordinary heterosexual girl takes for granted from the age of adolescence onwards. But it was hardly a practical solution, and it came all the more oddly from a young woman whose school record had earned her a place at a university.

The first open and avowed organization to cater exclusively for lesbian interests in Britain was established at the beginning of 1964 under the title, Minorities Research Group (M.R.G.). It was largely the result of an article, 'A quick look at lesbians', by a woman journalist named Dilys Rowe, which appeared in *Twentieth Century* in the previous winter, and which suggested that English lesbians consisted for the most part of elderly well-brought up women who shared a house, a garden and a female dog and almost certainly had erotic dreams about each other without daring to think about them; sometimes they bred dogs and kept tea shops and when one of them died the other behaved exactly like a widow. The writer quoted a lesbian as saying, 'The thing that hurts a homosexual woman most is that the heterosexual does not recognize the spiritual quality of her love.'[1]

This article evoked a reply in the following issue of the magazine from an anonymous lesbian who argued that what was resented by the female homosexual was not that the spirituality

[1] *Twentieth Century* (Winter 1962–63), 67–72.

of her life was doubted by the heterosexual, but its *authenticity*. 'I believe that male is always attracted to female,' she wrote, 'but that the body does not always correspond to the sex experienced.' What heterosexuals did not realize was that a homosexual woman finds it very difficult, often impossible, to imagine what it is like to be in love with a man.

> The love experienced may be spiritual or may be carnal, it is more likely to be a mixture of both just as normal love is. However, I think that the average reaction to a knowledge of Lesbian love tends to be: 'Oh she'll get over that when she meets the right man.' Indeed, with a young woman this may be the case, but when a woman reaches her middle thirties and has never been emotionally stirred by a man, but has experienced these feelings only towards members of her own sex, then it would appear more realistic to recognize that this is her mode of sexual self-expression, and not relegate it contemptuously to the level of the unrequited love for the games mistress.[1]

The Minorities Research Group was formed by five professional and business women—an engineer, a sociologist, a librarian, a shop assistant and a journalist—including the lesbian whose words have just been quoted, with the aim of providing advice on personal problems and helping lesbians who are lonely and insecure. It is a responsible organization under the direction of the founder journalist member Esmé Langley, who also serves on the Albany Trust Development Committee. It publishes a monthly newsletter called *Arena Three*, and through its medium as well as press notices it is the means of introducing women to others 'with interests and hobbies in common'. Furthermore, it organizes social functions both in London and the provinces, refers members in need of advice to appropriate professional aid, and participates in university and other research projects.

'At the moment there seems to be a veil of secrecy over the subject which is just beginning to lift,' says Miss Langley. If it is not the profoundly scientific body that its name suggests, at least M.R.G. has changed the lives of numbers of previously most unhappy people. 'You don't know what a relief it is just to be able to talk about it all!' is the most frequent immediate reaction of those who benefit from the Group's counselling. A significant feature was the large number of married lesbians who have communicated with or joined M.R.G., which suggested

[1] *id.* (Spring, 1963), 147–8.

that the problem of lesbianism in marriage was more considerable than the Wolfenden Committee thought, an impression amply confirmed by the Albany Trust's case work also.

For example, a divorced school teacher, whose family does not know that she is a lesbian, is now living happily with a woman friend in a semi-detached house. She is an intelligent woman, who does not feel that she is doing anything wrong. 'I can only hope that M.R.G. and responsible publicity will help the public to understand,' she has said. 'After all, why should we be ostracized for something we cannot help?'

'Now I realize to my joy that I am not, after all, alone,' another member of M.R.G. has recently admitted. 'There are many women like myself who are isolated from the normal pattern of social and sexual intercourse, who want and need the kind of warmth, companionship and love which I have to offer. And in this knowledge lies hope—hope that the future may hold meaning through contact with other human beings, that we might work together to remove this horrible feeling of isolation each one of us has suffered. Now in M.R.G., as we approach each other, we need not have that devastating fear of being rejected for our homosexuality.'

The criticism has been made, not without reason, that M.R.G. is too much a middle-class organization and is to a great extent unrepresentative of the mass of the female population which leaves school at the age of fifteen. This was no doubt inevitable from the manner in which it came into being. A questionnaire circulated among its members after M.R.G. had been in existence for two years reveals that teachers and nurses provided the largest segment, hardly surprising when one considers that these pro-fessions are largely staffed by women. Secretaries and civil servants came next, followed by writers, artists and other creative workers, while there were a few doctors, barristers, dress designers, hair stylists, antique dealers, masseuses, and even a theology student—but no factory workers. Also *Arena Three*, at least in its earlier issues, tended to be too much like a girls' school or house magazine, and there was a tendency to over-emphasize the merits of being a lesbian in a crusading spirit, occasionally going so far as to indicate antipathy towards the opposite sex. On the other hand, M.R.G. has already achieved a good deal in the promotion of its objects of counselling, education, and the improvement of the public image of lesbianism 'by freeing it from the prurience, sensationalism and vulgar voyeurism with which in some minds it has become associated'.

At least two other lesbian groups—Kenric in London and the New Group in Manchester—exist with aims broadly similar to M.R.G. Kenric was founded in 1965 in the Kensington and Richmond areas of London (hence the name) to combat loneliness among lesbians. 'Society still disapproves of lesbianism sufficiently to deter lesbians from confiding in their parents,' says Miss Cynthia Reid, a prime mover in the foundation. 'But a more pressing problem for the young lesbian is how to meet suitable partners . . . Kenric's main function is to give lesbians a chance to meet socially and take part in a wide range of activities. Last year we had talks, debates, parties, a treasure hunt and visits to the theatre.' To reach isolated women the society advertises discreetly in the *New Statesman*. Like M.R.G., Kenric does not accept married lesbians except with the knowledge and consent of their husbands. In the words of a consulting psychiatrist, 'they want the companionship of someone of their own age, class and outlook, and to be accepted by society. There is no reason why society should not accept them, unless they are the rare delinquent type, when they are likely to be psychopaths and harm others. One way society can help is by being more sympathetic, and in realizing that the odd-man out syndrome can be a very painful one to bear.'[1]

In other words, all these women's groups see it as an essential part of their function to integrate their members into general society more satisfactorily by helping to alleviate their personal problems of loneliness, guilt and maladjustment, and also to educate the general public to a more realistic understanding of the nature of the homosexual women's condition and needs.

[4]

Unlike certain European continental countries and also the United States, Britain has yet no organization which caters for the male homosexual's social needs on the same level that the Minorities Research Group and Kenric do for lesbians. Possibly encouraged by the success of the continental experiments, particularly in Holland, there have been several well-intentioned attempts to establish social organizations for the male homosexual such as the Esquire Clubs; but, as has been seen, they have run into difficulties and so far are regarded somewhat

[1] *Daily Telegraph.* January 10, 1969. ('The Women Condemned to Lead Lonely Lives.')

askance by the law enforcement authorities. At this point, it may be convenient for the purpose of comparison to take a brief look at some of the organizations at present operating outside Britain.

The best known and most successful of these is the Dutch Association of Homosexuals, popularly known by the initial letters of its original name, C.O.C. (*Cultuur-en Ontspannings-centrum* or 'Centre for Culture and Recreation'). Founded in 1947 by a Dutch actor (pseudonym Bob Angelo) in Amsterdam 'to promote humane and informed attitudes towards and treatment of homosexual men and women, and to provide psychological, moral and legal assistance against prejudice or harmful legal codes, and to discourage homosexual prostitution', it now has altogether about 4,000 members—3,500 men and 500 women—with branches in Rotterdam, The Hague, Utrecht, Groningen, Arnhem and Eindhoven. The club premises in each town usually consist of discussion and lecture rooms, also a bar and a restaurant-cum-night-club, where both the male and female members are allowed to dance with each other. Since it started over twenty years ago, the C.O.C. has achieved a remarkable degree of success in establishing close and mutually helpful co-operation with the Dutch police and probation services, and with the clergy, psychiatrists and other social welfare organizations. For example, it is sometimes consulted when the courts have to deal with offenders against young persons. According to Mr Antony Grey, the Albany Trust's secretary, who has visited it, 'the most noticeable feature of the club is its far more relaxed and secure atmosphere, compared with any English homosexual meeting place that I know'. Its Amsterdam headquarters are located at Korte Leidsedwarsstraat 49a—P.O. Box 542. Asked by a correspondent of the *Observer* whether the C.O.C. did not serve as a 'pick-up-joint', Mr Angelo replied: 'That possibility of course exists in about the same degree as you would find in any heterosexual social club. Our whole aim is to encourage members' capacity for more lasting relationships, and I think we have a high degree of success there.'[1]

Mr Bryan Magee, who has produced several TV documentaries about homosexuals in England, has written of the Dutch clubs:

> The C.O.C. struck me as being an organization that does good. It acts, above all else, as a counselling service for homosexuals. It engages psychiatrists who specialize in the problems of homosexuals, and homosexuals in trouble get sent to them

[1] *Observer*, January 13, 1968.

by welfare organizations, even by the law. It is a non-profit-
making organization, rather middle-class in membership, a
little do-goody in atmosphere perhaps, but very respectable.
It is much the most solid of the Dutch organizations. But it is
not the only one. Even the night club on their premises in
Amsterdam is not the only homosexual night club in the city.
There is one other big one, and quite a large number of smaller
bars. The other big one, a very different proposition from
C.O.C., is D.O.K. (short for *De Odeon Kring*, 'The Odeon
Club'). D.O.K. is frankly a profit-making organization, much
more commercial, more classless, swingier—I found its atmos-
phere altogether more congenial.

The D.O.K. is camouflaged behind an anonymous green door
beside one of the canals in central Amsterdam and is a favourite
resort of homosexual tourists from less tolerant lands who are
eligible for temporary membership on showing their passports
and paying the nominal entrance fee. English homosexuals
regularly charter airplanes for week-end visits to the D.O.K.
Mr Magee, who spent several hours there, found it well-run, free
from rowdiness, drunken disturbances and similarly embarrassing
scenes. The customers included some lesbians, who kept themselves very much to themselves, not mixing with the boys but
dancing passionately with each other and drinking in a small
group in the corner. Ages varied between twenty and forty.

By about two o'clock in the morning the scene was like that
in any swinging night club. The dance floor was crammed with
something like a hundred and fifty couples, the lights were
red and low, and all about one loudspeakers poured out the
recorded sounds of copulatory music. The dancers were
crushed up against each other, locked in each other's arms,
entwined round each other, kissing as they danced, nuzzling,
nibbling at each other's ears, their hands wandering over each
other's bodies—exactly, as I say, as you would find in any
successful night club, except that the dancers were all men. I
had a curious feeling that it was all, at one and the same time,
ordinary and extraordinary. In every respect except the identity
of sex between dancers it was a scene I must have witnessed
hundreds of times in my life, even down to the details, on the
side of the dance floor, of people at tables drinking out of each
other's glasses, or interlocking their arms to drink; or a hand
casually resting on the thigh of a partner; the giggling, the
flirting, the squeezing, the laughing.

Mr Magee's nocturnal experiences in Amsterdam impressed two things upon his mind, which seem to have come as a revelation to him for the first time. One was that homosexuals, or at least those he saw at the D.O.K., do have all the emotions and responses towards each other that are normal between the sexes—that their feelings are authentic and natural and spontaneous and involuntary. 'The other is something I can only describe as a feeling for the *normality* of homosexuality—the fact that when all is said and done it is just like what other people do, just a question of individuals who in other respects are unremarkable behaving in ways which are familiar to everyone.'[1]

Denmark has a similar but smaller homosexual association than Holland, and it also publishes several magazines for homosexuals, of which *Vennen* (P.O. Box 183, Copenhagen K) is the best known. The main feature of Danish homosexual life is the extremely tolerant social atmosphere which characterizes the country's attitude towards sexual matters generally, including the publication of all forms of erotica. In Denmark the age of consent for homosexuals is 18, whereas it is 21 in Holland, and homosexual affairs between young Danes in their late teens and twenties and thirties arouse no adverse comment. On the other hand, social attitudes in France are far more disapproving of homosexual behaviour, in spite of the liberality of French law embodied in the Code Napoleon. Nevertheless an organization known as *Arcadie* does exist in Paris, and it has a clubhouse and publishes a magazine under the same title (74 Boulevard de Neuilly, Paris, 12e). But its officials experience great difficulty in promoting serious public discussions about homosexuality, and they have little success in their repeated attempts to initiate discussions with the Catholic hierarchy and other official bodies in the country which has produced such famous homosexual writers as Verlaine, Rimbaud and Gide.

By contrast, the American scene is quite unlike anything to be found in Europe. The existence of fifty different state laws, all except one (Illinois) prohibiting not only homosexual acts between consenting adults in private but also 'unnatural' heterosexual behaviour (i.e. anything other than normal *coitus*), even between married couples, results in a yawning credibility gap between United States sex laws and surface mores and the actual behaviour of 95 per cent of the American population. The emphasis upon Civil Rights in recent years has resulted in the formation of a number of militant 'homophile' organizations,

[1] Bryan Magee. *One in Twenty* (1966), 98–107.

which campaign against what they allege to be the unconsti-
tutional lack of equality experienced by homosexuals and the
discrimination against them as a minority group. But with the
exception of California, where a Supreme Court decision has
upheld the homosexual's right to peaceful assembly, these
organizations work through conferences and publicity. The
Mattachine Society of Washington (P.O. Box 1032, Washington
D.C. 20013), which publishes *The Homosexual Citizen*, con-
centrates upon legal issues and endeavours to fight test cases
through the courts, such as contesting employment discrimination
in Government agencies alleged by unprosecuted homosexuals.
Lesbians are catered for by *The Ladder*, which is published
monthly by the Daughters of Bilitis, Inc., founded in 1955 in
San Francisco (3470 Mission Street). The older established
Californian societies, such as One Incorporated of Los Angeles,
prefer to give more emphasis to long-term public education and
to better social adjustment for the homosexual, while the newer
groups, notably the Society for Individual Rights (S.I.R.) of
San Francisco, tend to devote most of their energies to promoting
homosexual social functions such as reviews and dancing.
S.I.R's clubhouse, with its dance floor is probably the nearest
English-speaking equivalent to the Dutch C.O.C. clubs; its weekly
dances are licensed by the San Francisco police department,
which also advertises for police recruits in its monthly magazine.

[5]

There are other problems besides those of teen-age offenders
and suitable meeting places for homosexuals generally which the
recent English legislation has left unsolved. One of them is the
risk of infection by venereal disease through casual and
promiscuous association, a problem which is of course equally
serious for heterosexuals. According to Dr R. S. Morton, con-
sultant venereologist at the Royal Hospital, Sheffield, and
president of the Medical Society for the Study of Venereal
Diseases, more people are suffering from V.D. in this country
than at any time during the past fifteen to twenty years. 'This
has happened in spite of modern and effective treatment,' says
Dr Morton. 'People of all ages and social classes are involved.'
A few years ago the infection rate in the 15–19 age group was
one in 1,000 per annum. Now it is about one in 660, suggesting
that 'many more young people are having casual intercourse'.

Apparently immigrants, who are sometimes blamed by the ignorant and prejudiced, seldom bring venereal diseases into Britain; with few exceptions they are infected in this country. Dr Morton quotes one London venereologist to the effect that of all the male patients he sees and treats, one in five is a homosexual. 'Gonorrhoea and syphilis, and occasionally non-specific urethritis, are more commonly acquired in homosexual activity than ever before,' adds Dr Morton. 'It has been a matter of concern to venereologists that young homosexuals, especially, should be found ignorant of this fact.'

Rectal gonorrhoea or gonococcal proctitis occurs almost exclusively in passive homosexuals. Similarly male homosexuals may develop primary syphilitic lesions around the anus or actually inside the wall of the rectum, although primary sores may also occur on the lips or inside the mouth through kissing an infected partner. A noteworthy example was Oscar Wilde's French friend Marcel Schwob, who, as already noted, died from the effects of a syphilitic tumour in the rectum. Male homosexuals with rectal infections are today effectively treated with penicillin, an antibiotic unknown in Schwob's time. Sometimes they prove difficult to cure and require repeated treatment. According to Morton, it is thought that these initial failures are due to organisms producing an antidote called penicillinase, which may be present in the bowel, thus inhibiting the action of the antibiotic.

In his valuable treatise *Venereal Diseases*, Morton cites the findings of other venereologists, notably F. J. G. Jefferiss, who works in St Mary's Hospital, London. According to the latter's investigations, only 12 per cent of early male syphilis cases treated in this hospital in the middle 1950s were homosexuals. But by the years 1960–62 the figure had risen to 65 per cent. Similar figures of V.D. cases treated in the provinces are much lower, which may be attributed to the fact that London is 'something of a magnet for homosexuals'. Of 224 consecutive male homosexuals treated by Jefferiss in London, 164 had gonorrhoea, 10 syphilis, 16 non-specific urethritis, while the remaining 15 per cent had no apparent disease. At the same time, 97 of the 224 considered themselves 'passive', 127 were 'active' and 24 described themselves as 'versatile'. As might be expected from this classification, ano-rectal and penile disease was more or less evenly distributed. The fact that 15 per cent of the homosexual patients had been previously treated for venereal infection supported the general impression, in the venereologist's view, that many male homosexuals are promiscuous.

Writing shortly before the 1967 Act became law, Morton
thought it doubtful that the proposed legislation, if passed, would
make any marked impact on venereal disease rates in Great
Britain. In the event he has been proved right, since the figures
continue to rise in an alarming degree, apart from syphilis which
is better controlled than other venereal diseases. The overall
figures for gonorrhoea and non-specific urethritis have doubled
and trebled respectively since 1951.[1]

Another risk to which the homosexual is exposed by casual
encounters is that of being violently assaulted as the result of a
request for money. Admitted this has diminished lately, since
there is no longer the incentive that there formerly was to blackmail consenting adults for homosexual acts committed in private;
but unfortunately there are still occasional cases of violent homosexual crime comparable with the notorious 'Studio Murder'
which has already been described. Such a case occurred in 1968
in the Earl's Court district of West London, where the homosexual victim, who was a lecturer at a provincial university,
shared a flat with two other men who were not homosexuals.
The lecturer used the flat at week-ends and in vacations. According to the prosecution, he was in the habit of meeting men in
London and taking them back to the university where 'they
would be popular among his friends'. When in London the
lecturer would also pick up men and take them to his flat
for homosexual practices. He said he did not pay them money but
rewarded them with presents.

One day during the summer vacation he saw a man selling
obscene post cards in Earl's Court. The man was a twenty-three-
year-old labourer of no fixed address named Gerald Hopewell,
and the university lecturer took him back to his flat, where he
produced a bottle of champagne. Prosecuting counsel stated that
'Hopewell knew perfectly well why he had been taken to the
flat'. They had several drinks together, after which the lecturer
made homosexual advances. Hopewell's reaction was to ask for
money, and when the lecturer said that all he had was £2 10s.
Hopewell took it and then attacked him. Two days later the
lecturer was found lying badly injured and dehydrated in his
room. The reason why he was not found before, prosecuting
counsel told the court when Hopewell pleaded guilty at the Old
Bailey to a charge of attempted murder, was that the lecturer's
flatmates who were not homosexuals knew of his proclivities

---

[1] R. S. Morton, *Venereal Diseases* (1966), 57, 71, 128–30, 164. *The Times*,
July 30; *Observer*, August 4, 1968. Information communicated by R. S. Morton.

and were careful not to go into his room when the door was shut.

Hopewell described the assault in a statement he made to the police after his arrest:

> I hit him half a dozen times with a bottle and kicked him in the face. There was blood all over the place. I broke a bottle and slashed him across the face and kicked him. I kept hitting him but when I saw the state he was in I felt sorry for him. I put him to bed. Every time he breathed blood pumped out from him somewhere.
>
> I started crying. Then I grabbed a broken bottle and slashed him down the leg. I stuck the bottle in his face and all over his body. I looked over the flat, but could find no money and went back to the bedroom and tried to cut his throat. I thought he would die and, if he did not, he would be a key witness so I decided to kill him.
>
> I started hitting and kicking him and I thought he was dead. I meant to kill him as I don't like queers.

Mr Justice Ashworth, the trial judge, remarked that Hopewell was 'an absolute menace' and he told him so in passing sentence. 'If that is the way you are going to live, by "rolling homos", ' he said, 'I must send you away for a long time.' The judge did so, for ten years.

It was a miracle that the unfortunate lecturer survived this appalling attack. As it was, his wounds required fifty stitches and his face was marked for life.[1]

Known or suspected homosexuals who visit public lavatories are still in danger of being arrested for importuning or indecent assault by plain clothes police acting as *agents provocateurs*, even though they should be perfectly innocent of any such offence. A case of this kind recently occurred involving three officers of the Hampshire Constabulary and a thirty-five-year-old unmarried teacher, who was head of the Geography Department of Portsmouth College of Technology. The teacher was accused of masturbating in the lavatory and smiling at the police officers who were in plain clothes, as well as touching the genitals of one of them. 'I was acting as an *agent provocateur*, which was part of my duty,' said Sergeant Cyril Walker of the Hampshire Vice Squad. 'I was waiting to see if his actions were those of a homosexual. I was not acting in such a way that anybody would think I would welcome a homosexual advance.' The lavatory in question was

[1] *The Yorkshire Post*, September 28, 1968.

near Southsea Common, and it appeared that the police kept the place under observation, particularly late at night. On the occasion in question one of the officers was a probationary constable undergoing training and presumably being instructed in the *agent provocateur*'s distasteful technique.

The teacher's story, which was accepted by the jury, was that he had been to a party, where he had drunk some wine and eaten pâté. The combination, he said, had upset his stomach. He did not wish to go home and be sick for fear of disturbing his aunt and a young girl, a friend of his aunt's, who were staying in the house and occupied rooms beside the bathroom and lavatory. He therefore drove to Southsea Common where he walked for a little and then visited the public lavatory, where he saw two men in civilian clothes who proved to be police officers. He immediately left, walked again on the Common, and returned to the lavatory when he judged it would be empty. This time the two policemen had been joined by a third. He again left the lavatory without having done anything improper and was arrested shortly afterwards in a dark alleyway where he had put his fingers in his mouth and was trying to vomit. 'Got you!' said the police sergeant, pouncing on him. 'I've been watching you all night.'

The teacher was duly acquitted, having been suspended from his teaching post for the period of two months between his arrest and his trial. He was defended by a Queen's Counsel who made no application to the court for the costs of the defence, which amounted to £475. In rendering this bill to his client the solicitor explained that, if the application had failed, the recorder who heard the case might have made some adverse comment. 'For example he might well say that in his view your behaviour that night was rather peculiar and you really brought this matter upon yourself. That might not be entirely true but it is difficult to stop a recorder making a comment of that kind.'

Not suprisingly the teacher concluded that, while his acquittal formally disproved the homosexuality charges, he was still being punished for 'undefined behaviour which did not conform to the norm—behaviour, however, which was in his view no more eccentric than that of the three policemen'.[1]

The law of importuning, which derives from the old Vagrancy Acts, is now expressed in the Sexual Offences Act, 1956, s. 32, which states that 'it is an offence for a man persistently to solicit or importune in a public place for immoral purposes'. The

---

[1] *Sunday Times*, August 11, 1968.

essence of the offence is that the act should be done 'persistently'. There is no difference between importuning and soliciting in this context, although in the case of Mr W. T. Field, the Labour M.P., it was attempted to argue otherwise. Field, who was convicted at Bow Street magistrate's court in January 1953 and fined £15, had been arrested as the result of police surveillance of two West End urinals one evening between 9.25 and 10.15 p.m. According to the police evidence, Field stood beside or in front of various young men in these urinals, smiled at them and 'looked in the direction of their persons'. None of the people in the urinals appeared to be affected by his conduct. On appeal to a Queen's Bench Divisional Court, Field's counsel argued that what his client had done did not amount to importuning within the dictionary meaning of pestering, although it might have amounted to soliciting, i.e. 'inviting'. But the Lord Chief Justice, Lord Goddard, rejected this argument. 'There is no real distinction to be drawn between persistently soliciting and persistently importuning,' he said in dismissing the appeal; 'the draftsman put in those words to make it more emphatic.'[1]

Incidentally a 'public place' for the purpose of the statute has been held to be a place where the public go no matter whether they have a right to go or not, and to include, besides a public lavatory, *inter alia* an omnibus and a railway carriage in transit. Nor is it necessary for the prosecution to prove that the solicitation reached the mind of the person intended to be solicited so as to attract his attention. In a case decided in 1912, which is still the leading case on the subject, a man named Horton, while under police observation in the West End, entered seven public lavatories and remained a few minutes in each. While in the lavatories and in the street, he smiled in the faces of men, pursed his lips and wriggled his body. But he did not speak to or touch anyone, nor did he attempt to do so. No one complained that he had been solicited and there was no evidence other than that of the police. He was arrested on leaving the notorious 'Clarkson's Cottage', and taken to the police station, where on examination he was found to have his face 'artificially reddened' and in his pocket was found a powder puff with pink powder upon it, as the Lord Chief Justice later remarked, 'not unimportant in connection with an offence of this kind'. Convicted by the magistrate and sentenced to ten weeks' imprisonment with hard labour, Horton appealed to the Divisional Court on the ground that no one had in fact been solicited or importuned. His appeal

[1] *Field* v. *Chapman, The Times*, October 9, 1953.

was dismissed. 'To say that, because on the particular occasion he does not succeed in attracting the attention of anyone, there is no evidence upon which he can be convicted,' said Lord Chief Justice Alverstone, 'is an argument which we cannot adopt.'[1]

Michael Schofield takes the view that in some ways this law may have been and may continue to be the cause of more injustice than the Labouchere Amendment was before its repeal.

> Although the use of the word 'persistently' in the original wording of the act suggests that the intention was to protect members of the public from interference or at least annoyance, the interpretation by the courts means that in practice no one except a plain-clothes policeman need be aware of the importuning; and convictions are usually obtained on the sole evidence of the policeman who makes the arrest. In such a situation it is not necessary to stress the possibility of perjury, or indeed of provocative actions, on the part of the arresting constables. It is not sufficient to argue that the penalties are comparatively slight, for the disgrace that follows a conviction for importuning can be shattering.

Of course, the consequences of such a conviction vary according to the circumstances and position of the accused. While Mr Field had to resign his seat in Parliament and could take no further part in political life, the actor Sir John Gielgud, who was convicted of a similar offence later the same year in a Chelsea mews, found that his theatrical career was unaffected. Indeed he received a sympathetic ovation on the first occasion on which he appeared on the stage after the incident. As we have seen, this greatly upset the old-fashioned Conservative peer Lord Winterton, who publicly protested against it. It was rumoured at the time that Sir John might even be deprived of his knighthood, which he had recently received for his outstanding services to the theatre. Of course, this could not legally have been done, since Sir John's offence was a misdemeanour and not a felony, an anachronistic difference dating from the time when all felonies from treason to sheep stealing were punishable by death. The last knight to be degraded was Sir Roger Casement, not for his homosexual practices, for which he was not tried, but for his treasonable conduct towards the sovereign.

The law of importuning was originally aimed at the male prostitute, protector or 'bully', but in practice its application has been considerably extended. As Schofield emphasizes in his

---

[1] *Horton* v. *Mead* [1913] 1 K.B. 154.

latest comparative study, only a very few of the homosexuals charged with the offence of importuning are male prostitutes. 'The great majority are merely trying to find out if the other man is homosexual by the use of words or an inquiring look which would go unnoticed by the man who is heterosexual. If the other man does not respond, the homosexual will go away and seek a sexual partner elsewhere. A homosexual would be stupid to importune persistently and pressingly as he is well aware that the vast majority of men look upon homosexual activities with repugnance.'[1]

[6]

In spite of the recent change in the law affecting England and Wales, though not Scotland and Northern Ireland, the million or so male homosexuals in Britain are still legally worse off than their heterosexual brothers or lesbian sisters, since they must theoretically remain 'chaste' until they are twenty-one, while the others are under no legal prohibition in the matter of consenting sexual relations once they have reached their sixteenth birthday. Also the remaining homosexual offences on the statute book are generally punished with greater severity than corresponding heterosexual delinquencies; in one instance, where the act takes place between a man over twenty-one and another man under that age, although the act has taken place in private and the parties are consenting, the penalty on conviction has actually been increased. As has been seen, the purpose of this change is to protect adolescents against seduction by their elders; yet minors frequently make the initial advances and from time to time they are also charged with indulging in homosexual acts with others under twenty-one.

Besides these legal disabilities, homosexuals are still subject to considerable built-in social prejudices and hostility, which may adversely affect their relations with their families, employers and workmates. Even when they were acquitted on charges under the old law, they were liable to lose their jobs simply for being homosexual. 'I'm broadminded', the manager would say, 'but the chaps on the shop floor wouldn't like it if you stayed.' This antipathy persists just as it does in the case of coloured immigrants and Jews. 'Only the other day,' said Mr Antony Grey of

[1] Michael Schofield. *Sociological Aspects of Homosexuality* (1965), 200. Sir John Gielgud pleaded in mitigation that he had been drinking: *Evening News* (London), October 21, 1953.

the Albany Trust, 'I heard of a case in a Midland town where eight homosexuals, who worked in the same factory, met and talked together to the extent that it became noticed. They were all given the sack because it was felt that they had a bad influence on the place.' Mr Grey also quoted examples of discrimination in housing. 'Of course, landlords never openly state their prejudice. They say that they are looking for a married couple, or that two men aren't suitable as tenants.' Middle-aged bachelors are frequently and wrongly assumed to be homosexual, because they have not got married by the time they are thirty, and still more unfairly to be in the habit of committing homosexual acts. As Michael Schofield has pointed out, social pressure to marry is very strong on both sides of the Atlantic. 'A bachelor is liable to be regarded as eccentric and unstable, or even as unfit for posts of responsibility.'[1] Of course, there are bachelors of un-blemished character in public life, such as Edward Heath, the English Conservative Party leader, and J. Edgar Hoover, the Director of the U.S. Federal Bureau of Investigation, but they are the exception, and certainly in Heath's case the lack of a wife has been in some ways a handicap.

Although homosexual behaviour forms the theme of plays, films, radio and television features, as a subject it is still taboo in some British newspapers. Recently the *Sunday Express* (circulation 4,206,000) refused to accept an advertisement for a popular educational publication entitled *The Book of Life* until the word 'homosexuality' was removed from it. 'We are a family newspaper', the editor was reported as saying, 'and I don't want anything in the paper that our readers shouldn't read.' The word appeared as part of the caption of a picture of two men, one resting his hand on the other's shoulder, 'Homosexuality—is it natural?' This was not acceptable to the *Sunday Express*, which asked the ad line to be changed to 'Lawful—but is it natural?' And this was how it eventually read to *Express* families. 'A childish form of censorship,' commented the publishers of *The Book of Life* on the enforced alteration.[2]

In sophisticated and in particular artistic circles, it is fashion-able to express tolerance for homosexuals and sympathy for their problems. But relatively little has been achieved in Britain in the way of translating these laudable sentiments into practical action. The idea of subscribing money to help homosexuals is regarded as akin to heresy by large sections of the public, who willingly

[1] *Forum*, Vol. 2, No. 1 (1969), 12–19. *Schofield*, 148.
[2] *Campaign* (London), January 10, 1969.

contribute towards the relief of alcoholics, drug addicts, unmarried mothers, animals and other causes sponsored by 'do
gooders'. Apart from the slenderly financed and sadly under-
staffed Albany Trust, which grew out of the Homosexual Law
Reform Society, there are practically no sources to which the
anxious homosexual may turn for specialized aid in Britain
today. It is unfortunate that in many instances he should fight
shy of his family doctor, whose initial help might forestall later
recourse to the psychiatrist's couch. There is a crying need for a
better education of the public, including sex instruction in
schools. As Antony Grey says, 'the majority of society has to
come to a better understanding of homosexuality. People must
enlarge their comprehension and compassion. . . . While the
homosexual tries to adjust to society, society must also try to
adjust to the homosexual.'

During 1968, over five hundred individuals of both sexes
sought the advice of the trust in their sexual difficulties. Not a
great number in relation to the total homosexual population, but
more than enough for the trust to cope with. About a quarter
consisted of women. The great majority were straightforward
homosexual types, but there was a small minority of transvestite,
pederastic and other deviants. Ages varied from fifteen to fifty and
over. Four typical examples follow.

'I am in desperate need of help,' wrote a twenty-two-year-old
male homosexual from a north country town.

> Through this affliction I have tried to take my life twice as I
> feel I can't face the world like this. I am so depressed, having
> lost two good jobs through workmates finding out, and am
> now out of work. I am so frightened of people finding out,
> as up to recently I went about with normal company, and they
> looked on homosexuals as some kind of filth and this sickened
> me knowing I was one of the filth they spoke of; and when one
> of the lads found out, through malicious mouths, they seemed
> to drift away and now I am afraid to face anybody.
>
> I have left a good home where I have two sisters who used
> to look up to me for advice, but have now found out and look
> at me with disgust, having heard all sorts of nasty tales about
> what they call 'poufs'. I am now living in a one-room flat and
> at such a stage I am contemplating taking an overdose as I
> don't think I could carry this burden with no job. I don't like
> mixing with other homosexuals round here where I live as they
> are so well known. . . .

Please help me, I am still young and able to work. I have
seen my doctor but he is no use and doesn't understand what
it's like. I am sure if I don't get away from here soon I will
just give up and kill myself.

The next example is a woman in her early thirties. Although
she is a graduate in economics, her real interest is art, and the
possession of some private income, supplemented by teaching at
evening classes, enabled her to spend most of her time painting.
When she was in her teens, she had two affairs with women and
she prefers her own to the opposite sex, though she admits that
her orientation is probably bisexual. But for the past ten years
she failed to establish a suitable relationship with another woman,
as a result of which she had come to feel 'very much alone'. She
finds it difficult to get on with what she described as 'extremely
obvious types' of lesbians and feels that she has little in common
with other homosexual women whom she has met from time to
time. She tried a course of psychotherapy, but without any
success. Clearly her main difficulty was lack of communication
caused by isolation, partly physical and partly mental, since she
deliberately cut herself off from human contact for most of the
day. This is never easy to resolve even when the person affected
is eager to do so. Mental isolation—very common in people
who feel themselves to be outsiders socially—is something which
tends to build up over the years and can only be eradicated,
slowly and painfully, through a change in the attitudes of the
individual and of society.

The third example was a former successful headmaster of a
boys' secondary school, married with a teenage son and daughter.
A Rotarian, prominent in his Masonic lodge, commander of the
local cadets, and president of his local professional organization,
he led a full and interesting life until nearing the age of fifty,
when he was accused of an act of indecency with one of his pupils.
At first he denied the charge, but eventually, not wishing to
subject the boy concerned to an unnecessary ordeal by lying, he
admitted it. He was allowed to resign, but in other respects was
less fortunate than Harrow's Dr Vaughan. While awaiting trial,
he attempted unsuccessfully to gas himself and was taken to
hospital suffering from almost total amnesia. From hospital he
was brought to court, where he pleaded guilty and was sentenced
to a year's imprisonment. But after serving four months his
mental condition had deteriorated to such an extent that he was
transferred to a psychiatric hospital. When he returned home

on his release from prison his reception by his wife and children was so frigid that his doctor, fearing further suicide attempts, felt it necessary to return him to hospital. Eventually, after his wife had announced her intention of divorcing him and his children declared that they would have nothing further to do with him, he went to live with his elderly mother, with no job, since he had lost his licence to teach, and practically no money.

'I make no excuses for the conduct which caused my downfall,' he told the Trust.

Headmasters obviously should not be pederasts. Nevertheless, although I can find explanations for this tendency towards homosexuality—an only child whose father died very early etc.—I cannot bring myself to regard myself as an out-and-out homosexual. After all I was married for 20 years and did father two children. . . . Now, after all I have been through, I regard myself as practically sexless! Certainly I should be a far safer proposition, if I were allowed to return to teaching, than some youngster straight out of training college who may not know of what perils can lie ahead. . . . All I want is to get down to some real work again.

The last example was a married woman, who works as an attendant at a petrol filling station in the Midlands.

Although I am a woman of 25 years, I have never felt like one. All my life I have had to dress like one and try to act like one because of the embarrassment to myself and my family if people knew how I feel like. 'I've got to the stage where I've had enough of life as it is. I've felt like a chap all my life, and I find women very attractive; I try not to show it, I don't like the thought of everyone knowing I'm a bit queer. Apart from that, there's not many women around who want to get involved with another. There's only one thing I want and that's to be a chap. I want to know if this could be possible. I was advised to see a psychiatrist, but he would just try and make me think like a woman, but I like my mind as it is. I want my body to match it, then I will find all the happiness I've missed in my life.

The subject of these four case histories each received appropriate counselling and other help. The first was put in touch with an experienced social worker in his locality who helped him to find a suitable job. The second was advised to begin to alter the pattern of her life by engaging in work which brought her into contact with other people and by making more positive endeavours to meet others who shared her interests. The third, at the Trust's suggestion, entered for a Civil Service examination which he passed with distinction, as a result of which he was able to get back to a full-time satisfying job. The fourth, who lacked the opportunity to meet other women with the same homosexual disposition and interests as herself, was surprised to learn that there were perhaps over half a million other women in the country with the same problem. She was asked to consider the proposition that she should stop wanting to be a man and begin to see herself as a different sort of woman. She also helped through a local social worker to adjust herself to her condition and she was put in touch with two of the lesbian organizations, which have already been mentioned.[1]

It is abundantly clear that intense loneliness is the lot of far too many homosexual men and women. Their pleas for more adequate meeting places than exist at present in Britain pose the question of whether, with an important measure of law reform an accomplished fact, the time has not come for the establishment of a responsibly run social organization offering them recreational facilities and therapeutic help. Above all they need love. When Oscar Wilde spoke for himself he spoke for a million other homosexuals. 'I cannot live without the atmosphere of Love,' he told his friend Robert Ross: 'I must love and be loved, whatever price I pay for it.'[2]

[7]

While considerable progress has been made during recent years in improving the British public's knowledge of and attitude towards homosexuality and other sexual deviations from the norm, much remains to be done. Those primarily involved are themselves often in need of educating; many homosexuals and other deviants are quite ignorant of their own condition, as some of the case histories cited above show, and they need to have matters explained to them and put into the right perspective. There is still a great deal of prejudice to be eliminated on the part of politicians, government civil servants, professional people, social workers and those given to 'good works', thus lending point to Wilde's remark that 'it is not so much public opinion as public officials that need educating'. Recently a medical social

---

[1] Communicated by the Albany Trust.
[2] *Letters of Oscar Wilde*, ed. Hart-Davis, 644.

worker telephoned the Albany Trust for help in finding accommodation for a homosexual patient about to be discharged from her hospital after recovering from a nervous breakdown. She said that, immediately after his homosexuality was mentioned, all the doors usually open to patients had been slammed firmly shut: she had never experienced such difficulty in placing anyone before and was amazed at the extent of the prejudice revealed by this episode. The Trust also had considerable difficulty a short time ago in arranging treatment for a young girl drug addict who was also a lesbian—not because she took heroin, but because it was feared that she might have a sexually corrupting influence on other patients!

Then there are the problems posed by the families of homosexuals. 'The discovery that one of their children is homosexual is a tremendous shock for most parents,' says Antony Grey. 'Here again, one is up against the lack of proper sex education and the harmful results of the conspiracy of silence which society forces upon homosexuals. Parents think this is something which could never happen to them because they are usually not aware of ever having met a homosexual. When it does happen, they often refuse point blank to believe it. They certainly don't come to terms with it very easily. We have dealt with some most distressing cases where young people have been rejected by their families and are slung out into the street when their homosexuality becomes manifest.'

In this context Mr Grey has drawn attention to an interesting scheme in Holland, where week-end conferences are arranged through the Dialoog Foundation, an Albany Trust type offshoot of the C.O.C., at which parents of homosexual sons and daughters meet for two days, in groups, to discuss the whole thing with their children, with other homosexuals and with each other.

The opening session is called 'the crying day' because they are all so upset, but at the end of the two days they finish up discussing the practical difficulties of homosexual living, realizing how they can best help their children. I would very much like to see such a scheme operating in Britain.

Parents must realise that their homosexual son or daughter needs love and acceptance, perhaps even more than a child who does not have this problem. One remaining legal difficulty is that, as the law stands now, homosexual behaviour is only legal between two consenting adults aged over twenty-one. Therefore, parents and counsellors of homosexuals who are minors must make it clear that if they have sexual relationships they are breaking the law and must try to be as discreet and responsible as possible in their behaviour, as well as being prepared to accept any untoward consequences. But it is, of course, utterly unrealistic to expect teenagers who—as Kinsey showed— are at the age of most intensive sexual drive, to remain celibate until their twenty-first birthday if they happen to be attracted to others of their own sex.[1]

The Albany Trust's case work during the past few years has revealed three potential crisis periods in the average homosexual's life in Britain, where counselling and other help may be urgently needed. No doubt they have their counterparts in other countries. The first crisis is one of identity and occurs in the teens or early twenties when the homosexual discovers that he or she is 'different' in sexual response from other members of the community and that they are both drawn emotionally and physically towards individuals of their own sex instead of, or more than, to the opposite. For the male teenager there is a real need for reliable homosexual friends of his own age, but at present meeting them exposes him and those who may introduce him to them to the risk of prosecution. The second crisis may come in the late twenties or early thirties when the homosexual has failed to find a permanent partner, has become tired of casual relationships or 'one night stands' and craves for more stable company of his own kind. This is where a responsible social organization on the Dutch model, something more than a club, could fill a vital need. Finally, there may be a crisis for the middle-aged or elderly homosexuals, in their fifties or sixties, who have either lost their partners or no longer have any prospect of finding others, and who experience the same problems of increasing loneliness and isolation that beset many heterosexuals. They too are deserving of sympathy and help where necessary.

Although there is some considerable way yet to go before homosexuals become fully integrated in the community of Britain, my personal belief is that their complete social acceptance here is only a matter of time. Admittedly the old prejudices die hard, but with their gradual disappearance and incidentally the lowering of the 'age of consent' to a more realistic figure than twenty-one, the homosexual's socially disruptive potential will diminish while his or her value to the community comes to be recognized as being in its way as socially useful and productive

[1] *Forum, loc. cit.*

as that of the heterosexual. So long as homosexuals are recognized as being 'different', there is no logical reason why they should continue to be regarded as inferior or second-class citizens. Something of this attitude is already apparent among the younger generation, particularly those who subscribe to the gospel of 'make love not war'. Thus in Britain the love that formerly dared not speak its name may in the fullness of time come into its own without fear and without reproach as the expression of a satisfying and socially acceptable human relationship.

Select Bibliography

ACKERLEY, J. R. *My Father and Myself.* London, 1968.

ALLEN, CLIFFORD. *Homosexuality.* London, 1958.

BAILEY, D. S. *Homosexuality and the Western Christian Tradition.* London, 1955.

BLOCH, IVAN. *Sexual Life in England.* London and New York, 1934.

CARPENTER, EDWARD. *The Intermediate Sex.* London, 1908.

— *My Days and Dreams.* London, 1916.

CHESSER, EUSTACE. *Live and Let Live.* London, 1958.

— *Odd Man Out.* London, 1959.

COLE, WILLIAM G. *Sex and Love in the Bible.* London, 1962.

CROFT-COOKE, RUPERT. *The Verdict of You All.* London, 1955.

DAVIDSON, MICHAEL. *The World, the Flesh and Myself.* London, 1962.

EGLINTON, J. Z. *Greek Love.* New York, 1954.

ELLIS, HAVELOCK. *Sexual Inversion.* Watford, 1897. Reprinted with revisions in *Studies in the Psychology of Sex*, Vol. 2. New York, 1936.

FOSTER, JEANNETTE H. *Sex Variant Women in Literature.* London, 1958.

GARDE, NOEL I. *Jonathan to Gide: The Homosexual in History.* New York, 1964.

GROSSKURTH, PHYLLIS. *John Addington Symonds.* London, 1964.

HAUSER, RICHARD. *The Homosexual Society.* London, 1962.

HIRSCHFELD, MAGNUS. *Die Homosexualität des Mannes und des Weibes.* 2nd ed. Berlin, 1920.

HOLROYD, MICHAEL. *Lytton Strachey.* 2 vols. London, 1967–68.

HYDE, H. MONTGOMERY. *The Trials of Oscar Wilde.* London, 1948 and 1962.

— *The Trial of Sir Roger Casement.* London, 1960 and 1964.

KINSEY, A. C., POMEROY, W. B. and MARTIN, C. *Sexual Behaviour in the Human Male.* Philadelphia and London, 1948.

— and GEBHARD, P. *Sexual Behaviour in the Human Female.* Philadelphia and London, 1953.

MAGEE, BRYAN. *One in Twenty*. London, 1968.

MAYNE, XAVIER. (Edward I. Stevenson). *The Intersexes*. Florence, 1910.

MORTON, R. S. *Venereal Diseases*, London, 1966.

PISANUS FRAXI (Henry S. Ashbee). *Notes on Curious and Uncommon Books*. 3 vols. privately printed, London, 1877–85.

PITTENGER, NORMAN. *Time for Consent? A Christian's Approach to Homosexuality*. London, 1967.

PLUMMER, D. *Queer People*. London, 1963.

Report of the Committee on Homosexual Offences and Prostitution, London, 1957.

SCHOFIELD, MICHAEL. *Sociological Aspects of Homosexuality*. London, 1965.

STEVAS, N. ST. JOHN-. *Life, Death and the Law*. London, 1961.

SYMONDS, J. A. *A Problem in Modern Ethics*. Privately printed, 1891.

— *Memoirs*. Unpublished MS in the London Library.

WALKER, KENNETH. *Sexual Behaviour*. London, 1966.

WEST, D. J. *Homosexuality*. 3rd ed. London, 1967.

WESTWOOD, GORDON. *A Minority. A Report on the Life of the Male Homosexual in Great Britain*. London, 1960.

— *Society and the Homosexual*. London, 1952.

WILDE, OSCAR. *Letters of Oscar Wilde*. Ed. Rupert Hart-Davis. London, 1962.

WILDEBLOOD, PETER. *Against the Law*. London, 1955.

WORSLEY, T. CUTHBERT. *Flannelled Fool*. London, 1960.

Index

Pakenham, Lord, 233, 234
Palmerston, Lord, 112
Park, Frederick William, 94, 95, 96, 97, 98, 122, 123
Parke, Ernest, 124, 126, 127
Parke, Mr Justice, 92
Parker, Charles, 140
Parker, Lord Chief Justice Lord, 248, 266
Parliamentary History of England, 39 n.
Parry, Serjeant, 96
Passingham, Col. Robert, 77, 78
Pater, William, 109
Pederasty, 103, 104, 105, 116
  Burton's essay on, 155
Peel, Robert:
  reforms criminal law, 90, 91
Pemberton Billing, Noel, 171, 173, 174, 176
  on the 'Black Book', 171–2
Penitent Death of John Atherton, 58 n.
People, The, 252, 281 n.
Pepys, Samuel, 60
Percy, Lord Eustace, 179
Perfumed Garden, The, 155
Petre, Lady, 57
Philby, 'Kim', 213
Phoenix of Sodom, The, 79, 80
Picture of Dorian Gray, The, 143, 163
Pilar, James, 133
Pillory, the, 64, 69, 82
Pinorman, 191 n.
Pisanus Fraxi, 59 n., 60 n., 71, 72 n., 82 n., 155
Pitt-Rivers, Michael, 216, 222, 223, 224
Plain Reasons for the Growth of Sodomy in England, 65
Plummer, Douglas, 7 n.
Police:
  attitude to homosexual clubs of, 256–7
  blackmail by members of, 255
  homosexuality in the, 19

searching without a warrant, 216
zeal against homosexuals of, 4–5, 213, 214–16
Pollock, Sir Frederick, 38
Ponsonby, Sarah, 182–3
Portland, Lord, 62, 194
Powell, Enoch, 243
Pretor, Alfred, 111
Priestley, J. B., 236
Primrose, Neil, 173, 174
Prison service:
  homosexuality in, 19–20
Problem in Greek Ethics, A, 101
Problem in Modern Ethics, A, 101, 102, 103, 107, 119, 128 n.
Procuring, 273–4
Profumo, John, 250
Public houses:
  and homosexuality, 275–6
  Running Horse, Piccadilly, 27
  White Swan, 79, 80–1
Public lavatories:
  agents provocateurs in, 26, 209–210, 293–4
  as meeting places, 26
  homosexuality in, 207
  railway station, 207

Queensberry, 9th Marquess of, 143, 144, 146, 147
Queensberry, 11th Marquess of, 147 n.
Queensberry, 12th Marquess of, 263
Queer People, 7 n.
'Queers', 18, 22, 257
Quest for Corvo, 170

Radclyffe Hall a Case of Obscenity, 187 n.
Raffalovich, André, 143, 163–5, 166
Ralph Roister Doister, 41
Ransome, Arthur, 141
Rattigan, Terence, 247
Raven, Simon, 271